Blessed Are Those Who Ask the Questions

A volume in
Contemporary Perspectives in Management Spirituality and Religion
J. Goosby Smith, *Series Editor*

Blessed Are Those Who Ask the Questions

What Should We Be Asking About Management, Leadership, Spirituality, and Religion in Organizations?

edited by

J. Goosby Smith
The Citadel

Erin D. Renslow
The Citadel

INFORMATION AGE PUBLISHING, INC.
Charlotte, NC • www.infoagepub.com

Library of Congress Cataloging-in-Publication Data

A CIP record for this book is available from the Library of Congress
http://www.loc.gov

ISBN: 978-1-64802-430-6 (Paperback)
       978-1-64802-431-3 (Hardcover)
       978-1-64802-432-0 (E-Book)

Copyright © 2021 Information Age Publishing Inc.

All rights reserved. No part of this publication may be reproduced, stored in a retrieval system, or transmitted, in any form or by any means, electronic, mechanical, photocopying, microfilming, recording or otherwise, without written permission from the publisher.

Printed in the United States of America

To my "babies," Daniel and Aiah—
Thank you for loving me. Keep asking questions!

To Joseph, JC, and Jerrod—
Thank you for being my surrogate family here in SC.

To Vivian—
If I had a sister, it would be you!
—J. Goosby Smith

To my family—Dad, Mom, Lisa, Angela, Erica, and Braden.
This would not have been possible without your unwavering love, faith,
and support. Thank you for always believing in me.
—Erin D. Renslow

CONTENTS

Foreword ix
J. Goosby Smith and *Erin D. Renslow*

1 Is God Greater Than Tenure? 1
   Quintus R. Jett

2 Can Work Be Redeemed Through Play? (Or Why Is Playing
   Not an Option) 25
   Raymond Carr

3 Is the Spirit "Missing" in the Discourse of Management,
   Spirituality, and Religion? 41
   Shoaib Ul-Haq

4 Inspiring Inclusion: What Is the Evidence for a Faith-Based
   Approach to Leadership Development? 71
   Valerie L. Myers

5 What Happens When Classical Hollywood Narrative and
   American Mythos Converge? 95
   Joi Carr

6 Should Transformational Leadership Theory Include an
   Ethics Component? Insights From the Cupbearer to the King 119
   Tom Clark

7 What Are the Biblical Roots of Servant Leadership?...................... 139
  Michael J. Mlynarczyk

8 The Strategy of Spirituality: How Best Can Spiritual
  Leadership and Spirituality at Work Support and Sustain
  Organizational Strategy? A Christian Perspective.......................... 163
  Richard Peters and Joe Ricks

9 Motivation or Justification: How Is Religiosity Used in the
  Decision to Engage in Environmental Sustainability Practices? 187
  Shalei V. K. Simms and Dorothy M. Kirkman

10 Is Today's Focus on Innovation Enticing Global Managers
   Away From Religious and Spiritual Principles?.............................. 197
   Matthew Guah

11 (What's) The Matter With Babel? 221
   Daniel Q. Vass-Goosby

12 Religious and Wealthy: Can One Be Both? 247
   Miles K. Davis and Clifford F. Thies

13 How Can an Understanding of and Acknowledgment of the
   Effects of Sin and Evil Inform Solutions to Organizational
   and Societal Problems? 267
   Larry G. Daniel

14 How Can the Newest Global Religion—the Baha'i Faith—
   Impact the Future of Business? 291
   Payam Zamani

15 "Nuns" to Nones? Revisiting Management, Spirituality,
   and Religion in the Workplace for the New Generation................ 307
   Latha Poonamallee

About the Contributors.. 329

FOREWORD

As a reader, my first questions when I pick up a book are, "What is the meaning of this book's title?" and, "What is this book's genesis story?" The title of this volume, *Blessed are Those Who Ask the Questions*, came from a memorable scene[1] in one of my favorite late 1980s to early 1990s American television shows. *A Different World*[2] was a *Cosby Show* sequel in which the character, Denise Huxtable, attended a fictitious college: Hillman College (whose façades were, in actuality, my alma mater, Spelman College, and Clark Atlanta University, both in Atlanta, Georgia). I remember watching the exteriors filming and staging in the fall of 1986. Fans of the show will remember the scene portraying the character "Dwayne Wayne's" struggle between remaining silent or ruining the wedding of his perennial love interest, character Whitley Gilbert. Dwayne Wayne walked in and stopped partway down the center aisle just as the minister officiating the ceremony said "If there is any man who can show just cause...why they cannot be lawfully joined together...." Dwayne Wayne coughed, and all heads turned back to look at him. His friend, Ron, encouraged him to say something. Instead, Dwayne Wayne sat down. As the minister read the vows to Whitley Gilbert, she hallucinated that Dwayne Wayne was the minister. She became confused and she paused. As the drama mounted during that pause, Dwayne Wayne stood up, walked down the aisle, and said, "Will you...," *immediately* followed by a character who said, "Blessed are those who ask the questions, brotha." After a scuffle with ushers trying to maintain order, Whitley Gilbert left her intended groom, Byron, walked up the aisle and ran into the arms of Dwayne Wayne. That phrase, "blessed are those who ask the questions," stuck with me for over two decades because I believe that asking the right questions transforms our fields of inquiry. Thus, when conceptualizing this volume in which scholars and practitioners would be free to pose (sometimes provocative) questions in the field of management, leadership, spirituality, and religion, this title emerged.

The focus of the book emerged from the book of Genesis in the Hebrew and Christian Bibles. Genesis 32:22–32 relays the story of how Jacob is on the run: both from his uncle Laban, and now from his brother Esau (from whom he stole their father Isaac's birthright). Jacob sent his family ahead of him to safety, but he stayed put. Starting at verse 24, the New International Version of the Christian Bible reads

> 24 So Jacob was left alone, and a man wrestled with him till daybreak. 25 When the man saw that he could not overpower him, he touched the socket of Jacob's hip so that his hip was wrenched as he wrestled with the man. 26 Then the man said, "Let me go, for it is daybreak." But Jacob replied, "I will not let you go unless you bless me." 27 The man asked him, "What is your name?" "Jacob," he answered. 28 Then the man said, "Your name will no longer be Jacob, but Israel, because you have struggled with God and with humans and have overcome." 29 Jacob said, "Please tell me your name." But he replied, "Why do you ask my name?" Then he blessed him there. 30 So Jacob called the place Peniel, saying, "It is because I saw God face to face, and yet my life was spared."

While these two stories, Dwayne Wayne's wedding-crashing and Jacob's God-wrestling God may seem unrelated, to me they are intimately connected. In this story from Genesis, Jacob not only does not fear the uncertainty of a spirit wrestling with him, he refuses to let it go unless it blesses him. He keeps the ambiguity proximal as he displays the courage to make a demand of it, and to ask it to reveal its name. In the story from *A Different World*, Dwayne Wayne does much the same thing. He finds himself in uncertainty and wrestles with the ushers to ask Whitley the question, will she marry him. But, while the questioning in the midst of angst and ambiguity are clear, the supporting character's statement remains: "Blessed are those who ask the questions, brotha." This is the nature of Jacob's wrestling, to procure his blessing, this time legitimately from God. Had he not wrestled God, the question remains as to whether or not the Hebrews or Habiru, would have ever come to be.

However, questioning as an admirable act of struggling with God is not the same in all religions, which vary in their values for questioning.[3] However, questioning is necessary to ascertain truth(s). While people of diverse religions pray and meditate in different ways, many times we have questions. In the New International Version of the Christin Bible, James 1:5–8 advises

If any of you lacks wisdom, he should ask God, who gives generously to all without finding fault, and it will be given to him. 6 But when he asks, he must believe and not doubt, because he who doubts is like a wave of the sea, blown and tossed by the wind. 7 That man should not think he will receive anything from the Lord; 8 he is a double-minded man, unstable in all he does.

Given scriptural value for wisdom, an examination of how spirituality and religion, writ large, impact and are impacted by humans in organizations, requires inquiry. We must ask. We must wrestle. But, asking questions is not enough. As Rev. Floyd Thompkins, Jr. says,[4]

> The answers and solutions to our struggle for justice and peace can only come when we ask the right questions. Until everyone is in the room with a voice, those questions will not be raised and the emotional breakthroughs, revelations, and strategies will never happen...

As Rev. Thompkins says, we need multiple voices in the room so that a diverse set of questions can be asked. Consequently, for this project we intentionally sought people of multiple belief systems, faith traditions, and religions to ask the questions that burned in their hearts about management, leadership, spirituality, and religion in various workplaces. We freed our authors to express their questions in varying forms: prose, personal narrative, case studies, and scriptural

exegesis. We also freed them to explore various topics: advocacy for integrating a faith paradigm into management and leadership; explorations of the intersection of faith, leadership theories; application of religion to entrepreneurship; critical examinations of our American media; theological treatments of work and play; the juxtaposition of religion and wealth; a critical examination of innovation through a faith lens; an analysis of the impact of religiosity on environmental sustainability; the exploration of evil, sin, and redemption from diverse perspectives; application of quantum dynamics to the metaphors we communicate; and, examinations of religiosity and its inverse. For this project, we prioritized inclusiveness over expediency. We wanted a variety of voices and we got them! We are confident that as you read this book, you will, like us, crave the answers to new questions. We welcome you to delve into the questions that our "Blessed Authors" ask.

—**J. Goosby Smith** and **Erin D. Renslow**, Editors

NOTES

1. Swanard, M. (2012, December 6). *Dwayne shuts Whitley and Byron's Wedding Down*. [YouTube Channel]. https://www.youtube.com/watch?v=t095dapDIbY

2. *A Different World* (n.d.). IMDb. Retrieved July 10, 2020 from https://www.imdb.com/title/tt0092339/
3. Greenham, A. (2012). *The questioning God: An inquiry for Muslims, Jews, and Christians.* Gonzales, FL: Energion.
4. Thompkins, F. (n.d.) *The incubator network.* https://jpf.world/incubator-network/

CHAPTER 1

IS GOD GREATER THAN TENURE?

Quintus R. Jett

ABSTRACT

As a management scholar, I had a walk with God. In the aftermath of Hurricane Katrina, I sought to aid residents in the flood-damaged city of New Orleans, Louisiana (NOLA), through my knowledge and use of organizational theories. I created a project inspired by my academic interest in crowdsourcing, which at the time was an emerging phenomenon of organized volunteering and pooling of efforts and resources. This chapter chronicles how the Gentilly Project, originally inspired by my combined science and public service motivations, became a catalyst for transforming how I conceived and enacted my scholarly identity. Using an autoethnographic approach, I present a series of devotionals to review and reflect on the episode that recast how I envisioned myself and operated as a scholar. Leaning into relation with God to order my steps, I led local residents and volunteers to complete a district-wide survey of NOLA's Gentilly neighborhoods—without budget, fundraising, and project plan—within 32 days.

> The writing of history is a conceit of the survivors. Since survival is temporary, history is ephemeral. So, I will tell a story. It is not the only such story that could be told in the world of organizational studies, but it happens to be the one I know... (March, 1996, pp. 278–287)

I had my burning question when I arrived. English Professor Gretchen Holbrook Gerzina (2009) had released a new book, *Mr. and Mrs. Prince: How an Extraordinary Eighteenth-Century Family Moved Out of Slavery and Into Legend*. At Dartmouth College (Hanover, NH), there was a gathering of Black faculty and staff to celebrate the book's release and to discuss the book with the author. Professor Gerzina told the story of Mr. and Mrs. Prince, a free African American couple and their family living in the state of Vermont during the late 1700s. In telling the story, she shared how she conducted the research, identified archival sources, and made discoveries. I had finished reading the book before the gathering. I had enough years with academic peer review and the norms of academic publishing to be startled by something near the book's close.

When she ended her remarks, it was time for conversation. I stood up to raise my burning question:

> Towards the end of your book, you described visiting the property in Vermont that Mr. and Mrs. Prince owned centuries ago. And you wrote that you saw their ghosts. You are a scholar who committed to seeing a ghost in publication! Did you have reservations about doing that?

Yes, she said. She did. And for this chapter, so do I. It has taken me years to reach a point where I am comfortable sharing this in print, within an academic forum. I had a walk with God.

FAITH INQUIRIES IN ACADEMIC CIRCLES

Understandably, personal encounters with the supernatural are unaddressed in academic forums and publications. Norms of objective inquiry dominate in science, and among scholars in most academic fields. Going "on the record" about encountering spirits and looking to holy books or a deity for direction risks one's own professional credibility. Within academic realms, such disclosures and exploration about the supernatural, or the divine, occur instead informally. Dialogues take place within "in-group" spaces, where testimonies of faith and spirituality might occur with trust, safety, and mutual understanding.

Consideration and deliberations of God in decision-making are more naturally inquiries for researchers to address about others such as business managers (Schwartz, 2006), not themselves. In her edited book *Finding God at Harvard*, Kelly Monroe Kullberg (1997) counters this norm with contributors who reflect on their faith experiences and journeys from within the academic. Perspectives include: Christian faith bringing fulfillment to the life of a tenured professor (Loury, 1997), Judeo-Christian faith serving as counter to the pride and illusions of academic intellect (Berman, 1997), and faith journeys being consistent with the mysteries and discoveries experienced through intellectual inquiry (John, 1997). Hammett (1997) reflects on his spiritual faith and his professional identity as a natural scientist being fundamentally integrated. Kullberg's book illuminates the generative spaces where religious belief and intellectual thinking coincide, without being antithetical.

Few of the contributors to Kullberg's book are faculty members or research scientists. Most are authors reflecting on their present day's faith in reference to their paths through higher education and the intellectual life these paths fostered (e.g., university alumni). Loury (1997) is a professor of economics who reveals how his own religious awakening occurred about five years after he became tenured at Harvard. He describes vividly how it revitalized his marriage, restored him from addictions, and further transformed and gave new meaning to his life. Given he is reflecting and testifying holistically, the effect of this transformation on his identity as an academic scholar is not the focus.

In comparison, faith's impact on scholarly identity is the focus of this chapter. Specifically, I reflect and examine adoption of faith, belief, and practice as part of my decision-making while pursuing academic and public service motivations at a time when I was untenured but aspiring for it.

INCITING QUESTION

Is God greater than tenure? This question cannot be answered through our physical senses or research instruments. Even for academic scholars, first thoughts on the question are fundamentally subjective: shaped by personal assumptions and biases, including passionate (or unexamined) feelings. Within the logic of seeking academic tenure and promotion, entertaining open discourse about God is peripheral to our work, at best. Or it is a subject that lends itself to distraction from the path of "publish or perish."

New faculty members have relatively little time. The probationary period for evaluation for promotion to tenure from doctoral degree is less than seven years. Meanwhile, there are uncertainties of time and outcome involved in creating publishable research, finding a relevant (and preferably high status) outlet for it, and waiting and responding to editors and reviewers in the publication process. Furthermore, faculty members have additional expectations with research contributions and productivity: teaching, grantsmanship (in some fields), and service to their institution and within their fields. Junior scholars with full-time faculty appointments have high levels of expectation across competing professional priorities, in addition to commitments and responsibilities in their personal lives.

The core moments I share in this chapter occurred in December 2006, starting just over one year and three months following Hurricane Katrina's near miss of the city of New Orleans, Louisiana—an event which caused significant breaches in the city's levee system and resulted in extensive flooding throughout many of the city's districts and neighborhoods. My new experience of faith and practice, recounted in this chapter, was born in the midst of uncertainty and stress, both in my academic career and personal life.

The next section ("Into the Unknown") summarizes my career and other circumstances during the 3 months prior to what occurred within the 32 days that are central to this chapter. The subsequent section (Methods) summarizes my methodical approach: How does one revisit times over a decade in the past, in order to provide depiction of a journey and relationship with God? In layman's terms, how do I share with you the reader my testimony, in a form that also reflects an understanding of and respect for academic decorum and values?

What then follows is the section ("Devotionals") that chronicles what occurred within the 32 days, focusing on recollections and reflections of specific days within the Gentilly Project. The final section ("The Science of Charity") provides my concluding reflections about my faith and scholarly identity, further informed by the next stages of my career in the years since my first intentional walk with God in December 2006.

While the Gentilly Project itself might be observed as a kind of outlier that signals what a more inclusive and engaged scholarship could be (Avery, 2008), the impacts for an untenured scholar committing such a project must not be ignored. I am an African American, and perhaps scholars like me from underrepresented groups have additional appetite to expand academic norms. This story offers opportunity for new discourse and frontiers, to alleviate crises of meaning among scholars within and across our respective academic fields.

The most significant idol in today's professional scholarship is academic tenure, which emerged in the United States less than 80 years ago through declarations and recommendations of the American Association of University Professors (AAUP). Promotion to full professor post tenure is a pinnacle of general status and rewards within the academic profession, providing a means of permanence, deference, and opportunities for administrative authority and leadership within higher education institutions and fields. How is a faith and belief in God relevant to academic promotion and tenure? Here is my testimony.

INTO THE UNKNOWN

It was well over a decade ago when I started my walk with God. In September 2006, I believed in God and prayer, and did not belong to a church. I was at a transitional point in my faculty career. For the previous 12 months, I had been on a mission to make a difference in New Orleans following Hurricane Katrina, inspired by my research interests in "open source" solutions (popularly referred to today as *crowdsourcing*). September 2006 was also when my spouse and I separated. The project in New Orleans seemed the only area of my life where I might see progress.

Faith

If you had asked me if I believed in God in September 2006, my answer would have been yes. I am an African American. My parents were each born in the segregated South of the 1930s, with lineages back to American slavery in the 19th century. When they were raising me, we sometimes went to church, but I do not remember it being consistent. Sometimes, I remember seeing my mother on her knees praying by the bed when she was troubled. My father spoke about philosophy more than God or faith, yet I learned a bedtime prayer from his mother (one she taught her grandchildren when we would visit).

In graduate school, I collaborated with Reverend Thompkins to start a lunch-time series called "What Matters to Me and Why?" Several times a quarter, a faculty member would be featured for an intimate gathering of students and staff members in the side chapel of Stanford Memorial Church. It would begin with the speaker sharing for 20 minutes their response to the question "What matters to you and why?" and then there would be questions and conversations with the audience.

As I was completing my doctoral program, I was asked to give a baccalaureate speech on commencement weekend. On a sunny day, on stage facing an audience of graduating students and their families and a grand mural of Jesus delivering the Sermon on the Mount on the front of Stanford Church, I began with sharing how graduate school, although a blessing, nearly crushed my spirit at times. The title was "Praying for the Academy," and I spoke to the power of prayer in seeing me through. The speech was well received, but something appeared to bother one of the invited dignitaries on the stage. Afterwards, he turned to me privately: "Who are you praying to?" I had no answer.

About seven years from that time, not much about my faith had changed. At the beginning of 2006, it was a form of gratitude for my survival and blessings, not a petition to change my circumstances. Praying was for me an anxiety management technique for my difficult times. While I believed in God, I was not asking God for purpose or direction.

Career

In September 2006, I was uncertain about what to do next with my academic career. My appointment as visiting faculty member at Dartmouth College's Thayer School of Engineering had expired, and I had secured a 1-year interim appointment as a senior research fellow at Dartmouth's Tuck School of Business. Before I came to Dartmouth in 2003, I was a Rice University business school professor who had been denied contract renewal halfway to a promotion and tenure evaluation decision.

I had doubts about my marketability in the academic world. I was published, yet lacking a thematic pipeline of academic journal articles. Years before, my advisor and I had hit a rift in the process of completing my dissertation. I was on my own. To my detriment, I was a junior-level management scholar with unfocused multidisciplinary backgrounds: a PhD in industrial engineering, specializing in organization studies, who conducted field research on the strategies of high-tech companies; a business school professor who had taught operations management; an engineering management professor who taught operations research and statistics. Which academic job market was I best suited for?

With this interim appointment at Dartmouth's business school, I had that academic year to execute a move to return to a tenure-track position. I would have 50% of my prior salary in Dartmouth's engineering school plus health care benefits. Fortunately, I had no teaching responsibilities, so I had time to focus on the research expectation of the appointment and a job search. But I had no idea who would want to hire me. And I had doubts about my own discipline (and strategy) to effectively pursue another faculty position.

Project

In September 2006, being leader of a humanitarian project for New Orleans seemed the most promising thing I might offer the world, and it was a mission that excited me.

I was interested in open source as an organizing framework for 2 years prior to Hurricane Katrina and the flooding of New Orleans. With the increasing prevalence, access, and use of web-based platforms, in the early 2000s, it became possible for numerous contributors to volunteer their time remotely for community goals and projects. After seeing and participating in such activity in a nationwide grassroots political campaign, it had become a research interest: Under what conditions would distributed volunteers, independent and with diverse affiliates and skills, come together, like a school of fish, to fulfill a common cause? When the New Orleans levee-system collapsed as a result of Hurricane Katrina, I thought about how to apply what I was learning about open source organizing to support the city's residents in their return and recovery.

I had spent 12 months looking for a means to help people in New Orleans, while remaining based at Dartmouth College in New Hampshire over a thousand miles away. During the early months, I created a class project in my engineering management course. I traveled to New Orleans several times as the previous academic year progressed. I received $6,000 dollars in seed funding from Dartmouth's provost. I was introduced to Dartmouth geography professor, Xun Shi, who became a collaborator. Our focus turned to Gentilly, a district in New Orleans whose population roughly seemed representative of the whole city's socioeconomic demography (about two-thirds African American; mixed income levels).

By September 2006, the focus and features of the project were clear. It was about providing an organized system to motivate and direct volunteers to document, on an ongoing basis, the status of damage/recovery of every address in the Gentilly district using a simple coding system: RED (devastated), YELLOW (under construction), BLUE (renovated/occupied), or GREEN (vacant lot). Classifying collections of addresses would show the levels of recovery needs across and within Gentilly's 22 neighborhoods. This allowed us to deliver widespread support quickly to the areas where it was most needed.

Marriage

In September 2006, my wife and I separated after 7 years of marriage. We were not a religious couple, so our separation's effect as a catalyst for an awakening of faith and relationship with God was unexpected. It began with an encounter with a marriage restoration ministry, one which encouraged reflection and more engaged relationships with God as a source of change in one's own life, instead of laying judgement on the separated spouse. It continued with my visit, before the Thanksgiving holiday, to my spouse's grandmother, who was indeed religious.

Listening to her talking about the influence of God in her life moved me. When I scanned her Bible one morning after breakfast, I was inspired by the presence of a curriculum addendum to it: A collection of scriptures organized around the subject of financial breakthroughs, and other collections of scriptures organized on the subject of spiritual warfare.

I decided to order my own copy of this Bible edition, with intentions to start reading it as I would be field surveying in New Orleans within the coming 2 weeks. It was like adding another perspective to an upcoming professional adventure, so that I could maybe learn and enrich myself while seeking to advance the Gentilly Project.

METHODS

I used autoethnography to develop this testimony of what occurred during 32 fateful days in New Orleans during the year after Hurricane Katrina. Autoethnography is a qualitative research approach which facilitates connecting my autobiographical experiences to the broader theme and meanings of faith and academic careers. I applied it as an approach to engage in an inventory of my past experiences, through a conscious lens of self-reflective inquiry, in order to explore the story of when my faith (i.e., my belief in and experience of God) shifted, which subsequently affected my resilience within the academic profession and transformed my conceptions of scholarly identity.

In order to address this experience as more than a subjective one, I took steps to rediscover and verify specific events, including the context and timing of events and my particular perceptions and expressed states of mind during these events. This search and revisiting of available documentation provided the foundation of this autoethnographic approach.

Records

As I began to revisit this period of my life over ten years ago, I sought, assembled, and reviewed archival records. This time (December 8, 2006 to January 8, 2007) was acutely fast paced, uncertain, and emotional for me, so I was wary of accepting my memories and interpretation of significant events and their details at face value. Discovery and use of these records, which were mostly digital and from both personal and public sources, informed my recalling, correction, and corroboration of events (their timing, their substance, their context) from the 32-day period.

I used calendars from late 2006 and early 2007 to verify and serve as a check against my memories. These records refreshed specifics of what happened when, on which dates, and in relation to the timing and sequence of other events. Revisiting this information at times led me to remember specific perspectives and considerations that had been salient to me at particular moments long ago.

Public online records, in particular the project's blog (Jett, 2006), were useful to reconstruct with greater precision and context the project's progress during the 32 days, including what tactical goals were on particular days, when goals were met or exceeded, what barriers and concerns weighed most heavily at critical moments, and further when my expectations for the project were frustrated or elevated. I also searched public online records to check for possible discrepancies between a blog post's publication date and the actual date of events within and outside the project. If, for example, on a particular day where a blog post described rain, warmth and sun, or freezing temperatures in New Orleans, was this indeed the case?

Personal digital records, such as information contained in personal emails, revealed instances when I incorrectly assumed the timing of events. For instance, a religious advertisement I saw shortly before the separation from my spouse led me to discover a marriage-restoration ministry online. I assumed I must have signed up in September 2006, but a confirmation email receipt indicates it was late October.

Another instance is the timing of when I purchased a particular Bible after visiting my wife's grandmother during the Fall of 2006, before commencing my launch of field mapping operations in early December. I thought the visit must have been in October, assuming there might be a period of weeks between purchasing the Bible and deciding to bring it with me to read on downtime while leading the project in New Orleans. However, it was a more compressed time window than I remembered. My personal email records showed that I visited my wife's grandmother several days before Thanksgiving. I purchased the same Bible edition that she had on the day after Thanksgiving (Friday, November 24, 2006), for delivery the week before the start of field operations on December 8.

Private email records further revealed my thoughts and feelings at particular moments in my own words, such as my describing the state of my religious belief to the author of the slate.com series "Blogging the Bible" on Christmas Day 2006.

Gentilly Project (October–November, 2006)

The 32 fateful days of the Gentilly Project addressed in this chapter originally began as the goal of address-level field mapping of a single Gentilly neighborhood called Pontchartrain Park in about two weeks. Pontchartrain Park is an historic neighborhood, the first in the city of New Orleans developed and permitted for African-American homeowners. At the time of Hurricane Katrina, many of its residents were upper-middle class, college-educated seniors, and the neighborhood's houses had significant flooding with accompanying mold damage.

The originally scheduled field survey dates (December 8 to December 22) were chosen to coincide with the operating window of Dartmouth College's student group service initiatives in the New Orleans area. I had hoped that by choosing dates aligned with Dartmouth students' presence in town for service activities, I might have access to students as volunteers—if they had spare time—or learn of and gain access to other potential volunteers through them.

Spiritual Warfare

In parallel with seeking to complete address-level color code mapping in Pontchartrain Park, I was also engaged on a personal journey of seeking understanding and relationship with God.

My main instrument and object to achieve this was the Bible I purchased in November 2006, less than two weeks before the start of Gentilly surveying on December 8. It was a King James version special edition: *God's Victorious Army—Financial Breakthrough Spiritual Warfare Bible*, with commentaries by Pentecostal evangelist Morris Cerullo, 1996.

After receiving my edition in the mail, I began a routine of reading. I began with the selected scriptures and commentaries focused on spiritual warfare, starting with the first thematic subject with plans to continue in sequence through the additional 15 spiritual warfare subjects during the months ahead. I hoped to maintain study of one scripture with its commentary per day within the subject area I was reading. During the 32 days that are the focus of this chapter, my readings were within the first three spiritual warfare subjects:

1. *What Must We Do That We Might Work the Works of God?* We can be proof producers and prove that Jesus is alive by manifesting these same miracles in our lives (17 scriptures).
2. *Who is a Minister?* A true minister is a servant who is willing to give of himself in every area of his life, just as Jesus poured Himself out by laying aside His divinity and giving His life as a sacrifice for the world (10 scriptures).
3. *Go Beyond The Point of Blessing.* God wants you to operate in the same power and anointing that was upon His Son, Jesus Christ. Beyond the point of blessing is a spiritual relationship that will enable you to walk in power (4 scriptures).

Devotionals

As I reconstructed my path with support of archival records, I retraced my path reading these biblical themes of spiritual warfare with associated scriptures.

Reflecting on these themes and scriptures, I partitioned my combined spiritual and managerial leadership journey into six devotionals, each focused on a particular day that offered a pivotal sign or moment. I present each passage using a simple structure. Each leads with a selected scripture from the Bible that reflects the meaning I see today in that day's events. Each continues a descriptive, synoptic story of what happened that day. Each ends with my reflection on the significance of that day in terms of my own spiritual, emotional, and intellectual journey.

DEVOTIONALS

Day 1

And we know that in all things God works for the good of those who love him, who have been called according to his purpose.
—Romans 8:28, NIV

When I arrived in New Orleans the day before, there were reasons to be hopeful. My research assistant Christiana and I had arrived uneventfully by flight in the afternoon, then picked up a rental car. We visited the Gentilly neighborhood briefly: First, to check in and obtain keys to the lab space provided to us by the dean of the science school at the University of New Orleans; then to compare our census-block mapping assignments to the addresses on the street. We met with John, a business owner I met during an executive program at Dartmouth. He drove from Atlanta to volunteer with us for a week. Another business owner from the program, named Pamela, had offered to help find us volunteer housing in the city, using her networks. She called about an hour before dusk to tell us what she had located. As the sun set, John, Christiana, and I moved into a large empty house with three dozen beds.

However, on the previous day, I had also seen a reason for despair. When Christiana and I had visited Pontchartrain Park, the focus of our surveying the next 2 weeks, we learned that our census-block sheets were not matching the addresses we were seeing on the street. I was confused and alarmed by this. The system I expected to use to achieve our goal was wrong, and our plan to survey the neighborhood systematically had gone awry.

The barracks house was so cold that night, I had problems sleeping. The weather was much colder that night and the following morning than we had expected or planned. My winter coat and heavier layers of clothing were back in New Hampshire.

I had packed my new Bible, though. Two inches thick, it took up space and added great weight to my travel bag. I wondered briefly if I should have left it home instead, but let the thought go remembering its purpose. I would do my best to read at least one scripture with commentary per day, and recopy the commentary in a notebook to reinforce the words and idea. I was in the first thematic set of scriptures on spiritual warfare: *What Must We Do That We Might Work The Works of God?*

That morning after we got up, the three of us (John, Christiana, and I) dressed as warmly as we could and went to Pontchartrain Park to begin our 2 weeks of surveying. The one scheduled appointment in the late morning was Norbert, a city resident who had emailed me the week before. He was curious about my project and wanted to learn more and perhaps help.

As Norbert joined us walking the neighborhood, I explained the census-block assignment problem to him. He asked for one of the sheets for that part of the neighborhood. He looked at it and smiled. Then he used the sheet to predict addresses on the approaching sheets. There was no problem with the assignments! The issue was simply that I did not know how to read them. He promised to show me that evening.

That afternoon, I received a call from the group of Dartmouth students that I knew would be in the city. There were safety issues at the site of the service organization where they were staying and volunteering, and they asked for my help finding a new place to stay. I thought: The volunteer house has two or three dozen extra beds! We might make arrangements for the group to move in, and after I confirmed with the property manager, they did.

As Norbert was visiting the house to explain and show me how census blocks were organized and matched with addresses on the street, the group of 14 undergraduate students from Dartmouth arrived.

Significant Reflective Moment

In the beginning of the Gentilly field surveying, we had circumstances working to our favor and according to our plans: safe travel and arrival, access to free work space at a university, and just-in-time provision of volunteer housing for our core team of three. Yet, there were new circumstances that seeded confusion and doubt: specifically, problems using our intended surveying method, and also forces outside my control (e.g., outlier cold weather in New Orleans).

As Day 1 progressed, the circumstances causing me trepidation seemed to naturally settle and resolve themselves. That morning was uncharacteristically cold for New Orleans (it was, in fact, record setting), and it would not be that cold again during the remainder of our stay. A stranger whom I had already scheduled to meet had the answer to the survey method problem and would have useful suggestions and offer property-lot maps to apply the method more easily. A group of Dartmouth students with whom I was in contact suddenly needed a new place to stay (and volunteer) within the city, and the night before I had moved into a large house with many empty beds that could provide them shelter.

In uncertain circumstances, I often assumed unforeseen events would be a threat or harmful to me. That day vividly showed me how the fortuitous and helpful might arise from uncertainty. It was like I had received proof that serendipity does indeed exist, and it might reliably appear for my good when I was publicly working for a purpose greater than my private interests and needs.

Day 7

> *He said: "Listen, King Jehoshaphat and all who live in Judah and Jerusalem! This is what the Lord says to you: 'Do not be afraid or discouraged because of this vast army. For the battle is not yours, but God's."*
> —2 Chronicles 20:15, NIV

Mapping Pontchartrain Park was finished 2 days early. Here is how it happened.

On Day 1, the group of 14 Dartmouth undergraduates moved into our volunteer house barracks during the evening. On Day 2, they joined us in mapping the neighborhood, based on our understanding of how to properly survey by census tract and the property-lot maps provided by Norbert. That day, a student leader of another Dartmouth service group in the city contacted me. It was a team of graduate students who were in the same conditions that the undergraduate group had recently left. The leader asked: Would I possibly have housing and a different service opportunity for them too? On Day 3, the team of nine graduate students moved into the volunteer house.

On Day 5, over a week ahead of schedule, we completed the address-level survey of Pontchartrain Park. On Day 6, we completed a second neighborhood, one adjacent to Pontchartrain Park, that had approximately the same number of addresses.

On this day (Day 7), we started a third neighborhood and expected to finish it by day's end. We already had plans to meet with residents from a fourth neighborhood on Day 9 to enlist their volunteer help. Yet, at our current pace, I thought we might complete their neighborhood before meeting with them.

Significant Reflective Moment

I was in the midst of something wonderful. While I could conceive and communicate what was occurring in academic and professional terms, I felt a bold spirit inhabiting the project too.

From an operations management perspective, our capacity was growing. Our output completing address-level field surveying per hour and per day was increasing. I could measure, estimate, and project where our collective progress might be some days ahead, as well as see the levers that might either grow or interrupt our output during the course of a day. As a team, we began to anticipate and plan how we started, transitioned, and ended our surveying: For instance, more intentionally planning for lunch and breaks, and deciding which volunteers would be needed where for what purposes to complete mapping of neighborhoods more expediently. These were all the features one would expect in managing a project, technically speaking.

At the same time, I was experiencing something beyond project management techniques. It felt like guiding a mission, where the inspiration and talents of any of the volunteers might lead or result in the operation adapting or taking on new and unforeseen directions to fulfill its goals: successively mapping Gentilly neighborhoods by address (Red, Yellow, Blue, or Green). More than my knowledge and understanding were behind the pull and momentum we were experiencing. It felt astonishing, delightful, and miraculous.

Day 10

> *"For I know the plans I have for you," declares the Lord, "plans to prosper you and not to harm you, plans to give you hope and a future."*
> —Jeremiah 29:11, NIV

It was Sunday, December 17, a sunny day with blue skies. The New Orleans Saints, the city's football team, had a winning record, and there was much excitement about town for the afternoon's home game. The previous Sunday, in response to an invitation from a Gentilly resident, I attended mass at St. Leo The Great Catholic Church. While I was not attending church that morning, a form of sabbath and setting time aside for God (for both myself and the project) was part of my thinking.

The project had a pace and rhythm to it. Local residents were joining the Dartmouth student volunteers in the field on a regular basis. We had conducted outreach through a variety of methods, including distributing flyers, contacting neighborhood associations, setting up an information table in the field, and relying on the word-of-mouth of previous volunteers who had mapped with us.

I think what attracted residents the most as volunteers was them seeing us organized in pairs, circling multiple blocks in their neighborhoods during the same 2–3 hour period. When residents were curious and asked what we were doing, we had a real story to tell about why we were there and could refer to the specific progress we were making (e.g., which neighborhoods we had already finished).

However, the project was also in transition. The house where we were all staying, due to its previous commitments to other volunteering groups, was unable to house our full group moving forward. The undergraduate group moved out and pursued another service project they had created. The rest of us relocated to a box-trailer camping site at the edge of the city near the airport, and the graduate group planned to continue Gentilly mapping.

While I had confidence from the unexpected progress (i.e., mapping more than several neighborhoods within 2 weeks, not one), I was also questioning how I would know I was proceeding in the right way.

I went to a fast food restaurant for breakfast. When I was in line, two brothers (brothas) behind me were talking about God. One made the point that God sees the love in what you do, even if you don't get the results you intend. He went on to say it's the love in the act, not just the act in isolation, that God wants to see.

I turned around and acknowledged I was listening. We joked together for a quick minute. However, the line was hardly moving, so they decided to go eat somewhere else.

As they left, the brother who made the points about God turned around to me and smiled: "I think you got what you needed though."

Significant Reflective Moment

I was gradually making my way through different scriptures in my Bible and commentary, still under the theme: "What Must We Do That We Might Work the Works of God?" The reading and reflection fostered a comfort with uncertainty and consideration of bold steps within the project, yet I still naturally had doubts. I knew it was unclear what I might do or change or stop within the project during the coming days. I could see there was plenty in the project beyond my control. What would be my anchor during these remaining several days in New Orleans? How would I look for it?

On this day, I learned I might not always struggle for a sign. The sign will sometimes find me, providing answers to questions I want answered but have not clearly formulated. When I do not see or have a plan, God might already have a plan for me.

Day 14

> *But he said to me, "My grace is sufficient for you, for my power is made perfect in weakness." Therefore, I will boast all the more gladly about my weaknesses, so that Christ's power may rest on me.*
> —2 Corinthians 12:9, NIV

It was several days before Christmas. I was leaving New Orleans soon, and I had already decided to return after Christmas to continue and finish the other Gentilly neighborhoods.

We had completed 5 of the 22 neighborhoods, covering about a third of the roughly 15,000 district addresses. What remained included several of the largest neighborhoods. I had asked one of the graduate students to spend the full day researching how many total census blocks were there in Gentilly. He found over 800, and I recalled that once the team completed (i.e., collection with data entry) about two dozen blocks in a full day. There was a lot more to do, but it seemed feasible having identified the total blocks and having estimates of what might be achieved in a day.

I asked if the graduate students were willing to return to New Orleans after Christmas Day. It would be for a week, ahead of the close to Dartmouth's winter break. I would cover our expenses: the roundtrip flights from New Hampshire, and our housing, rental cars, and food in New Orleans. Three of the nine graduate students volunteered. Meanwhile, my research assistant Christiana had received a full-time employment offer, and the employer's preference was for an immediate start. She and I discussed the situation. Although she was a great help and was willing to ask for a postponed start, I wanted her to seize that opportunity.

With the achievements and relationships with Gentilly residents who had already volunteered, I envisioned a post-Christmas completion of the remaining 17 neighborhoods of the district, hopefully before Dartmouth's winter term started the first week of January. However, although I could envision this, I understood what a leap this would be. I did not need to delve into the calculations to see: The increase in our scale of mapping capacity must greatly exceed the past 2 weeks. Although I had seen significant increases in mapping capacity the past 2 weeks over what I had imagined on Day 1, I knew I probably lacked the resources and plan on this Day 14 to achieve the vision I had.

I was scared. I said to myself: "God help me."

Significant Reflective Moment

Given the collective progress on the project in 2 weeks, more than I had reasonably imagined, it seemed unthankful to God or the universe to stop. Perhaps a complete surveying of Gentilly might be achieved quickly and soon, although I was unclear exactly how.

The gap between what had been surveyed and the completion of the whole district was significant, but would it not be more interesting and important in scholarly perspective to complete a survey of more (all) of the Gentilly neighborhoods in a continuous short span of weeks, instead of interrupted over a period of months?

I also asked myself: What must I do that I might work the works of God? Although the gaps to achieve this seemed impossible, I had no doubt. That I might work the works of God, I would pursue a complete survey of Gentilly quickly and soon, even if I might fail.

Day 23

> *Direct my footsteps according to your word; let no sin rule over me.*
> —Psalm 119:133, NIV

The moment I woke up and opened my eyes in bed, I was curious and excited. I thought: What will God have us do today?

It was December 30, a day the team had been anticipating and planning for over a week. This was our most ambitious goal to date: mapping three neighborhoods in one day. This was Saturday; we had scheduled ahead before Christmas, and had contacted local residents and neighborhood associations to volunteer for a critical surveying day.

There were five of us on the core team: three graduate students, plus one spouse and myself. It was our third day back in New Orleans. In spite of a couple of obstacles we had to overcome with our flights and preparing our mapping assignments, we had made progress the past 2 days. We had finished three more Gentilly neighborhoods, bringing the project's total to 8 of 22.

However, there was a problem. Yesterday, a heavy rain had been forecast for today. One of the neighborhood association presidents we had collaborated with for today's ambitious mapping day had had access to a couple dozen volunteers to help. By last night, those volunteers had already cancelled.

Sarah was co-leader of the Dartmouth graduate team participating with me before Christmas. Sharing her experience with her spouse had convinced him to join the team for this after-Christmas effort. She had come to me last night, asking for a decision. Should we cancel mapping tomorrow?

I had answered, thinking about it, that if it indeed poured rain tomorrow, we could and should not be mapping. Our process involved the use of clipboards and paper lists of addresses. Surveying in a downpour made little sense. So my final decision before going to bed that night:

"If it rains, we're not going to map. If it doesn't rain, we will. We'll see in the morning." When I woke up in the morning, I jumped out of bed. I ran to the window, listening for rain, and I pulled the curtain open. With faint light outside, I saw the pavement. The parking lot was dry. Not a drop.

I turned on the television for the latest weather. The early-day forecast said no rain in the morning, but heavy rain starting after the noon hour. I immediately called Sarah.

Our original plan was to map the three neighborhoods at separate times throughout the day: one in the morning, another in the midday, and a final one in the afternoon. I asked Sarah to call the three neighborhood presidents. We would complete all three neighborhoods concurrently.

Residents from the midday scheduled neighborhood would come to the morning scheduled neighborhood, to help quickly complete the surveying. Then residents from both neighborhoods might go together to complete the midday neighborhood.

We began with the first neighborhood. When it was near complete mid-late morning, I went to the afternoon scheduled neighborhood to guide mapping of its residents.

All three neighborhoods were completed by not long past the noon hour. As we finished the final neighborhood, the sky grew dark and heavy. It poured rain hard for the rest of the afternoon and evening.

Significant Reflective Moment

I trusted God's will, not my own. I was prepared to submit to whatever conditions provided. If it was raining that morning, I imagined us staying inside because God had another purpose. If rain was no longer anticipated for the day that morning, I was prepared to proceed as our team had planned, grateful for having suitable conditions that I knew were outside our ability to control and influence.

When I saw the Lord supplied neither one of the dichotomous choices I expected, I remained obedient to my purpose. When I learned it would rain hard in the afternoon and not much at all in the morning, my mind did wrestle with what to do. The idea to pursue the three neighborhoods concurrently instead just appeared in my head, and my focus turned to connecting with Sarah about execution.

Day 29

> *"For it is by grace you have been saved, through faith—and this is not from yourselves, it is the gift of God."*
> —Ephesians 2:8, NIV

Late in the afternoon of January 5, I was alone in the project's lab space at the University of New Orleans. The building was so quiet, I wondered if I might be the only one there. It was now 9 days since returning to New Orleans after Christmas. We had mapped nine neighborhoods in that time, leaving a total of 14 completed of 22. The remaining 8 neighborhoods included the three largest in Gentilly.

Yesterday had been the start of Dartmouth's winter term. The team of three students plus spouse had returned to New Hampshire, and I had postponed my return flight indefinitely. I would not return home until all of Gentilly was completed.

It was unclear when that might be. I was unable to specify a date, because the completion would depend on the level of participating volunteers each day. I had a rough estimate that I shared with the team before they left. If I had about 50 volunteers for one day, I thought I could finish the remaining neighborhoods.

I considered that I might recruit residents to volunteer. However, there were two things I had not considered. First, it was January 5, the end of the holiday season. It would be harder to find residents and other volunteers to participate moving forward, especially during the weekdays, since more people were returning to work. Second, I had overestimated my time and ability to actively recruit volunteers. For the past several weeks, student volunteers were doing that with and for me, sometimes when they were out in the field surveying.

As I realized these things, I began to despair. It might be weeks before the remaining neighborhoods were completed. I thought of the solitude and comfort of my home in New Hampshire. Even with the frigid outdoor temperatures up north, I imagined the house warm and appealing. I wanted to go home.

I was sitting at the desk, lost in my head, when the office phone rang.

"Hello."
"Hello, I'm looking for Dr. Jett"
"Speaking..."
"We have about 50 volunteers here at our church..."
"I'll take them!"
"All of them?!"
"Yes!"

Within 2 hours, I was meeting with the leaders of the large student group, who were from the University of Massachusetts at Boston. The next day, there were over fifty volunteers mapping several neighborhoods. I had never yet had so many volunteers at once surveying, and at times I lost track and we had to retrieve and transport groups of several volunteers who had been lost.

The group could only volunteer for the one day. The largest neighborhoods were completed, but the two least flood-damaged neighborhoods and portions of others were incomplete.

Two days later, Gentilly residents finished the mapping and, led by one of their own, brought me the results as I rested and prepared to return to New Hampshire.

Significant Reflective Moment

I had doubts and was exhausted. I did not see a way out due to the constraints imposed by a lack of resources and ability. Then, suddenly like the wind, I had help.

If you had told me on Day 1 that the Gentilly Project would be completed in 32 days, I would not have believed you. I was without a plan, a budget, or a team to credibly expect it would be done. Yet, it happened. In pursuing this effort, I had a purpose (why I was mapping Gentilly) and an end-in-mind (what I was mapping in Gentilly: field classification of each address in each neighborhood as Red, Yellow, Blue, Green), and the knowledge that I lacked the means to achieve it within such a short period of time. I thought that I would maybe have a complete mapping of the district done in 6 months if I was fortunate and smartly applied my knowledge and use of organization and management theories.

Instead, I experienced and learned a different kind of favor. My knowledge and use of theories were insufficient to achieve this surprising collective achievement with volunteers. What provided me with resilience and envisioned steps forward through the uncertainty and constraints in my circumstances, and the means to live beyond my fears and doubts, was my intentional pursuit and walk in relationship with God.

THE SCIENCE OF CHARITY

"The life I am living is not the same as the life that wants to live in me."
—Palmer, 2000

After completing this first district-wide survey of Gentilly in 32 days (January 2007), I would be divorced within three months. I would also join a church for the first time, eventually becoming a background vocalist on its worship team. Two years after the fateful 32 days in Gentilly, I had a tenure-track faculty offer: an assistant professorship position in the School of Public Affairs and Administration at the Newark campus of Rutgers University in New Jersey. After nine more months, I began the appointment. I taught undergraduate public service majors in my home school, as well as undergraduate social entrepreneurship courses in the Rutgers Business School.

During the next 5 years, I sought to adapt and conform to the academic research disciplines of public administration and nonprofit management. In public administration, I saw that my management research background and interests were closest to the subfield of performance management, but the journals, theories, and empirical research were significantly different without cross-fertilization. A promising topic to bridge my fundamental identity as a scholar of organization management and innovation with the public administration research realm was *governing emergent public responses to disasters*. The nonprofit management research realm was more interdisciplinary, and thus a better fit with my research style and interests. Research topics attractive to me included food charities (e.g., food pantries and food rescue) and the religious foundations of contemporary philanthropy (in Christianity and also Islam). In teaching, I became comfortable redesigning course curricula in public/nonprofit administration to infuse my business management, innovation, and STEM backgrounds.

Finally, almost eight years after the fateful 32 days mapping Gentilly (November 2014), I sat in the large multipurpose room in Rutgers University–Newark's student center. I was watching the live-stream of a funeral. And I had learned by email 2 hours before that I had been denied tenure.

Resilience

The funeral was for Professor Clement Price, a beloved longtime professor at Rutgers University–Newark. I knew him, and I had once attended a Black faculty/staff event at his house. I cannot say we were personally close. I put attending his funeral virtually at the student center on my calendar, given how crowded it was expected to be (and was) at the church homegoing service. Professor Price's field was history. In addition to being a tenured professor at Rutgers, he was the official historian of the city of Newark, New Jersey. With my eclectic interests within fields of management and organizations, I was always captivated by his perspective and remarks about Newark as a place and institution. However, it was mostly a small but poignant sense of overlapping journeys that drew me to his funeral. Clement Price was an African-American faculty member in the generation ahead of me. Also, he had died following complications from a stroke 2 weeks before. About two years before, my blood pressure was so high as I was submitting for contract renewal, I was in territory medically to have a stroke myself. Thank God, I did not.

Professor Price's (Clem's) funeral happening on the same morning I learned I was denied tenure at Rutgers was coincidental. Yet, it was a mournful moment that centered me, brought me closer to God, and protected me. Being denied tenure is painful, invoking powerful feelings of sadness, anger, and disappointment. But while virtually attending the church homegoing service for Clem that morning, I realized that being denied tenure was a blow that did not sting. At a moment I was expecting to be broken, I felt surprisingly undefeated.

Public Scholarship

During a peak of music and spirit and emotion during Clem's funeral, there were suddenly words in my head. It was an answer to a question I had not yet formed, so was not struggling with yet. God spoke to me: "You will contribute to the science of charity."

All the varied and seemingly disorganized experiences that I had had since the 32 fateful days of Gentilly 8 years before, and even extending back further to the start of my days in middle school, my undergraduate years, and my initial years as a doctoral student all made holistic sense for an instant. The unified sense of what I have been doing all my life faded relatively quickly, but I remembered the lesson. I do not need the academic profession for validation. The excellence I seek that empowers me and gives me resilience does not come from the professorship, or being employed by a college or university, or from seeking or having tenure.

Seeking an ongoing and more intimate relationship with God has given me courage to overcome the pressures of academic careerism. My faith journey has enabled me to hear and accept the call and responsibility to contribute as a scholar to the public's good and well-being. Placing God above tenure has enabled me to claim joy, creativity, and hope as fundamental values of my scholarly identity, serving as antidote to the pessimism and misanthropy which at times flourish within academic cultures. I am a scholar and a human being who wants to care and make a difference for people and the world with the talents that God has given me.

My faith walk during the 32 fateful days of Gentilly did more than make scholarship tolerable. It began another dimension of living as a scholar. Thirteen years later, I see that not only did I discover the fruits of intentionally walking with God with a scholarly mind and identity intact, but I also see that God has been walking with me the whole time in my career and life.

REFERENCES

Avery, D. (2008). Assessing our impact: In search of a metric for multicultural research. *The Industrial-Organizational Psychologist, 45*(3), 65–70.
Berman, H. J. (1997). Judeo-Christian versus pagan scholarship. In K. M. Kulberg (Ed.), *Finding God at Harvard: Spiritual journeys of thinking Christians* (pp. 291–298). Downers Grove, IL: InterVarsity Press.
Gerzina, G. H. (2009). *Mr. and Mrs. Prince: How an extraordinary eighteenth-century family moved out of slavery and into legend.* New York, NY: Amistad.
Hammett, G. (1997). Why be a scientist? In K. M. Kulberg (Ed.), *Finding God at Harvard: Spiritual journeys of thinking Christians* (pp. 275–282). Downers Grove, IL: InterVarsity Press.
Jett, Q. R. (2006, December 31). Get on the good foot. *Gentilly Project.* Retrieved from http://gentillyproject.blogspot.com/2006/12/
John, B. (1997). A sense of mystery: Reflections of a monk. In K. M. Kulberg (Ed.), *Finding God at Harvard: Spiritual journeys of thinking Christians* (pp. 307–312). Downers Grove, IL: InterVarsity Press.
Kullberg, K. M. (1997). *Finding God at Harvard: Spiritual journeys of thinking Christians.* Downers Grove, IL: InterVarsity Press.
Loury, G. (1997). A professor under reconstruction. In K. M. Kulberg (Ed.), *Finding God at Harvard: Spiritual journeys of thinking Christians* (pp. 67–76). Downers Grove, IL: InterVarsity Press.
March, J. G. (1996). Continuity and change in theories of organizational action. *Administrative Science Quarterly, 41*(2), 278–287.
Palmer, P. J. (2000). *Let your life speak: Listening for the voice of vocation.* San Francisco, CA: Jossey-Bass.
Schwartz, M. S. (2006). God as a managerial Stakeholder? *Journal of Business Ethics, 66*(2/3), 291–306.

CHAPTER 2

CAN WORK BE REDEEMED THROUGH PLAY?

(Or Why Is Playing Not an Option)

Raymond Carr
Pepperdine University

I begin with a confession. I experienced something akin to a guilty pleasure and pangs of conscience when I began thinking of the concept of play, especially while enduring a world rife with social, political, and economic turmoil. To put it frankly, we live in perilous times. But it is exactly during such times that a "redemptive spirituality" can be most instructive. The question "Can work be redeemed through play?" is in fact aimed at helping readers negotiate these times.

In my view, the customary framing of the conflict between work and play has produced misinterpretations. The tendency to see play or leisure as the reward of labor or as radically separated from work reveals a failure of insight as to the meaning of theological play. A theology of play, particularly as informed by deeper insight into aesthetics of spirituality, can actually liberate work from alienation in relation to God, human vocations, and self-understanding. To illuminate the significance of theological play, I will first attend to various theologies of play, offer suggestions for how these positions coincide with human labor, and close with what I hope are inspirational insights into the way a redemptive spirituality can redeem work through play.

The term redemptive spirituality—because of its religious overtones—often sounds more dogmatic and rigid than free and inspiring to some ears, but I have no such narrow connotations in mind. In this chapter, I posit redemptive spirituality as a peculiar, mundane, and sometimes even profane way of freely living—a free mode of human being which finds its ground tone in a spontaneous and improvisational relationship to the living God. This framing is opposed to more regimented, even mechanical, modes of being that emerge in industrial complexes that are often encountered in American workplaces and bootstrap moralities. As I will demonstrate, this mode of being also transcends religious conventions on one hand and ideological convictions on the other.

To commend these insights to students of theology, I have created the following tightly developed statement about being human: "Biblical faith is not about being religious, it is about being *radically* human; but being radically human includes God and the religious things we do—properly situated."[1] For this reason I will try to frame and properly situate play in relation to work—interpreted as an age old problem—especially in our modern post-industrial, technocratically driven societies. I believe a deeper sense of humanity can come from (re)considering the relationship between work and play which is evident in the joy, thanksgiving, and glorious liberty to which the element of play is a fruitful, though broken, witness.

But because the tension between work and play is an age-old problem, properly situating this part of human life means acknowledging the problem of how humans engage each other in work environments. As the Anglican lay theologian William Stringfellow (2006) noted "no form of idolatry is more cynically practiced or more empirically corrupted" than the ethic of work (p. 23); thus, in alienated forms of labor, life encroaches on human freedom, twisting and turning its subjects in unintended directions—as the world and its institutions, ideologies, and imaginaries stake their claims on human priorities. Religion and work, especially religious understanding as a justification for work, ironically leads the way in making such claims on the deeper more resourceful notions of human freedom. It is as if religion and work jostle with one another as they dialectically compete for the lion's share of human attention, framing human behavior so that achievement and productivity become self-justifying modes of living. God, religion—or the more contemporary common term—spirituality coalesce as shibboleths so-called "believers" often use to justify themselves over against wary unbelievers and perhaps even lazy co-workers. Religion even reinforces ideological notions of work; and work reinforces religion.

The speciously healthy relationship between work and religion is what partly encourages me to plant seeds on the first day of class in order to help students walk more confidently in a freedom that first of all leads away from religious ideology—not from God or various faith traditions, but a freedom from religious conventions that occlude human beings from living in a way that is "more radically human." Ironically, this way of thinking represents the first step for students who are on a journey to deepen and (re)orient their relationship to various faith traditions and society in general and to that most basic and cynically practiced mode of being, that is, human work. In beginning this discussion among students, I make an important distinction between faith *in God* and religious acts, puritanical notions of self-control, and even spiritual formation, ideas typically presented as some type of moral self-justification.

This brings me closer to the goal of this text since the editor has suggested that one way of thinking more deeply about faith relates to the freedom to ask questions. Blessed, indeed, are those who ask the questions! Thomas Merton (1970), a Trappist monk, once declared that "in the progress toward religious understanding, one does not go from answer to answer but from question to question. One's questions are answered, not by clear definitive answers, but by more pertinent and more crucial questions" (pp. 29–30). Questions in fact are often more important than our answers. Questions, if left uninterrogated, remain freighted with presuppositions and suppositions that shape and determine our ultimate conclusions. Questions can be abstract and speculative and pedantically theoretical, running roughshod over the complexity of human experience or so deeply shaped by the concrete that there is no room for the metaphysical. Merton is commending the reader, from a theological vantage point, to a more free way of being. In this regard, the need for better questions has led me to reconsider what "play" has to say to work. And, more specifically, to ask a question that on the surface may sound blasphemous or even sacrilegious, that is, "Can work be redeemed by play?" I am feeling that guilty pleasure again.

Again, to explore this question—or perhaps to come to a more pertinent question—I will first introduce a few examples of theologies of play, attend to the dialectic between work and play (and their common experience as alienated realities). I will then close with a return to a deeper engagement with what the fragmentary nature of play suggests as I reconsider our provocative question theologically. In the end, I hope to corroborate the wisdom of another exclamatory statement I use to remind students of their need to interrogate their questions, that is, "You must question your questions!"

THEOLOGIES OF PLAY

When referring to theologies of play, the critical literature of this genre has been growing, although theologies of play remain relegated to the margins of the discipline itself. There were, however, theologians whose approach to the task of theology had already gestured in this direction.[2] Karl Barth provides such an example. Barth (1960) offered a subtle hint toward play when he described 19th century theologians as being "a little too serious at being professors, taking themselves too seriously" (p. 17). Barth remained suspicious of the bourgeois person who did not know how to play. His eschatological view of God did not ignore human experience or achievement, but harnessed it, bracketing it so that people did not revel in their egotism. Barth (1962) suggested that the church and the community of faith should approach the world "not as a spoilsport, but in the knowledge that art and science, business and politics, techniques and education are really a game—a serious game, but a game, and *game* means an imitative and ultimately ineffective activity—the significance of which lies not in its attainable goals but in what it signifies" (p. 349). For Barth (1963), this way of viewing the world gave way to a type of playful humor tied to his understanding of God whom he called the "bounteous God," and he cast theology as not merely a science, but because of its special "subject matter," theology came to be a free and joyful science in light of the mystery of God (p. 9). Mozart's music even functioned as an analogy of the freedom of God in Barth's theological thinking; and he furthermore thought a theology of redemption should be a theology of play—because God has redeemed (or liberated) the world.

God therefore liberates human beings to a peculiar freedom; dare I say it—they are given the *freedom to play*; so when God comes, according to Barth (1981b), God brings a "loosening, release, and relaxation" into obedient play—a play that is the mode of being for children of God (p. 502). This coming of God reorients our attitudes to work: "our work in relation to his [God's] is more play than work" (p. 502). This element of play has been lost in our modern preoccupations with personal achievement. Interpreted in Barth's way, however, play revolutionizes our vision of work beyond limitations that shape and color the more radical ways of being human in the world, limitations that stifle imaginations, ratchet up our apprehensions, and steal our relaxation. Perhaps this is what Jesus means when the Bible says, "For my yoke is easy, and my burden is light" (Matthew 11:30, NIV). The free play of the Gospel does not burden because it represents the unearned gift of good news, whereas human beings often seek heavy burdens as a form of self-justification.

William Stringfellow, who is often described as graduating from Harvard and moving into Harlem, lawyered among poor Blacks. Partly, because of his recognition of how Blacks identified deleterious institutional powers,

Stringfellow became more aware of the way "death" functioned in the world, an experience which simultaneously gave him a more acute sense of play, informing his theopolitical work. Stringfellow (1982), for instance, loved the circus. Whenever a circus came to town, he visited when possible, and even found occasions to spend "summer weeks traveling with the Clyde Beatty-Cole Brothers Circus through New England and part of New York State" (p. 89). For Stringfellow the circus was *not* an escape from the realities of the world. The circus was a commentary that gave him perspective for engaging in the common life of the world. He called the circus a "parable of the eschaton," meaning that the circus in some way became an analogy or parable of the end times, the promise of God, that is, a parable of what is ultimate. Stated differently, the circus should be considered with a profound seriousness which reminded him of what should ultimately shape his mode of being in the world. One could even ask, what Stringfellow saw in the circus that made it witness to the ultimate? The answer is that during this golden age of the circus in America, Stringfellow (1982) witnessed what he described as "human 'oddities' and 'curiosities'—giants, [little persons], and the exceptionally obese; [conjoined] twins, albinos" and more (p. 89).

For him the circus represented an "eschatological company in which all sorts and conditions of life are congregated" (p. 89). In terms of both its gathered style of life and the circus performances, he could see how the circus made a parody of life. It was a witness to a grand participation in life by all kinds of people; and although Stringfellow does not entertain this point, the circus performers themselves made a parody of work even as they participated in a form of play. Said differently, what appears as play for circus performances was actually work.

Others also attempted to write theologies and philosophies of play, respectively. James H. Cone (1972), the father of Black theology, found his orientation in the playfulness of the spirituals and the blues. The blues for him were "secular spirituals" where he heard affirmations of life; and the spirituals were identified as "religiously social," songs where he heard the liberation of God in the midst of life—including work, sociopolitical communities, and the larger society (pp. 30–35). These spirituals provided slaves, and later victims of de jure and de facto segregation, with a way to endure the profound tensions that existed in the interstices of social chaos where even God seemed to be absent. Cone thus used the spirituals and the blues to negotiate the dialectical relationship between faithful political engagement and joyful self-affirmation, eliciting all kinds of responses, including playful humor.

Angela Davis (1998), a political activist, academic, and author, was also a connoisseur of the blues engaging in "blues practices" that informed "working-class women as capable of exercising some measure of agency in choosing their partners" (p. 46). Davis, for instance, utilized the blues to stimulate profound reflections on the autonomy and resiliency that the blues provided to working class Black women::

> I want to emphasize for the moment, the importance of women's blues as a site for the independent elaboration and affirmation of subjectivity and community for women of the black working class. Through the blues, black women were able to autonomously work out as audiences and performers—a working class model of womanhood. This model of womanhood was based in part on a collective historical memory of what had been previously required of women to cope with slavery. (p. 46)

The point of these examples is to raise important questions for the reader. How do *you* play? And, perhaps more importantly, how does your form of play inform and reconcile you to the work you do? To be sure, one of the ways to work more humanly is to understand work from the vantage point of play.

In terms of my personal analogical point of contact for play, the genre of jazz provides insight to my constructive theological development. In particular, the musical aesthetic of the so-called Bebop jazz artist, Thelonious Monk, has helped to shape my theological vision. Monk was a brilliant artist whose music contained a lighthearted ludic element. Even when he played a tune like "round midnight," which routinely played as a ballad for most artists because of its "wounding melody," Monk executes the song with his characteristic harmonic delight.[3] And although Monk was technically informed, he freely broke with conventional technique in order to play what he desired. While this makes sense in jazz, since it is an art-form that is profoundly personal and individualistic, Monk endured a peculiar kind of obscurity because his aesthetic required risky choices that broke with musical conventions. Monk summed up his attitude about the issue in an interview that has led to one of his most prescient responses about what he was doing musically: "I say play your own way. Don't play what the public wants—you play what you want and let the public pick up what you are doing—even if it *does* take them fifteen, twenty years" (Hentoff, 1961, p. 184).

Monk's comment is not simply a throwaway line. For despite his grand contributions to the genre of jazz, Monk waited for more than 15 years for steady work while many of the most celebrated jazz musicians of his day benefited from his contributions (Hentoff, 1961, p. 178). Jazz critics often portrayed Monk as somewhat of a curiosity with captions such as "Mad Monk" or "The High Priest of Bop." And as Nat Hentoff (1961) writes, "There was no attempt to discuss the nature or seriousness of his musical intentions" (p. 184). Nevertheless, artists who "played" with Monk witnessed his grand contributions to jazz, including such greats as Miles Davis, Mary Lou Williams, Charlie Parker, Dizzy Gillespie, and many others.

Monk was a jazz master and several texts and documentaries witness to his genius. His composing, acknowledged for its delightful ludic quality, is spontaneous, lighthearted, and filled with juxtapositions, dissonances, and rhythmic displacements. Even a cursory hearing of his songs, such as "Lu Lu is Back in Town" or "Nice Work if You Can Get It" reveals the playfulness of Monk's music and the disarming nature of his aesthetic. These features cause critics to make misjudgments about his contributions, assuming his aesthetic is unsophisticated and lacks a profound technical understanding. Such interpretations of Monk's music are far from reality and such misjudgments reveal the tendency to judge an artist who is "at play" as lacking seriousness when, paradoxically, it is often the one at play who is perhaps the most candid and seriously concentrating on a particular task. Perhaps these oversights also reveal why Harvey Cox (1969), the Harvard divinity professor, is correct when stating that "there is an unnecessary gap in today's world between the world-changers and life celebrators" (p. viii). Indeed, a soul at play does not lack seriousness. A soul at play functions as a creative commentary on those who take themselves too seriously and, therefore, to be at play is to place a limit or critical proviso over those who arrogantly prejudge others and themselves.

Challenging Work

It is customary to juxtapose carelessly the activities of play with work in common experience. *Work and play, play and work*: these two seeming polarities form a thesis and antithesis akin to darkness and light or harmony and disharmony; moreover, the two activities are assumed to interact as somehow part of the cycle of life. There is even the old saying: "I work hard so I can play hard." It is as if there is a cat and mouse game between work and play, rather than a more fundamental way of thinking about the interrelationship between these activities. Such clichéd views about work demonstrate that the deeper biblical meaning of work and play—understood as being subject to alienation—is not a serious consideration for modern people.

On the contrary, from the standpoint of redemptive spirituality, both work and play are subject to alienation and capable of being turned into an ideology that binds people to certain agendas and alienates them from a deeper sense of freedom. This is where the hoary biblical term "fallen" comes in. It means—if I may demythologize the term—that human beings become *alienated* in their work and are often estranged from one another in work and in play; they become alienated from the joyfulness of creation, insubordinate, lacking identity and integrity in the workplace and at the playground. Theologically, such insights amount to the elementary knowledge of faith, and while some may hear in this wisdom a profound cynicism or a negative view of the world, the Bible nevertheless presents this insight as a kind of critical realism as if it is *the* true situation for human beings who live in the time between the curse and the promise (Bonhoeffer, 1960, pp. 85–86).

Alienation when at work, then, is a peculiar mode of being for everyone. A person can in fact be alienated from work for a number of reasons. Eric Fromm (1968), the agnostic psychoanalyst who had a Jewish formation, described the humanist idea of alienation as the same thing as the biblical concept of idolatry, that is, "in the prophetic sense of worshiping the work of one's own hands" (p. 136). He ventured so far as to describe alienation as a "common fight" that believers and nonbelievers share together to resolve. These differences are secondary to their common humanity and the common need to resist alienation (p. 136). Moreover, because people mistakenly reduce alienation to individual differences in social and cultural experiences, they often miss the role alienation plays in institutional life and an institutions concern for its own survival. Thus, people overlook the way they become necessary to institutions, serving institutional agendas rather than their own concrete human concerns. Theologically speaking, institutions function according to their primary concern as living realities, as created things (Barth,1931a; Stringfellow, 1964, p. 49ff.). It is therefore necessary for human persons to express their concern for the good of common humanity beyond any mere individualisms. I will briefly mention several other types of alienation in the context of work that immediately come to mind.

The first common way moderns become alienated through work is when mechanistic modes of production or an overemphasis on products functions to reduce people to being mere "cogs in a machine." These processes often focus on human usefulness, that is, production of materials rather than construction of human communities. Long work hours, unrealistic emphasis on productivity, and excessive workplace routines extract the joy out of work and diminish the spontaneity of human fellowship. In such conditions product takes precedence over the promise of human life.

These problems proliferate in academic environments, for example, where emphasis on intellectual production and utility reigns over service. Students become the commodified products without any real compensation because the substance of what one produces is sacrificed at the altar of production and the relationship therefore suffers alienation. During his sole visit to America in 1962, Karl Barth (1963) registered concern about the "ambiance of the academy" and its impact on theological thought (p. 14f). While a problematic ambiance can include a number of problems, Barth's concern seemed aimed at the deleterious way academic culture pressed theological thought towards a type of self-justification. A preoccupation with achievements encroached upon the discipline and its claims to be what Barth described as a "modest, free, critical, and happy science *sui generis* in such an environment" (pp. 15–16). Publishing houses and other institutions reinforce the estrangement in the academic industrial complex. These institutions potentially commodify the "raw products" of theological work and constrain those who would freely engage in theologizing.

In other words, theology in such environments loses its place as a response to the mystery of God and fails to exude playfulness from the discovery and enchantment surrounding the theological subject matter. To acknowledge this truth is not to ignore the need for some type of production within academic circles, but rather to track the commodifying agency of the academic industrial complex. Ironically, Barth is arguably one of the most prolific theologians in history, but he nevertheless remained sensitive to the dangers theology must face within its academic environment.

Another common way human labor is corrupted is in a corrupted spirit of competition, especially when progress based on competition juxtaposes one person in competition with another. Martin Luther King, Jr. (1967) often criticized this problem using the language of the *ends versus the means* in human endeavors, arguing that "the ends and the means cohere." For instance, when interrogating the immorality of segregation, King (1967) exposed the problem that occurs when ideology treated human beings "as means rather than ends, and thereby reduces them to things rather than persons" (pp. 96–97). King's criticism leads me to ask if there is a spirit of competition and progress that lies at the root of the race problem in America? Could it be that conspicuous consumption and competition drive human alienation? Could the cultural anxiety in the nation be tied to the profound constellation of issues that are immediately connected to the sense of economic conflict we experience with one another; and therefore people retreat and retrench to preserve personal property; thus what is really at work is a spirit of competition functioning as the zeitgeist that determines the spiritual health of our nation?

Martin King's special criterion of ends versus means also applies to the corporate world. When one lives in the corporate world s/he must always be alert to modes of exploitation—whether they issue from the framework of the structure itself, as mentioned above, or whether it makes its appearance through graft, deceit, or a lack of integrity that corrupts the joyfulness of the corporate workspace. Alienation (and reification) can be both an internal or external problem, and in agreement with Erich Fromm (1968), we must not make human beings "subservient to things, and in this process becoming a thing [themselves]" (p. 136). The third and final form of alienation may come as a surprise.

A Caveat for Play

Before addressing the problem of play theologically, I must consider a third form of alienation that, ironically, pertains to how one interprets the concept of play. Play paradoxically resides closer to the truth of redemption (or liberation) since it parodies the good humor and unburdened lightness of God's free grace. For this reason, I must offer a caveat for any emphasis on play interpreted as a natural form of freedom, that is, freedom under its own capacity. Some forms of play even thrive on obsessive and compulsive drives aimed at fulfilling various egotistical lusts and superficial self-satisfactions. These forms can render play as alienated, perverted, and subject to exploitation. The taxonomy of play therefore benefits when distinguished and discussed in light of its unique relationship to work.

It is important to remember that alienation can potentially take up residence within play. Salvation to be sure is not grounded in whether one plays or not. Play, like work, suffers a kind of estrangement that is common to all forms of human vocational life. Alexander Schmemann (1990), a Greek Orthodox theologian, criticized the Puritan worldview—a prevalent part of American society—for its reliance on moral distinctions and failure to recognize the significance of estrangement:

> The American society in which I live assumes that tomato juice is always good, and that alcohol is always bad; in effect, tomato juice is not fallen. Similarly the television advertisements tell us, "Milk is natural"; in other words, it is also not fallen. But tomato juice and milk are equally part of the fallen world, along with everything else. (p. 98)

Following Schmemann's logic, work is certainly subject to alienation, but play is also part of the so-called "fallen" world. Play has the potential to be misused; and as I will demonstrate below, in the wrong hands play can be weaponized over against some of its greatest proponents. This phenomenon is nowhere more evident than in the abuse of Black ritual play. And while ritual play is a feature of many societies, Blacks have a peculiar relationship to such forms of play.

J. Deotis Roberts (1978), a Black theologian who also pioneered Black theology, argued that Blacks have "the gift of laughter." He highlighted the celebratory nature of Black religion, yet he remained aware of the tragicomic nature of Black experience in America, even where it seemed to echo the "release and hope" of the Christian Gospel. Occasionally, however, in American society the light, joyful, and cathartic notions of constructive play known for sustaining Black life are stereotyped and weaponized, portraying Blacks as childlike, naïve, and uneducated. This way of interpreting Black "capital P" play has roots in the American beginnings. Even some of the most important statesmen interpreted play in a way that missed the genius of Black cultural life in America. For instance, after witnessing slaves enjoying amusements, Thomas Jefferson (1999), wrote the following in his book *The Notes on Virginia*:

> They seem to require less sleep. A black, after hard labour through the day, will be induced by the slightest amusements to sit up till midnight, or later, though knowing he must be out with the first dawn of the morning. They are at least as brave, and more adventuresome. But this may perhaps pro-

ceed from a want of forethought, which prevents their seeing a danger till it be present. When present, they do not go through it with more coolness or steadiness than the whites... Their griefs are transient. Those numberless afflictions, which render it doubtful whether heaven has given life to us in mercy or in wrath, are less felt, and sooner forgotten with them. In general, their existence appears to participate more of sensation than reflection. (p. 146)

Jefferson pathologized the therapeutic role of "black play," viewing the "amusements," and perhaps even the way Black slaves negotiated grief—as peculiar and less than cultured. Rather than recognizing these incipient blues practices as, "weighted heavily in the direction of release and hope rather than in the direction of doubt and skepticism," reflecting a mode being through which black people have been able "to maintain sanity and trust in life," Jefferson interpreted Jefferson interpreted the mediation of the blues as a hindrance to productivity and a rational deficit (Roberts, 1978, pp. 242–243). His writings stand as a genealogical testament to the pathologization of play and the need for an approach that includes critical realism.

Jefferson prototypes those who live in the cultural vanguard, including American statesmen, cultural leaders, and ordinary citizens, who later fueled anti-Black racism by using affable and jovial characters who in midst of suffering magically overcame tragedy. These caricatures of Blacks, whose so-called ability to transcend suffering, justified an unjust status quo in the minds of many American Whites; moreover, they were deployed to besmirch the character of African Americans by depicting them as having a naïve childlike character and ability to overcome evil. Any theology of play must therefore interrogate with a hermeneutic of suspicion the way play, as a theological phenomenon, can be misinterpreted to parody truth and undermine human agency, dignity, and integrity.

The history of Jim Crow laws in America provides an example of the abuse of constructive elements of play. The term *Jim Crow* developed from Whites playing the role of minstrels who mimicked Black dance steps. Thomas "Daddy" Rice achieved national fame imitating Blacks; moreover, "Jim Crow" became the first form of national popular entertainment designed to demean and dehumanize Black Americans. And similar to Jefferson's musings in his book *Notes on the State of Virginia*, the history of Jim Crow provided another early example of weaponized forms of play that were caricatures and tailored to demean and parody the gifts and talents of oppressed Black Americans. More disastrously, the term "Jim Crow" came to be the moniker for racial segregation or the "quasi-legal, or customary practice of disfranchising, physically segregating, barring, and discriminating against black Americans" (Packard, 2002, p. 14). A similar problem exists in the American film industry with examples from *Birth of a Nation* (1915) and other landmark moments that link the history of play and entertainment to exploitation in America; however, these examples are beyond the scope of this chapter.

Even positive cultural models of play can paradoxically distance one from reality. As noted earlier an element of play opens the door to substitutes for more hopeful living. These substitutes actually have their telos in a form of nihilism that promotes detachment from responsible human behavior. An example of this problem is seen in the disruptive, boundary crossing play of tricksters whose gamesmanship gives way to a dispassionate opportunism, witnessing to the pathology of play—a death knell to human solidarity.

(RE)TURNING TO THEOLOGICAL PLAY

How do you take seriously this dilemma of play as a fallen reality and engage in a sense of play that informs the workplace as modeled in examples above? Can work be redeemed through play?

Answering this question requires a profound (re)conceptualizing of the concept of play or playfulness. While it is customary to view concepts like justice, peace, freedom, and even play, from a generic viewpoint derived from the center of American linguistic parlance, theological play is not generic or generalized. As Barth (1968) correctly pointed out, *latet periculum in generalibus* [danger lurks in generalities] (p. 61), so theological play should be understood more specifically. Thus, the play I am referencing is a corollary of biblical or redemptive spirituality. This form of playfulness materializes out of Christ-responsive love rooted in the freedom of God. As the French theologian, Jacques Ellul (1969) wrote, "Nothing could have responded to God except the spontaneous free gift. Nothing could have loved God except the free play of the creature turned toward his Creator" (p. 59). Theological play is therefore observed in the spontaneous and free response to the Creator's gift of life, and when interpreted in this way, "life should be play—not constraint" (2018, p. 87).

But this freedom from constraint resides in an inversion of our typical way of speaking about freedom. It means thinking of freedom as a gift rather than as an accomplishment. It means inverting our common logic. Ellul (1998) wrote that the Holy Spirit intervenes in order to "make us reason in reverse" (p. 22). Thus, in theological thinking one often engages in a transposed sense of history, a counterintuitive way of considering the beginning from the end, viewing time from the vantage of eternity, the cross from the resurrection, creation from redemption—and, of course, *work* from the standpoint of joyful *play* before God. It also means that play is not an ultimate reality. Play exists as a spontaneous and fragmentary mode of witnessing to what is ultimate; and in its fragmentariness, in its brokenness, play asserts itself in relation to any style of life as life is captured in the rhythm and momentum of work. Even in its most superficial sense play, disrupts the momentum of work, ameliorating the redundancy of its rhythms.

And while there are a number of forms of play, theologically speaking, play has its orbit around the redemption of God, the mysterious center of theology, where notions like unity, peace, and freedom are gifted with new meanings. Redemptive play suggests therefore that those who would participate in play must (re)orient their thinking and understanding of the world in such a way that s/he can again identify, discover and discern the signs, wonders, and even mundane things that playfully witness to God.

If it is true that God materially changes all things [*der Ganz-Ändernder*], then God gives the world parabolic form and transposes everything within common history so that the whole world comes alive (Barth, 1956, pp. 316–317). For workers gifted with this knowledge, it means that spontaneity and playfulness should be cultivated precisely during the routine and redundancy of work. Perhaps, a scheduled break to visit a neighbor's workstation, a paused moment to watch an old inspiring basketball clip of your favorite player, or casually listening to a bluesy jazz tune can all be reminders of the sabbatic life and the truth that "life should be play—not constraint" (Anderson, 2018, p. 87). In fact, with a more enchanted view of the world one can find sparkles of surprise in even the smallest things. The sagacious words of the biblical psalmist resounds with this sentiment: "The heavens declare the glory of God; the skies proclaim the work of his hands" (Psalm 19:1, NIV). This insight reframes what it means to interpret work from the vantage of theological play. Redemptive spirituality in fact suggests that the whole cosmos gains a new cosmic density when faith is fired by the eschatological play of the bounteous God. Such critical awareness about the world should also remind us of the provisional nature of work and help galvanize the heroic energy that arises from the playfulness of the rhythm of creation.

When growing up in Petersburg, Virginia, I often experienced a sense of play when participating in local breakdancing contests throughout the city. During that time, I did not know breakdancing echoed ritualistic forms of play that were all too common in Black folklife. This interest in dancing had its impetus in the encouragement of my mother who died just as I began to hone my dancing skills and mastery of the art form; and although I no longer dance in the same way, I am reminded of how the aesthetic forms achieved in breakdancing are designed to create illusions that transcend the routines of the body and expose their limitations. Following bell hooks (1991), breakdancing deconstructs the body and demonstrates "how you can move and control parts of a body one didn't realize existed within the realm of self-discipline or control" (p. 78). Looking beyond hooks' point, such artful play functions as a form of parabolic suggestiveness that makes a parody of the body and witnesses to our pending emancipation from its limitations. In the act of such playfulness breakdancers are icons of the eschaton, meaning they remind us that limitations of the body are only temporary, and that we should constantly seek to challenge the routines of work. To be sure, I am often mindful—especially when the redundancy of work ushers me to the altar of alienation about my own body—of the playful encouragement of my mother whose words still inspire and reframe how I feel about the gravity of routines that seek to exploit human labor. Such experiences are fruitful reminders that there is a redemptive spirituality that recasts, reorients, and recaptures the true meaning of earthly work.

In sum, I close with some insights into what redemptive spirituality means practically. First, it means that there is a need for a sharper aesthetic awareness. Theological play must remain joyfully open to deploying resources, searching for analogies and finding spaces to revel in the superabundance of creation. Recently, I treasured the words of a young caretaker of the elderly who offered a thoughtful response when asked, "What do you do to relieve the burden of work after attending to so many problems from so many people?" She responded, "I bought a trampoline." In other words, she found a way to play and marshalled her resources to witness to hope beyond work. When people live more freely from a deeper, more resourceful freedom, creation becomes the space where we find ways to recreate and benefit from the world's superabundance. It becomes a playground. In this kind of play, the rhythms of work and commodified forms of labor are unmasked and challenged. As noted earlier, God's "loosening or unshackling" of the created order frees us for spontaneous play that redeems work (Barth, 1981b).

Secondly, in order to play we must find ways to re-enchant and restore the workaday world to ourselves. Cornel West (1999), the pragmatist philosopher, once stated that "we as teachers must ask ourselves, how do we tease out that sense of awe and accent the wrestling with the mystery of being," noting that televisual culture has flattened human perceptions of the world (p. 557). As a result, common history is no longer viewed as an enchanted world. Schmemann (2003) also identifies this common problem of modern, scientific worldviews, writing that this mechanistic worldview has "gradually stripped [people] of a deeper and richer vision of the world [and it is as if] we have been told that all questions of life, of the world and of everything in it can be approached and understood exclusively through the use of a computer." Revelation, however, he argues, can come to human beings "in nature, in another person, in love, in joy and in suffering" (pp. 39–44). Allow me to add that revelation can also come to us *in play*. Indeed, what if, as Schmemann suggests, "*everything* is revelation." Certainly redemptive spirituality should be open to such an enchanted and mysterious view of the world... that *everything is revelation!*

Third, and finally, the (re)cultivated vision of the world needs a corollary *wisdom* to accompany it. Wisdom, of course, is not a form of abstract learning or mere intellect. Wisdom evidences itself in actual practical engagement with cultural others in effectual, multi-dialogical human conversations—intersections that allow shared experiences—especially when critically sharpened from the insights of theological play to enhance our ability to redeem and reframe how we understand human labor. In this regard, the Bible has much to teach moderns since it draws from its immediate sociopolitical and aesthetic environment. Christoph Barth (1991), an Old Testament scholar, argued that "if the OT [Old Testament] could tap such sources, there is no reason why Christians should not listen cheerfully to the religious and secular wisdom of the peoples among whom they live" (p. 251). The point is that in an intellectually overdeveloped world, sapiential metaphors become indispensable to more radical ways of knowing and living. This form of wisdom encourages us to transcend the limitations of modern worldviews, including narrow religious conceptions and rules-based morality which forfeit the mandate to joyfully live in grace and attend to the wisdom in the world.

We stand at a threshold moment, and notwithstanding this truth, if we open our eyes to the playful rhythms of the bounteous God, we will discover a world "charged with the grandeur of God" that inspires us with the heroic energy to recapture a sense of awe, and engage in acts of advocacy in light of the wisdom of God (Ephesians 3:10, RSV). With this inspiration we can enter into the rhythm of a joyful correspondence between the living God and humanity, a relationship which ultimately answers the question of whether work can be redeemed through play.

NOTES

1. The term radical comes from the Latin term *radix* which means "root," that is, I want to grasp and articulate the root of what it means to be human. It is not a mere religious or political shibboleth for those who would engage in partisan politics either on the left or the right.
2. Literature on a theology of play has increased in scope and complexity since many of the seminal studies mention in this chapter. For insight into this type of literature in philosophy, theology, and other fields (see Miller, 1971).
3. An excellent online example is Thelonious Monk Quartet playing "Round Midnight" in 1966 (Domtheodore, 2010).

REFERENCES

Anderson, R. (2018). *New Testament micro-Ethics—On trusting freedom: The first Christians' genotype for multicultural living.* Eugene, OR: Wipf and Stock.
Barth, C. (1991). *God with us: A theological introduction to the Old Testament.* Grand Rapids, MI: Eerdmans.
Barth, K. (1956). *Church dogmatics* (Vol. 4.1). London, England: T&T Clark.
Barth, K. (1960). *The humanity of God.* Louisville, KY: Westminster John Knox Press.
Barth, K. (1962). *Theology and church: Shorter writings 1920–1928.* Eugene, OR: Wipf and Stock.
Barth, K. (1963). *Evangelical theology.* Grand Rapids, MI: Eerdmans.

Barth, K. (1981a). *The Christian life: Church dogmatics IV, 4 lecture fragments.* Edinburgh, Scotland: T & T Clark.
Barth, K. (1981b). *Ethics.* Edinburgh, Scotland: T&T Clark.
Bonhoeffer, D. (1960). *Creation and fall: A theological interpretation of Genesis 1–3.* London, England: SCM Press.
Busch, E. (1986). Deciding moments in the life and work of Karl Barth. *Grail, 2*(4), 51–67.
Cone, J. (1972). *The spirituals and the blues: An interpretation.* Ossining, NY: Orbis Books.
Cox, H. (1969). *The feast of fools: A theological essay on festivity and fantasy.* Cambridge, MA: Harvard University Press.
Davis, A. (1998). *Blues legacies and Black feminism: Gertrude "Ma" Rainey, Bessie Smith, and Billie Holiday.* New York, NY: Vintage Books.
Domtheodore. (2010, April). *Thelonious Monk Quartet—Round Midnight* [Video]. https://www.youtube.com/watch?v=-yg7aZpIXRI
Ellul, J. (1969). *To will or to do: An ethical research for Christians.* Philadelphia, PA: Pilgrim.
Ellul, J. (1998). *On religion, technology, and politics: Conversations with Patrick Troude-Chastenet.* Atlanta, GA: Scholars Press.
Fromm, E. (1968). *Revolution of hope: Toward a humanized technology.* New York, NY: Harper & Row.
Hentoff, N. (1961). *The jazz life.* New York, NY: The Dial Press.
Hopkins G. (1953). *Poems and prose.* London England: Penguin Books.
Jefferson, T. (1999). *Notes on the state of Virginia.* New York, NY: Penguin Books.
King, M. (1957). *Where do we go from here.* Boston, MA: Beacon Press.
Merton, T. (1970). *Opening the Bible.* Collegeville, MN: The Liturgical Press.
Miller, D. (1971). Theology and play studies: An overview. *Journal of the American Academy of Religion, 39*(3), 349–354.
Packard, J. (2002). *American nightmare: The history of Jim Crow.* New York, NY: St. Martin's Press.
Roberts, J. D. (1978). Liberation theism. In C. E. Bruce & W. R. Jones (Eds.), *Black theology: Essays on the formation and outreach of contemporary Black theology* (pp. 233–246). Lewisburg, PA: Bucknell University Press.
Schmemann, A. (1990). Liturgy and eschatology. In T. Fisch (Ed.), *Liturgy and tradition: Theological reflections of Alexander Schmemann* (pp. 89–100). New York, NY: Saint Vladimer's Seminary Press.
Schmemann, A. (2003). *I believe: Celebration of faith.* New York, NY: St. Vladimir's Seminary Press.
Stringfellow, W. (1964). *Free in obedience.* New York, NY: Seabury Press.
Stringfellow, W. (1982). *A simplicity of faith: My experience in mourning.* Nashville, TN: Abington.
Stringfellow W. (2006). *Imposters of God: Inquiries into favorite idols.* Eugene, OR: Wipf and Stock.
Watkins, G. & West, C. (1991). *Breaking bread: Insurgent black intellectual life.* Boston, MA: South End Press.
West, C. (1999). *The Cornel West reader.* New York, NY: Civitas Books.

CHAPTER 3

IS THE SPIRIT "MISSING" IN THE DISCOURSE OF MANAGEMENT, SPIRITUALITY, AND RELIGION?

Shoaib Ul-Haq
HEC Liege, Belgium

ABSTRACT

The community of MSR (Management, Spirituality, and Religion) can be conceptualized as a "discourse community" since it is a group bound by similar social practices and a common focus on the relationship between spirituality/religion and contemporary organizations. This community is guided by certain normative assumptions including humans as physical creatures endowed only with reason and sense perception, this-worldly focus and neglect of other-worldly concerns, rationality as the dominant mode of knowing, independence of spirituality from religion, lack of engagement with transcendental issues and an instrumental use of spirituality in organizations. It seems that MSR is locked in these modernist epistemic commitments and if it wants to grow as a discipline, it would need to critically evaluate these commitments and rework its discourses. Here, Sufism or Islamic mysticism can

Blessed are Those Who Ask the Questions, pages 41–70
Copyright © 2021 by Information Age Publishing
All rights of reproduction in any form reserved.

help by pointing out the nature and characteristics of the human spirit and the ways it can be transformed. In this way, Sufism provides a radical point of departure in order to save the MSR community from the blind alley in which it is currently trapped.

In the contemporary age of high complexity, hyper-speed, and increasingly fluid business environments, organizations are realizing the importance of nourishing employees' spirituality. With the complex, conflicting, and stressful workplace dynamics, employees and managers need to bring their whole self to work in order to make informed and wise decisions (Sheep, 2006). This is possible only when the daily activities of employees are marked by a deep sense of purpose and significance which allows them to meaningfully engage with their work. One method to achieve this is through spiritual practices such as yoga and mindfulness meditation which are supposed to provide personal strength and mental soundness. Consider for example Aetna's CEO, Mark Bertolini, extolling the virtues of meditation for his employees (Gelles, 2015) or the Xerox executive who inspires his employees to engage in "vision quests" (spiritual retreats) for more creative output in terms of product development (Bradbury, 2003). In fact, in his recent book, David Gelles (2015) documents the proliferation of such organizationally driven spiritual programs in the business world adopted by firms such as General Mills, Apple, Google, Monsanto, LinkedIn, to name a few.

In order to fulfill the supply needs of this corporate market, many spiritual gurus, healers, occult tutors, and mythologists have emerged. Examples of such gurus include Sri Sri Ravi Shankar (founder, "Art of Living"; owner of the consumer goods maker Sriveda Sattva Pvt Limited), Devdutt Pattanaik, Serge Benhayon, and others are regularly invited by large and medium size companies to teach spirituality to their employees. As part of their teaching, these gurus impart love, wisdom, self-control, and the capacity to think outside the box. Their "services" (Zaidman, Goldstein-Gidoni, & Nehemya, 2009) are available at a hefty price and most of them have built a business empire that runs spiritual workshops around the world and also offer spiritual goods for corporate consumption. It is important to note that, unlike the traditions from which these gurus draw their inspiration from, they don't support the idea of any form of asceticism or renunciation of the material world. In fact, their philosophy is perfectly aligned with enlightenment rationality, neoliberal capitalism, and a global consumer culture (Upadhya, 2013). An important requirement of participation in this culture is to buy and consume indigenous, sacred symbols embodied in the form of crystals, stones, psychic readings, Ayurveda medicines, sculptures, incense, and so forth. Hence, a part of the organizational move to spiritual enlightenment and health is realized through commodification of indigenous paraphernalia (Zaidman, 2003) as well as consumption of the spiritual experiences, places, and services (Rinallo, Scott, & Maclaran, 2013). Gradually, this spiritual teaching and learning became a legitimate domain of corporate leaders giving rise to a new breed of spirit-oriented managers responsible for creating a link between spirit and work (Hawley, 1993; Moxley, 1999). Consequently, organizations are now no longer dependent on spiritual gurus since managers can carry out the same functions (Fry & Cohen, 2009; Rothausen, 2017). As a guru is considered to be a charismatic man with higher intellect, enlightenment, and wisdom, managers are expected to exhibit similar capabilities and then pass them on to their employees.

Due to the reasons outlined above, a kind of spiritual turn is sweeping across the corporate world (Driver, 2007) which is also reflected in the scholarly domain by a surge of academic and practitioner focused papers and books on the topic of "workplace spirituality" (Lund Dean & Fornaciari, 2007), especially since 1996. This new domain was further legitimized when a MSR interest group was created in the Academy of Management (AoM) in 2000. Due to the incessant efforts of its founding members including Judith Neal, Jerry Biberman, Robert Giacalone, and many others, MSR group was able to institutionalize as a fresh but important area of inquiry within the broader management discipline (Tackney, Chappell, & Sato, 2017). An important contribution of MSR founders is the creation of an academic space for discussion of spiritual matters and for imagining alternative perspectives.

One would assume, however, that the most important "object" of study in the academic discipline of workplace spirituality (WPS) would be the human "spirit" itself. However, a glance at the WPS discourse informs us that a discussion of the nature or characteristics of the spirit is totally missing (Ul-Haq, 2020). This neglect of the main object of knowledge in the WPS discourse is the topic of this chapter. It is my contention that the reasons for this neglect are rooted in the modernist epistemic commitments of the MSR community. After a brief discussion of these commitments, I introduce *Sufism* (Islamic spirituality) as an alternative paradigm which recognizes spirit as a central object of inquiry while challenging the contemporary modes of its representation. Towards the end, I briefly discuss implications of engaging with this rich ancient heritage mainly in terms of new insights for reconfiguring organizing and organizations.

In this chapter, I have taken a Bourdieusian research stance which emphasizes awareness of a researcher's personal sociohistorical subject positioning (Bourdieu, 2007) with the assumption that production of social knowledge cannot be understood independently of the social world inhabited by the researcher. In this regard, I need to declare that my interest in the topic of "spirit" is determined by my personal background as a member of an Islamic Sufi order, *Naqshbandiya Owaisia*, in Pakistan. My doctoral training as a critical management scholar in the postcolonial context of Muslim global South shaped my research agenda towards the deconstruction of existing dominant imaginaries and promotion of a spiritually inspired way of seeing the world and being in the organization. The WPS discourse (mainly generated in the Anglo-American context) and its lack of engagement with the spirit are observations that stem from my personal reflections and introspection. As Arthur Zajonc has argued, self-reflection as a method does not rest on a systematic analysis of texts or empirical data but on an authentic commitment by the researcher to be contemplative and reflexive (Zajonc, 2009). Despite this commitment, I am fully aware that my Islamic worldview and spiritual disposition (habitus in Bourdieu's terms) played a significant role in providing me an interpretative framework that underpins my argument in this chapter. Nevertheless, my critique emerges from within the WPS paradigm and I used Western sources for problematizing the discipline and only mobilized some non-Western sources while positing the Sufi alternative. I do believe that new and valuable insights can be drawn from the well of Sufi wisdom spanning more than 1,400 years. Please also note that some parts of the section on Sufism have already been published as a book chapter (see Ul-Haq & Khan, 2018).

MSR AS A DISCOURSE COMMUNITY

Following Berger and Luckmann's (1966) sociology of knowledge, the community of MSR can be conceptualized as a "discourse community" (Bizzell, 1992; Porter, 1986) with a distinct boundary since it is a group bound by similar social practices and a common focus on the relationship between spirituality/religion and contemporary organizations. This community generates knowledge and exchanges ideas through approved channels including specific journals as well as conferences, including the domain-specific journal, *Journal of Management, Spirituality & Religion*, publication of special issues in mainstream management journals (e.g., *Leadership Quarterly, Journal of Organizational Change Management, Journal of Management Education*, etc.) as well as the prestigious Academy of Management annual conference through the platform of the MSR Division. These channels, however, are regulated by disciplinary practices of knowledge production (Whitley, 2000) that determine the object of inquiry, the presuppositions underlying knowledge as well as the conditions of knowability. Hence, as a "discourse community," MSR is guided by certain normative epistemic assumptions as well as accepted theories and methodologies thus forming a shared belief system (van Dijk, 1995). On the contrary, some researchers have pointed out that MSR is an inherently multidisciplinary domain encompassing such diverse fields such as religion, ethics, social work, management, education, nursing, and psychology (Lund Dean & Fornaciari, 2007). In other words, the possibility of a common shared representation is remote. Nevertheless, some ideologies can cut across disciplinary boundaries and carry with them certain common representational standards which underlie the definitions, methods as well as theories of the discourse community. The famous French philosopher, Michel Foucault, for instance, has labeled these standards as an *episteme*. A common standard in the modern episteme, for example, would be its reliance on "man" as the arbiter of all knowledge claims of objects and actions and as a "subject" which can be "known" (Foucault, 1973). In other words, knowledge as the product of individual men as subjects reflecting on objects in order to create universal abstract concepts is quite a "modern" phenomenon when contrasted with previous epistemes, such as those of the classical age. Following the same line of argument, the episteme of the MSR community provides certain implicit "rules of formation" (Foucault, 1973, p. 38) that constitute the legitimacy of knowledge claims. These epistemic assumptions generally go unquestioned and hence certain beliefs are taken for granted in the community (with some notable exceptions). The community members are normally unaware of the existence of this episteme but unconsciously play by its rules since it controls social representations as well as the discourse (O'Leary & Chia, 2007; van Dijk, 1995).

Consider the topic of "spirit" in the WPS discourse as an example of these unconscious but productive structures within which knowledge is produced by the MSR community members. One would assume that the most important "object" of study in WPS will be the human "spirit" itself. Nevertheless, there is a complete absence of knowledge about this object in WPS. There is no discussion, whatsoever, on what is spirit, what is its nature, and what are its characteristics as well as functions (Ul-Haq, 2020). The closest that the discourse reaches its object is to study the consequences which result when the object is "in action." Hence, the most sophisticated articulation in the discourse is to study the construction of meanings when the spirit is alive (Braud, 2009). However, there is no discussion of what it means that the spirit is alive and how it is related to construction of meanings. Most of the meditative practices espoused in WPS are meant for improving mental and physical health instead of developing one's spirit.

Recently, a Buddhist inspired set of meditative practices known as "mindfulness" has gained popularity among some of the MSR community members (Vu & Gill, 2018). The religious sounding terminologies of these practices, however, were replaced by secular and scientific language in order to increase its acceptability as a therapeutic device (Brown, 2016). Mindfulness is defined as "the self-regulation of attention so that it is maintained on immediate experience, thereby allowing for increased recognition of mental events in the present moment" (Bishop et al., 2004, p. 282).

As the definition illustrates, the focus is on the control of one's mind instead of the spirit. Moreover, the Buddhist intention of such meditation is to dispel the illusion of ego while corporate mindfulness is presented in a functionalist and decontextualized manner with a focus on stress reduction of employees, enhancing their creativity, and boosting their emotional intelligence (Baas, Nevicka, & ten Velden, 2014; Purser & Milillo, 2015). Paradoxically, such outcomes might actually inflate one's ego instead of diminishing it. Moreover, it is not necessary that meditation will always lead to a heightened sense of awareness. As illustrated by Hugh Willmott (2018),

> the meditator may fall asleep or become completely carried away by, rather than become more aware of, the normal stream of consciousness. By default, the ostensible normality of the status quo is undisturbed. The primary obstacle to meditative awareness is distracting—ego-threatening or alluring—thoughts or sensations. Unless this obstacle is recognized and removed, meditating makes little difference, except perhaps to provide a spiritual or "cool" badge of identity. (pp. 262–263)

This spiritual identity, however, performatively constitutes the managerial self in neoliberal capitalist relations (Purser, 2019) with an objective of maximizing its organizational functionality. This instrumentality of the spiritual self is reflected in WPS discourse which is replete with studies showing its positive benefits for organizations. Some of these benefits include higher job satisfaction, joy at work (Rego & e Cunha, 2008), innovation and creativity in product development and process improvement (Tischler, Biberman, & McKeage, 2002), organizational identification (Demirtas, Hannah, Gok, Arslan, & Capar, 2017), greater commitment and trust (Krishnakumar & Neck, 2002), higher productivity (Karakas, 2010), and higher levels of corporate social responsibility (Pruzan, 2008). However, there is no explanation or proof of why these positive objectives will be achieved through developing or nurturing the spirit or what does it even mean to "nurture" the spirit. Since the spirit was never an object of study, there is no scientific ground for conferring credibility on causal imputations in this discourse. Hence, it becomes very difficult to link the meditative practices and their causal impact on work practices. As argued by Lychnell (2017),

> Empirical management research on how people let the meditative attitude spread to work in order to further personal growth has been limited. Prior literature has focused on how simple activities, such as washing dishes, chopping wood, or writing emails may contribute to cultivating mindfulness...Also, previous writings have, to a large extent, been based on various authors' experiences or conceptual ideas rooted in Buddhism...rather than systematic, empirical management research. (p. 2)

In fact, one important "modern" criteria of any discipline to achieve a "scientific" rank is the ontological status of its objects of knowledge (Nickles, 2013). Any knowledge claim about this object will be dealt with suspicion in the scientific circles if it is far from the methodology of experimental observation (Webster & Sell, 2014). Nevertheless, there is no method or procedure to test the causal connections or theories in the WPS discourse by an experiment or observation as they cannot capture the "personal, experiential, and even supernatural nature of spirituality" (McKee, Mills, & Driscoll, 2008, p. 191). Hence, from a purely Popperian perspective, these theories are not falsifiable which would make the whole WPS discipline a pseudoscientific endeavor (Popper, 1963). It is no wonder then that organizations are still struggling with the problems that WPS was supposed to solve.

In the sections below, I set out to show that what explains the difficulties of the MSR community in understanding their object is actually not the complexity of the object but rather the social nature of their ideological commitments. The discourse generated by this community is trapped in the problems generated by following a particular modernist episteme. It is my contention that in order to productively rethink their discipline, the MSR community would need to engage with profound questions such as the complex nature of the self, the real sources of knowledge, the possibility of an afterworld, relationship of spirituality with religious traditions, importance of metaphysical issues and the problems of focusing blindly on performativity. Afterwards I will introduce how Sufism (Islamic spirituality) provides an alternative episteme in which these problems don't exist. In what follows below, I attempt to uncover some of the assumptions of the MSR community.

Nature of the Self

In order to start developing an understanding of the epistemic commitments of this discourse, let me try to unearth the modern notions of what it means to be a human being. The scientific rationalism of the modern episteme is grounded in the Western pre-enlightenment period when the principle perspective of man changed from reliance on revelatory or spiritual knowledge to sense perception coupled with disengaged reason (Schmidt, 1996; Zafirovski, 2011). The whole organic universe including man is now to be understood purely mechanically, taken apart piece by piece (Wagner, 1994) in the form of "correct" linear symbols (Lagerlund, 2007). Hence to know some object is to have an accurate image of it in our minds along with its distinct position in the man-made scheme of things. This modern tendency of fragmentary perception and coherent understanding is, of course, entirely opposite to the ancient idea of perceiving reality as a paradoxical whole (in Taoism and Buddhism for instance) or as an elastic band in a dynamic push and pull state (Izutsu, 1983; Schneider, 1999) without imposing a priori conceptual categories.

The most famous Western philosopher who was instrumental in developing the modern concept of the self is Descartes. He declares, "I can have no knowledge of what is outside me except by means of the ideas I have within me" (Descartes, 1642, 1970, p. 123). This inward idea of knowledge meant that humans have to now *build* the ideas of their self through some intrapsychic activity. This also implies that the self would need to be objectified which is only possible if we conceptualize it as a functional and mechanical entity (Markie, 1992). Nevertheless, this disembodied view of the self stripped it of any spiritual, immaterial dimension which ultimately resulted in a rejection of classical ontology (Taylor, 1989). This modern view of self was taken to its extreme by John Locke who professed a deep anti-teleological view of human nature. He argued that there is no need for an external source (such as God) to tell us about ourselves since this revealed truth is also discoverable by reasoning based on sense-experience (Dybikowski, 2004). Man's rational self-responsibility demands that we disengage from our traditions and make them an object of scientific inquiry. However, this meant that man needs to be aware of his thought processes and is fully capable of radical scrutiny of his self that emerges from objectification (Taylor, 1989).

Hence, we enter an era in which a lot of things which were known to man through revelation or spiritual intuition suddenly became not only irrelevant but were even portrayed as the oppositional other. All the traditional knowledge was cast aside as dogmatic and unscientific. Now new knowledge about man, nature, and the cosmos have to be discovered and described in secular rational and machine-like terms by following the scientific methodology. However, the tools of science are not designed for capturing the spiritual elements or the substance of consciousness of the self. This is due to the fact that "spirit," for science, is an unobservable entity without any real referent (Agazzi & Pauri, 2000).

Overall, the turn towards an inward view of generating knowledge through disengaged reason and the scientific methodology is responsible for a movement from the classical understanding of spirit to its denial or obscurity in the modern discourse. It is no wonder, then, that there is no discussion of the actual spirit in WPS. This makes the term *spirituality* an empty container hollow from inside and without any meaning since meaning belongs to semantics instead of simple language elements. Echoing the same thought, Reva Brown (2003) writes,

> The more I read on the topic of organizational spirituality (OS), the more apparent it became that the concept is not unclear—it is opaque. The literature

provided as many definitions of OS as there were authors writing about it, and this is to ignore those papers where the authors took for granted that their readers knew what was meant when they used the term, so they never got as far as defining OS. (p. 393)

Due to the lack of a clear concept, WPS can signify altogether different meanings for different organizational researchers and managers. This problem is highlighted by Michal Izak (2012) in the following way:

> How are we supposed to give an account of the rapidly developing domain of organizational spirituality, without having the notion of "spirituality" at hand? It does not seem plausible. (p. 28)

Hence, nature of a human being is totally obscure in the workplace spirituality discourse.

Rationality as the Dominant Source of Knowledge

Another problematic assumption of this community is their dominant focus on logical empiricism grounded in positivism (Krahnke, Giacalone, & Jurkiewicz, 2003) and the fundamental belief that knowledge of the researchers in this community is central and secure. It is claimed that this knowledge is valid because it is based on hard and "objective" data which the individual minds of these researchers can somehow access. The "data" have been analyzed through conceptual thought, which implies privileging this particular medium over all other mediums such as intuition (Armstrong, 1914). The logical inferences that can be drawn from data analysis are claimed to be independent of the researcher's preferences, attitudes, and beliefs as if the knower was absent while knowing. This allows the community to claim that the postulated relationships between different data and the theories built on these relationships are universal, objective, and value neutral.

Any other knowledge source such as revelation or even spiritual intuition is subjective and uncertain and therefore is unreliable and invalid (Schneiders, 1989). However, believing in such objectivity immediately generates two problems which are known in philosophy as (a) the problem of thought, and (b) the problem of knowledge (Davidson, 2004; Sceski, 2007). The first problem is related to the constraints on knowledge claims and the second is related to the justification of our beliefs in a mind-independent world. These two problems point out that the community needs to recognize some basic limitations of what they know through brute empiricism. For example, once knowledge is restricted to sense-experience, it becomes impossible to claim anything about reality or "truth" since that would imply extending knowledge beyond sense data (Layder, 1985). Moreover, as Thomas Kuhn, has convincingly argued, the process of generating theoretical knowledge in a discipline is influenced by psychological, social, and historical elements (Kuhn, 1962). In other words, the hard and objective data cannot provide a foundation for generating knowledge claims. The assumption that such data is simply available in the world and can be simply "read off" has been severely attacked by philosophers of science. Due to these criticisms, this assumption is now replaced by a "theory-ladenness" notion, meaning that our observations for collecting data are partly determined by the researchers' or his/her community's theoretical assumptions (Brewer & Lambert, 2001). At best, the data underdetermines theories and is pliable due to which it cannot be used to settle theoretical disagreements (Quine, 1975).

Nevertheless, despite awareness of the dangers and limitations of privileging rational thought over other mediums, the faith in this practice remains strong in the WPS community.

This Worldly Focus and Disregard of Otherworldly Concerns

The WPS discourse emphasizes life in the here and now, relationships between individual organizational members and the alleviation of suffering in this world during this lifetime (Giacalone & Jurkiewicz, 2010). However, what the discourse totally ignores are otherworldly concerns as there is no discussion of existential questions such as life after death. Categorizing the discourse by using this dichotomy (this-worldly vs. otherworldly) is important as it depicts the thrust of the discourse and shows where the community members spend their valuable time, energy, and thought. No one even posits the existence of a supernatural plane, or a metaphysical realm, or a domain of the spirits. This exclusive focus on the material world is epistemologically linked to positivism and materialism which manifest themselves in scientism (Rosenberg, 2017). The latter is a reductive epistemology that posits a belief in a world composed of only material things (Sorell, 1994) with all other objects as manifestations of matter including the brain. According to this materialist doctrine, the belief in another possible world is irrational. This worldview caused the otherworldly concerns to gradually disappear from the WPS discourse. This also results in a certain reordering of priorities away from the accumulation of spiritual benefits to an accumulation of purely material benefits of this world resulting in "dark satanic mills" (Blake, 1976) instead of spiritual workplaces.

Independence of Spirituality From Religion

As many scholars have noticed, Western spirituality, originating out of the Judeo-Christian tradition, was not conceived outside of religion, at least traditionally (Gavrilyuk & Coakley, 2012; Ritskes, 2011; Herrick, 2003). However, the modern processes of secularization meant practicing spirituality in a nonreligious and nonsacred setting (Heelas, Woodhead, Seel, Szerszynski, & Tusting, 2005). The assumption of these practices is that spirituality can be secular as it is extracted from religion through rational thought. This is necessary because religion and any transcendental concern is assumed to be incompatible with the postmodern society (Griffin, 1989). Yet the perennial human desire to find a better route to a meaningful life remains which now has to be searched outside the boundaries of formal religion (Camus, 1991).

In their rejection of religion, the locus of Western civilization shifted from the public to the private and from the collective to the autonomous and disinterested individual (Shapin, 1994). This privileging of the disembodied individual subject resulted in a utilitarian search for exquisite spiritual sensations from different spiritual traditions of the world in a form of religious consumerism (Redden, 2016). As argued by Ritskes (2011),

> These forms of spirituality were transplanted into Western society as exotic and different, being positioned as a counter-discourse to the hegemonic influence of religion, as an alternative way of reaching personal fulfillment. (p. 19)

This results in "deracination" which implies dislocating certain spiritual features from their religious grounding and mix and matching these features to create what is now called a "New Age spirituality" (Sutcliffe & Gilhus, 2014; Zaidman, 2007). However, this means that individuals are simply consuming secular spirituality for gathering and enhancing sensations instead of transforming their spirit.

Performativity

Many scholars have pointed out the strong link between the current WPS movement and neoliberal capitalism (Heelas, 1999; Walsh, 2018). It is interesting to note, however, that some have construed spirituality as the savior of failing capitalism (Thompson, 2000) while others consider it as an essential part of the "cultural logic" of contemporary capitalism (Possamai, 2003). Regardless, the assumption behind all such conceptualizations is that the purpose of organizations is only related to instrumental, efficiency-oriented performance and WPS is a tool to achieve this performance. Hence, the inherent performativity in organizations work to place an economic value upon spiritual practices. Consuming spirituality in this manner leads to its commodification and exploitation. Consider, for example, the corporate contemplative training programs such as the Google "Search Inside Yourself" project which is a spiritual mindfulness-based training with a clear objective of improving creativity and emotional intelligence of employees. The program focuses on neuroscientific evidence to promote the concept of employee "optimization" which can be achieved by becoming more emotionally competent. The steps of the training highlight the total neglect of "spirit" and an inadvertent focus on mental relaxation as is evident from the passage below:

> Trainees start with step one—focusing their attention—which is regarded as the basis of all higher cognitive abilities and is believed to make the mind calmer and more stable. With step two—self-knowledge and self-mastery—the new attention skills are used to gain a deeper understanding of thoughts and emotions. The third training step—creating useful mental habits—encompasses contemplative practices thought to cultivate compassion for others and happiness. (Rupprecht & Walach, 2016, p. 316)

As the above steps show, the assumption is that Google employees are material beings instead of spiritual beings with material needs instead of spiritual needs. The most important of these material needs is the need to bring one's mind back to a balanced stage. This stage is conceptualized as one where the mind is relaxed and stress free so that it can be effectively used to serve the organization. Nevertheless, this selfish hedonism doesn't even consider the structures of power that are making people stressed. As argued by Lychnell (2017), this commodification acts to mask organizational inequalities which are the source of employee suffering in the first place. In his own words,

> Using meditation to become more productive and efficient could be seen as an instrumental intention. In original Buddhist practice, however, the ultimate goal is to eliminate suffering, a spiritual intention, which goes deeper than the instrumental one as, ironically, the source of suffering might be one's drive to become more efficient at work. (p. 2)

Nevertheless, for managers, spirituality and mindfulness have utilitarian functions including employee motivation, stress reduction, as well as enhanced efficiency. Due to its ethically challenged presuppositions, management appropriates spirituality in an instrumental fashion to augment the economic value of workers which is equivalent to killing their spirit (Allcorn, 2002).

It seems that MSR is locked in these epistemic commitments and if it wants to grow as a discipline, it will need to critically evaluate these commitments and rework its discourses. Here, Sufism or Islamic mysticism can help. However, before I introduce the main ideas of Sufism and its conceptualization of human spirit, let me clarify the usage of certain terms. First, Sufism (*Tasawwuf* in Persian) or Islamic mysticism or spirituality are simply labels which are good for orientation but lack the semantic capacity to cover the diverse phenomena and teachings that are part of this branch of Islam (Chittick, 2000). Therefore, to use the term "Sufism" for such diversity is only to provide a direction to the reader and focus more on the reality behind the term. What I would try to represent in these pages is the classical formulation of this discipline mainly using Western sources which would be beneficial for the Western audience. Although I am using male pronouns in this chapter, this does not imply that females are not part of Sufism. Avoiding the use of double pronouns was a conscious choice in order to save space but should not be misconstrued as sexist pronoun usage. Finally, Arabic and Persian terms (in italics) were used in order to convey the language spoken by Sufis. I used honorific titles for prophets and saints since this is also part of a Sufi's etiquette (*adab*).

SUFISM

Sufism is a branch of knowledge in Islam which is not discursive or acquired knowledge (*'ilm*) but a more infused, experiential, intimate, and spiritual knowing or what has been named as intuitive knowledge (*ma'rifa*; Nguyen, 2016). Although the former is more concerned with the tools of knowledge that the Western audience is generally familiar with including reason, sense perception, and logical argumentation, the latter is broader in its scope. It extends the traditional tools of knowledge through spiritual intuition and a direct awareness of reality through the process of illumination (Schimmel, 1975). The objective of this knowledge is closeness with *Allah* (God) and attainment of His love by perfecting sincerity of intention and action (Bashir, 2011) through purification (*tazkiya*) of the spirit. This perfection is possible through positive transformation of the spirit by walking in the footsteps of the Prophet Muhammad (Peace be Upon Him; PBUH). As the spirit grows and increases in stature, it is able to grasp and internalize metaphysical realities and attain higher spiritual stations (*maqamat*; Khan, 1965).

The most important *hadith* (sayings and actions of the Prophet) which has been accepted collectively by Muslim scholars, as representing the central core of their faith, is known as *Hadith* of the angel Gabriel. This angel visited Prophet Muhammad (PBUH) and questioned him about the three main dimensions of religion; namely, *Islam* (submission), *Iman* (faith), and

Ihsan (sincerest devotion; Chittick, 2000). The Prophet's answer shows three dimensions encompassing the outward and inward expressions of the religion. The first dimension, the dimension of Islam, is based on *Tawhid* (the oneness and uniqueness of God), five daily prayers, offering of *Zakat* (almsgiving), fasting in the holy month of *Ramadan*, and performing pilgrimage to Mecca. These "five pillars" are the building blocks of the domain of knowledge which later was called Islamic jurisprudence or *Shariah* (Chittick, 1992, p. 3). The second dimension, the dimension of *Iman*, is an expression for a specific conviction in the belief in *Allah* (God), His messengers, His angels, the Last Day, His books, and the good and evil fate as ordained by Him. These beliefs form the core of Islamic theology which was then elaborated by Muslim *mutakallims* (theologians). Nevertheless, the most important part of this hadith relates to the third dimension, the dimension of *Ihsan*, which adds spirituality to the religion (Campo, 2009, p. xxiv). *Ihsan* reminds Muslims that they are always in the presence of *Allah*, and that one should consider this "presence" in all his thoughts and actions (Buehler, 2015). In the words of the Prophet (PBUH), *Ihsan* is described as:

> Worship *Allah* as if you see Him, for if you see Him not, yet He sees you. (Khan, 1965, p. 13)

The inner contemplations and manifestations which will inculcate this state as a substance of man's consciousness is the subject of Sufism. All the leading Sufi sheikhs (masters of the Sufi path and the friends of God) believe that acquiring the inner esoteric state of *ihsan* is obligatory for all Muslims. It is not just a part but the essence of the religion since this consciousness will permeate in all the beliefs and actions of a Sufi (mystic). Although these three dimensions are distinct, they are thoroughly intertwined with each other and collectively represent the Islamic tradition. Imam al-Ghazali (may *Allah*'s mercy be upon him; 1058–1111) was a distinguished Sufi master and he was strongly of the view that Sufism is not distinct from the religion of Islam. His views are expressed by Rev. Gardener (1917) as follows:

> Sufiism, he (Ghazali) maintains, will never enable a man to dispense with revealed religion, or free him from the duty of performing its prescribed observances. (p. 133)

This implies that *ihsan* is built on the doctrines and practices preached by the Prophet (PBUH) and cannot be alienated from formal religion. Hence, a Sufi having the right belief and following the right practices along with engaging in *dhikr* (remembrance) and *taffakur* (spiritual meditation) will aim to perfect his faith and submission to the will of *Allah* (Chittick, 2000). This deliberate choice of mystics to submit and love *Allah* is not merely mental or theoretical but "so totally sincere that it has shaken them to the depth of their being and set them in motion upon the path" (Lings, 1975, p. 30). Another Sufi master, ibn al-Arabi, understood this perfection of self as the first step toward fulfilling human destiny and becoming a mirror that reflects the beauty of *Allah* (*mir'at al-haqq*; Chodkiewicz, 1993). Every aspect of creation reflects the Creator and since *Allah* is the most beautiful, so too are all His reflections but one would have to reach the stage of *ihsan* in order to become such a mirror (Corbin, 1969). In ibn Arabi's own words, "God (*al-haqq*) is your mirror, that is, the mirror in which you contemplate yourself, and you, you are His mirror, that is, the mirror in which He contemplates His divine names" (Corbin, 1969, p. 271).

The knowledge one gains by becoming this mirror is true knowledge (*ilm al-haqiqa*) which is an experiential knowledge conditional on the state of moral and spiritual excellence of the Sufi (Kabbani, 2003). One important question that this knowledge addresses at the outset is the relationship between *Allah* and His creation including human beings. The nature and etiquette of this relationship cannot be known through discursive thought or by employing the mechanisms of logic but is accessible only through revelation or *ma'rifa* (intuitive knowledge; Chittick, 2005). For both Rumi (1207–1273) and ibn Arabi, the two great Sufi masters, the creation is a multiform and multi-chrome manifestation of the divine through relationships with *Allah*'s names and attributes, however delimited this might be (Lamptey, 2014; Lewis, 2000). Ibn Arabi (may *Allah*'s mercy be upon him) describes the relationship between God and His creation through the metaphor of the light and the rays. God's being is symbolized by light, and creation constitutes the rays emanating from this iridescent center. To the extent that the rays reflect the light, they are at one with it, and inasmuch as they are not the light itself, they are in darkness. And so a creature is constituted both by its reflection of being and by a lack thereof—what ibn Arabi calls the reality of "He/Not He" (Chittick, 1989, p. 7). Hence, *Allah* alone possesses the true being (*wujud*) while all the creation receives its being from this same source. Please note that this does not mean that the Sufi Sheikhs are referring to pantheism (Chittick, 1989, p. 79). Rather, they are explaining oneness in a sophisticated manner.

Nevertheless, this knowledge cannot be obtained without an educator or a guide. Correct comprehension of the Quran, *hadith* as well as the spiritual training at a personal level depends on an experienced teacher called a *Sheikh* (Buehler, 2016; Stepaniants, 1994). He will often be the spiritual leader of a *tariqah* or a specific Sufi order which can be conceptualized as a standard organizational form of Sufism (Le Gall, 2004). Although there are numerous such Sufi orders, the most famous are Qadri, Chishti, Naqshbandi, Shadili, and Suhrawardi. If one wants to tread on this spiritual path, he needs to join a Sufi order as the conditions, experiences, understanding of the spiritual stations, and the introspection necessary for spiritual development cannot be learned through any text since there is no linguistic tool available to describe them. These blessings (*barakah*) are achieved directly from the spirit, body, and the heart of a *Sheikh* as well as by following his ethical conduct (*akhlaq*).

Nevertheless, before we turn to the topic of the human transformations that takes place during this spiritual journey, let me first delineate the Sufi conceptualization of what it means to be "human."

VIEW OF HUMAN NATURE

While addressing the question of self or the nature of being, Sufis often reveals a specific preoccupation with ontology, or the nature of reality. Drawing both on contemplative interpretations of the primary Islamic sources, the Quran and *hadith*, and mystical experiences, they address most questions, including that of human nature, in relation to the ultimate nature of reality. The nature of the created universe and its origin can be judged from its purpose which can be explained from another *hadith*. According to this *hadith*, *Allah* said,

> I was a hidden treasure and desired/loved to be known, so I created you (humans) that I might be known. (Brown, 2009, p. 193)

This implies that this whole cosmos is a mirror of the divine and our purpose in it is to actively seek God. The universe acts as a bridge that can be used by humans to potentially cross the chasm between the hidden divine treasure and *Allah*'s self-revelation through His attributes. Hence, any ontological definition needs to be situated within this broader framework of Islamic cosmology.

Traditional Western sciences have assumed that a human being is nothing more than a physical creature functioning through a nervous system and controlled by a physical mind (Brown, Murphy, & Malony, 1998). Nevertheless, this conception is challenged in Sufi anthropology where a human being is composed of *nafs* (the animal spirit) and *ruh* (the human spirit/soul) which are both contained in the chamber of *jism* (the human body; Hermansen, 1988; Milani, 2013). The latter provides an original characteristic to the whole human race since it distinguishes them from all other creatures (Adamson, 2015). This human spirit or *ruh* is also a created body with a certain beginning but it is different in nature to the corporeal body (Sharifian, 2013). The best explanation is provided by Maulana Allah Yar Khan (may *Allah*'s mercy be upon him; 1904–1984) as follows:

> It (*ruh*) is luminous, radiant, incorporeal, subtle, living, dynamic and permeates all the organs of the physical body. It is a delicate circulation and diffu-

sion just as water in a rose, or oil in an olive branch or fire in a pile of coal. (Khan, 1965, p. 29)

Hence, the spirit is a refulgent and subtle body which resembles the physical body in its shape. It is sanctified with wisdom, maturity, and moral consciousness right from the moment of its creation. It exists in the realm of command (*aalam e-amr*) and is transferred to the realm of creation (*aalam e-khulq*) when an angel breathes it (*nafakh*) into the physical body. It then animates the physical body and all of its corporeal potentialities including the stages of life (childhood, youth, maturity, and old age). It does not follow the boundaries of space, time, tangibility, and causality but can see, speak, and hear without using material means (Khan, 1965). The understanding of the nature and characteristics of the spirit are not possible through rational thought or sense-experience but through spiritual intuition (*ma'rifa*) and spiritual unveiling (*kashf*). The famous scholar and Sufi, Qadi Thanaullah Panipati (may *Allah*'s mercy be upon him; 1731–1810) wrote in his exegesis of the Quran:

> The realm of creation comprises the Tremendous Throne and whatsoever is in between the heavens and the earth. It comprises of four elements: fire, water, air and clay and things created therefrom... The realm of command comprises incorporeal beings, i.e., *Lataaif* (subtle parts of the spirit), the *qalb*, *ruh*, *sirri*, *khaffi* and *akhfa* all above the Tremendous Throne... These *Lataaif* are attributed to the realm of command because they have not been created from any matter but are created through His direct command. (Khan, 1965, p. 34)

As is evident from the above quotation, Sufis believe that there are five vital organs of the spirit. These organs derive life from Divine Light, *nur* (Bowering, 2001). Just as the spirit is the driving force for the physical body, the Divine Lights which originate from *Allah* are the driving force for the spirit. This *nur* is manifest in itself and makes other things such as the human spirit manifest by shining upon it. In this sense, *nur* is responsible for existence and being of the nonexistent and non-manifest entities. It purifies and purges the spirit from base desires so that it can attain *Allah*'s nearness, pleasure, and eternal salvation. Every vital organ of the spirit is illuminated when this *nur* is bestowed upon them. However, the color of the lights, their fragrance, and their moral effects vary from one organ to the other.

Human spirit is the main agent for Sufis and its development is the main objective of their ritual practices. This does not mean, however, that the body is irrelevant; on the contrary, it is instrumental for remolding of the spirit and a medium for its knowledge (Rozehnal, 2007). The mystical journey of a Sufi starts from his heart which is not only the central organ of the body but also the vital center of the spirit (Burckhardt, 1976). The Prophet

(PBUH) said, "Verily there is in the body a small piece of flesh; if it is good the whole body is good and if it is corrupted the whole body is corrupted and that is the heart" (as narrated in Bukhari). What the Prophet (PBUH) is referring to is not the physical heart but *Qalb*, the subtle heart or the inner heart which is the center of the spirit. The same reality has been mentioned in the Quran: "But *Allah* has endeared the faith to you and has beautified it in your *qalb* (hearts)" (Quran, 49:7).

This implies that *qalb* is the focal point of responsibility, the sovereign of the human body and also the most important organ of the spirit. Although the eyes and the ears act as its sensory organs, the tongue acts as its translator and the mind acts to provide logical reasoning, the real decision maker and the commanding master is the *qalb*. All other organs of the human body are subservient to it while it understands and decides. Moreover, *qalb* is also a reservoir of atemporal spiritual knowledge which is based on spiritual intuition and beyond any characterization (Shafii, 1988). Sufism is concerned with how *qalb* and other vital organs can be purified, and how this as well as one's actions, thoughts, and personal consciousness can be perfected while going through spiritual development stations.

TRANSFORMATIONS OF THE HUMAN SPIRIT

The above discussion hints at the possibility that a spiritual transformation in the spirit is possible and desirable. Participation in this process is one of the most important functions performed by Sufi Sheikhs who provide a devotional path to their disciples in order to change their selves from a lowly instinctual nature to an ultimate state of timeless proximity to God. This path or journey teaches the disciples through discipline, repentance (*istighfar*), introspection (*muraqaba*), continuation of prayers especially God's remembrance (*dhikr*), and strictly following other commandments of the *Shariah*.

The Sufi Sheikhs have divided this metamorphosis in three stages, based on three Quranic verses which explicitly address this topic (Milani, 2013). The first verse refers to a self which is at the lowest stage and it is characterized as *al-ammarah* (that which incites to evil). This stage indicates the urge of the animal spirit to have its way and corrupt the spirit. The second stage is that of *al-lawwama* (that which blames) and is regretful. Regret is the result of the new consciousness, which reveals the imperfections of the spirit and the futility of its unconscious ways of being in the world. This gradual growth of awareness will result in a lack of recourse to the previous base tendencies. A Sufi disciple in the second stage can also be characterized to be in a state of "abstinence"; actively avoiding all forms of inferior impulses and tendencies by observing high ethical code of his *Sheikh*. Nevertheless, it needs to be clarified at this point that this "abstinence" does not lead to asceticism. It also does not lend itself to develop a pious self which becomes judgmental and critical of others, which further separates one from the others. In summary, the goal here is the deconditioning of the self from its original habits and addictions.

The third and the final stage represents the state of *al-motma'ena* (that which is at peace). This stage is characterized by joyful satisfaction and removal of all doubts. The spirit, at this stage, is in full compliance with divine will and becomes a mirror of God's attributes. This is also the stage of *ihsan* where the Sufi is continually in the Presence of God and is humbled by the ever-increasing God-consciousness (Brown, 2009).

The outward manifestation of this spiritual awakening will be reflected in not only a higher form of self-consciousness but also in one's strict observance of ethical values (*akhlaq*) and one's lofty character. For Sufis, ethics and morality are a domain of *qalb* and the blessings of *Allah* cleans one's *qalb* from moral ailments while also generating positive moral virtues. This clearly depicts that Sufism is not just concerned with spiritual experiences but wants to translate those experiences as a higher form of ethical conduct in the daily lives of Sufis. The ultimate goal of this spiritual quest is to become what ibn Arabi calls the "perfect man" (*insan al-kamil*): a "complete and total human being who has actualized all the potentialities latent in the form of God" (Chittick, 1994, p. 23; Schimmel, 1975). The concept of *insan-e kamil* represents the ideal to which human beings can aspire. Such a positive philosophy places before us the grandeur of humanity since God's love to "be known" can be fully instantiated in *insan al-kamil*. This perfect man is the object of God's love and realizing this excellence is/should be the main objective of any human being and will be a culminating point of human love for God (*ishq*). Let us turn to a Prophetic saying regarding God's love,

> Those who seek nearness to Me seek nearness through nothing I love more than the performance of what I have made incumbent upon them. My servant never ceases to seek nearness to Me through supererogatory works until I love him. Then, when I love him, I am his hearing through which he hears, his sight through which he sees, his hand through which he grasps, and his foot through which he walks. (Chittick, 2014, p. 235)

This presents the status of the self which reaches the state of *al-motma'ena* where it is totally engulfed by love. In that state, man loses volition and self-centeredness and becomes aware of his situation of being separated from what he truly loves, God. This concept also informs us that all life including human life and all other creation of God cannot be separated from the Original. In this sense, love for anything other than God is illusory and metaphorical in nature (Chittick, 1995). In the words of ibn Arabi:

> The entities of the cosmos are all lovers because of Him, whatever the beloved may be, since all created things are the pedestals for the Real's self-disclosure. Their love is fixed, they are loving, and He is the loving...In the case of the created thing, you know the entity and you love. It may be that the name is not known. However, love refuses anything but making the beloved known. Among us are those who know God in this world, and among us are those who do not know Him until they die while loving some specific thing. Then they will come to understand, when the covering is lifted, that they had loved only God, but they had been veiled by the name of the created thing. (Chittick, 1995, p. 13)

Hence, *ishq* or love is actualized only by humans by loving the Real and even when they are loving a specific thing, they are loving Him since all are His creation. Hence, transformation of the spirit is actually an increase in capacity for *ishq*. In order to develop this capacity, man needs to understand the characteristics, qualities, and dispositions of his spirit wherein nobility exists. These qualities include *Taqwa* (piety), *Wara* (scrupulous fear of *Allah*), *Zuhd* (abstention), *Khushu* (reverence), *Khudu* (humility), *Sabr* (patience), *Sidq* (truthfulness), *Tawakkul* (reliance), *Adab* (etiquette), *Tawba* (repentance), *Inaba* (turning to *Allah*), *Hilm* (forbearance), *Rahma* (compassion), *Karam* (generosity), *Haya* (modesty), and *Shajaa* (courage). These are the essential hallmarks of a Sufi which are, in essence, inspired by the Prophet (PBUH) himself and the Sufi attains such qualities by following *Shariah* under the guidance of an accomplished Sheikh. Another important devotional practice in attaining such qualities is communal *dhikr* within a circle or *halaqa* (Elias, 2013). The importance of *dhikr* in achieving spiritual transformation has been underscored by many scholars. For example, consider the following:

> Dhikr is considered to be a torrent which in addition to eliminating the undesirable qualities of the disciple and substituting Divine attributes for them, in the final analysis effaces the individual ego in such a way that not a trace of the "I" remains. (Nurbakhsh, 1990, p. 5)

The above quote depicts that *dhikr* is far more complicated and organic than simple "remembrance" since it introduces the disciple to a powerful spiritual passage with its own microcosmic dimensions. Many Sufi masters have documented how this Quranic validated means of meditation can cause the removal of barriers (*hijab*) between the Sufi and reality as it actually is (Ridgeon, 2015).

SPIRITUAL EXPERIENCE

One manifestation of this removal is mystical revelation or divine disclosure (*kashf*) in which time, history, and all other forms of creation lose their independence and reveal their true ontological and epistemological nature

(Saniotis, 2007). According to ibn Arabi, such a man is in the realm of the "immutable entities" (*a'yan thabitah*) and he can now look at the things of the sensible world (Izutsu, 1983) in order to transform social realities. Imam Ghazali has termed this spiritual tasting as *dhawq* and described it as a kind of perceptive faculty of the spirit which allows it to discern truths. In his own words,

> [*dhawq*] is a light which appears in the heart after it is purified of its blamable characteristics. Through this light are revealed many matters of which one had heard only the name and about which one had imagined vague and general meanings. As a result the meanings become clear until one has true knowledge of the nature of God, His attributes, His acts, the meaning of the term angels and devils...and the meaning of prophecy, prophet, and the meaning of revelation. (Shehadi, 1964, p. 46)

Another meditative practice followed by the Sufis in order to generate this spiritual experience is contemplation (*muraqaba*; Ernst & Lawrence, 2002). The Sufi masters consider *muraqaba* as a channel to attain spiritual "states of consciousness beyond the limits of the rational, discursive mind and the descriptive power of language" (Rozehnal, 2007, p. 197). When a disciple engages in these contemplative exercises with the blessings of his Sufi master, he can attain certain spiritual stations (*maqam*). Each station has its own unique spiritual taste and feelings which produces an enhanced state of consciousness (Buehler, 2015). In Imam Ghazali's account, this spiritual experience provides a direct spiritual experience of reality and in this sense is better than reason which only provides an indirect and mediated sense-experience of reality. Such states produce the capacity to maintain focus of the disciple on different names and attributes of God and control his ego while absorbing spiritual energy. The two important stations on this journey include annihilation (*fanaa*) and permanent union (*baqaa*; Ernst & Lawrence, 2002, p. 16). Hence, these contemplative practices are used to attain a veridical cognition of realities as they really are (Hermansen, 1997).

However, the communication of this spiritual experience is limited by human cognition and inadequacies of language (Tymieniecka, 2011). This is the reason why most Sufis have resorted to rich allegorical poetry in order to demonstrate the depth of communication with the Divine. The abnormal state of Sufi consciousness and the experiences it entails are conveyed via apparent paradoxes and symbols (Pskhu, 2011). Although another individual on the same spiritual path might understand these symbols, others might get confused due to the semantic polysemy of Sufi texts. The most famous among these poetical works are Shaikh Saa'di's *Gulistan* and *Bostan*, Hafiz's *Divan* and Jalal-ud-Din Rumi's magnum opus, *Masnavi Maulana Rumi*. Consider, for example, a poem by Maulana Rumi titled "Mystical poems of Rumi" (Yarshater, 2009):

Again I am raging, I am in such a state by your soul that every bond you bind, I break, by your soul

I am like heaven, like the moon, like a candle by your glow; I am all reason, all love, all soul, by your soul

My joy is of your doing, my hangover of your thorn; whatever side you turn your face, I turn mine, by your soul

I spoke in error; it is not surprising to speak in error in this state, for this moment I cannot tell cup from wine, by your soul

I am that madman in bonds who binds the 'divs'; I, the madman, am a Solomon with the 'divs', by your soul

Whatever from other than love raises up its head from my heart, forthwith I drive it out of the court of my heart, by your soul

Come, you who have departed, for the thing that departs come back; neither you are that, by my soul, nor I am that, by your soul

Disbeliever, do not conceal disbelief in your soul, for I will recite the secret of your destiny, by your soul

Out of love of Sham-e-Tabrizi, through wakefulness or night rising, like a spinning mote I am distraught, by your soul

ORGANIZATIONAL IMPLICATIONS

I hope that even a brief discussion of Sufism is sufficient for one to realize the depth of understanding of spirituality that exists in this ancient well of wisdom. By using pearls from this well, we can provide a radically transformative and regenerative imaginary to rethink the role of organizations in society. The first revolutionary social implications of the nonperformative intent of Sufism is in shaping the purpose of organizations. Within the Sufi framework, organizations are simply tools available to humans to be closer to God and seek His pleasure and love. Hence, people can only make those decisions which are morally responsible according to *Shariah's* injunctions while also serving the wider public. This sense of altruism for humanity and the associated social obligations are not just an afterthought but are the central organizing principles. Therefore, organizations produce goods and services to serve humanity while generating a nonexploitative rate of return. This also implies that blind obedience to producing efficiency at all costs is discouraged or in the words of critical theory, performativity is avoided (Spicer, Alvesson, & Kärreman, 2016). The nonperformative organizational purpose or intent, however, is not focused on critical emancipation but surrender to the will of God.

Sufism can also generate meanings for employees since it links organizational actions with an ultimate purpose that goes beyond the performance of mundane tasks. The organization recognizes its particular place in the whole divine scheme of things and starts contributing to the greater community since this community represents God's creation. It rises above its individual entity and becomes part of an integrated whole. Another implication of such a transcendent organizational purpose is to conceptualize other firms not as "competitors only" whom we have to "beat" in this game. Rather, firms in the same industry need to collaborate with each other due to their common objective of seeking God's pleasure.

Similarly, the role of leader of a contemporary spiritual organization is to look after and care for his employees. Any leader is simply a vicegerent or agent of God whose duty is to love God and His creation in this world and the business organization is simply a tool or means to achieve this end. This purpose and vision of the organization should be made clear by the leader through his personal example of patience, gratitude, reliance on God, and humility. The purpose gets legitimized whenever this leader makes important organizational decisions which then become part of the organizational culture through specific routines and procedures. This significantly improves the meaning of organizational actions and practices for employees. Moreover, the genuine caring attitude of the leader towards his workers is going to energize them as they reciprocate with a sense of heightened responsibility. The more the employees are socially integrated in this organization's culture and value system, the more they feel committed towards the organization since their inner being, their spirit, starts believing, and embracing the organizational vision. This implies that the experience of their work will become increasingly important in their personal lives since it will serve as a conduit for spiritual transformation. As employee understanding and appreciation of their work increases, they start caring not only for the organization but also for each other. This will have positive consequences since it will inculcate an atmosphere of trust where people can provide each other honest feedback without any fear of marginalization.

Finally, Sufism can help avert the identity crisis in modern organizations since there is a lot of emphasis on creating awareness of the presence of *Allah* and the fundamental reality of one's relationship with one's creator. The contents of such an awareness determines who we are or in other words, our identity. As Maulana Rumi beautifully explains in his magnum opus, *Masnavi*:

> "You are your thought, brother,
> The rest of you is bones and fiber
> If you think of roses, you are a rose garden,
> If you think of thorns, you're fuel for the furnace"

Mankind's everlasting search for a sense of meaning and purpose require rethinking of our deepest intentions as well as a radical transformation of work and the workplace. Hence, engaging with Sufism will provide us a radical imaginary of a humane world which can help us in not only generating a nonperformative intent but also reinvigorating the emancipatory commitments of WPS discourse. This, I believe, is a change full of possibilities for the future.

REFERENCES

Adamson, P. (2015). *Philosophy in the Islamic world: A very short introduction.* Oxford, England: Oxford University Press.

Agazzi, E., & Pauri, M. (Eds.). (2000). *Boston studies in the philosophy of science, volume 215: The reality of the unobservable: Observability, unobservability and their impact on the issue of scientific realism.* Dordrecht, Netherlands: Springer.

Allcorn, S. (2002). *Death of the spirit in the American workplace.* Westport, CT: Quorum Books.

Armstrong, A. C. (1914). Bergson, Berkeley, and philosophical intuition. *The Philosophical Review, 23*(4), 430–438.

Baas, M., Nevicka, B., & ten Velden, F. S. (2014). Specific mindfulness skills differentially predict creative performance. *Personality and Social Psychology Bulletin, 40*(9), 1092–1106.

Bashir, S. (2011). *Sufi bodies: Religion and society in medieval Islam.* New York, NY: Columbia University Press.

Berger, P. L., & Luckmann, T. (1966). *The social construction of reality: A treatise in the sociology of knowledge.* Garden City, NY: Doubleday.

Bishop, S. R., Lau, M., Shapiro, S., Carlson, L., Anderson, N. D., & Carmody, J. (2004). Mindfulness: A proposed operational definition. *Clinical Psychology: Science and Practice, 11*(3), 230–241.

Bizzell, P. (1992). *Academic discourse and critical consciousness.* Pittsburgh, PA: University of Pittsburgh Press.

Blake, W. (1976). Milton. In A. Kazin (Ed.), *The portable blake.* New York, NY: Penguin.

Bourdieu, P. (2007). *Sketch for a self-analysis* (R. Nice, Trans.). Cambridge, England: Polity Press.

Böwering, G. (2001). The light verse: Qur'anic text and Sufi interpretation. *Oriens, 36*, 113–144.

Bradbury, H. (2003). Sustaining inner and outer worlds: A whole-systems approach to developing sustainable business practices in management. *Journal of Management Education, 27*(2), 172–187.

Braud, W. (2009). Dragons, spheres, and flashlights: Appropriate research approaches for studying workplace spirituality. *Journal of Management, Spirituality & Religion, 6*(1), 59–75.

Brewer, W. F., & Lambert, B. L. (2001). The theory-ladenness of observation and the theory-ladenness of the rest of the scientific process. *Philosophy of Science, 68*(S3), S176–S186.

Brown, C. G. (2016). Can "secular" mindfulness be separated from religion? In R. E. Purser, D. Forbes, & A. Burke (Eds.), *Handbook of mindfulness: Culture, context, and social engagement* (pp. 75–94). Dordrecht, Netherlands: Springer.
Brown, J. A. C. (2009). *Hadith: Muhammad's legacy in the medieval and modern world.* Oxford, England: Oneworld.
Brown, R. B. (2003). Organizational spirituality: The sceptic's version. *Organization, 10*(2), 393–400.
Brown, W. S., Murphy, N. C., & Malony, H. N. (Eds.). (1998). *Whatever happened to the soul? Scientific and theological portraits of human nature.* Minneapolis, MN: Fortress Press.
Buehler, A. F. (2015). Sufi contemplation: 'Abdullah Shah's *Suluk-i Mujaddidiyya*. In L. Komjathy (Ed.), *Contemplative literature: A comparative sourcebook on meditation and contemplative prayer* (pp. 307–358). Albany: State University of New York Press.
Buehler, A. F. (2016). *Recognizing sufism: Contemplation in the Islamic tradition.* London, England: I. B. Tauris.
Burckhardt, T. (1976). *Introduction to Sufi doctrine* (D. M. Matheson, Trans.). Wellingborough, England: Thorsons.
Campo, J. E. (2009). *Encyclopedia of Islam.* New York, NY: Facts on File.
Camus, A. (1991). *The myth of Sisyphus and other essays.* New York, NY: Vintage.
Chittick, W. C. (1989). *The Sufi path of knowledge: Ibn al-'Arabi's metaphysics of imagination.* Albany: State University of New York Press.
Chittick, W. C. (1992). *Faith and practice of Islam: Three thirteenth-century Sufi texts.* Albany: State University of New York Press.
Chittick, W. C. (1994). *Imaginal worlds: Ibn al-'Arabi and the problem of religious diversity.* Albany: State University of New York Press.
Chittick, W. C. (1995). The divine roots of human love. *Journal of the Muhyiddin Ibn 'Arabi Society, 17,* 55–78.
Chittick, W. C. (2000). *Sufism: A short introduction.* Oxford, England: OneWorld.
Chittick, W. C. (2005). *The Sufi doctrine of Rumi.* Bloomington, IN: World Wisdom.
Chittick, W. C. (2014). Love in Islamic thought. *Religion Compass, 8*(7), 229–238.
Chodkiewicz, M. (1993). *An ocean without shore: Ibn Arabi, the book, and the law* (D. Streight, Trans.). Albany: State University of New York Press.
Corbin, H. (1969). *Creative imagination in the Sufism of Ibn 'Arabi.* Princeton, NJ: Princeton University Press.
Davidson, D. (2004). *Problems of rationality.* Oxford, England: Clarendon Press.
Demirtas, O., Hannah, S. T., Gok, K., Arslan, A., & Capar, N. (2017). The moderated influence of ethical leadership, via meaningful work, on followers' engagement, organizational identification, and envy. *Journal of Business Ethics, 145*(1), 183–199.
Descartes, R. (1970). *Descartes: Philosophical letters* (A. Kenny, Trans.). Oxford, England: Oxford University Press. (Original work published 1642)
Driver, M. (2007). A "spiritual turn" in organizational studies: Meaning making or meaningless? *Journal of Management, Spirituality & Religion, 4*(1), 56–86.
Dybikowski, J. (2004). The critique of Christianity. In M. Fitzpatrick, P. Jones, C. Knellwolf, & I. McCalman (Eds.), *The enlightenment world* (pp. 41–56). London, England: Routledge.

Elias, J. J. (2013). Sufi *dhikr* between meditation and prayer. In H. Eifring (Ed.), *Meditation in Judaism, Christianity and Islam: Cultural histories* (pp. 189–200). London, England: Bloomsbury.

Ernst, C. W., & Lawrence, B. B. (2002). *Sufi Martyrs of love: The Chishti order in South Asia and beyond*. New York, NY: Palgrave Macmillan.

Foucault, M. (1973). *The order of things: An archaeology of the human sciences*. New York, NY: Vintage.

Fry, L. W., & Cohen, M. P. (2009). Spiritual leadership as a paradigm for organizational transformation and recovery from extended work hours cultures. *Journal of Business Ethics, 84*(2), 265–278.

Gardener, W. R. W. (1917). Al-Ghazali as Sufi. *The Muslim World, 7*(2), 131–143.

Gavrilyuk, P. L., & Coakley, S. (Eds.). (2012). *The spiritual senses: Perceiving God in western Christianity*. Cambridge, England: Cambridge University Press.

Gelles, D. (2015). *Mindful work: How meditation is changing business from the inside out*. Wilmington, MA: Mariner Books.

Giacalone, R. A., & Jurkiewicz, C. L. (Eds.). (2010). *Handbook of workplace spirituality and organizational performance* (2nd ed.). Armonk, NY: M.E. Sharpe.

Griffin, D. R. (1989). *God and religion in the postmodern world: Essays in postmodern theology*. Albany: State University of New York Press.

Hawley, J. (1993). *Reawakening the spirit at work: The power of Dharmic management*. San Francisco, CA: Berrett-Koehler.

Heelas, P. (1999). Prosperity and the new age movement: The efficacy of spiritual economics. In B. R. Wilson & J. Cresswell (Eds.), *New religious movements: Challenge and response* (pp. 51–78). London, England: Routledge.

Heelas, P., Woodhead, L., Seel, B., Szerszynski, B., & Tusting, K. (2005). *The spiritual revolution: Why religion is giving way to spirituality*. Malden, MA: Blackwell.

Hermansen, M. K. (1988). Shah Wali Allah's theory of the subtle spiritual centers (*Lataif*): A Sufi model of personhood and self-transformation. *Journal of Near Eastern Studies, 47*(1), 1–25.

Hermansen, M. K. (1997). Visions as 'good to think': A cognitive approach to visionary experience in Islamic Sufi thought. *Religion, 27*(1), 25–43.

Herrick, J. A. (2003). *The making of the new spirituality: The eclipse of the western religious tradition*. Downers Grove, IL: InterVarsity Books.

Izak, M. (2012). Spiritual *episteme*: Sensemaking in the framework of organizational spirituality. *Journal of Organizational Change Management, 25*(1), 24–47.

Izutsu, T. (1983). *Sufism and Taoism: A comparative study of key philosophical concepts*. Los Angeles: University of California Press.

Kabbani, M. H. (2003). *Classical Islam and the Naqshbandi Sufi tradition* (2nd ed.). Fenton, MI: ISCA.

Karakas, F. (2010). Spirituality and performance in organizations: A literature review. *Journal of Business Ethics, 94*(1), 89–106.

Khan, A. Y. (1965). *Dalael us-Suluk* (A. Talha, Trans.). Chakwal, Pakistan: Idarah-e Naqshbandiah Owaisiah.

Krahnke, K., Giacalone, R., & Jurkiewicz, C. L. (2003). Point-counterpoint: Measuring workplace spirituality. *Journal of Organizational Change Management, 16*(4), 396–405.

Krishnakumar, S., & Neck, C. P. (2002). The "what," "why," and "how" of spirituality in the workplace. *Journal of Managerial Psychology, 17*(3), 153–164.

Kuhn, T. S. (1962). *The structure of scientific revolutions.* Chicago, IL: University of Chicago Press.

Lagerlund, H. (Ed.). (2007). *Representation and objects of thought in medieval philosophy.* Farnham, England: Ashgate.

Lamptey, J. T. (2014). *Never wholly other: A Muslima theology of religious pluralism.* Oxford, England: Oxford University Press.

Layder, D. (1985). Beyond empiricism? The promise of realism. *Philosophy of the Social Sciences, 15*(3), 255–274.

Le Gall, D. (2004). *A culture of Sufism: Naqshbandis in the Ottoman world, 1450–1700.* Albany: State University of New York Press.

Lewis, F. D. (2000). *Rumi–past and present, east and west: The life, teachings, and poetry of Jalal al-Din Rumi.* London, England: Oneworld.

Lings, M. (1975). *What Is Sufism?* London, England: Allen & Unwin.

Lund Dean, K., & Fornaciari, C. J. (2007). Empirical research in management, spirituality & religion during its founding years. *Journal of Management, Spirituality & Religion, 4*(1), 3–34.

Lychnell, L. (2017). When work becomes meditation: How managers use work as a tool for personal growth. *Journal of Management, Spirituality & Religion, 14*(3), 255–275.

Markie, P. (1992). The cogito and its importance. In J. Cottingham (Ed.), *The Cambridge companion to Descartes* (pp. 140–173). Cambridge, England: Cambridge University Press.

McKee, M. C., Mills, J. H., & Driscoll, C. (2008). Making sense of workplace spirituality: Towards a new methodology. *Journal of Management, Spirituality & Religion, 5*(2), 190–210.

Milani, M. (2013). The subtle body in Sufism. In G. Samuel & J. Johnston (Eds.), *Religion and the subtle body in Asia and the west: Between mind and body* (pp. 168–184). London, England: Routledge.

Moxley, R. S. (2000). *Leadership and spirit: Breathing new vitality and energy into individuals and organizations.* San Francisco, CA: Jossey-Bass.

Nguyen, M. (2016). Sufi theological thought. In S. Schmidtke (Ed.), *The Oxford handbook of Islamic theology.* Oxford, England: Oxford University Press.

Nickles, T. (2013). The problem of demarcation: History and future. In M. Pigliucci & M. Boudry (Eds.), *Philosophy of pseudoscience: Reconsidering the demarcation problem* (pp. 101–120). Chicago, IL: University of Chicago Press.

Nurbakhsh, D. (1990). Sufism and psychoanalysis. *Sufi, 5,* 5–10.

O'Leary, M., & Chia, R. (2007). Epistemes and structures of sensemaking in organizational life. *Journal of Management Inquiry, 16*(4), 392–406.

Popper, K. R. (1963). *Science: Conjectures and refutations.* New York, NY: Harper & Row.

Porter, J. E. (1986). Intertextuality and the discourse community. *Rhetoric Review, 5*(1), 34–47.

Possamai, A. (2003). Alternative spiritualities and the cultural logic of late capitalism. *Culture and Religion, 4*(1), 31–45.

Pruzan, P. (2008). Spirituality as a firm basis for corporate social responsibility. In A. Crane, A. McWilliams, D. Matten, J. Moon, & D. S. Siegel (Eds.), *The Oxford handbook of corporate social responsibility* (pp. 552–559). Oxford, England: Oxford University Press.

Pskhu, R. (2011). Poetic expressions in Sufi language (based on al-Niffary's "kitab al-mawaqif"). In A.-T. Tymieniecka (Ed.), *Sharing poetic expressions: Beauty, sublime, mysticism in Islamic and occidental culture* (pp. 213–216). Heidelberg, Germany: Springer.

Purser, R. E. (2019). *McMindfulness: How mindfulness became the new capitalist spirituality*. London, England: Repeater Books.

Purser, R. E., & Milillo, J. (2015). Mindfulness revisited: A Buddhist-based conceptualization. *Journal of Management Inquiry, 24*(1), 3–24.

Quine, W. v. O. (1975). On empirically equivalent systems of the world. *Erkenntnis, 9*, 313–328.

Redden, G. (2016). Revisiting the spiritual supermarket: Does the commodification of spirituality necessarily devalue it? *Culture and Religion, 17*(2), 231–249.

Rego, A., & e Cunha, M. P. (2008). Workplace spirituality and organizational commitment: An empirical study. *Journal of Organizational Change Management, 21*(1), 53–75.

Ridgeon, L. (2015). Mysticism in medieval sufism. In L. Ridgeon (Ed.), *The Cambridge companion to Sufism* (pp. 125–149). Cambridge, England: Cambridge University Press.

Rinallo, D., Scott, L. M., & Maclaran, P. (Eds.). (2013). *Consumption and spirituality*. New York. NY: Routledge.

Ritskes, E. J. (2011). Connected: Indigenous spirituality as resistance in the classroom. In N. N. Wane, E. L. Manyimo, & E. J. Ritskes (Eds.), *Spirituality, education, & society: An integrated approach* (pp. 15–36). Rotterdam, Netherlands: Sense.

Rosenberg, A. (2017). Strong scientism and its research agenda. In M. Boudry, & M. Pigliucci (Eds.), *Science unlimited? The challenges of scientism* (pp. 203–224). Chicago, IL: University of Chicago Press.

Rothausen, T. J. (2017). Integrating leadership development with Ignatian spirituality: A model for designing a spiritual leader development practice. *Journal of Business Ethics, 145*(4), 811–829.

Rozehnal, R. (2007). *Islamic Sufism unbound: Politics and piety in twenty-first century Pakistan*. Basingstoke, England: Palgrave Macmillan.

Rupprecht, S., & Walach, H. (2016). Mindfulness at work: How mindfulness training may change the way we work. In M. Wiencke, M. Cacace, & S. Fischer (Eds.), *Healthy at work: Interdisciplinary perspectives* (pp. 311–328). Dordrecht, Netherlands: Springer.

Saniotis, A. (2007). Mystical mastery: The presentation of *Kashf* in Sufi divination. *Asian Anthropology, 6*(1), 29–51.

Sceski, J. H. (2007). *Popper, objectivity and the growth of knowledge*. London, England: Continuum.

Schimmel, A.-M. (1975). *Mystical dimensions of Islam*. Chapel Hill: University of North Carolina Press.

Schmidt, J. (Ed.). (1996). *What is enlightenment? Eighteenth-century answers and twentieth-century questions*. Berkeley: University of California Press.

Schneider, K. J. (1999). *The paradoxical self: Toward an understanding of our contradictory nature.* Buffalo, NY: Humanity Books.

Schneiders, S. M. (1989). Spirituality in the academy. *Theological Studies, 50*(4), 676–697.

Shafii, M. (1988). *Freedom from the self: Sufism, meditation, and psychotherapy.* New York, NY: Human Sciences Press.

Shapin, S. (1994). *A social history of truth: Civility and science in seventeenth-century England.* Chicago, IL: University of Chicago Press.

Sharifian, F. (2013). Conceptualisations of *ruh* 'spirit/soul' and *jesm* 'body' in Persian: A Sufi perspective. In R. Caballero & J. E. D. Vera (Eds.), *Sensuous cognition: Explorations into human sentience: Imagination, (e)motion and perception* (pp. 251–264). Berlin, Germany: Walter de Gruyter.

Sheep, M. L. (2006). Nurturing the whole person: The ethics of workplace spirituality in a society of organizations. *Journal of Business Ethics, 66*(4), 357–375.

Shehadi, F. A. (1964). *Ghazali's unique unknowable god.* Leiden, Netherlands: E. J. Brill.

Sorell, T. (1994). *Scientism: Philosophy and the infatuation with science.* London, England: Routledge.

Spicer, A., Alvesson, M., & Kärreman, D. (2016). Extending critical performativity. *Human Relations, 69*(2), 225–249.

Stepaniants, M. T. (1994). *Sufi wisdom.* Albany: State University of New York Press.

Sutcliffe, S. J., & Gilhus, I. S. (2014). Introduction: "All mixed up"-thinking about religion in relation to new age spiritualities. In S. J. Sutcliffe & I. S. Gilhus (Eds.), *New age spirituality: Rethinking religion* (pp. 1–15). London, England: Routledge.

Tackney, C. T., Chappell, S. F., & Sato, T. (2017). MSR founders narrative and content analysis of scholarly papers: 2000–2015. *Journal of Management, Spirituality & Religion, 14*(2), 1–25.

Taylor, C. (1989). *Sources of the self: The making of the modern identity.* Cambridge, MA: Harvard University Press.

Thompson, C. M. (2000). *The congruent life: Following the inward path of fulfilling work and inspired leadership.* San Francisco, CA: Jossey-Bass.

Tischler, L., Biberman, J., & McKeage, R. (2002). Linking emotional intelligence, spirituality and workplace performance: Definitions, models and ideas for research. *Journal of Managerial Psychology, 17*(3), 203–218.

Tymieniecka, A.-T. (Ed.). (2011). *Sharing poetic expressions: Beauty, sublime, mysticism in Islamic and occidental culture.* Heidelberg, Germany: Springer.

Ul-Haq, S. (2020). Spiritual development and meaningful work: A Habermasian critique. *Human Resource Development International, 23*(2), 125–145.

Ul-Haq, S., & Khan, F. R. (2018). A Sufi view of human transformation and its organizational implications. In J. A. Neal (Ed.), *Handbook of personal and organizational transformation* (pp. 833–865). Cham, Switzerland: Springer.

Upadhya, C. (2013). Shrink-wrapped souls: Managing the self in India's new economy. In N. Gooptu (Ed.), *Enterprise culture in neoliberal India: Studies in youth, class, work and media* (pp. 93–108). London, England: Routledge.

van Dijk, T. A. (1995). Discourse semantics and ideology. *Discourse & Society, 6*(2), 243–289.

Vu, M. C., & Gill, R. (2018). Is there corporate mindfulness? An exploratory study of Buddhist-enacted spiritual leaders' perspectives and practices. *Journal of Management, Spirituality & Religion, 15*(2), 155–177.

Wagner, P. (1994). *A sociology of modernity: Liberty and discipline.* London, England: Routledge.

Walsh, Z. (2018). Mindfulness under neoliberal governmentality: Critiquing the operation of biopower in corporate mindfulness and constructing queer alternatives. *Journal of Management, Spirituality & Religion, 15*(2), 109–122.

Webster, M., & Sell, J. (2014). Why do experiments? In M. Webster & J. Sell (Eds.), *Laboratory experiments in the social sciences* (2nd ed.; pp. 5–22). Burlington, MA: Academic Press.

Whitley, R. (2000). *The intellectual and social organization of the sciences* (2nd ed.). Oxford, England: Clarendon Press.

Willmott, H. C. (2018). Madness and mindfulness: How the "personal" is "political." In S. Stanley, R. E. Purser, & N. N. Singh (Eds.), *Handbook of ethical foundations of mindfulness* (pp. 259–283). Dordrecht, Netherlands: Springer.

Yarshater, E. (Ed.) (2009). *Mystical poems of Rumi.* Chicago, IL: University of Chicago Press.

Zafirovski, M. Z. (2011). *The enlightenment and its effects on modern society.* New York, NY: Springer.

Zaidman, N. (2003). Commercialization of religious objects: A comparison between traditional and new age religions. *Social Compass, 50*(3), 345–360.

Zaidman, N. (2007). The new age shop–Church or marketplace? *Journal of Contemporary Religion, 16*(3), 361–372.

Zaidman, N., Goldstein-Gidoni, O., & Nehemya, I. (2009). From temples to organizations: The introduction and packaging of spirituality. *Organization, 16*(4), 597–621.

Zajonc, A. (2009). *Meditation as contemplative inquiry: When knowing becomes love.* Great Barrington, MA: Lindisfarne Books.

CHAPTER 4

INSPIRING INCLUSION

What Is the Evidence for a Faith-Based Approach to Leadership Development?

Valerie L. Myers
University of Michigan

How does a nation's incremental ascent toward intercultural understanding and economic recovery tumble into xenophobia and cascading crises? Leadership.

> Then Pharaoh said to Joseph, "Since God has made all this known to you, there is no one so discerning and wise as you. You shall be in charge of the palace, and all of my people are to submit to your orders. Only with respect to the respect to the throne will I be greater than you." (Genesis 41:39–40, NIV)

> Then a new king, to whom Joseph meant nothing, came to power in Egypt. "Look", he said to his people, "the Israelites have become far too numerous for us. Come, we must deal shrewdly with them or they will become even more numerous and, if war breaks out, will join our enemies, fight against us and leave the country." (Exodus 1:8–10, NIV)

Under different leaders, the same country lurched from implementing to eviscerating ethnically inclusive policies. Leaders determined whether difference became a resource for societal progress or the justification for human cruelty. The human, economic, and environmental consequences that followed are legendary in Judeo-Christian traditions.

Together, these iconic stories about the Pharaohs of Genesis and Exodus illustrate contemporary issues in the workplace diversity literature. At a macro level, they showcase nationalism vs. immigration, economic scarcity vs. profitability, and how a lack of diversity leads to stagnation vs. diversity as a catalyst for innovation and growth. At the organization level, these stories reveal tensions between exclusion vs. inclusion, conflict vs. cooperation, conformity vs. positive deviance, prejudice vs. positive regard, oppression vs. empowerment, talent attrition vs. attraction, and bias vs. objectivity. More importantly, these stories reveal how a leader's view of power as self-service vs. responsibly serving others influences diversity, equity, and inclusion at multiple levels.

Indeed, Judeo-Christian scriptures are replete with examples of optimal and abysmal diversity and inclusion practices. Therefore, I contend that a faith-based approach to diversity and inclusion merits exploration; research supports this view. During the course of my analysis of phenomena at the intersection of faith and organizations (Mattis et al., 2004; Myers, 2003b, 2005, 2011, 2013a, 2013b; Wallace, Myers, & Osai, 2004), I discovered research that demonstrates the efficacy of faith-based interventions in the United States (DiIulio, 2002; Johnson, Thompkins, & Webb 2002; Myers, 2003a).

In this chapter, I integrate diversity management and intervention planning literatures to propose a faith-based alternative to typical corporate diversity, equity, and inclusion (DE&I) training. Toward this end, I explicitly focus on Christianity in the United States because it is the dominant religion; 71% of Americans identify as Christians (Pew Research Center), thus it crosses boundaries of politics, race, gender, education level, ability, and economic status (Kosmin & Keysar, 2009). Among Christians, 40% are Mainline or Evangelical Protestants and 21% are Catholic; those denominations are predominantly White (86%, 76%, and 59% respectively; Pew Research Center). Therefore, Christian ideology is uniquely positioned to influence a large segment of the population, its leaders, and the behavioral ecosystem (e.g., peers, social groups, congregations, cultural institutions, and communities).

Regarding the ecosystem, an enduring, complicated relationship exists between religion, U.S. culture, capitalism, and diversity. Specifically, institutionalized biases and diversity conflicts seeded the nation's founding and are reinforced by national culture, subcultural beliefs, and sometimes errant religious beliefs. Although this problem is not unique to the United

States, it is an extreme and intractable case that presents an intriguing research context. Despite these complicating factors however, I am optimistic about a faith-based approach. Why? Because religious ideology putatively transcends U.S. culture, patriotism, politics, capitalism, and social identities (although religion is used to promote political agendas, see Sharlett, 2008). Religious faith therefore, may be uniquely situated to counter discriminatory beliefs and behaviors that infect individuals, organizations, and society.

The goal of this chapter is to delineate the ways in which a faith-based DE&I intervention might lead to more profound, lasting, positive changes than secular ones, particularly among people who are ambivalent about or resist diversity (e.g., privileged, willfully oblivious, or bigots). I begin by presenting evidence indicating the need for alternative approaches to typical, secular diversity training. Next, I share insights from intervention research that provide empirical support for a faith-based approach. I draw upon my expertise as a professor and researcher of diversity leadership (Dreachslin & Myers, 2007; Myers & Dreachslin, 2007; Myers, 2009; Myers & Wooten, 2009; Myers, 2015; Myers et al., 2016) to apply management insights to aforementioned Bible passages, describing ways that a faith-based intervention can promote lasting cognitive, affective, and behavioral change. Bear in mind that, although this chapter focuses on Judeo-Christian beliefs and the United States, many insights are transferable to other countries and religious faiths.

THE CURRENT STATE OF U.S. DIVERSITY, EQUITY, AND INCLUSION

Progress

Civil Rights legislation of the 1960s and the emergence of diversity scholarship in the 1990s (Cox & Blake, 1991; Roberson, 2019) have resulted in a voluminous literature about moral, legal, normative, and pragmatic reasons (e.g., business case) to embrace diversity (Thomas & Ely, 1996). The "business case" has led corporations to invest millions in diversity initiatives, executives, and to compete for national awards that acknowledge: exemplary diversity recruitment and hiring, increased supplier diversity, mentoring, and pipeline programs (DiversityInc.com). Is there a return on these investments? Yes.

Research shows that diverse corporate boards, with women and people of color, are also more profitable (Hunt, Yee, Prince, & Dixon-Fyle, 2018). Other returns on diversity investments can now be quantified with sophisticated analytic tools (Hubbard, 2012, 2019). Research also shows that diversity can add value to team performance via social learning that enhances problem-solving, decision-making, and innovation (Page, 2005; Pentland, 2013). Consequently, corporations have made incremental gains to increase diversity and promote inclusion. But the results of those efforts are anemic; they flow from broader social trends.

Problems

Despite decades of trying, discrimination persists in the United States, resulting in relative inertia in corporations, which in turn reinforces the social status quo.

- *Inclusiveness.* The U.S. ranks 23rd in inclusiveness, among 29 advanced economies (World Economic Forum, Inclusive Development Report, 2018.)
- *Inequality.* On a scale of absolute equality "0" to absolute inequality "1," the U.S. scores .45, lagging 108 of 144 countries (Gini Index, 2020). Adverse effects of inequality disproportionately impact people of color (Lee, 2018).
- *Hate Crimes.* After a 20-year decline from 1995–2015, hate crimes surged 11%. Racial animus was the main cause of single-bias hate crimes (59%), followed by religion (20%) and sexual orientation (18%; FBI, n.d.).
- *Leader Demographics.* Whether corporate boards members (Farber, 2017), government leaders (Geiger, Bialik, & Gramlich, 2019), or leaders of all major cultural institutions (e.g., university presidents, news editors, music and television producers, sports team owners, military advisors; Park, Keller, & Williams, 2016), minority rule by Whites and men persists (see Table 4.1).

  These disparities persist despite studies showing that a lack of diversity compromises problem-solving and decision-making (Page, 2005), including ethical decisions.
- *Corporate Ethics.* The United States ranks 23rd in public ethics and corruption, and 19th in corporate ethics (World Economic Forum,

TABLE 4.1 Demographics of the U.S. Population Compared to Business and Political Leaders

	% Whites	% White Men	% All Women	% People of Color
U.S. Population	60%	31%	51%	40%
Corporate Boards	86%	65%	20%	14%
116th U.S. Congress (House, Senate)	78%	62%	24%	22%

n.d.; Global Competitiveness report 2018). Ethical indifference and lapses reinforce conditions that perpetuate myriad social dysfunctions and human suffering (Zimbardo, 2008).

These statistics expose the intransigence of diversity challenges, their embeddedness in national and business culture, and resulting inertia in society and organizations.

Symbiotic Inertia

Inertia and uneven DE&I progress are predictable given paradoxical circumstances of the United States' founding. Aspirations for independence, prosperity, freedom from tyranny, and justice-for-all were pursued with abominable wars, genocide, broken treaties, slavery and oppression, theft, deception, racism, sexism, and injustices-against-many (Baptist, 2014, Grann, 2017; Isenberg, 2016). So it is not surprising that 240+ years of celebrating the aspirational history, while ignoring or minimizing abominable methods are no match for mere decades of DE&I activism, legislation, research, and investments.

Three decades of diversity scholarship, corporate training, and the proliferation of diversity executives have yielded modest to disappointing results (Harvard Business Review, 2016; Roberson, 2019). Even recipients of corporate diversity awards (e.g., DiversityInc), fall short. MBA students who have worked for those esteemed firms often state that their company's diversity ranking is more virtue signaling than substance; business leaders and scholars agree (Bush & Peters, 2016; Harvard Business Review, 2016). Further, research refutes the efficacy of trendy implicit bias training (Lai et al., 2016), despite popular press and HR expectations. This confluence of disappointing results has rendered the word "diversity" somewhat meaningless, evoking cynicism and eye-rolls (Dobbins & Kalev, 2016).

In order to overcome inertia and entrenched ideologies, I contend that a more authoritative, compelling, transcendent ideology is needed. Religion is one such ideology.

An Ideological Alternative

Christianity inherently supports DE&I with passages that prescribe esteeming people who are different (e.g., differently gifted); showing empathy and care for the marginal, vulnerable, and strangers; and conveying positive regard (Rogers, 1957, 1959) for the disregarded. Hence, one might logically expect Christians to value diversity, exemplify ethical behaviors, and enact inclusive policies. Yet, preceding statistics suggest that some

Christians do not practice their professed beliefs or are unaware of their faith's teachings about diversity. Nevertheless, research suggests that faith-based interventions, informed by religious teachings, may be a catalyst for positive change.

Faith-based interventions combine expert, theological, and local knowledge to promote cognitive, behavioral, and emotional change (see Myers, 2003a,b). They have long been used to ignite positive change at individual, organizational, and societal levels (Brown, 1937; Engs, 2000). Although intuitive, folk practices predate social science research, scholars now understand many of the psychosocial mechanisms that contribute to the effectiveness of faith-based and secular interventions.

PLANNING EFFECTIVE INTERVENTIONS: SECULAR AND FAITH-BASED APPROACHES

Before presenting ideas for a faith-based DE&I intervention, it is important to lay a theoretical and empirical foundation. I begin by summarizing intervention planning basics that are derived from the behavioral health literature. This synopsis reveals limits of extant corporate DE&I training and merits of a faith-based approach. After providing empirical support for the efficacy of faith-based interventions compared to secular controls, I present a case example and discuss transferrable insights for a faith-based DE&I intervention.

Intervention Planning Basics

The aim of interventions is to promote health and well-being in a specific population, while reducing or eliminating factors that compromise their well-being (Green & Kreuter, 2004). Effective intervention planning entails: (a) customizing instruction to serve people at different stages of change, (b) using a proven intervention planning model, and (c) designing a culturally relevant experience to achieve maximum impact.

Customize for People at Different Stages of Change

The target population for an intervention is not monolithic; it is typically distributed across five stages of change, each requiring a custom approach (Prochaska, DiClemente, & Norcross, 1992; Prochaska, Redding, & Evers, 2008). For example, interventions for people at advanced stages of change (e.g., *action* and *maintenance*) may be limited to infrequent, one-size-fits-all sessions that reinforce existing knowledge or skills to promote action and prevent relapse. Whereas people at earlier intermediate stages

> **TABLE 4.2 Customize Intervention for People at Different Stages of Change**
>
> - *Early Stage:* Identify and address resisters' faulty beliefs and behaviors; convey risks of not changing.
> - *Intermediate Stage:* Provide repeated instruction to increase awareness, knowledge, skills, and build relationships that support change.
> - *Advanced Stage:* Reinforce and maintain prior learning and change, equip for action, and prevent relapse.

(e.g., *contemplation* and *preparation*) need more frequent, intensive expert instruction and social supports to increase their awareness, knowledge, and skills. Still, interventions designed for the intermediate stage will not produce results among people at the earliest stage of change (e.g., *precontemplation*) and who are most resistant. Resisters reject expert knowledge, conformity pressures, and therefore require an intervention-before-the-intervention. Planners must first identify and address resisters' counterproductive values, faulty beliefs, defeating behaviors, and undermining social influences—and educate them about the negative consequences of *not* changing.

Addressing this array of complex needs requires sophisticated planning frameworks.

Use a Proven Intervention Model: PRECEDE–PROCEED

The PRECEDE–PROCEED model is the gold standard in behavioral health and has been used to design interventions that promote individual, group, organizational, and system-wide change (Green & Kreuter, 2004). A strength of PRECEDE–PROCEED is its multidimensional framing of problems, solutions, and factors that support change. Specifically, P-R-E in PRECEDE stands for *predisposing, reinforcing,* and *enabling* factors that increase the likelihood of change.

Predisposing factors include thoughts, feelings, knowledge (or lack of it), cultural beliefs, and childhood experiences that increase or decrease a person's inclination to change. *Reinforcing factors* include direct benefits from enacting desired behaviors; social support and acceptance; and affirmation from organizational leaders and members. *Enabling factors* are easily summarized as a credible message, messenger, and methods.

Enabling messages should be derived from recent and rigorous subject matter research, rather than mere opinion and anecdotes. Effective messengers may be trained experts, community leaders, and/or peers. Instructional methods may include lectures, self-study, demonstrations, courses, conversations, and immersion experiences. These P-R-E factors are supported and sustained by Policy, Regulatory, and Organizational factors (P-R-O).

As Table 4.3 shows, cultural relevance is a vital factor that influences, supports, and sustains change.

TABLE 4.3 PRECEDE–PROCEED: A Multi-Dimensional, Multi-Level Framework for Change

P-R-E-CEDE Factors Influence Change	P-R-O-CEED Factors Support and Sustain Change
Thoughts, feelings, knowledge, beliefs, and cultural practices that predispose or prevent change.	Policy advocacy and goals.
	Regulatory supports, barriers, and legislative goals.
Behavioral benefits, social support and recognition that reinforce change outcomes.	Organizational leader, culture, communication, and norms.
Instructional message, messenger, and methods that enable change.	

Make It Culturally Relevant to Achieve Impact

Culturally relevant interventions customize the message, messenger, and methods to further *predispose and reinforce* change within a target audience. Cultural relevance is achieved by including: language, rituals, symbols, role models, shared meaning, peers, leaders endorsement/involvement, and organizational practices that are valued within a given community (P-R-O). Research shows that strategic cultural customization can significantly increase an intervention's credibility, accelerate progression through stages of change, and have a powerful transformative impact (Myers, 2003a; Yaneck, Becker, Moy, Gittelsohn, & Koffman, 2001).

Impact = reach × efficacy (Rimer, Glanz, & Rasband, 2001). *Reach* means educating the largest number of people and meeting them where they are—geographically, cognitively, and emotionally. *Efficacy* is achieved by providing an adequate number of treatments (i.e., typically 4–6, at minimum) that convey expert knowledge, local/cultural knowledge, and use best practices. Hence, cultural customization increases an intervention's *reach, efficacy,* and *impact* (see Table 4.4; Green & Kreuter, 2004).

Figure 4.1 illustrates the interdependence of aforementioned elements. A proven intervention planning framework is the foundation for embedding subject matter expertise, a custom experience for people at various stages of change, and culturally relevant instruction that results in a

TABLE 4.4 Cultural Relevance for Maximum Impact: Reach × Efficacy

- Reach the greatest number of people (location); address their thoughts, feelings, behaviors, education level, beliefs, and social influences.
- Empower efficacy to change with an adequate number of treatments, credible messages, messengers, and methods that facilitate learning, skill building, and provide culturally meaningful reinforcements.

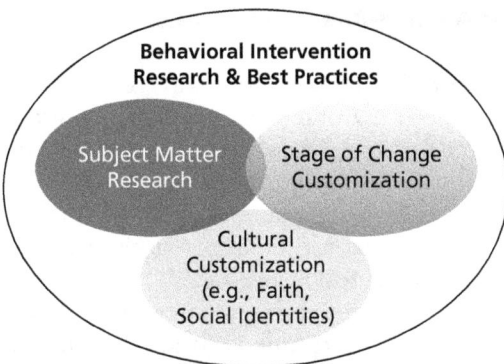

Figure 4.1 Interdependent elements of effective intervention planning.

transformative, high-impact learning experience. Figure 4.1 also provides a framework for understanding potential gaps in secular DE&I training and benefits of a faith-based approach.

Reasons to Have Faith in Faith-Based Interventions

Numerous studies show that, compared to secular controls, faith-based interventions (FBIs): lead to more significant change, accelerate transition through stages of change, produce greater magnitudes of change, and result in change being sustained over a longer period of time (see DiIulio, 2002; Johnson, Thompkins, & Webb, 2002; Myers, 2003a, 2003b). Research also shows that FBIs promote the adoption of desired behaviors (e.g., exercise, plant-based nutrition, cardiovascular health behaviors)[1] and cessation of undesirable behaviors (e.g., smoking, sedentary lifestyle, substance abuse).

Greater impact is achieved via the enhanced reach and efficacy of FBIs. *Reach* expands due to a convenient location that attracts voluntary members, provides organic support among natural peers, and typically has norms of positive regard that welcome all people (e.g., various stages of change). Shared beliefs and practices (e.g., narratives, rituals, songs, iconic stories, and leader behaviors) heighten cognitive, emotional, cultural, and spiritual resonance.

Efficacy is enhanced by a unique synthesis of credible expert, religious, and local knowledge; trusted messengers; and culturally appropriate methods (P-R-E). The context facilitates the completion of multiple treatments that are supported and sustained by clergy endorsements and sermons, church policies, community gatherings, and routine communication (P-R-O). Studies show that FBIs are especially effective for people who resist change (see Myers, 2003a).

Case Example: A Faith-Based Intervention for Resisters

The *Learn, Share, and Live* intervention was created to help a community of senior, African American women overcome their resistance to life-saving or life-extending breast cancer detection behaviors (Skinner et al., 1998). Planners assessed women's baseline heath knowledge, behaviors, and beliefs, which revealed their deeply-rooted fears about the healthcare system, faulty moral beliefs about breast self-exams, lack of knowledge about the disease, and absence of medical screening.

Content and methods were informed and endorsed by local pastors (*organizational support*). A pre-intervention utilized religious scriptures to counter women's spiritual justifications for inaction (e.g., "it is in God's hands") and reframe self-exams as "stewardship of the body." Women's faulty beliefs were further challenged with accurate medical information, survivor testimonials, and presenting the extreme risks of *not* changing (e.g., preventable, early death). These preliminary steps facilitated women's transition from resistant to reluctant but ready to change.

The next phase entailed four instructional sessions held in a community organization. Content was customized to address women's literacy (e.g., average 10th grade education) and failing vision. A bead stringing activity was used to demonstrate how to identify lumps during self-exams and dandelion images were used to illustrate how the disease spreads. In addition to pastors' support, participants' learning was reinforced by the social support of group members and spiritual support from their faith. At this point, a woman's continued resistance to change might raise questions about her commitment to her faith and community (which has risks).

Learn, Share, and Live resulted in significant advancement through stages of change, and change in knowledge, feelings, and behaviors that support breast cancer prevention. Although FBIs are not a panacea, I present this example because it is illustrative of how the FBI might similarly influence change among people who resist diversity and inclusion.

Transferable Insights for Faith-Based Approaches to DE&I

Resistance to DE&I is deeply rooted in U.S. culture, the ecosystem (e.g., media, education, and community), faulty religious beliefs, and animating beliefs of different social identity groups. Those powerfully reinforcing factors diminish and neutralize the impact of generic DE&I training—particularly for people at the resistant stage of change. Therefore, it is pointless to simply offer counter-factual knowledge or attack a person's passionately held ideology with a less meaningful, opposing one (e.g., the business case for diversity). To overcome their resistance, counter negative reinforcing factors, and influence change, a more authoritative, culturally relevant, and transcendent ideology is needed—like religious faith.

Let's return now to passages from Genesis and Exodus, at the beginning of this chapter, to explore ways that expert knowledge and religious ideology can be combined to create a high *impact*, culturally relevant, FBI that promotes DE&I. These narratives can be customized to *reach* different audiences (e.g., leaders, followers, Whites, people of color, and various political and social identity groups) and people at various stages of change. *Efficacy* can be attained by crafting messages that are delivered by credible messengers who use best practices to provide instruction with four or more sessions in a nonwork setting, where *policies, regulations,* and *organizational* factors (e.g., leaders, norms, rituals) support desired DE&I outcomes.

LEADING EGYPT: FAITH-BASED DE&I INTERVENTION FOR PEOPLE IN ALL STAGES OF CHANGE

Here, I describe frameworks for two customizable faith-based DE&I interventions. The first intervention is for people who are "ready to change"; it uses a business case that is derived from the book of Genesis (Myers, 2013b). The second proposed pre-intervention is for people who *resist* change: it uses the Exodus passage. Both interventions include religious text, virtual role models, social science theory, and have practical applications for DE&I training and education.

Ready for Change: Diversity, Equity, and Inclusion in Genesis 28–50

Audience and Cultural Customization

I teach an inclusive leadership course for MBA and graduate students at the University of Michigan's Ross School of Business. As such, it is a one-size-fits-many DE&I intervention for people who are contemplating and curious about change. The capstone business case that I use is derived from the Genesis story (Myers, 2013b), which we will refer to as "Joseph's Journey." Joseph's story is common to Abrahamic religions (e.g., Judaism, Christianity, and Islam) and is therefore relevant to domestic and international students, typically *reaching* 2/3 of the class. For the remaining 1/3 it is cognitively and emotionally resonant (or sometimes repugnant). Our explicit ground rule: We will not discuss religious beliefs. Instead, the culturally relevant framing is business and the social science of diversity.

To promote *efficacy*, the case is introduced during the 4th class session, preceded by sessions that convey expert knowledge about diversity and inclusion, such as: the "business case"; routine organizational DE&I practices (including religious accommodation); and diversity research (e.g., innovation, neuroscience of biases, ethical decision-making, team dynamics). At this juncture, students have acquired basic knowledge and skills to help them overcome any ambivalence they may have about diversity and inclusion; they've also practiced applying their new knowledge and skills to traditional business cases and with team members.

Joseph's Journey (Myers, 2013b) presents several workplace scenarios with variations in: inclusive leadership, team dynamics, cultural influences, and categories of difference (e.g., individual, ideological, sociodemographic, and power). Here, I focus on the Pharaoh in Chapter 41 as an exemplar of inclusive leadership because his curiosity about Joseph, a Hebrew prisoner with unique capabilities and sterling character, led to an unlikely and highly productive partnership. Together, these leaders increased diversity and cross-cultural collaborations to positively transform society.

Faith-Based Content

Despite Joseph's difference, and because of it, Pharaoh modified traditional recruitment and selection criteria, suspended judgment about perceived deficits, and hired Joseph because he possessed skills that a homogenous team of Egyptian advisor's lacked.

> Then Pharaoh said to Joseph, "Inasmuch as God has shown you all this, there is no one as discerning and wise as you. You shall be over my house, and all my people shall be ruled according to your word; only in regard to the throne will I be greater than you. (Genesis 41: 39–40, NKJV)

Pharaoh sponsored Joseph, publicly supported him, compensated him well, respected their religious differences, and included him in elite social circles—somewhat. Joseph was excluded from informal leader gatherings because Hebrews and Egyptians dined separately. Still, Joseph distinguished himself as an exemplary leader, developed new economic policies, and learned from Egyptians in order to create innovative environmental management tactics. Joseph later recruited and mentored other qualified people from his ethnic group (his family), further increasing diversity and improving performance with their unique skills. Hebrew immigrants' contributions were ultimately viewed as essential to national vitality and renewal.

As Pharaoh and Joseph's relationship evolved, animus between Egyptians and Hebrews dissolved and morphed into cross-cultural respect. Pharaoh's infectious positive regard toward Joseph and the Hebrews is apparent in how Egyptian leaders responded when Joseph's father died (Genesis 50).

> 7 So Joseph went up to bury his father. All Pharaoh's officials accompanied him—the dignitaries of his court and all the dignitaries of Egypt—8 besides all the members of Joseph's household and his brothers and those belonging to his father's household.... 11 When the Canaanites who lived there saw the mourning at the threshing floor of Atad, they said, "The Egyptians are holding a solemn ceremony of mourning." That is why that place near the Jordan is called Abel Mizraim.

Egyptians who once reviled Hebrews, shared their grief and traveled with them to memorialize Joseph's father. Hebrews mourned him 40 days; Egyptians mourned him 70 days (Genesis 50: 1–3). This kind of intercultural empathy, understanding, and exchange might have been unimaginable decades earlier, when Joseph entered Egypt as a teenage slave. But with Pharaoh's transformational leadership and Joseph's exceptional performance, ethnic biases abated, anti-immigrant attitudes and behaviors declined, and the nation flourished. Together, Egyptian and Hebrew citizens prospered because of Joseph's revolutionary, counter-cyclical economic policies (Buttonwood, 2009).

Practical Application

This excerpt from Joseph's Journey illustrates how a leader's deliberate, albeit imperfect, inclusive actions resulted in more diversity at senior levels and throughout an organization, more intercultural understanding, more learning, more innovation, more economic resilience, and a more cohesive society. Yet, despite Pharaoh's efforts, institutional norms remained the same, remnants of social segregation persisted, and social learning across cultures never reached its *full* potential. We consider additional DE&I actions that Pharaoh could have taken to foster more progress. Such tension between progress and the status quo is common in modern organizations, making this case highly instrumental for students' learning and growth.

Students' reactions to this case are always mixed, yet their weekly journal entries indicate significant learning and change. Foremost, all students are surprised by the case. Their heightened emotions (+/–) create opportunities for greater self-awareness, learning, and opportunities to practice their skills.

Several students are routinely offended by this case and challenged to recognize, suspend, and overcome their religious biases so that they can absorb management lessons. As we discuss the case and diagnose cultural norms, leader biases, ethical lapses, and exclusive behaviors, students soon discover what they too must do to create an inclusive workplace (e.g., challenge institutional norms, speak up, be an ally, etc.). In this sense, Joseph's Journey and this class session constitute a secular DE&I intervention, despite faith content.

For students who are adherent of Abrahamic faiths, this case is both a secular and faith-based DE&I intervention. Even though we do not discuss religious beliefs, the case is culturally relevant for believers; it indirectly activates existing beliefs and valued memories that further predispose, reinforce, and enable their professional growth. Other students who are ambivalent about or have weak attachments to religion, recognize parallels between their secular beliefs, management lessons, and sometimes write about becoming more curious about religion.

In sum, the *reach* of this case and the engagement that it evokes are among the most robust throughout the semester. I hypothesize that engagement and *efficacy* would be even more powerful in the context of an actual FBI, in which participants freely discuss the intersection of business norms, cultural ideologies, and their religious beliefs. Nevertheless, this Genesis narrative alone is insufficient to evoke meaningful change in ardent resisters.

Resisting Change: Diversity, Oppression, and Exclusion in Exodus 1–14

Audience and Cultural Customization

Resisters are neither ready, willing, or interested in receiving expert knowledge about the diversity "business case," the benefits of inclusion, or in interacting with people who are different. Hence, the ideal audience for this intervention is people who share social identities, backgrounds, or animating beliefs. Increasing e*fficacy* for this group will require preliminary intervention that addresses faulty, entrenched beliefs about one's own and others' social identities (e.g., stereotypes), the "acceptable" social order, and counterproductive behaviors. The Exodus passage is ideal in this regard. Even though it follows Genesis sequentially, it can be a preliminary intervention for resisters.

The Exodus story begins centuries after Joseph's reign. The new Pharaoh's hatred toward Hebrews is palpable, as he responds to demographic shifts with fear, callousness, and brutality.

Pharaoh's bigoted emotional appeals revived dormant anti-Hebrew sentiments and fomented intercultural hostility and cruelty throughout the country. Thus, this story may *reach* people who similarly detest diversity, "others," and seek to harm them. However, as resisters identify with Pharaoh's anti-DE&I emotions and actions, they can also be challenged to reconcile dissonance between their shared emotions, actions, and their espoused religious beliefs; Pharaoh rejected God.

The story also enumerates myriad risks of *not* changing, which is vital to influence change among resisters. Specifically, the consequences of Pharaoh's hatred toward diversity and failure to change are analogous to the waning support of peers, reputational damage, organizational decline, financial loss, and societal instability that participants may also experience. Thus, the valued cultural lens of religious faith is used to reframe their faulty beliefs and behaviors as profane.

Faith-Based Content

> Now there arose a new king over Egypt, who did not know Joseph. And he said to his people, "Look, the people of the children of Israel are more and mightier than we; come, let us deal shrewdly with them, lest they multiply, and it happen, in the event of war, that they also join our enemies and fight against us, and so go up out of the land. (Exodus 1:8–10, NKJV)

Successive chapters (1–14) describe Pharaoh's abuses of power and how he co-opts minions to enact his punitive policies against Hebrews—and against reason, against opposition from Egyptian advisors, and against mounting physical evidence that the country was headed in the wrong direction (e.g., plagues, economic downturn, death). Pharaoh demonized diversity, fomenting Egyptians' fear and resentment toward a growing Hebrew population, enacting anti-Hebrew labor policies, and snatching Hebrew babies from their parents to kill them. Through it all, Pharaoh remained indifferent to their suffering, reveled in his duplicity, and repeatedly rejected Moses' appeals for mercy and freedom. Pharaoh's repeated broken promises to free them were simply tactics to avoid God's wrath.

Pharaoh's hard-hearted, tough leadership (see Exodus 7:3, 14, 15, 22; 8:15, 19, 32; 9:12, 34, 35; 10:1, 20, 27; 11:10) brought unnecessary calamity to the country, Egyptian elites, and his own family. In response to Pharaoh's treachery, God sent ten plagues to Egypt (e.g., poisoned water and fish, hordes of frogs, locusts and gnats, and disease). Unrelenting, Pharaoh ignored cabinet members' warning that the plagues were indeed divine judgment against him. Frustrated Egyptians began turning against Pharaoh saying, "How long will you refuse to humble yourself?" How long will this man [Moses] be a snare for us? Do you not realize that Egypt is destroyed?" (Exodus 10: 3, 7). Slowly, Pharaoh's loyalists defected, resisted his demands, and were spared negative consequences. But Pharaoh, impervious to the toll of his impudence, hubris, and anger, allowed his son to die as collateral damage.

By the time more Egyptians perceived the Divine judgment against their immoral actions, it was too late. Egypt was plundered as the Hebrews left with their treasure (Exodus 14:25). Recalcitrant to the end, Pharaoh changed his mind after finally freeing the Hebrews, followed them, and tried to kill them. Hebrews escaped on dry ground; Pharaoh and his army were overthrown by a great wave of the sea (Exodus 14:27).

Practical Application

The Exodus story powerfully illustrates the systemic nature of oppression, exclusion, ethnic hatred, and unethical leadership in a nonaccusatory yet culturally valued way. Its cautionary lessons can be used to ignite change at societal, organizational, individual, and relationship levels.

Society. At a macro level, this story is presciently instructive for our time, echoing modern headlines about: escalating hate crimes, demonization of immigrants, refugee children being taken from their parents, conscientious defection of political elites from their party, contamination of water (e.g., Flint, Michigan) and food supplies, increasing frequency and ferocity of environmental disasters (e.g., hurricanes, floods, fires, pestilence), the COVID-19 pandemic and related economic collapse. Group discussions might examine parallels to U.S. history and the ways in which powerful people have similarly misused their authority and racial tropes to manipulate pliable people to act against their own self-interest (Isenberg, 2016), consequently destabilizing society.

Organizations and leaders. Institutionalized biases, unethical corporate cultures, and wide-spread costs of discriminatory practices on profitability are among the theoretical topics that can be explored through the Exodus lens. Of particular interest, is how corporations and institutions reflect the values, psychological well-being, or psychopathy (Bakan, 2004) of society and its leaders.

Leaders in Genesis and Exodus portray senior leaders who use or abuse their power to help or harm others, depending upon their own social identity (Scholl, Sassenberg, Scheepers, Ellemers, & de Wit, 2017, 2018). In Exodus, the Pharaohs were energized by their worst primitive instincts (Kahneman, 2011; Sapolsky, 2017), demonstrating a lack of cognitive development. The story is replete with examples of the psychological dysfunction and distortions that animate discriminatory behaviors that are antithetical to Christian faith. Select verses can be used to evoke profound cognitive dissonance and discussion among participants that previously justified their own similar thoughts, feelings, and behaviors. Pharaoh said:

> Who is the Lord, that I should obey His voice to let Israel go? I do not know the Lord, nor will I let Israel go. (Exodus 5: 2, NKJV)

> Pharaoh quickly summoned Moses and Aaron and said, "I have sinned against the Lord your God and against you. Now forgive my sin once more and pray to the Lord your God to take this deadly plague away from me. (Exodus 10: 16, 17, NKJV)

Pharaoh's contempt for God and Moses, an esteemed religious hero, nullifies any prior religious justifications of discrimination and exclusion.

Ideally, structured discussions about this content will help diminish spiritualized resistance and facilitate progress to the next stage, "ready to change."

Individuals. Interventions that are designed for people who are "ready to change" combine culturally relevant *and* expert knowledge. Here, we might begin by comparing Pharaoh's behaviors with symptoms of psychopathology as defined in the *Diagnostic and Statistical Manual of Mental Disorders, 5th Edition* (American Psychiatric Association, 2013), which include: deceitfulness, reckless disregard for the safety of others, and inability to experience guilt and so forth.

Exodus is replete with other examples of arrested cognitive development (Kohlberg, 1976; Piaget, 1932) and character deficits (e.g., self-interest, brutality, lying, murder, disregard for facts, blame-shifting; Peterson & Seligman, 2004) that undermine inclusion and societal well-being. Group discussions might explore: the psychology of ethical decision-making (Haidt, 2012), the neuroscience of fear and bias (Kahneman, 2011; Sapolsky, 2017), and the need to adopt mental habits that enable one to triumph over toxic traditions (Baldwin, 1962). However, knowledge alone is insufficient. Participants need skills to act on their new knowledge and role models to guide them.

Relationships. Although leaders' (un)ethical beliefs and behaviors trickle-down to teams and individuals (Ambrose, Schminke, & Mayer, 2013), followers can resist. Members of Pharaoh's cabinet and the Egyptian community slowly recognized the adverse consequences of his immoral decisions, defected, and took concrete steps to reject his bigotry (e.g., thwarted plots, speaking up). They serve as powerful virtual role models for participants that seek to similarly make incremental behavioral shifts. These virtual positive deviants (Cameron, Dutton, & Quinn, 2003) can inspire and illustrate alternative behaviors that promote diversity, equity, inclusion, and ethical transformation.

In sum, Genesis and Exodus narratives are so dense with management and DE&I concepts that an intervention could span 4, 20, or more treatments.

IMPLICATIONS FOR PRACTICE AND RESEARCH

The accelerated pace of global demographic shifts and hyper-connectedness demand more effective DE&I leadership. But statistics suggest that many Americans are more resistant to DE&I than they think and existing training lacks *impact* to help them overcome it. Although corporate training has the potential to *reach* an entire employee population, it typically lacks customization to address the needs of people at different stages of change, rendering it out of reach for many. One-size-fits-all training ignores the interests and impediments of ardent resisters, while "preaching" to an already converted group of social justice advocates in an advanced stage of change.

Reach may be further diminished by a lack of cultural customization—or because of it. To what degree is DE&I training culturally relevant for all subcultural groups in the workplace? Does training reinforce a dominant group's or the organization's ideology? Although potentially inspiring, customization that conforms to the organization's DE&I ideology has risks (e.g., leader hypocrisy, indifference) that can undermine desired change and breed cynicism (Ashforth & Vaidyanath, 2002). In fact, aforementioned DE&I statistics suggest that P-R-O factors in the workplace (e.g., senior leader demographics) may unintentionally reinforce the status quo and undermine training effectiveness.

The *efficacy* of corporate DE&I training is variable and questionable. For example, how many training programs provide 4–6 treatments, which are essential for significant change? Are training protocols guided by the latest management trend, robust PR in the "right" business outlets, or intervention science? Does training address *predisposing factors* that inhibit change? Does it provide sufficient *reinforcements* from leaders and peers? Does evidence *enable* learning and skill building, or do content and methods simply reflect a facilitator's preferences? Indeed, Figure 4.1 provides a framework for understanding the impotence of existing corporate DE&I training and ways that they might immediately be improved. Even so, research suggests that a faith-based DE&I intervention will likely yield even more significant and lasting change.

This chapter extracts insights from the health behavior literature to describe the ways in which an evidence-based, culturally relevant, stage appropriate, faith-based DE&I intervention might yield more impactful results than secular ones. Research shows that FBIs have been powerful catalysts for change in a variety of domains (e.g., health, education, workplace). Future research might compare the efficacy of faith-based versus secular DE&I interventions and their effects on people at various stages of change. Studies might also examine discrete outcomes such as changes in thoughts, feelings, and behaviors, giving particular attention to the magnitude of change among *resisters*.

Research might also compare cultural adaptations of FBIs targeted at different subcultural groups (e.g., high status White leaders, people of high and low income, high and low education levels, and people from different geographic regions). For example, it would be useful to know which messages, messengers, methods, and iconic figures *reach* specific audiences and are associated with more statistically significant and lasting change. Likewise, it would be useful to understand the contextual effects of organization supports (e.g., business leaders vs. clergy and community) on intervention outcomes for different populations.

CONCLUSION

Existing tactics to facilitate DE&I are inadequate to address the challenges of our time. According to the Fourth National Climate Assessment Report (Reidmiller et al., 2018), forthcoming climate changes will cause rising sea levels, food crises, and mass migration, similar to the Genesis story. Like Joseph's family during the famine, vulnerable "strangers" will seek food, refuge, and work wherever they can to survive. Coming changes will disproportionately affect people who are "different"—indigenous people, people of color, the aged, infirm, and poor. Although we are different, our fate as human beings is connected. No one will be immune to the dire consequences of climate change and resource scarcity, which was also true in ancient Egypt—and may soon be again (Walsh & Sengupta, 2020).

If leaders are open-minded and ethical, like the Pharaoh in Genesis, they will discover that, like Joseph, those "strangers" possess unique skills and capabilities that can help us successfully meet coming challenges. The question is: How will leaders respond to increasing demographic shifts? What behavioral tone, policies, and trajectory will leaders set for their nation and organizations? Will they stoke tribal fear of "others" to justify injustice, exploitation, and cruelty, as in Exodus? Or will leaders inspire inclusion, like the Pharaoh in Genesis, leveraging Joseph's and Hebrews' talents to benefit all? And finally, how will we respond? Will we feign faithfulness to our espoused religious beliefs while cowardly conforming to the status quo? Or will we be positive deviants who courageously practice the Christian faith of inclusion that we profess?

REFERENCES

Ambrose, M. L., Schminke, M., & Mayer, D. M. (2013). Trickle-down effects of supervisor perceptions of interactional justice: A moderated mediation approach. *Journal of Applied Psychology, 98*(4), 678–689.

American Psychiatric Association. (2013). *Diagnostic and statistical manual of mental disorders* (5th ed.). Arlington, VA: Author.

Ashforth, B. E., & Vaidyanath, D. (2002). Work organizations as secular religions. *Journal of Management Inquiry, 11*(4), 359–370.

Baldwin, J. (Ed.). (1985). The creative process. In *The price of the ticket: Collected nonfiction, 1948–1985* (pp. 315–318). New York, NY: St. Martin's Press.

Bakan, J. (2005). *The corporation: The pathological pursuit of profit and power.* New York, NY: Free Press.

Baptist, E. E. (2014). *The half has never been told: Slavery and the making of American capitalism.* New York, NY: Basic Books.

Brown, R. C. (1937). The national Negro health week movement. *Journal of Negro Education, 6*(3), 553–564.

Bush, M., & Peters, K. (2016, December 5). How the best companies do diversity right. *Forbes Magazine.* Retrieved from http://fortune.com/2016/12/05/diversity-inclusion-workplaces/

Buttonwood. (2009, April 8). Spin and substance: What the G20 did and did not achieve. *The Economist.* Retrieved from http://www.economist.com/node/13447131

Cameron, K., Dutton, J., & Quinn, R. (2003). *Positive organizational scholarship: Foundations of a new discipline.* San Francisco, CA: Berrett-Koehler.

Cox T. H., & Blake S. (1991). Managing cultural diversity: Implications for organizational competitiveness. *Academy of Management Executive, 5*(3), 45–56.

DiIulio, J. J. (2002). Reasons for objective Hope in the two faith factors. In B. R. Johnson, R. B. Tompkins, & D. Webb (Eds.), *Objective hope: Assessing the effectiveness of faith based organizations: A review of the literature* (pp. 5–6). Philadelphia: Center for Research on Religion and Urban Civil Society, University of Pennsylvania.

Dobbins. F., & Kalev, A. (2016, July–August). Why diversity programs fail and what works better. *Harvard Business Review.* Retrieved from https://hbr.org/2016/07/why-diversity-programs-fail

Dreachslin, J. L., & Myers, V. L. (2007). A systems approach to culturally competent and linguistically appropriate care. *Journal of Healthcare Management, 52*(4), 220–226.

Engs, R. C. (2000). *Clean living movements: American cycles of health reform.* Westport, CT: Praeger.

Farber, M. (2017, February 6). Board diversity at Fortune 500 companies has reached an all-time high. *Forbes Magazine.* Retrieved from https://fortune.com/2017/02/06/board-diversity-fortune-500/

Federal Bureau of Investigation. (n.d.). *Hate crime statistics 1995–2015.* Retrieved from https://ucr.fbi.gov/hate-crime

Geiger, A. W., Bialik, K., & Gramlich, J. (2019, February 15). The changing face of congress in 6 charts. *Pew Research Center.* Retrieved from https://www.pewresearch.org/fact-tank/2019/02/15/the-changing-face-of-congress/

Gini Index. (2020). Retrieved from https://worldpopulationreview.com/countries/gini-coefficient-by-country/#dataTable

Grann, D. (2017). *Killers of the flower moon: The Osage murders and the birth of the FBI.* New York, NY: Doubleday.

Green, L.W., & Kreuter, M.W. (2004). *Health promotion planning: An educational and ecological approach* (4th ed.). Mountain View, CA: Mayfield.

Haidt, J. (2012). *The righteous mind: Why good people are divided by politics and religion.* New York, NY: Pantheon-Random House.

Harvard Business Review. (2016). *The latest diversity research—Special issue,* July/August.

Hubbard, E. E. (2012). *The diversity scorecard: Evaluating the impact of diversity on organizational performance* (Improving Human Performance). New York, NY: Routledge Press.

Hubbard, E.E. (2019). *Introduction to diversity return on investment (DROI®): Building diversity initiatives with a demonstrated ROI impact on the bottom-line.* Petaluma, CA: Global Insights.

Hunt, V., Yee, L., Prince, S., & Dixon-Fyle, S. (2018). *Delivering through diversity*. Retrieved from https://www.mckinsey.com/business-functions/organization/our-insights/delivering-through-diversity

Isenberg, N. (2016). *White trash: The 400-year untold history of class in America*. New York, NY: Viking Press.

Johnson, B. R., Tompkins, R. B., & Webb, D. (2002). *Objective hope—Assessing the effectiveness of faith-based organizations: A review of the literature*. Philadelphia: Center for Research on Religion and Urban Civil Society, University of Pennsylvania.

Kahneman, D. (2011). *Thinking fast and slow*. New York, NY: Farrar, Straus & Giroux.

Kohlberg, L. (1976). Moral stages and moralization: The cognitive-developmental approach. In T. Lickona (Ed.), *Moral development and behavior: Theory, research and social issues* (pp. 31–53). New York, NY: Holt, Rinehart and Winston.

Kosmin, B. A., & Keysar, A. (2009). *American religious identification survey*. Hartford, CT: Trinity College. Retrieved from https://commons.trincoll.edu/aris/files/2011/08/ARIS_Report_2008.pdf

Lai, C. K., Skinner, A. L., Cooley, E., Murrar, S., Brauer, M., Devos, T., . . . Nosek, B. A. (2016). Reducing implicit racial preferences: II. Intervention effectiveness across time. *Journal of Experimental Psychology, 145*(8), 1001–1016.

Lee, S. (Ed.). (2018). *Save our cities, powering the digital revolution: The state of Black America 2018*. Retrieved from http://soba.iamempowered.com/2018-report

Mattis, J. S., Beckham, W., Saunders, B., Williams, J., McAllister, D., Myers, V., . . . Dixon, C. (2004). Who will volunteer? Religiosity, everyday racism, and social participation among African American men. *Journal of Adult Development, 11*(4), 261–272.

Myers, V. L. (2003a). *An interdisciplinary analysis of faith-based human services: Identifying latent organizational, social and psychological processes* (Unpublished doctoral dissertation). University of Michigan, Ann Arbor, MI.

Myers, V. L. (2003b). Planning and evaluating faith-based interventions: Closing the theory–practice divide. In *The role of faith-based organizations in the social welfare system: 2003 spring research forum working papers*. Washington, DC: Independent Sector and the Roundtable on Religion and Social Welfare Policy.

Myers, V. L. (2005). Black church culture, social programs & faith-based policy: Using organization theory to reconcile rhetoric and reality. *African American Research Perspectives, 11*(1), 116–138. (National Congregation Study National Data Set)

Myers, V. L. (2009). Pilot of a diversity leadership competency course for graduate students in healthcare administration. *Journal of Health Administration Education, 24*(4), 273–300.

Myers, V. L. (2011). *Calling and talent development: Not your average working Joe—Part A*. Ann Arbor: Business Case Study, William Davidson Institute, University of Michigan. (Revised in 2013)

Myers, V. L. (2013a). *The power of a calling: Insights from Joseph's journey – Parts A, B & C*. Ann Arbor: Business Case Study, William Davidson Institute, University of Michigan.

Myers, V. L. (2013b). *Conversations about calling: Advancing management perspectives*. New York, NY: Routledge.

Myers, V. L. (2015). Diversity ideologies in action: Energizing renewal and excellence in healthcare. In K. D. Elsbach, A.B. Kayes, & D. C. Kayes (Eds.), *Contemporary organizational behavior: From ideas to action* (p. 419). Upper Saddle River, NJ: Prentice Hall.

Myers, V. L., & Dreachslin, J. L. (2007). Recruitment and retention of a diverse workforce: Challenge and opportunity. *Journal of Healthcare Management, 52*(5), 290.

Myers, V. L., Griffith, J. R., Banaszak-Holl, J., Raghunathan, T., Wooten, L.P., & Zhu, J. (2016). *Organizational climate and diversity management in southeast Michigan hospitals*. Retrieved from https://sph.umich.edu/glc/news/pdf/UnivOfMichiganHospitalStudy_FINALREPORTOct2016.pdf

Myers, V. L., & Wooten, L. P. (2009). The transformational power of a mission driven strategy: Extraordinary diversity practices & quality of care in a multi-state healthcare system. *Organization Dynamics, 38*(4), 297–304.

Page, S. E. (2005). *The difference: How the power of diversity creates better groups, firms, schools, and societies.* Princeton, NJ: Princeton University Press.

Park, H., Keller, J., & Williams, J. (2016, February 28). The faces of American power, nearly as White as the Oscar nominees. *New York Times.* Retrieved from https://www.nytimes.com/interactive/2016/02/26/us/race-of-american-power.html

Pentland, A. S. (2013, November). Beyond the Echo Chamber: When making decisions, seek ideas from diverse sources and test them with a wide network. *Harvard Business Review.* Retrieved from https://hbr.org/2013/11/beyond-the-echo-chamber

Peterson, C., & Seligman, M. (2004). *Character strengths and virtues: A handbook and classification.* Oxford, England: Oxford University Press.

Pew Research Center. (n.d.) Religion in public life: Religious landscape study. Retrieved from http://www.pewforum.org/religious-landscape-study/

Piaget, J. (1932). *The moral judgment of the child.* London, England: Kegan Paul, Trench, Trubner and Co.

Prochaska, J. O., DiClemente, C. C., & Norcross, J. C. (1992). In search of how people change: Applications to the addictive behaviors. *American Psychologist, 47*(9), 1102–1114.

Prochaska, J. O., Redding, C. A., & Evers, K. (2008). The transtheoretical model and stages of change. In K. Glanz, B. K. Rimer, & K. V. Viswanath (Eds.), *Health behavior and health education: Theory, research, and practice* (4th ed., pp. 170–222). San Francisco, CA: Jossey-Bass.

Reidmiller, D. R., Avery, C. W., Easterling, D. R., Kunkel, K. E., Lewis, K. L. M., Maycock, T. K., & Stewart, B. C. (Eds.). (2018). *Impacts, risks and adaptation in the United States: Fourth national climate assessment, Volume II.* Washington, DC: U.S. Global Change Research Program.

Rimer, B. K., Glanz, K., & Rasband, G. (2001). Searching for evidence about health education and health behavior interventions. *Health Education and Behavior, 28*(2), 231–248.

Roberson, Q. M. (2019). Diversity in the workplace: A review, synthesis, and future research agenda. *Annual Review of Organizational Psychology and Organizational Behavior, 6,* 69–88.

Rogers, C. R. (1957). The necessary and sufficient conditions of therapeutic personality change. *Journal of Consulting Psychology, 21*(2), 95–103.

Rogers, C. R. (1959). A theory of therapy, personality, and interpersonal relationships: As developed in the client-centered framework. In S. Koch (Ed.), *Psychology: A study of a science* (pp. 184–256). New York, NY: McGraw-Hill.

Sapolsky, R. M. (2017). Behave: The biology of humans at our best and worst. New York, NY: Penguin Press.

Scholl, A., Sassenberg, K., Scheepers, D., Ellemers, N., & de Wit, F. (2017). A matter of focus: Power-holders feel more responsible after adopting a cognitive other-focus, rather than a self-focus. *British Journal of Social Psychology, 56*(1), 89–102.

Scholl, A., Sassenberg, K., Scheepers, D., Ellemers, N., & de Wit, F. (2018). Highly identified power-holders feel responsible: The interplay between social identification and social power within groups. *British Journal of Social Psychology, 57*(1), 112–129.

Sharlett, J. (2008). *The family: The secret fundamentalism at the heart of American power.* New York, NY: Harper Collins.

Skinner, C. S., Sykes, R. K., Monseos, B. S., Andriole, D. S., Arfken, C. L., & Fisher, E. B. (1998). Learn, share and live: Breast cancer education for older, urban minority women. *Health Education & Behavior, 25*(1), 60–78.

Thomas, D., & Ely, R. (1996, September/October). Making differences matter: A new paradigm for managing diversity. *Harvard Business Review.*

Wallace, J. W., Myers, V. M., & Osai, E. (2004). *Faith matters: Race/ethnicity, religion and substance use in America.* Baltimore, MD: Annie E. Casey Foundation Press.

Walsh, D., & Sengupta, S. (2020, February 9). For thousands of years, Egypt controlled the Nile. A New dam threatens that. *New York Times.* Retrieved from https://www.nytimes.com/interactive/2020/02/09/world/africa/nile-river-dam.html

World Economic Forum. (n.d.). *The global competitiveness report 2017–2018.* Retrieved from http://reports.weforum.org/global-competitiveness-index-2017-2018/competitiveness-rankings/#series=GCI.A.01.02.01

World Economic Forum. (2018). *Inclusive development index 2018.* Retrieved from http://www3.weforum.org/docs/WEF_Forum_IncGrwth_2018.pdf

Yaneck, L. R., Becker, D. M., Moy, T. F., Gittelsohn, J., & Koffman, D. M (2001, July). Project Joy: Faith based cardiovascular health promotion for African American women. *Public Health Report, 116*(Suppl 1), 68–81. doi: 10.1093/phr/116.S1.68. PMID: 11889276; PMCID: PMC1913665.

Zimbardo, P. (2008). *The Lucifer effect: Understanding how good people turn evil.* New York, NY: Random House.

CHAPTER 5

WHAT HAPPENS WHEN CLASSICAL HOLLYWOOD NARRATIVE AND AMERICAN MYTHOS CONVERGE?

Joi Carr
Pepperdine University

> We die. That may be the meaning of life. But we *do* language. That may be the measure of our lives. (Morrison, 2002, p. 22)

> The spectator recognizes himself [herself] and his [her] own finiteness in the face of the power of fate... To see that "this is how it is" is a kind of self-knowledge for the spectator, who emerges with new insight from the illusions he [she], like everyone else, lives. The tragic affirmation is an insight that the spectator has by virtue of the continuity of meaning in which he [she] places himself [herself]. (Gadamer, 1989, p. 133)

The complex intersection of classical Hollywood cinema, American identity politics, and American national mythos converge every day in our lives. The confluence of these dynamic ideological spheres constructs a reality for some people and as a result, creates the perfect storm for a great deal of chaos and pain in inclusive organizational and workplace environments, especially when left unchecked. The crux of this text explores the ideological reservoir that resides *in* all of us and the cinematic lore we carry into every space we enter. Cinematic arts are—arguably—the most popular art form in the last 100 years because it touches a deep part of the human psyche and emotional state of being. Movies reflect aspects of American culture/society, but also embodies a determining refracting power. Our shared assumptions about our reality, and the people in it, are passed down from generation to generation and classical Hollywood narrative helps concretize these controlling social narratives. I will begin with the theoretical import of this journey toward examining how the cinematic apparatus functions through encounter with the spectator and then explore the classical Hollywood narrative and its ideological framing. I will engage hermeneutical scholar, Hans-Georg Gadamer and Nobel laureate, Toni Morrison to help elucidate my claim.

THEORETICAL IMPLICATIONS

"You are what you eat." I grew up hearing this cautionary aphorism and in some instances at the very moment I was about to eat some delicious morsel or creamy yumminess. I never gave this old adage a second thought until adulthood. I quickly learned that food is chemical information for the body. Once it goes into the mouth and down the esophagus this information is processed through an amazing system that ties consumption to controlling consequences. For some, this daily food reality guided by this invaluable pithy truth becomes a blessed gift when coupled with a modicum of discipline and discernment. *I know* this is an *odd* place to begin a critical exploration of cinematic arts and classical Hollywood narrative. However, eating is a perfect metaphor for this critical journey. Please bear with me.

We all know that eating self-indulgently without critical pause can wreak havoc in one's life. For instance, when there is transgression from healthy choices, one could confess, "That delightful double serving of butter pecan ice cream cake—yes, ice cream cake—momentarily slayed me" while another could confess, "I am an impulsive eater because food satiates me, my ailing heart." In both of these circumstances, there is a conscious awareness of one's behavior and as such perhaps a positive outcome is plausible for both scenarios. For the first confession, perhaps a little exercise will counterbalance the dietary splurge and for the later confession, perhaps a therapeutic journey toward healing. Nonetheless, self-awareness is key. In an essay written in 1863–1864 entitled, *Concerning Spiritualism and Materialism*, German philosopher, Ludwig Feuerbach, is credited for the maxim, "Man is what he eats." Feuerbach's contribution led to the notion that if what we eat affects the body, it also affects the mind whether we assent to it or not. The process of chewing and swallowing food—consumption—cannot be disrupted after the transference of information has begun. Ingestion equals consequences. Thus, we *are* what we eat in no uncertain terms. Everything we eat becomes a part of our being and transmits information—literal energy—to our brain, arguably the most powerful organ in the body. Simply put, we are the sum total of what we consume both body and mind. This process of consumption can be a conscious journey or one freighted with a great deal of passive self-inflicted victimization.

The very nature of the byproduct of the cinema-going experience is akin to the process of eating, one of consumption and consequential ideological resonance. The film apparatus is developed to function through the natural way we perceive information through visual and auditory inference. The flicker of the movie screen in all its fragmentation and segmented communication coalesces in our minds as a whole and renders an expressed narrative that speaks profoundly to our inner lives. Why? It just does! Movies offer powerful stories and potentially deep emotional resonance. Ergo, in the last 100 years, cinema has been the most dominant art form on the planet. Right after the turn of the last century, movies swiftly decentered other major forms of national leisure pastime for the working class initially "a medium supported by 'the nickels of the working class,'" but then for the nation as a whole after the introduction of "movie palaces" (Ross, 1998, pp. 19–20).

In fact, in the United States movies soon became one of the first shared mass pop cultural experiences across socioeconomic class, race/ethnicity, religion, and gender. When individualized kinetoscope viewing shifts to indoor nickelodeon film exhibitions between 1905–1910, upwards of 25 million people are purported to have become weekly "patrons" by 1910 (Gomery, 1992, pp. 18–33; see also Robinson, 1996). This shift to the communal theatrical space created a new kind of collective socialization and resultantly, a communal American experience effectively came into being. With the advent of celluloid and the film projector, this turn to general audiences in theatrical venues, irrespective of a patron's annual income, ushered in a new powerful "democratic" form of ideological communication to the masses. In *Working-Class Hollywood: Silent Film and the Shaping of Class in America,* Steven Ross (1998) states, "Movies attracted a wide range of patrons. Young and old, black and white, native-born and foreign-born, men and women, poor and well-to-do, Protestants, Catholics, and Jews could all be found at the cinema" (p. 19). This pre-Hollywood studio system period tested the validity of the medium as a purveyor of identity politics beyond the normal divisive social categories that typically drive wedges in society. Until about WWI, this medium of entertainment served as a vehicle for community building for a particular class of American citizens who felt disenfranchised. Ross (1998) argues,

> By creating a common link between millions of working-class people who were often divided by ethnicity, religion, race, and gender, movies emerged as a vehicle capable of expressing a new public identity dominated by working-class sensibilities. Reformers such as Frederic C. Howe wrote worriedly about films that "tended to excite class feelings," and warned of the day when movies would become "the daily press of industrial groups, of classes of socialism, and radical opinion." (p. 12)

The rapid pace of technological innovation effected change in labor industries which created a fertile context for movies to flourish as a primary social activity for many. A decrease in working hours, with more pay, and an emerging commercial cinema as an affordable entertainment option laid the framework for the discovery of the medium as a viable social opiate and communal acculturating space.

The flurry of activity was related to cinema's evidenced powerful underlining seduction as an art form. Everyone, the rich and poor alike, felt this palpable new reality in this *new* theatrical space. However, two distinct perspectives emerged regarding the sphere. On the one hand, the nickelodeon theaters became a whimsical space for play and imagination that was affordable and felt comforting. Ross (1998) adds that for the burgeoning new middle class population (working class, white collar, and blue collar workers) they sought fulfillment, they felt unsettled with life and looked "to leisure to provide their lives with new meaning" (p. 13). In movie theaters, the boundaries of social identity collapsed into exploration and a particular kind of freedom of expression; there a *particular* agency emerged that was a kind of elixir for the soul. The imaginative theatrical realms—the nickelodeon space—became "fluid social spaces over which audiences exerted considerable control, places where anything might happen and where boisterous patrons frequently transgressed middle-class boundaries of acceptable behavior" (Ross, 1998, p. 12). By contrast, social advocates and upper-class elites took issue with such exposure to questionable movie content and such expressive space. Moreover, there was a great deal of disdain for the seeming tawdriness of the low-brow activity of cinema going and the potential for amoral degradation. Ross asserts that there was an effort to suppress the frequency of such leisure activity that might have the potential for social rebellion and the development of class affinity groups. Ross (1998) explains that during this time before WWI the working class and middle class boundaries began to splinter in a few directions, yet there was an effort to "shut them [movies and movie theaters] down completely" by "politicians, clergy, reformers, and civic leaders" because the art form and spaces were "perceived as [posing] political, moral, and physical dangers" (p. 12). The shift from private screening of short actualities, to individualized screening of short films, to general public commercial communal screening changed America and the world forever.

CINEMA GOING AND CULTURAL RITUAL

Why is this shift so important? Film-going consumption quickly began to take a central role in U.S. cultural ritual—like weekly church going. The historic early period in cinematic arts marks a shift. Film as an art form becomes a cultural phenomenon, an industry, and a sociocultural institution with verve and unquestioned loyal consumer following. Part of the power of this aesthetic comes from its ability to be intimate beyond its form and moor the spectator in a reality beyond the screen. Cinematic language transcends its form and speaks beyond words. It embodies the inexpressible that requires language to point to and into. This art form reaches beyond its audio/visual linguistic mode and captures flashes of overwhelming human meaning. In *Truth and Method*, hermeneutical scholar Hans-Georg Gadamer (1989) explores art as a cite of encounter for the spectator beyond the artwork as subject (I will return to this notion when I discuss how the cinematic apparatus functions). Film is a unique form of truthing the human experience in a faithful inarticulable form. This notion may seem oxymoronic in nature, however, consider Gadamer's premise on language. In Chapter 5, "Language and Hermeneutics," Gadamer turns to examining "language as the medium of hermeneutic experience" (p. 419). The significance of this section buttresses my point regarding language and communication—that is, the attempt to use language as a mode of expression is often incomparable to art's ability to render meaning. Gadamer (1989) argues that there is a real consequence of language's remarkable—real—liminal quality. He states,

> Indeed, language often seems ill-suited to express what we feel. In the face of the overwhelming presence of works of art, the task of expressing in words what they say to us seems like an infinite and hopeless undertaking. The fact our desire and capacity to understand always go beyond any statement that we can make seems like a critique of language. But this does not alter the fundamental priority of language. The possibilities of our knowledge seem to be far more individual than the possibilities of expression offered by language. (p. 419)

Cinematic language is aesthetic—in audio/visual form—and breaks with this normative aspect of language. Film form is an artful mode of communication and, as a result, its resonance is penetrating and deeply emotive in nature, both cognitive and affective. Moreover, cinematic language, although functioning through codes and conventions, connotes knowledge and understanding of the human condition in and through its form of artistic expression. The aesthetic form of communication drives connection and tethers spectators to its commanding discourse.

Thus, cinema's form of entertainment is also cathartic in nature and draws masses to its comforting presence. Film by nature is a healing balm. It reassures the spectator of a constituent reality. Habitual imbibing of its storytelling affect can be restorative like a church community/setting. Cultural rituals have many forms and can fundamentally function as a "homeostasis" agent for individuals and a collective. In *The Strange Order of Things: Life, Feeling, and the Making of Cultures,* author and neuroscientist, Antonio Damasio (2018), in a biological and social science context explores homeostasis—"the condition that regulates human physiology within the range that makes possible not only the survival but also the flourishing of life" (p. 167). For the context of my major point here, Damasio's transdisciplinary investigation supports the notion that feeling, and a sense of flourishing are interconnected. Cinematic screen reality is a steady cultural resource that can provide a sustaining critical narrative toward enriching one's life psychologically. Damasio (2018) explains the interconnection of feeling and cultural practices in this manner:

> How does one connect the state of homeostasis to the making of a cultural instrument capable of correcting a homeostatic deficit? As I suggested, the bridge is provided by feeling, a mental expression of the homeostasis and because of the upheaval they can generate, feelings operate as motives for engaging the creative intellect, the latter being the link in the chain that is responsible for the actual construction of the cultural practice or instrument. (p. 167)

In this case, early cinema going becomes a ritualized meditative societal practice for millions of people. However, the efficacy of this faithful salve is doubled edged. If I can now return to the eating metaphor, for the masses, cinematic arts deliver socializing narratives that can both affirm the status quo and/or challenge it. Movies speak with authority and are a socializing and acculturating force. So beyond the old adage, "You are what you eat," the more pressing concern may very well be, "What is eating you?" Film texts devour its spectators—subjects—veritably by the way cinematic language functions.

Film: Language, Culture, Encounter

> Narrative has never been merely entertainment for me. It is, I believe, one of the principle ways in which we absorb knowledge. (Morrison, 2002, p. 7)

Story is powerful and it functions through dialogical encounters. Story in the form of cinematic language is imbued with an inordinate power for seduction since it feels familiar and true. We have been trained to believe that movies are safe spaces, primarily for entertainment purposes. Albeit somewhat true, the way in which we watch movies places us, as spectators, in a vulnerable positionality with its content. Sure, cinema going allows the spectator to experience taboo imagery without censure. This socially accepted sphere of violence, sexuality, and language protects aberrance. A myriad of improprieties and even fetishization is permissible in this imaginative sphere and part of the allure. Still, the movie screening process is like digesting food. We literally become subject to the will of the narrative—what goes *in* encounters us. Just like food delivers information to the brain so too does cinema. The film text provides us with a reading by carrying us along a particular journey that is derived through seeming passive participation. The filmic apparatus requires the spectator to suspend disbelief and become subject of the text—in other words, the spectator is required to assent to the veracity of each given story in order to get through the narrative to its end. Classical Hollywood narrative counts on this surrender and as such the construction of its cinematic language requires the spectator to identify with the protagonist and his/her journey. This type of verisimilitude—narrative truthing—functions through tight artifice and drives a particular perspective from shot to shot. Spectators are carried along through explicit causality to a film's conclusion—and in American cinema, it's usually satisfying, meaning happy or at least embodies a semblance of "status quo-ness" or a modicum of perceived justice from the dominant culture's perspective. Though quite entertaining, movies *are* a dialogical encounter. In order to understand/digest the art form one must contend with his/her personal history.

In other words, as the spectator experiences the film, the film constructs—colonizes—the viewer. Ironically, the art form is rarely perceived as embodying ideological particularity, but it does. Film form lulls us as it speaks profoundly and decidedly to us. *We* are present in this experience. Gadamer (1989) argues that "situatedness"[1] is a criterion for understanding:

> Rather, I maintain that a work of art, thanks to its formal aspects, has something to say to us either through the question it awakens, or the questions it answers. A work of art "says something to someone."... In this assertion is contained the dismay of finding oneself directly affected by what was said there, in order to make it understandable to oneself and to others. I therefore continue to maintain that the experience of art is an experience of meaning, and as such this experience is something that brought about understanding. To this extent, then aesthetics is absorbed into hermeneutics. (Gadamer & Dutt, 2001, p. 70)

In other words, Gadamer's hermeneutical aesthetics contends that art—film in this case—happens to us and in us. Art speaks to *us* and as such offers a unique kind of pleasurable experience. Yet art in its formal aesthetic language connotes a cultural reality one encounters with the form. This space is an opportunity for rich critical reflection. In fact, Gadamer argues that meaning in this encounter with art happens when the art form masters "the interpreter." Hence, "here it really is true to say that this event is not our action upon the thing, but the act of the thing itself" (Gadamer, 1989, p. 463). Film has a certain amount of agency and autonomy that it leverages. In *Gadamer on the Contemporary Understanding of Art: An Evaluation*, Peter Alawa (2017) expounds on this encounter by suggesting that this experience with art can enrich us so much so that we have the possibility of deeper communal understanding. He states,

> In the experience of art, we are not merely given a 'moment' of vision, but are able to "ideal" along with the work in a way that takes us out of ordinary time into what Gadamer calls "fulfilled" or "autonomous" time. Thus, the artwork has a festive, symbolic and playful character. Since the festival similarly takes us out of ordinary time, while also opening us up to the true possibility of community. (pp. 58–65)

With art, time and space is altered in the experience and this event of dialogue is potentially transformative.

With film, the experience goes even deeper. Gadamer (1989) believes the dialogical encounter with art, this "event," truths in a particular way that forges meaning—"fusion of horizons" (p. 317). The interpreter—in this case the moviegoer—has "prejudices" (Gadamer, 1989, pp. 289–291). These presuppositions/predispositions are not prejudice in the modern sense of the word, but they do affect one's encounter and understanding. Gadamer (1989) states, "The prejudices and fore-meaning that occupy the interpreter's consciousness are not at his [her] free disposal. He [She] cannot separate in advance the productive prejudices that enable understanding from the prejudices that hinder it and lead to misunderstandings" (p. 307). In sum, when we encounter cinematic art, we negotiate levels of our positionality implicitly and explicitly. Movies feel like home because they speak to us via the most intimate form of language: our hearts, our minds, and personal histories. This affective experience with cinematic art reaches beyond its aesthetic and draws on our life experiences as we explore film form. The "truth" one feels when experiencing cinematic narrative happens to us in this encounter—and at times provides meaning for one's life and cultural understanding. Gadamer (1989), in a discussion of Aristotle's definition of tragedy in *Poetics*, speaks of this aspect of "event" as "extra-aesthetic, an ethical and metaphysical phenomenon that enters into the sphere of aesthetic problems only from outside" (p. 130). Movies have the ability to point outside of the text into a sociocultural reality in the spectator's life and all of this happens by simply watching and understanding film form (audio/visual language).

Movies, Meaning, and Matter

Now to the crux of the subject matter at hand, consuming movies without critical consciousness means the ideological content of cinematic narrative will consume you. Critical self-reflection through dialogical encounter creates an opportunity for emancipatory learning—the kind that helps one identify and challenge meaning and develop an awareness of underlying assumptions (Mezirow, 1991, p. 87; see also Mezirow, 1990). However, without space for this kind of work in one's life there are serious consequences. The audience often assumes that this critical ideological aspect of storytelling is absent in film, unless the film is a documentary or a narrative film explicitly created by someone from a "minority" group (i.e., people of color, women, or other class categories). The zeitgeist—the spirit and/or beliefs of a particular age—is at the center of this art form and drives consumer patterns, industry production, and distribution norms. Movies are not created in a vacuum and these particular artifacts are tethered to the people who create them: what they value, what they love, hate, or are indifferent toward (Eisenstein, 1949, pp. 150–178).[2] This art form is popular because it *is* for everyone.

However, classical Hollywood narrative structure creates a facade of inclusion (narrative understanding). Movies do not make money if audiences feel alienated. Film art, as an industry, is constructed in a way that on the surface messages inclusion. In its exclusivity regarding narrative content, that then becomes the norm. Everyone who watches movies, to an extent, accepts this tacit exclusionary practice and typically agrees and understands that the normative gaze is "White"—meaning stories created by dominant culture are the norm and are universal, cultureless. This classical Hollywood cinematic exclusionary practice under the guise of inclusivity has socialized the world to believe that "Whiteness" stands for universal. In his historical analysis of cinema, *The Birth of Whiteness: Race and the Emergence of U.S. Cinema,* Daniel Bernardi (1996) argues that with the advent of cinema "racial formation" is a central creedal matter of the aesthetic language:

> In studying and critically engaging the articulation of race in popular culture, particularly the ways in which cinema represents and narrates race, I have come to understand that this term also names a hegemonic way of knowing and seeing. Race is not only identity, but also a socio-historical formation. In the United States, this amounts to what sociologists Michael Omi and Howard Winant call a "racial formation," a ubiquitous and enduring color-line based on cultural and physiognomic differences that inform and at times determine our access to institutions, our social organization, our self-perception and our self-expression. "From a racial formation perspective," the sociologists explain, "race is a matter of both structure and cultural representation." (p. 3)

Although "Whiteness" drives much of the ideological framing, the apparatus functions in a way that makes this ideological work invisible—seemingly universal—yet felt. The industry and the art form work hand in hand.

Moreover, this sociocultural ideological frame in film often reifies pernicious ideology such as patriarchy, racism, sexism, classism, ageism, and the like, and are often cloaked as normative behavior, though in reality promulgates pernicious forms of cultural imperialism. What does this artful ideological reality mean for the workplace? To be sure, ideology controls attitudes, values, and behavior which could manifest in the workplace in a myriad of negative ways or positive ones. How can organizations develop a clear understanding of how movies impact our social and organizational spaces? What can individuals, organizations, and industries do to create thriving environments that are equitable and inclusive? First, organizations must uncover how classical Hollywood narrative has a deep connection with American mythos and identity politics and learn of its global implication on organizations and industries.

Closing the Theoretical

I will close on this theoretical conversation with an important mantra: Language embodies and transmits culture. Be careful what you eat because it might well be eating you...up. Nobel Laureate and author, Toni Morrison says she has always been aware of this constructive agency through narrative. In 1993, upon accepting the award of the Nobel Prize for literature, Morrison (2002) begins her speech with a personal confession of sorts, "Narrative has never been merely entertainment for me. It is, I believe, one of the principle ways in which we absorb knowledge" (p. 7). This insight into her perspective of story helps undergird my critical point about narrative. Movies are screen modes of reality yet have real world consequences for the viewer. Screening a film is like reading a book. However, while screening the movie, it reads you. Hence, my point in the overview of Gadamer's hermeneutic aesthetic above. Movies problematize our perception of our daily lives. Reuben Mikhael Castagno's (2014) *The Psychology of Cinematic Popular Culture and Educators' Reflective Practices*, discusses the impact of the film in pedagogical practices. In his discussion of Jürgen Habermas's, *On the Logic of the Social Sciences*, Castagno (2014) explores reflective practices and their import in the teaching and learning process:

> Habermas's project requires an uncritical and unreflective learning that usually takes place during early development. He argues that we are not able to reflect back on internalized norms until we have first learned how to follow them blindly through coercion imposed from without. Therefore, rational reconstruction depends on a prior uncritical assimilation of norms during our

formative years... It is the capacity to become critically aware of the meaning and of the sequence of identification and alienation, which comprises our life learning experiences. (p. 19)

Morrison's poignancy is echoed here. Narratives change who we become.

"What Is Eating You?": Movies and American Mythos

> There is a certain kind of peace that is not merely the absence of war. It is larger than that. The peace I am thinking of is not at the mercy of history's rule, nor is it a passive surrender to the status quo. (Morrison, 2003, p. 7)

> "Mama—does God live here?" (Hokinson, 1929)

Upon receiving a National Book Foundation medal for Distinguished Contributions to American Letters, Morrison (2003) strikes a provocative tenor in her acceptance, *The Dancing Mind*. She asserts,

> There is a certain kind of peace that is not merely the absence of war. It is larger than that. The peace I am thinking of is not at the mercy of history's rule, nor is it a passive surrender to the status quo. The peace I am thinking about is the dance of an open mind when it engages another equally open one—an activity that occurs most naturally, most often in the reading/writing world we live in. (p. 7)

Morrison suggests that there is an inner life we each have (at whatever level we experience it) that has the potential to gift us with a certain kind of peace that happens through dialogical encounters. She believes the life of the mind is an invaluable gift that is to be honored and fiercely protected. In her text, Morrison argues that this work begins internally and is often in tension with external phenomena in our lives, in the world that vies for our attention or sequesters us. She states, "Accessible as it is, this particular kind of peace warrants vigilance" (Morrison, 2003, p. 7). She shares two examples of individuals who find themselves in dilemmas: one, "the reader by an absence of solitude," a privileged American male PhD student, and the other, a "writer imperiled by the absence of a hospitable community," a woman from a "regime" that prohibits her from exploring her authorial voice freely (Morrison, 2003, p. 15). The two anecdotal stories she shares elucidates a vital point in her professed lifelong journey and for my critical endeavor here. Morrison states, "Securing that kind of peace—the peace of a dancing mind—is our work..." (Morrison, 2003, p. 17). I extend her call to action to those in organizational leadership, to corporate managers, and to leaders in faith-based organizations, and the like. Effective leadership management includes a vision that engages the whole person toward a kind of joy and fulfillment toward creating space for critical self-reflection.

Movies: Sacred Space?

In an iconic 1929 cartoon featured in *The New Yorker* on February 29, Helen Hokinson, staff cartoonist, asks a provocative question loaded with theological, sociological, and psychological import. Hokinson's cartoon imagery captures a satirical tone. The shift from storefront nickelodeon theaters to ornate cathedral spaces in the mid–late 1920s highlighted the cultural significance of movies and the centrality of moviegoing as an experience. Samuel "Roxy" Rothafel commissioned Walter Ahlschlager and Harold Rambusch to create a "Cathedral of the Motion Picture" on West 50th Street. New York's Roxy Theatre's opulence included a 110-seat orchestral space and a grand rotunda lobby that featured columns. The cartoon highlights the sheer spectacle and grandeur of the space. The image features a mother and her child trotting through the lobby, in the foreground, while others are in the background standing in line to enter the theater space. The mother and child are in motion, leaning forward with one foot in front of the other. The high ceilings and space dwarfs the size of people. The mother is focused on a destination, almost pulling the child forward, but the child, clutching an object in her hand, is craning her neck upward with her eyes straining upward, with her mouth parted, trying to catch her mother's attention as she asks, "Mama—does God live here?" For this child, the only logical conclusion she could fathom for such opulence to exist had to be for God. Hokinson's clever choice to have the child imagine and wonder is both humorous and telling. First, the child's question suggests that she has only seen churches that rival the magnitude of the movie theater. More importantly, this question rivals the reality that millions of people made cinema-going a priority in their lives. The lux nature of the theater equaled a powerful medium's shift to a mass cultural phenomenon. The child's question is disturbing too and touches quite close to the commanding nature that classical Hollywood narrative had and still has on the nation's imagination.

Movies explore the sociocultural matter of our lives; as a result, the complex intersection of classical Hollywood cinema and American national mythos meet at the most intimate levels in our lives. Cinema as a sociocultural institution functions ideologically since it represents a semblance of reality and the "apparatus" functions as such (Rosen, 1986).[3] Movies take up prevailing cultural beliefs—mythos—and systematizes them in axiomatic forms. The theatrical sphere can be perceived as a space that proffers a set of guiding principles or fundamental sociocultural beliefs that have sociopolitical ramifications. Does this notion feel familiar? Maybe like church? Movies appeal to us because we are the subjects of the narrative. All the visual and sonic representation we experience as spectators become personal (which I explored extensively in the theoretical conversation above). What we learn in this imaginative space affects our personal lives and interpersonal relationships.

For example, In *The Bluest Eye*, Morrison illustrates how the theatrical (movies) space functions doctrinally through its symbolic and technological language. Morrison describes Pauline Breedlove, Pecola's mother. For Pauline, movies save her. They become a safe haven, a "sacred" space. When her life felt chaotic, she retreated to this space she deemed safe. Morrison (2007) creates a disturbing picture of what actually happens to Pauline in this narrative space, while seated in the dark theater:

> She went to the movies instead. There in the dark her memory was refreshed, and she succumbed to her earlier dreams. Along with the idea of romantic love, she was introduced to another—physical beauty. Probably the most destructive ideas in the history of human thought. Both originated in envy, thrived in insecurity, and ended in disillusion. In equating physical beauty with virtue, she stripped her mind, bound it, and collected self-contempt by the heap... It would be for her a well-spring from which she would draw the most destructive emotions... She was never able, after her education in the movies, to look at a face and not assign it some category in the scale of absolute beauty, and the scale was one she absorbed in full from the silver screen... curtailing freedom in every way. (p. 120)

Pauline left the movie theater feeling free emotionally. But in fact, when she left, she was locked in sequestered space—ideologically. She no longer loved herself. What happened to her, in her? Movies are discourse-centered and narrative functions through codes and conventions; embedded at the center of classical Hollywood narrative technical and symbolic language is cultural information begging for discursive consideration. Pauline lost a bit of herself with each viewing. The redundancy of her absence on the screen (the absence of self-affirming and constructive representation) wreaked havoc on her psyche and emotional life.

Movies have to compress information into handy symbols in order to tell a story in such a brief period of screen time (approximately 90 minutes for a feature-length film). Screenplays become audio/visual worlds that express meaning through content and form: film content is the subject expressed in the narrative and film form is how the subject is expressed through cinematic language. Methods of film form include mise-en-scène (everything visual within a frame), editing (tempo/rhythm), lighting, camera movement and angles, focal length (depth of field, movement through space, proximity), and composition (arrangement of visual elements). For instance, films use flat stereotypes to heighten quick access to narrative content and connotative meaning. Characterization and social typage is used in cinema to help set up social categories and differentiation in story development. These character types then become universal symbols of meaning in storytelling practices that are easily recognizable to spectators. In a somewhat innocuous form, for example, overweight people in narratives become symbolic for greed: For example, characters like Kasper Gutman (*The Maltese Falcon*, 1941), Philip Stuckey (*Pretty Woman*, 1990), and Nedry (*Jurassic Park*, 1993). On the other hand, this shorthand cinematic language is a powerful socializing and acculturating force. I used *The Bluest Eye's* character, Pauline Breedlove, as an exemplar of this movie magic. Poor Pauline was swept into an ideological matrix. She did not and could not recognize herself on the screen and left the theater malformed by this dialogical encounter (Taylor, 1994).[4] At this level, social class, gender, and race/ethnicity play a greater symbolic role. For example, White men are competent leaders, superheroes (e.g., Clarke Kent [*Superman*, 1978]). The use of typage creates universal norms for everyone—an entire nation, regardless of class (socioeconomic class). Whether one contends with this practice oppositionally or not, the cinema-going audience learns and understands these ideological codes and conventions. Movies reflect our social reality and also refracts one, which reinforces cultural norms, a dominant discourse of power.

"Narrative Zeitgeist": Movies and Cultural Imperialism

Moreover, classical Hollywood narrative explores the American experience. As a national cinema it exposes a particular way of life and functions as a unique cultural institution. Movies and mythos are cultural partners. American film narratives reflect prevailing cultural attitudes through its symbolic language. To be sure, filmic language supports the practice of cultural imperialism in the United States and abroad. For instance, the first Black character to appear in American cinema was a White man in blackface (*Uncle Tom's Cabin*; Bogle, 2016, p. 1). This cultural oddity speaks volumes about American social and identity politics—that the first Black person to appear in cinema is controlled by the White imagination means the imagery that follows coheres to this foundational start. In the United States, commercial cinema from its inception has been created and controlled by dominant cultural ideas for success in the mass marketplace. The ideological messaging has been fairly consistent with exposing dominant cultural beliefs over the last century. Bernardi (1996) asserts that this kind of representational practice then develops codes that require contrastive imagery to concretize Whiteness as the normative gaze. He explains:

Culture is one of the main terrains where the white order is alternately supported and contested. In film, arguably the most popular and profitable form of culture in the last one hundred years, racist practices dominate the industrial, representational, and narrative history of the medium. Indeed, U.S. cinema has consistently constructed whiteness, the representational and narrative form of Eurocentrism, as the norm by which "Others" fail by comparison. People of color are generally represented as either deviant threats to white rule, thereby requiring civilizing or brutal punishment, or fetishized objects of exotic beauty, icons for racist scopophilia. (pp. 4–5)

This practice has experienced longevity and is encoded in film form. Although, countercultural cinematic voices were present from the beginning, these alternative representations could not thrive without funding and exhibition spaces: films produced by Hampton and Tuskegee Institutes (between 1909–1913), the Lincoln Motion Picture Company founded in 1916, and the Micheaux Film Corporation founded in 1918 by novelist and filmmaking pioneer, Oscar Micheaux (Bowser, Gaines, & Musser, 2001; Field, 2015).

In "Creating Space for a Hundred Flowers to Bloom," distinguished author and English and comparative literature scholar, Ngũgĩ wa Thiong'o (1993) argues that language creates the opportunity for cultural exchange. Culture and national traditions reside in language. He contends that the world benefits from literature in particular, especially when it is written in native languages; he maintains that "this vast heritage of human creativity... expressed in the particularities of our different languages and cultures" allows the world to become generative, plant "seeds for a new tomorrow" (wa Thiong'o, 1993, p. 24). This potential reality, he argues, at its worse can be a form of domination if the world only values the languages of the West and at its best, if inclusive of literature written in all languages, can reflect the "wealth of a common global culture" the "multi-coloured reality of the human creative stream" (wa Thiong'o, 1993, p. 24).

Imagine if American cinema was multilingual. What conversation would we be engaging in 100 years later. Instead of parsing out the beautiful historical nuances and complexities of gender, race, religion et al., representations that could have *been* in American cinema, we are still wrestling with examining the singular dominant cinematic ideological tenor. As Wa Thiong'o (1993) develops his plea for inclusivity, he imagines that

> if people were really to depend on European literature, even at its best, they would get a very distorted picture of the modern world, its evolution and its contemporary being. The twentieth century is a product of imperialist adventurism, true, but also of resistance from people of the Third World. This resistance is often reflected in Third World literature and is an integral part of the modern world. (p. 18)

The colonial seduction is not new, but it is different for each nation and person. In the United States, Daniel Bernardi (1996) argues that "early cinema has been a clear partner in the hegemonic struggle over the meaning of race" (pp. 3–5). Race is a low hanging fruit for American cinema so I will continue this as an exemplar for all the other pejorative missteps audience goers are barraged with.

We do not always conform to the messages we receive from film, but the message has been received, nonetheless. We are inundated with cultural information that vies for our attention and seeks to construct our collective reality, a reality that supports controlling cultural narratives that tell us how we "should" perceive ourselves and others in the world. Cultural imperialism functions to maintain inequitable relationships. Culture is just about everything we hold dear, aspects of everyday life that drives our beliefs, which drives our behavior, which includes our cultural identity and social identities. These cultural beliefs are also a set of shared values, attitudes, practices, and goals that characterizes organizations and institutions (corporate, church, etc.). Prolonged contact with messaging is a form of sociopolitical acculturation, which also supports a drive toward assimilation. In other words, cinematic language as a national cinema speaks in one native language that dominates cultural discourse. Let me provide two brief cinematic examples.

D. W. Griffith and **The Birth of a Nation** *(1915)*

The Birth of a Nation is considered a watershed moment in American cinematic history. This 3-hour feature, originally entitled, *Clansman* (for its Los Angeles debut and an adaption of Thomas Dixon Jr.'s novel and play), has been touted as the greatest film ever made. Melvyn Stokes (2008), in his extensive book on the film's history, reports that in the *New York Dramatic Mirror* newspaper "an anonymous reviewer," astounded by its brilliance exclaims, "If there is to be a greater picture than *Birth of a Nation,* may we live to see it" (p. 4). D. W. Griffith's film represents innovation in cinematic narrative storytelling. I will first just say people did not know cinematic arts were broken until Griffith fixed it. He literally created a blueprint for modern cinema and in fact, Griffith is credited with making film an art form. Most film buffs are familiar with the laundry list of Griffith's technological and narrative achievements: innovative editing that shaped a strong narrative flow and dramatic development (cutting for dramatic action from multi-camera perspectives), the use of parallel action (crosscutting) to heighten drama, modulating length of shots to effect the rhythm and tempo of the narrative (pacing), the use of montage and transitions between shots to suggest temporality (iris), split-screen shots, the use of an original musical score, creates lighting choices that evoke thematic content, and use of flashback sequencing to complexify the narrative linearity, features costume design steeped in historical realism, and more.

The Birth of a Nation is arguably seen as the first "blockbuster" film in the United States and is simultaneously "denounced as the most slanderous anti-Negro movie ever released" (Bogle, 2016, p. 10). Film historian, Donald Bogle argues that "Griffith introduces the final mythic type, the brutal black buck" (p. 10). The character, played by a White man in blackface, actor Walter Long, is depicted as a dastardly hyper sexualized "villain" who lusted after a White female, hoping to take her hand in marriage. One of the most important films in American history was "the first to deal with a black theme and at the same time to articulate fully the pantheon of black" stereotypes: the coon (buffoon), tom (submissive and good-natured), mulattoes (ill-fated due to racial identity), mammy (loyal and strong), and buck (violent sexual deviant; Bogle, 2016, pp. 10–18.) These cinematic narrative staples "all were character types used for the same effect: to entertain by stressing Negro inferiority" (Bogle, 2016, p. 4). The heroes of the story are Ku Klux Klan members and the antagonist are Black slaves also played by White actors in blackface. Griffith's effective use of title cards in the film fanned the flames of racial hatred in the nation. One title card reads,

> "The helpless minority," referring to White southerners. The climax of the story surrounds "a group of good Southern white men, members of an 'invisible empire,' who in white sheets and hoods, battle the blacks.... Defenders of white womanhood, white honor, white glory, and they restore to the south everything it has lost, its white supremacy. Thus, we have the birth of a nation. And the birth of the Ku Klux Klan. (Bogle, 2016, p. 12)

The film was screened at the White House, for members of Congress and judges of the Supreme Court. After screening the film, President Woodrow Wilson was reported as saying, "It's like writing history in lightning!" (Stokes, 2008, p. 111).

After its release in 1915, the persuasive narrative is responsible for the second and highest resurgence of the Ku Klux Klan in America ("increasing to 10.2 million by 1926"; Gordon, 2017, p. 20). Black American citizens lost their lives because of the incendiary nature of the story—lynchings follow in the film's wake. Film historian, Thomas Cripps describes the immediate backlash after the movie premiered. Led by the National Association for the Advancement of Colored People (NAACP), Cripps (1977) states that

> Afro-Americans had started the decade in the street with their angry protest... Negro war veterans in Washington picketed *The Birth of a Nation* with placards asking, "We represent America in France. Why should 'The Birth of a Nation' misrepresent us here?" (pp. 142–143)

The film also catalyzed African American independent cinema. *The Birth of a Race* by director Emmett J. Scott's was released in 1919 and Oscar Micheaux's *The Homesteader* (1919) soon followed and began his iconic filmmaking career. Cripps (1977) adds that

> during the rerelease of the film in 1930 with a soundtrack, the NAACP official line was that *The Birth of a Nation* was not art but mob incitement... The campaign against the birth of a nation has been the dawn of a new day. It provided the first occasion on which black men, long organized into local groups, stretched their muscles across the nation. (pp. 142–143)

Although some filmmakers are still contending with the inflammatory representation of African Americans in Griffith's *Birth of a Nation* (e.g., 2012's *Django: Unchained*, 2016's *Fences*, 2017's *Get Out*, 2018's *Black Panther*). These stereotypes have endured and still appear in modern American cinema and our nation is still reeling from D. W. Griffith and *Birth of a Nation's* powerful ideological blow.

How can one wonder why Black men in America are stigmatized? I will close on this narrative note about author and writer for *The New York Times*, Brent Staples. His story will punctuate the ideological power of cinema by illustration. In "Black Men and Public Space," Staples (1986) shares a bit of his journey as a Black man in America. He speaks of his real-world consequences of Griffith's type of aesthetic violence:

> It is not altogether clear to me how I reached the ripe old age of twenty-two without being conscious of the lethality nighttime pedestrians attributed to me... As a boy, I saw countless tough guys locked away; I have since buried several, too... Over the years, I learned to smother the rage I felt at so often being taken for a criminal... And on late-evening constitutionals I employ what has proved to be an excellent tension-reducing measure: I whistle melodies from Beethoven and Vivaldi and the more popular classical composers. Even steely New Yorkers hunching toward nighttime destinations seem to relax, and occasionally they even join in the tune. Virtually everybody seems to sense that a mugger wouldn't be warbling bright, sunny selections from Vivaldi's Four Seasons. It is my equivalent of the cowbell that hikers wear when they know they are in bear country.[5]

Snow White and the Seven Dwarfs *(David Hand, 1937)*

Most Americans are familiar with Disney's 1937 version of *Snow White and the Seven Dwarfs*, an adaptation of Jacob Grimm and Wilhelm Grimm's fairytale first published in 1812. Snow White's characterization is one of the primary texts that problematizes the way women and men live in the real world. Here I will frankly state through no fault of Disney's, this film embodies the "Cult of True Womanhood" also known as "The Cult of Domesticity." The narrative defines being the object of the normative gaze—standard form worthy "*to-be-looked-at-ness*"—as a gift (Mulvey, 1990, pp. 28–40). Whiteness, as a result, is bound to the standard. This film reifies the 19th century sentiment that a women's vocation is in the home. Historian Barbara Welter (1996), in "The Cult of True Womanhood: 1820–1860," describes the essential pillars of the virtuous womanhood as prescribed by the Bible—American cultural social norms. Welter (1966) describes the foundational principles and practices for a woman to succeed:

> piety, purity, submissiveness, and domesticity...without them, no matter whether there was fame, achievement or wealth, all was ashes. With them she was promised happiness and power...Religion and piety was the core of woman's virtue, the source of her strength. (pp. 151–174)

Snow White heightens this mandate and includes beauty and "Whiteness." As a character, she is presented as a woman in waiting; she is full of hope that she will fulfill her desire for marriage and her place in the home. Each of her songs center around cleaning (how much she enjoys it), courtship, and her passive role in it. She sings, "I'm wishing for the one I love to find me today...One love that has possessed me" (Disney & Cotrell, 1937). Moreover, beauty is Snow White's most valuable possession. The magic mirror states assuredly, "Rags cannot hide her gentle grace...She's beautiful like an angel." Her beauty allows her to have a special relationship with the animals; she garners their affection and companionship. The dwarfs are giddy over her beauty, but are also mesmerized by the way she organizes their lives in the cottage. Her beauty saves her life on her perilous journey: The huntsman has pity on her, and the dwarfs find her alluring: "She was so beautiful even in death. They could not bury her." The narrative fetishizes her beauty and her skin that was "white as snow." The queen is captivated by Snow White's beauty and wants to destroy her. The narrative offers a number of problematic social ideas under the guise of normative behavior and desire: mythology associated with love and the rescue, the divisiveness amongst women (jealousy), ugliness and evil associated with age, and her seeming innate desire to become Coventry Patmore's (1887) "angel in the house." Men are pathologized in this film too: either as a prince functioning under a mandate of coupling or a simple man with a great work ethic (the dwarfs). Snow White's characterization is not realistic for everyone. Women of color are posited in negation in *Snow White* since they are often depicted in films deviating from this standard. It actually is not a gift to become a thing, a fetish, but when the culture deems it valuable one might be willing to sacrifice herself to such a fleeting reward. Welter (1996) closes her essay on a humorous note, "Who can find a valiant woman?" was asked frequently from the pulpit and editorial pages [of magazines]. There was only one place to look for her—at home" (pp. 151–174).

CONCLUDING THOUGHTS

Cultural imperialism is framed out of the mythos of a given society, the way society stories themselves. Mythos is not purely myth; it is the "stuff" that helps construct a nation's identity—the core beliefs or presuppositions about a society. These stories have global import. Think of it as a metanarrative or tradition passed down from generation to generation that helps give a nation direction and meaning. Religious historian, Richard Hughes (2018), in *Myths America Lives By*, explores American identity by delving into five key myths that are central to how America perceives itself in the world. For this discussion, upon examining of these myths closer, one would find a great deal of resonance with the underlying ideology in classical Hollywood films. The theoretical portion of this discussion I developed above lands squarely at this juncture of sociocultural and political content that America, as a nation, holds dear. Much of the cultural resonance in filmic language begins here. Hughes investigates each myth in historical context in tandem with counter narratives by African Americans and other marginalized people: Chosen Nation, Nature's Nation, the Christian Nation, the Millennial Nation, and the Innocent Nation in the context of White supremacy (in his latest edition). By doing so, Hughes gets closer to wa Thiong'o's call for cultural exchange. Listening to this kind of ideological exploration helps ferret out important origins of cultural meaning that are embedded in movies. Film reifies these ideas subliminally through its aesthetic language. This sociocultural apparatus must be taken seriously and engaged with intention. America has one of the oldest written constitutions still in use. Much of our social behavior surrounds this document and the mythos that helped shape it. Societies benefit from critical self-reflection. Human dignity is a central tenet of the espoused goal of the American experience and dialogical encounters produces outcomes that, when leveraged, can gift our nation with deep self-awareness and community.

What happens when classical Hollywood narrative and American mythos converge? All kinds of chaos that one cannot quite articulate yet feel in organizational/work climates. Convergences *feel* a particular way. The kind of discomfort in spaces that one cannot quite give language to, but one feels right under the surface from day to day. An organization's climate left unchecked, could very well be a hostile space indeed—despite an organization's "culture" of values and shared missional assumptions.[6] Why? Because we love movies and they speak with deep resonance to our hearts and minds. They teach us through aesthetic conventions, social typage, and stereotyping. They build imaginative worlds, lyrical splendor that satiates us. However, the next time you experience some minor matter or egregious one that seemed a bit irrational from someone in your organizational space, you may have to wonder if cinematic language contributed to the behavior and/or transgression.

Constructing Work-Spaces: *Cultivating Critical Consciousness and Capacity*

> Do not conform to the pattern of this world, but be transformed by the renewing of your mind. Then you will be able to test and approve what God's will is—his good, pleasing and perfect will. (Romans 12:2, NIV)

Now, I hope you have fared sumptuously on this bountiful food for thought. And of late, I have been mulling over a perplexing statement Toni Morrison (2002) presents toward the climax of her Nobel Laureate acceptance speech: "We die. That may be the meaning of life. But we *do* language. That may be the measure of our lives" (p. 22). I have been troubled to a certain extent about the meaning of this statement. It is disturbing, profound. However, after exploring Gadamer's hermeneutical aesthetics in the context of cinematic language and American mythos, I feel I have a slightly better understanding of Morrison's critical point. The statement is asking an invaluable question. What is your life worth? Is it worth living well? Journeying toward becoming your best self. Dying is a mark of living—having had a life worth living—but *doing* language wrestles with the nature of one's journey, doing points to a profound knowing that life is a deep mystery and mastery is not the goal (mastery is not in the realm of possibility for the finite). Journey, however, is the gift of *doing* language well. Doing language opens up vistas of knowledge for the "dancing mind." There is life unto death and death (dying to hegemonic aspects of the human condition) unto life. Morrison continues by stating that language "arcs toward the place where meaning lie... Word-work is sublime... because it is generative; it makes meaning that secures our difference, our human difference—the way in which we are like no other" (2002, pp. 20, 22). Morrison makes a similar point to Gadamer's about language—that language is liminal. She asserts that "language can never 'pin down' slavery, genocide, war. Nor should it yearn for the arrogance to be able to do so. Its force, its felicity, is in its reach toward the ineffable" (p. 21). Our lives hang in the mystical realm of being and I have learned that the way we wield language has enormous consequences: unto life or death.

Here are a few pithy aphorisms to contemplate as you develop a plan:

Create a space (peaceful) for work in the work space.
Bias comes with each person due to cultural preferences.
It is hard to build community with people you do not trust.
Encourage spiritual and emotional health.
Encourage critical thinking.
Encourage active participation—think, feel, learn, grow!
Encourage media literacy.
Encourage bias training.
Wisdom is manifested in behavior.
Engage personal histories.
Develop critical thinking skills and problem-solving skills.
Name it and address it.
Ask for wisdom from each other.
Tap untapped talent. Competence comes in many shapes and sizes.
Remember you are what you eat!
Be reflective and respond with grace.

NOTES

1. See Gadamer, *Truth and Method,* p. 313. Gadamer's notion of "situatedness" includes one's personal history, which he terms "effective history." Here he discusses the potential for encounter: "We define the concept of 'situation' by saying that it represents a standpoint that limits the possibility of vision. Hence essential to the concept of situation is the concept of '*horizon.*' The horizon is the range of vision that includes everything that can be seen from a particular vantage point. Applying this to the thinking mind, we speak of the narrowness of horizon, of the possible expansion of horizon, of the opening up of horizons, and so forth" (p. 313).
2. For a discussion of film form see Sergei Eisenstein, *Film Form: Essays in Film Theory,* Trans. Jay Leyda (New York, NY: Harcourt and Brace, 1949), pp. 150–178. *The Film Sense,* Trans. Jay Leyda (New York, NY: Harcourt and Brace, 1947). Sergei Eisenstein, *Film Form: Essays in Film Theory,* p. 168.
3. See Phillip Rosen's edited text for a thorough exploration of filmic narrative, ideology, and film as an apparatus. Philip Rosen, Ed., *Narrative, Apparatus, Ideology: A Film Theory Reader* (New York, NY: Columbia University Press, 1986).
4. See Charles Taylor "The Politics of Recognition" in *Multiculturalism: Examining the Politics of Recognition,* Ed. Amy Gutman (New Jersey: Princeton University Press, 1994).

5. Brent Staples, "Black Men and Public Space," *Harper's Magazine*, December, 1986, pp. 19–20.
6. For an extensive exploration of organizational climate and strategies toward institutional change see Daryl Smith's *Diversity's Promise for Higher Education: Making It Work*. Baltimore: John Hopkins University Press, 2020.

REFERENCES

Alawa, P. (2017). Gadamer on the contemporary understanding of art: An evaluation. *International Journal of Philosophy and Theology*, 5(2), 58–65.
Bernardi, D. (1996). *The birth of Whiteness: Race and the emergence of U.S. cinema*. New Brunswick, NJ: Rutgers University Press.
Bogle, D. (2016). *Toms, coons, mulattoes, mammies, and bucks*. New York, NY: Continuum.
Bowser, P., Gaines, J., & Musser C. (2001). *Oscar Micheaux and his circle: African-American filmmaking and race cinema of the silent era*. Bloomington: Indiana University Press.
Cripps, T. (1977). *Slow fade to Black: The Negro in American film, 1900–1942*. New York, NY: Oxford University Press.
Castagno, R. M. (2014). *The psychology of cinematic popular culture and educators' reflective practices*. Potomac, MD: Bentham Science.
Damasio, A. (2018). *The strange order of things: Life, feeling, and the making of cultures*. New York, NY: Pantheon.
Disney, W. (Producer), & Cotrell, W. (Sequencing Director). (1937). *Snow white and the seven dwarfs* [Motion Picture]. United States: Walt Disney Productions
Eisenstein, S. (1949). *Film form: Essays in film theory*. New York, NY: Harcourt and Brace.
Eisenstein, S. (1947). *The film sense* (J. Leyda, Trans.). New York, NY: Harcourt and Brace.
Field, A. N. (2015). *Uplift cinema: The emergence of African American film and the possibility of Black modernity*. Durham, NC: Duke University Press.
Gadamer, H.-G. (1989). *Truth and method*. London, England: Bloomsbury.
Gadamer, H.-G., & Dutt, C. (2001). *Gadamer in conversation: Reflections and commentary* (R. E. Palmer, Trans.). New Haven, CT: Yale University Press.
Gomery, D. (1992). *Shared pleasures: A History of movie presentation in the United States*. Madison: University of Wisconsin Press.
Gordon, L. (2017). *The second coming of the KKK: The Ku Klux Klan of the 1920s and the American political tradition*. New York, NY: Norton.
Griffith, D. W. (Producer/Director). (1915). *Birth of a nation* [Motion Picture]. United States: D. W. Griffith Corporation and Epoch Production Company.
Hand, D. (1937). *Snow White and the Seven Dwarfs* [Motion Picture]. United States: Walt Disney Productions.
Hughes, R. (2018). *Myths America lives*. Chicago: University of Illinois Press.
Hokinson, H. (1929, February 23). Mama, does God live here? *The New Yorker*.
Mezirow, J. (1990). *Fostering critical reflection in adulthood: A Guide to transformative and emancipatory learning*. San Francisco, CA: Jossey-Bass.
Mezirow, J. (1991). *Transformative dimensions of adult learning*. San Francisco, CA: Jossey-Bass.

Morrison, T. (2002). *The Nobel Laureate in literature*. New York, NY: Knopf.
Morrison, T. (2003). *The dancing mind*. New York, NY: Knopf.
Morrison, T. (2007). *The bluest eye*. New York, NY: Vintage Books.
Mulvey, L. (1990). Visual pleasure and narrative cinema. In P. Erens (Ed.), *Issues in feminist film criticism* (pp. 28–40). Bloomington: Indiana University Press.
Patmore, C. (1887). *The angel in the house*. London, England: Cassell & Co.
Porter, E. (1903). *Uncle Tom's Cabin*. Edison Production Company.
Robinson, D. (1996). *From peep show to palace: The birth of American film*. New York, NY: Columbia University Press.
Rosen, P. (Ed.). (1986) *Narrative, apparatus, edeology: A film theory reader*. New York, NY: Columbia University Press.
Ross, S. (1998). *Working-class Hollywood: Silent film and the shaping of class in America*. Princeton, NJ: Princeton University Press.
Staples, B. (1986, December). Black men and public space. *Harper's Magazine*. Retrieved from https://harpers.org/archive/1986/12/black-men-and-public-space/
Smith, D. (2020). *Diversity's promise for higher education: Making it work*. Baltimore, MD: John Hopkins University Press.
Stokes, M. (2008). *D.W. Griffith's the birth of a nation: A History of the most controversial move of all time*. New York, NY: Oxford University Press.
Taylor, C. (1994). The politics of recognition. In A. Gutman (Ed.), *Multiculturalism: Examining the politics of recognition* (pp. 25–74). Princeton, NJ: Princeton University Press.
Wa Thiong'o, N. (Ed.). (1993). Creating space for a hundred flowers to bloom: The wealth of a common global culture. In *Moving the centre: The struggle for cultural freedoms* (pp. 12–24). Oxford, England: James Curry.
Welter, B. (1996). The cult of true womanhood: 1820–1860. *American Quarterly, 18*(2), 151–174.

CHAPTER 6

SHOULD TRANSFORMATIONAL LEADERSHIP THEORY INCLUDE AN ETHICS COMPONENT?

Insights From the Cupbearer to the King

Tom Clark
The Citadel

ABSTRACT

Does the Old Testament narrative of Nehemiah illustrate important leadership behaviors that could help bolster modern transformational leadership theory? Yes, absolutely! The Old Testament narrative of Nehemiah illustrates important leadership behaviors that align with transformational leadership, but it also highlights a missing component in the theory. Using narrative genre analysis, this chapter first explores the meaning of Nehemiah 2:1–20 and then compares the analysis with the modern leadership theory of transformational leadership. In the process, it assesses Nehemiah's leadership behavior, pointing out both the alignment with and divergence from transformational leadership to add insight and suggest possible refinement to the theory. The analysis identified an important difference between the pericope and transformational leadership: ethical boundaries. To integrate the insight

Blessed are Those Who Ask the Questions, pages 119–137
Copyright © 2021 by Information Age Publishing
All rights of reproduction in any form reserved.

from this exegesis into transformational leadership, the theory must adopt a component that serves to ethically constrain and direct a transformational leader's actions while preserving the positive leadership characteristics originally envisioned. Blending transformational leadership with ethical leadership may present a promising direction to investigate. Nehemiah's actions, which were constrained by his devotion to God, demonstrate that ethical transformational leadership is possible.

Does the Old Testament narrative of Nehemiah illustrate important leadership behaviors that could help refine modern transformational leadership theory? Serving as the cupbearer to Artaxerxes, the Persian king, Nehemiah stands out as a God-fearing member of the imperial court who successfully navigates its intricate challenges and proves himself to be a highly capable leader. The pericope Nehemiah 2:1–20 (see next section) first describes an interview with Artaxerxes where Nehemiah obtained permission to return and rebuild Jerusalem's walls. Next, it describes Nehemiah's arrival in Jerusalem, his covert inspection of the walls, and his proposal to the people that results in collaboration in the rebuilding project. As the story unfolds, Nehemiah confronts local opposition that objects with the restoration initiative. Using narrative genre analysis, this chapter first explores the meaning of Nehemiah 2:1–20 and then compares the analysis with the modern leadership theory of transformational leadership, as described by Bass and Riggio (2008). In the process, it assesses Nehemiah's leadership behavior, pointing out both the alignment with and divergence from transformational leadership to add insight and suggest possible refinement to the theory.

NEHEMIAH 2:1–20 (ENGLISH STANDARD VERSION)

1 In the month of Nisan, in the 20th year of King Artaxerxes, when wine was before him, I took up the wine and gave it to the king. Now I had not been sad in his presence. 2 And the king said to me, "Why is your face sad, seeing you are not sick? This is nothing but sadness of the heart." Then I was very much afraid. 3 I said to the king, "Let the king live forever! Why should not my face be sad, when the city, the place of my fathers' graves, lies in ruins, and its gates have been destroyed by fire?" 4 Then the king said to me, "What are you requesting?" So I prayed to the God of heaven. 5 And I said to the king, "If it pleases the king, and if your servant has found favor in your sight, that you send me to Judah, to the city of my fathers' graves, that I may rebuild it." 6 And the king said to me (the queen sitting beside him), "How long will you be gone, and when will you return?" So it pleased the king to send me when I had given him a time. 7 And I said to the king, "If it pleases the king, let letters be given me to the governors of the province Beyond the River, that they may let me pass through until I come to Judah, 8 and a letter to Asaph, the keeper of the king's forest, that he may give me timber to make beams for the gates of

the fortress of the temple, and for the wall of the city, and for the house that I shall occupy." And the king granted me what I asked, for the good hand of my God was upon me.

9 Then I came to the governors of the province Beyond the River and gave them the king's letters. Now the king had sent with me officers of the army and horsemen. 10 But when Sanballat the Horonite and Tobiah the Ammonite servant heard this, it displeased them greatly that someone had come to seek the welfare of the people of Israel.

11 So I went to Jerusalem and was there three days. 12 Then I arose in the night, I and a few men with me. And I told no one what my God had put into my heart to do for Jerusalem. There was no animal with me but the one on which I rode. 13 I went out by night by the Valley Gate to the Dragon Spring and to the Dung Gate, and I inspected the walls of Jerusalem that were broken down and its gates that had been destroyed by fire. 14 Then I went on to the Fountain Gate and to the King's Pool, but there was no room for the animal that was under me to pass. 15 Then I went up in the night by the valley and inspected the wall, and I turned back and entered by the Valley Gate, and so returned. 16 And the officials did not know where I had gone or what I was doing, and I had not yet told the Jews, the priests, the nobles, the officials, and the rest who were to do the work.

17 Then I said to them, "You see the trouble we are in, how Jerusalem lies in ruins with its gates burned. Come, let us build the wall of Jerusalem, that we may no longer suffer derision." 18 And I told them of the hand of my God that had been upon me for good, and also of the words that the king had spoken to me. And they said, "Let us rise up and build." So they strengthened their hands for the good work. 19 But when Sanballat the Horonite and Tobiah the Ammonite servant and Geshem the Arab heard of it, they jeered at us and despised us and said, "What is this thing that you are doing? Are you rebelling against the king?" 20 Then I replied to them, "The God of heaven will make us prosper, and we his servants will arise and build, but you have no portion or right or claim in Jerusalem."

Narrative Interpretation of Nehemiah 2:1–20

Explaining that biblical narratives blend history with theology into a story, Osborne (2006) highlighted four perspectives to consider during narrative interpretation: (a) source criticism, (b) form criticism, (c) redaction criticism, and (d) narrative criticism. Each perspective is a lens with which to view the scripture. When combined, they provide a balanced perspective of the historical and philosophical components that enhances scriptural interpretation. In the case of the pericope, they afford the reader an insightful vantage point from which to consider Nehemiah's leadership style and capability.

Source Criticism

Issues related to the source of scripture center on authorship. According to Blenkinsopp (1988), in the Hebrew Bible, the books of Ezra and Nehemiah comprise one book (p. 38), and Myers (2008) explained that as the biblical canon evolved, the books of Ezra and Nehemiah became distinct (p. xxxviii); therefore, any source-related discussion concerning Nehemiah typically includes Ezra and vice versa. Interestingly, Batten (1913) suggested that they ought to be recombined now (p. 1). Nevertheless, according to Williamson (1998), some scholars consider these two books to be the conclusion of a longer document that began with the book of Chronicles (p. xxi). Clarifying the situation, however, Loken (2011) concluded that these books were never intended to be a single, coherent text along with Chronicles despite their chronological continuation and similarity in themes and concepts. Throntveit (1992) also indicated that researchers had debated the authorship of these books (i.e., Chronicles, Ezra, and Nehemiah) in the past, but according to Williamson (1998), today scholars have agreed that most of Nehemiah, to include the subject pericope, is a personal account written by Nehemiah himself or a scribe under his direct supervision (p. xxiv).

Form Criticism

Buss (1999) explained that the examination of literary forms, or form criticism, analyzes speech patterns (p. 15), and Butler (2014) elaborated that this helps identify the genre that a literary unit represents (p. 12). According to Throntveit (1992), parallel arrangement, which he referred to as concentricity, was the primary literary device employed in the pericope, as well as throughout the Ezra-Nehemiah text (p. 6). He explained that the concentric arrangement of the text creates a literary echo, depicted by the form "AB...B'A'" (Throntveit, 1992, p. 4). For example, he provided the following illustration of parallel arrangement within the second part of the pericope:

A. Nehemiah's report and appeal: "Let us build the wall" (17)
  B. Rationale: Hand of God and words of the king (18a)
    X. People's response: "Let us rise up and build" (18b)
  B'. Rationale attacked: "Rebelling against the king?" (19)
A'. Nehemiah's retort: "The God of heaven will make us prosper, and we his servants will arise and build" (20) (Nehemiah 2:17–20; Throntveit, 1992, p. 73).

Throntveit (1992) explained that the reader mainly benefits from the parallel arrangement because it helps to recognize the literary organization while revealing the author's intended logic once the units have been identified (p. 6).

Redaction Criticism

The key to redaction criticism, according to Osborne (2006), is determining the way the literary editor (redactor) used sources and theological purpose behind any changes (p. 202). In the case of Nehemiah, Williamson (1998) described near universal agreement among researchers that the majority, and potentially all, of this Old Testament book came straight from a document called the Nehemiah Memoir (p. 166). Fensham (1982) concurred and indicated the portion of the Nehemiah Memoir accepted today includes the subject pericope (p. 5). He elaborated that although extra-biblical, corroborating sources are lacking, it is reasonable to accept its reliability (Fensham, 1982, p. 5). Williamson (1998) also emphasized that the Nehemiah Memoir developed in two distinct stages; therefore, the book contains a blend of literary genres, but he found it unsurprising that attempts to find other sources and comparison texts have been unsuccessful (p. xxviii).

Narrative Criticism

The final step in narrative interpretation involves narrative criticism, for which Osborne (2006) outlined the following steps: (a) structural analysis, (b) stylistic analysis, (c) redactional analysis, (d) exegetical analysis, (e) theological analysis, and (f) contextualization (pp. 216–220). He explained that this approach tends to highlight the factors that both create meaning and attract readers into the literary environment, but he cautioned that if considered in isolation, apart from the chronological and referential linkages, the approach quickly loses its effectiveness (p. 216). If done properly, however, narrative criticism provides a perspective of the author's artistry that permits the meaning and significance of the story to unfold.

Structural Analysis

The pericope neatly divides into two parts: (a) Nehemiah's conversation with King Artaxerxes (verses 1–8) and (b) his follow-on arrival in Jerusalem, inspection of the Jerusalem walls, and interaction with the local people (verses 9–20). Williamson (1998) explained that the date reference in verse 1 highlights a new paragraph and serves to effectively join Chapters 1 and 2 (p. 177). He also observed that the pericope has unity as a continuous narrative; however, the initial reactions of Sanballat and Tobiah in verse 10 indicate a division (p. 177). The first part, which includes verses 1–8, has only one section that relates exclusively to Nehemiah's conversation with King

Artaxerxes and highlights his reliance on God. The second part has three sections: (a) Nehemiah's arrival, covert inspection of Jerusalem's walls, and assessment of the overall task (verses 9–15); (b) his explanation of the situation to his fellow Jews and subsequent proposal for them to collaborate with him to rebuild the wall (verses 16–18); and (c) his conversation with the opposition: Sanballat, Tobiah, and Geshem (verses 19–20). Finally, Williamson (1998) explained that Nehemiah's actions were structurally parallel between the two parts of the pericope. That is, both in his conversation with the king and in his interaction with the people in Jerusalem, Nehemiah was fearful at first, subservient in his actions and speech, and cautious with his words (see verses 2–6 and 11–16) until he was certain of his position (p. 178). However, he moved forward boldly once satisfied that his actions were covered by prayer (see verses 4 and 18; Williamson, 1998, p. 178).

Stylistic Analysis

According to Fensham (1982), the original Hebrew of the text is postexilic (539–331 BC), sharing features with the Hebrew in Chronicles (p. 22). Myers (2008) concurred, adding that the text also contains Persian words and expressions (p. lxiv). Dorsey (2004) observed that the overarching theme woven throughout the fabric of the narrative in Nehemiah is returning to Judah, the homeland (p. 161). The Ezra–Nehemiah text employs a parallel patterned structure such that three times the reader is shown how Jews returned to their homeland, leaving relative comfort in the diaspora, and how God supported them, blessed them, and answered their prayers (Dorsey, 2004, p. 161). For example, encompassing both the pericope and its preceding chapter, Dorsey (2004) provided the following illustration of parallel arrangement:

  A. Nehemiah receives report of the problem (1:1–3)
   B. Nehemiah sits and mourns (1:4–11)
    C. Nehemiah asks the king to return to Jerusalem (2:1–5)
     X. TURNING POINT: The king grants the request! (2:6)
    C′. Nehemiah asks the king for letters of introduction (2:7–10)
   B′. Nehemiah arises and goes to Jerusalem (2:11–16)
  A′. Nehemiah gives a report to Jews and responds to opponents (2:17–20; p. 159)

Additionally, while focusing on Nehemiah's night ride in the second half of the pericope (verses 11–16), Throntveit (1992) provided the following example of a parallel arrangement:

  A. "I told no one" (11–12)
   B. "I went out by night by the Valley Gate" (13a)

X. "I inspected the walls of Jerusalem" (13b–15a)
B'. "I...entered by the Valley Gate" (15b)
A'. "I had not yet told the Jews..." (16; p. 73)

Dorsey (2004) explained that the repetitiveness of parallel arrangement helps the reader remember and allows the author to "compare, contrast, reiterate, emphasize, explain, and illustrate" (p. 29).

Redactional Analysis

There appears to be a consensus that the Nehemiah Memoir serves as the sole source for the pericope (Batten, 1913; Fensham, 1982; Williamson, 1998). The narrative was written in the first person, which Batten (1913) described as vibrant (p. 14). He elaborated that the character of the source material changes between that of a diary and journal at times, interspersed with prayers and curses, such that it may originally have been intended only for the author's personal use (p. 14). According to Williamson (1998), it presents a straightforward historical narrative (p. xlviii), and Kidner (1979) explained that the majority of Nehemiah is a personal record, accentuated with frank comments that make it among the liveliest narratives in the Bible (p. 83).

Exegetical Analysis

The exegetical analysis of the pericope illustrates several important leadership behaviors and concepts demonstrated by Nehemiah. Part I (verses 1–8) describes Nehemiah's conversation with King Artaxerxes. Part II (verses 9–20) describes Nehemiah's arrival, covert inspection of Jerusalem's walls, proposal to the people, and conversation with the opposition.

Part I: Verses 1–8. Nehemiah's conversation with the king in verse 1 followed a period of careful planning and preparation. Kidner (1979) pointed out that Nehemiah, following his prayer to God (see Nehemiah 1:11), had decided to raise this specific topic on that specific day (p. 87). According to Williamson (1998), it is possible that Nehemiah intentionally accepted the risk of allowing King Artaxerxes to see his emotions even though he had hidden them in the past (p. 178). Kidner (1979) agreed; however, Myers (2008) indicated that Nehemiah's appearance resulted from the stress related to a very serious situation and was not a ploy to gain attention (p. 99). Regardless, whether intentional or unavoidable, his visible emotions influenced the conversation. Complicating the situation, according to Williamson (1998), Nehemiah's depressed appearance could have been perceived as discourteous and an attempt to manipulate the king (p. 179). Nehemiah, however, had correctly anticipated the king's reaction. Fensham (1982) observed that Artaxerxes questioned different aspects of Nehemiah's disposition, to include his (a) inner spirit, reflected outwardly, (b) bodily illness, and (c) his heartfelt sadness (p. 160). He concluded that this multifaceted inquiry highlighted the king's keen observation skills and direct interest in the well-being of his servant (p. 160). Interestingly, Nehemiah reacts to this focused attention from the king with fear, which may not be surprising since Batten (1913) described the king's diagnosis as penetrating (p. 191). As a result, Nehemiah chose to move forward carefully. Williamson (1998) suggested that Nehemiah based his circumspect approach described in verse 3 on his desire to determine God's intentions and the right time to press forward with his plan of action (p. 179).

Williamson (1998) pointed out the linkage in verses 4 and 5 between Nehemiah's two ongoing conversations, first with his heavenly lord, followed immediately with the presentation of his petition to his earthly one (p. 179). Fensham (1982) also observed that by this point in the conversation, Artaxerxes was aware that Nehemiah desired to request something, and the king's willingness to listen provided proof of his tolerance (p. 161). According to Batten (1913), Nehemiah believed in God's direct interaction during important events, and he recognized the current time as the most important in his life (p. 192). Moreover, Fensham (1982) opined that Nehemiah was completely confident in God's guidance and that the king was likewise subject to God's will (p. 161). Throntveit (1992) observed in verse 5 that Nehemiah, growing in confidence, asked the king to send him home to restore his city (p. 68).

Additional dimensions of the situation begin to emerge in verse 6. Williamson (1998) indicated that most scholars believe Nehemiah was favored by the queen mentioned in verse 6, which may be evidence of her support of his request (p. 180). Fensham (1982) concurred that Nehemiah was likely a favorite, elaborating that Artaxerxes was strongly influenced by women during his reign (p. 162). Batten (1913) questioned the actual identity of the woman, indicating that "queen" was an inaccurate translation, but agreed that whomever it was, Nehemiah mentioned her because of her ability to influence the king (p. 193). According to Williamson (1998), verses 7 and 8 illustrate that Nehemiah felt certain of his position as he pressed forward, uninvited but with determination, with additional requests for letters of passage and timber for the rebuilding project (p. 181). Fensham (1982) explained that Nehemiah's petitions in these verses focused on two factors: (a) security, afforded by letters describing the king's intent and (b) supplies, with which to complete the rebuilding project (p. 162). Throntveit (1992) observed that this specific detail suggested that Nehemiah had spent the last several months both in planning and prayer (p. 69).

Throntveit (1992) stressed that in verse 8, Nehemiah gave the credit for the successfulness of his interaction with the king to God's influence and power (p. 69). Myers (2008) agreed, stating that Nehemiah was aware of God's influence in his life (p. 100). Loken (2011) noted with interest

Nehemiah's level of preparedness to respond to the king, and Kidner (1979) observed that Artaxerxes was struck by the bold and well-developed nature of Nehemiah's requests, pointing out that being vague would have characterized them as impulsive or dream-like (p. 88). He explained that Nehemiah had (a) prayed enough and (b) had faith enough to adequately envision the project in sufficient detail, to include the technique for building, that he subsequently gained the king's approval (Kidner, 1979, p. 88).

Part II: Verses 9–20. Part two of the pericope unfolds with Nehemiah arriving in Jerusalem. Kidner (1979) observed that Nehemiah's military escort in verse 9 served a greater purpose beyond simple security, explaining that it also permitted him to arrive with a sense of dignity and importance, certainly impressing the governors (p. 88). Throntveit (1992) agreed. Kidner (1979) opined that this also explained why the governors ultimately resorted to bluffing instead of using force in their opposition to the rebuilding project (p. 88). According to Fensham (1982), verse 10 demonstrates that Nehemiah's arrival and pending project immediately caused problems for the neighboring authorities and nations (p. 163). Furthermore, Throntveit (1992) observed that these problems established Nehemiah's mission as a good versus evil struggle, with the good elements (i.e., the human king and divine God) promoting success and the bad elements (i.e., Nehemiah's gloomy spirit, Jerusalem's predicament, and the opposition) foreshadowing failure (p. 70). Myers (2008) opined that someone with less courage might have quickly surrendered to the opposition facing Nehemiah (p. 101).

Williamson (1998) observed that Nehemiah's 3-day delay upon arrival in Jerusalem, described in verse 11, gave him time to (a) handle formalities, (b) address his family affairs, and (c) become familiar with the overall situation (p. 187). Nehemiah's accurate situational assessment here was critical, and Myers (2008) emphasized that his timing and method were significant (p. 104). After rhetorically questioning the need for a clandestine mission, Fensham (1982) explained that God had guided Nehemiah to complete the planning but that a personal inspection was still required to ensure the proposed concept would be successful (p. 165). This supports the explanation by Williamson (1998) that Nehemiah's desire for secrecy was reasonable given that (a) the Jerusalem wall had been destroyed, (b) the force that destroyed it was still in the vicinity (see Ezra 4), and (c) the opposition would have local allies to provide intelligence on his movement and activities (p. 187). Williamson (1998) observed that these facts made the need for secrecy and movement by night obvious and therefore justified any practical difficulty that it might have imposed on Nehemiah and his comrades (p. 188). Williamson (1998) explained that the "few men" described in verse 12 had to be aware of Nehemiah's plans and opined that they might have been family members from Jerusalem and possibly some who came from Babylon with him; regardless, they would have been trusted agents (p. 188). Williamson (1998) observed that Nehemiah's plans for the project were extensive, so a personal survey was necessary to confirm the accuracy of the plan and essential before enlisting the assistance of the citizens in Jerusalem (p. 191).

Based on his actions in verses 11–16, Throntveit (1992) described Nehemiah as a sharp administrator, who recognized the danger in presenting an ill-conceived plan to the local officials before gaining a full appreciation of the project's intricacies (p. 71). A miscalculation on Nehemiah's part at this point would have caused considerable harm and potentially jeopardized the entire initiative. Throntveit (1992) emphasized that Nehemiah realized that he had to present a simple yet precise proposal, convincing the local officials that he both understood and could handle the complexity of the project (p. 72). Myers (2008) explained that Nehemiah had been planning the restoration of Jerusalem's defenses since he first received the news of its predicament (see Nehemiah 1:1–2), but this initiative required personal evaluation, which led to his covert inspection shortly after arriving in Jerusalem, starting in verse 13 and concluding in verse 15 (pp. 103–104).

According to Throntveit (1992), the narrative does not mention any negative aspects, such as gloom or hopelessness, in Part II of the pericope but rather illustrates the initial steps to decisively implement Nehemiah's plan to correct the problem confronting Jerusalem (p. 72). By verse 17, Nehemiah had the information that he needed. Myers (2008) observed that following his nighttime inspection, Nehemiah understood that the problem facing Jerusalem would not be corrected until highly dedicated Jews took action (p. 105). Williamson (1998) explained that Nehemiah shared the concept of his plan in verse 17 with his fellow citizens by first describing their predicament and empathizing with them, while also accurately anticipating that the impact on them would be the same as he experienced previously (p. 191). Fensham (1982) pointed out that Nehemiah was careful in his selection of words because he recognized that they needed to resonate with the people (p. 167). Fensham (1982) described Nehemiah as being primed for action as he outlined his assessment of Jerusalem's meager defenses followed immediately by an earnest appeal to help him rebuild the wall, stressing that their disgrace must end (p. 167). Kidner (1979) drove this point home, stating that occasionally it requires an outsider to harshly point out that which has eroded over time (p. 90). Fensham (1982) observed that Nehemiah's presentation was favorably received since the people immediately agreed to start the work (p. 168). Williamson (1998) also described Nehemiah as forceful, but qualified this characterization by stressing that Nehemiah's attention was foremost on God, who would correct their misfortune, and only secondly to the king (p. 191). According to Myers (2008), Nehemiah's actions here solidify his religious justification for the mission: God had favored him, which resulted in the success he had in obtaining the king's approval (p. 105).

Williamson (1998) noted that the pericope ends with a final mention of the opposition but also observed that the speed of their reaction suggests that spies kept them apprised (p. 191). Throntveit (1992) observed that the fundamental mistake of the opposition in the pericope is that they consistently forget to consider God, completely ignoring the divine nature of the work, and concentrate instead on the political situation (see verses 10 and 19; p. 73). Nehemiah, however, did not make this mistake. Williamson (1998) explained that rather than countering his opponent's force with similar force, Nehemiah chose instead to express his reliance and confidence on God, the source of his authority (p. 192). Throntveit (1992) emphasized that Nehemiah was unmoved by the taunts from the opposition and responded by reasserting the divine mandate authorizing the project (p. 73). Batten (1913) suggested that Sanballat would have been much more impressed if Nehemiah had mentioned his authority from the king instead of God's grace (p. 204). Nehemiah, however, did not succumb to this temptation. Myers (2008) emphasized that Nehemiah did not retaliate with the opposition using his royal authority but rather with a statement regarding the role of God, who would allow them to flourish (p. 106). Fensham (1982) added that Nehemiah chose his words carefully in verse 20, explaining that the term "God of heaven" would have been very familiar to the Persian court (pp. 168–169). That is, according to Fensham (1982), the opposition should not have ridiculed or objected to the mission once they were aware that the Persian king endorsed Nehemiah, who invoked God's name to justify rebuilding the wall (p. 169).

Theological Analysis

Theologically, the overall significance of the pericope, according to Williamson (1998), emerges from God's role in the restoration of Judah through secular means (p. xlix). Throntveit (1992) explained that the theme of God's authority over human and political means runs through the pericope and maintains its relevancy today (p. 73). He also emphasized that Nehemiah understood this power structure (p. 73). This first becomes evident in Nehemiah's use of prayer during Part I of the pericope. Williamson (1998) highlighted that verses 1–10 illustrate that the king's royal authorization is a divine instrument (p. xlix). Throntveit (1992) explained that Nehemiah's prayer arose from his close relationship with God and need for his support (p. 68). He also suggested that it reminds the reader of an unseen third person, who remains hidden during the narrative (Throntveit, 1992, p. 68). God's role is similarly evident, according to Throntveit (1992), when Nehemiah credited his success with Artaxerxes (see verse 8) and authority to rebuild (see verse 18) to God's power (p. 69). Finally, in verse 20, Nehemiah built on this theme again by firmly reiterating his theological mandate for the proposed task; however, as Throntveit (1992) observed, he did not mention the king this time (p. 73).

Contextualization

Highlighting the significance of the pericope, several important leadership principles emerged during the exegesis. Perhaps the most obvious and important relates to Nehemiah's authenticity, as demonstrated by the modeling of his faith and his continuous reliance on God and habit of first seeking God's guidance. Several scholars made observations describing this behavior (Batten, 1913; Blenkinsopp, 1988; Fensham, 1982; Kidner, 1979; Loken, 2011; Myers, 2008; Throntveit, 1992; Williamson, 1998). Kidner (1979) expounded upon this during a description of Nehemiah's ability to handle and overcome confrontation with the opposition in verse 20. He stated that even with enemies, when accused of sedition, Nehemiah did not mention his earthly mandate but rather his divine one (p. 91).

Summary of Leadership Principles

Table 6.1 depicts the important leadership-related principles, characteristics, and behaviors that emerged during the exegesis.

TRANSFORMATIONAL LEADERSHIP THEORY OVERVIEW

Built on the leadership concept conceived by Burns (1978), transformational leadership, according to Bass (1999), serves to (a) raise consciousness regarding important issues among followers; (b) raise follower concerns for "higher-level needs on Maslow's hierarchy"; and (c) move followers to transcend self-interests, benefiting the organization (p. 5). Bass and Riggio (2008) explained that transformational leadership (a) motivates followers to accomplish more than originally intended or thought possible, (b) sets high expectations, (c) achieves superior performances, (d) results in more dedicated and fulfilled followers, (e) empowers followers by focusing on personal needs and development, and (f) helps followers enhance their leadership potential (pp. 3–4). They also acknowledged that in certain ways, transformational leadership is an extension of transactional leadership (Bass & Riggio, 2008, p. 4).

TABLE 6.1 Summary of Leadership Principles in Nehemiah 2:1-20 (by verse)

Principle	1	2	3	4	5	6	7	8	9	10	11	12	13	14	15	16	17	18	19	20
Authenticity			X	X				X			X	X	X	X			X	X		X
Circumspection		X					X		X				X							
Courage	X		X							X							X			X
Determination	X	X	X	X			X		X			X				X	X	X		X
Patience										X	X									
Persistence		X							X					X					X	
Respect					X	X											X			
Reverence				X				X										X		X
Risk Acceptance	X		X							X										
Sense of Mission	X						X		X		X	X	X	X	X	X	X	X		X
Trust					X	X											X			
Vision	X		X		X		X	X			X	X	X	X	X	X	X	X		X
Wisdom							X	X	X		X	X	X	X	X	X	X			X

According to Bass and Riggio (2008), transformational leadership has four components or dimensions: (a) idealized influence, (b) inspirational motivation, (c) intellectual stimulation, and (d) individualized consideration (pp. 5–6). First, they explained that transformational leaders are role models, who influence others resulting in admiration, respect, and trust (Bass & Riggio, 2008, p. 5). Second, the behavior of transformational leaders, according to Bass and Riggio (2008), inspires and motivates others by providing meaningful challenges in the work of their followers (p. 6). Third, they indicated that transformational leaders provide intellectual stimulation, which promotes innovation and creativity, by (a) being critical of assumptions, (b) looking at problems from new perspectives, and (c) finding new approaches to existing conditions (Bass & Riggio, 2008, p. 6). Fourth and finally, they explained that transformational leaders provide personal-level consideration by offering attention and acting as coach and mentor, addressing the desire for achievement and advancement in each follower (Bass & Riggio, 2008, p. 7).

INTERSECTION OF NEHEMIAH 2:1–20 AND TRANSFORMATIONAL LEADERSHIP

Nehemiah's behavior aligns with transformational leadership theory; however, the exegesis also highlighted a critical difference that could result in unethical or immoral outcomes if not acknowledged. An ethical boundary aligning with God's nature constrained Nehemiah's behavior, but transformational leadership theory does not address this issue. Therefore, this difference suggests a shortfall in the theory and potential area for refinement and enhancement.

Alignment

Nehemiah's behavior aligns with the four components of transformational leadership: (a) idealized influence, (b) inspirational motivation, (c) intellectual stimulation, and (d) individualized consideration. An interesting aspect of the pericope is that Nehemiah demonstrates capacity as a transformational leader twice but in very different contexts. The first time occurs in Part I of the pericope as he interacts with the king, up the organizational hierarchy, demonstrating his leadership capability from a subordinate position. The second time occurs in Part II, during his interaction with the people in Jerusalem that unfolds both horizontally, across the organizational hierarchy, with the opposition, and down, with his fellow Jews.

Nehemiah exercised idealized influence, clearly demonstrating his determination, persistence, and sense of mission. He also exhibited a readiness to take calculated risks. According to Williamson (1998), by allowing his emotions to show, Nehemiah intentionally exposed himself to significant danger by raising the topic about Jerusalem's distressed state with Artaxerxes, since it was unlikely that the king would quickly revoke his decree not to rebuild the city (see Ezra 4:21; p. 179). Based on the reactions of others, including the king, queen, and fellow Jews, he was well-respected and trusted. According to Williamson (1998), Nehemiah took the initiative in verse 5, after sensing God's reassurance and leveraging the king's trust (i.e., favor), by not simply describing his basic anxiety but also boldly requesting, uninvited, all necessary support and supplies that he would need (p. 179). The reactions of the king and queen may characterize admiration for Nehemiah. According to Kidner (1979), the queen influenced the king's decision, but he also emphasized that this interview with the king impresses upon the reader that it was Nehemiah's character that afforded him the opportunity to speak and assured the approval of the request, superseding any political impediments (pp. 87–88).

Nehemiah also demonstrated the ability to be inspirational and motivational, particularly in the second part of the pericope during his interaction with the people. He presented a compelling vision for rebuilding the walls, offered both meaning and challenge, and communicated his expectations. According to Williamson (1998), the positive, coherent response from Nehemiah's fellow citizens provided additional confirmation that his course of action was correct (p. 191).

By questioning the current imperial policy regarding Jerusalem and then reframing the problem, Nehemiah offered the king intellectual stimulation, albeit reluctantly. Throntveit (1992) explained that Nehemiah's fear came from uncertainty now that he had to make a request that required the king to change imperial policy (p. 68). He excelled as a transformational leader, however, when he went beyond problem identification and offered a creative, highly developed solution. Intellectual stimulation was clear during his interaction with the people when he reframed their predicament as one of shame and not mere insecurity. Stressing the significance of Nehemiah's proposal, Kidner (1979) explained that Nehemiah was struck not as much by the disheveled state in Jerusalem as by its disgrace, a fact that he successfully conveyed in his appeal to the people (p. 90).

Of the four transformational leadership components, individualized consideration may be the least evident in Nehemiah's actions; however, both with the king and with the opposition, he demonstrated well-developed listening skills, and with the people, he exercised encouragement, a key element in both teaching and coaching. Nevertheless, Fensham (1982) described Nehemiah as both clever and capable, someone who understood his people as well as his enemies (p. 165).

Divergence

The exegesis also highlighted the existence of ethical boundaries that constrained and channeled Nehemiah's behavior that are absent from transformational leadership theory. In Nehemiah's case, his ethical focus was a byproduct of his strong relationship with God, which was noted by several scholars (Batten, 1913; Blenkinsopp, 1988; Fensham, 1982; Kidner, 1979; Loken, 2011; Myers, 2008; Throntveit, 1992; Williamson, 1998). Fensham (1982) emphasized that Nehemiah prayed first to God, illustrating his faith and devotion and ensuring alignment with God's intent, such that the king would find the request acceptable (p. 161). Supporting this position, Kidner (1979) also pointed out that Nehemiah realized that his faith in God was not the pivotal factor in gaining approval, but rather it was God himself, the object of his faith, who directly guided his life and behavior (p. 88). The lack of ethical boundaries in the theory correlates with the observations made by Tourish (2013), who cautioned that despite its popularity and potential, transformational leadership could be destructive and promote negative leadership (p. 37). He explained that transformational leaders influence followers to change their goals, presumably for better ones, based on higher visions, that are supported by enhanced organizational goals (p. 21). However, if the leader's objectives are unethical or immoral, then this style of leadership becomes problematic. For instance, in its extreme, complicated problems similar to the ones Ciulla (1995) described surrounding Hitler begin to arise. According to Tourish (2013), charismatic cult leadership that resulted in Jonestown and Heaven's Gate also falls into this category. In Nehemiah's case, however, his actions were constrained by Judeo values, Jewish law, and his love of God.

That said, Ciulla (2015) expressed confusion over the expectation for a transformational leader to be ethical, indicating that Bass's original transformational leadership model lacked a values-based component; nevertheless, she also described a prevailing assumption that transformational leaders were moral (p. 28). According to Bradley and Charbonneau (2004), there is disagreement about whether transformational leadership has a moral component. Regardless, it is not uncommon for weaknesses in a leadership theory to be overlooked. Conger (1990) acknowledged the tendency to focus on the positive and productive aspects in a leadership style, cautioning that distinguishing leader behaviors have associated risks that may also be problematic and possibly destructive (p. 44). In the case of transformational leadership, evidently after accepting criticism (Ciulla,

2015), Bass (1997) provided clarification that differentiated between ethical and unethical leadership behavior, explaining that "pseudo-transformational leaders" use the same theoretical components to influence their followers but for purposes that may be unethical and exploit them (p. 133). Bass and Steidlmeier (1999) offered additional justification for authentic transformational leadership, arguing that critics (a) ignored the positive nature of inspirational leadership, (b) failed to differentiate transformational and pseudo-transformational leadership, and (c) overlooked that the identification of core values and a unifying purpose fosters effective leadership that benefits followers (p. 211). They acknowledged, however, that pseudo-transformational leaders should be categorized as immoral (Bass & Steidlmeier, 1999, p. 211). If Bass and Steidlmeier (1999) are correct, then a unifying organizational purpose, published core values, and a code of ethics in the secular organizational environment should suffice. The problem, of course, is that such strategies may mean very little if not reinforced throughout the organization. For example, the stated values of respect, integrity, communication, and excellence, may provide adequate ethical boundaries for some organizations, but they did little for Enron because they were not followed or enforced (Kunen, 2002). Unconvinced, Tourish (2013) argued that the transformational leadership model is fundamentally flawed (p. 39).

CONCLUSION

Does the Old Testament narrative of Nehemiah illustrate important leadership behaviors that could help bolster modern transformational leadership theory? Yes, absolutely! This analysis identified an important difference between the pericope and transformational leadership: ethical boundaries. As such, this critique highlights a shortcoming in transformational leadership and a missing theoretical component in the model. As discussed, attempts to provide additional specificity to the existing model with terms such as pseudo-transformational have been unconvincing. To integrate the insight from this exegesis into transformational leadership, the next steps should include the identification and inclusion of a theoretical component that serves to ethically constrain and direct a transformational leader's actions while preserving the positive leadership characteristics originally envisioned by Burns (1978). Blending transformational leadership with ethical leadership, as described by Brown and Trevino (2006), may present a promising direction to investigate. Nehemiah's actions, which were constrained by his devotion to God, demonstrate that ethical transformational leadership is possible.

REFERENCES

Bass, B. M. (1997). Does the transactional-transformational leadership paradigm transcend organizational and national boundaries? *American Psychologist, 52*(2), 130–139.

Bass, B. M. (1999). Current developments in transformational leadership: Research and applications. *The Psychologist-Manager Journal, 3*(1), 5–21. https://doi.org/10.1037/h0095852

Bass, B. M., & Riggio, R. E. (2008). *Transformational leadership* (2nd ed.). Mahwah, NJ: Erlbaum.

Bass, B. M., & Steidlmeier, P. (1999). Ethics, character, and authentic transformational leadership behavior. *Leadership Quarterly, 10*(2), 181–217. https://doi.org/10.1016/s1048-9843(99)00016-8

Batten, L. W. (1913). *A critical and exegetical commentary on the books of Ezra and Nehemiah.* New York, NY: T., & T. Clark.

Blenkinsopp, J. (1988). *Ezra-Nehemiah: A commentary.* Philadelphia, PA: The Westminster Press.

Bradley, P., & Charbonneau, D. (2004). Transformational leadership: Something new, something old. *Canadian Military Journal, 5*(1), 7–14.

Brown, M. E., & Trevino, L. K. (2006). Ethical leadership: A review and future directions. *The Leadership Quarterly, 17*(6), 595–616. https://doi.org/10.1016/j.leaqua.2006.10.004

Burns, J. M. (1978). *Leadership.* New York, NY: Harper & Row.

Buss, M. J. (1999). *Biblical form criticism in its context.* Sheffield, England: Sheffield Academic Press.

Butler, T. C. (2014). *Joshua, 1–12* (N. L. deClaissé-Walford [Ed.]; 2nd ed.; Vol. 7a). Grand Rapids, MI: Zondervan.

Ciulla, J. B. (1995). Leadership ethics: Mapping the territory. *Business Ethics Quarterly, 5*(1), 5–28. https://doi.org/10.2307/3857269

Ciulla, J. B. (2015). Conversations and correspondence with Burns on the ethics of transforming leadership. *Leadership and the Humanities, 3*(1), 26–31. https://doi.org/10.4337/lath.2015.01.04

Conger, J. A. (1990). The dark side of leadership. *Organizational Dynamics, 19*(2), 44–55. https://doi.org/10.1016/0090-2616(90)90070-6

Dorsey, D. A. (2004). *The literary structure of the Old Testament: A commentary on Genesis–Malachi.* Grand Rapids, MI: Baker Academic.

Fensham, F. C. (1982). *The books of Ezra and Nehemiah.* Grand Rapids, MI: William B. Eerdmans.

Kidner, D. (1979). *Ezra and Nehemiah: An introduction and commentary.* Downers Grove, IL: InterVarsity Press.

Kunen, J. S. (2002, January 19). Enron's vision (and values) thing. *The New York Times.* Retrieved from https://www.nytimes.com/2002/01/19/opinion/enron-s-vision-and-values-thing.html

Loken, I. (2011). *Ezra & Nehemiah: Evangelical exegetical commentary.* Bellingham, WA: Lexham Press.

Myers, J. M. (2008). *Ezra-Nehemiah: Introduction, translation, and notes.* New Haven, CT: Yale University Press.

Osborne, G. R. (2006). *The hermeneutical spiral: A comprehensive introduction to biblical interpretation* (2nd ed.). Downers Grove, IL: InterVarsity Press.

Throntveit, M. A. (1992). *Ezra-Nehemiah*. Louisville, KY: John Knox Press.

Tourish, D. (2013). *The dark side of transformational leadership: A critical perspective*. New York, NY: Routledge.

Williamson, H. G. M. (1998). *Ezra, Nehemiah*. Dallas, TX: Word Books.

CHAPTER 7

WHAT ARE THE BIBLICAL ROOTS OF SERVANT LEADERSHIP?

Michael J. Mlynarczyk
Colorado Christian University

ABSTRACT

With the global issues that the world is currently addressing, the researcher challenges that leaders at every level need to follow Jesus' servant leadership example. This biblical perspective is applicable to successful leadership in the nonprofit sector regardless of leaders' faith. This case study will compare servant leadership through a secular worldview and a biblical worldview in order to contribute to the advancement of the organizational leadership body of knowledge.

With the global issues that world leaders are currently addressing, the researcher challenges that leaders at every level need to follow Jesus' servant leadership example. Greenleaf (1970) defines a servant leader as someone who

> focuses primarily on the growth and well-being of people and the communities to which they belong. While traditional leadership generally involves the accumulation and exercise of power by one at the "top of the pyramid,"

Blessed are Those Who Ask the Questions, pages 139–162
Copyright © 2021 by Information Age Publishing
All rights of reproduction in any form reserved.

servant leadership is different. The servant-leader shares power, puts the needs of others first and helps people develop and perform as highly as possible. (TRKGCFSL, 2018, para. 4)

The Greenleaf (1970) definition of servant leadership supports the biblical perspective of servant leadership emulated by Jesus. Both view a servant leader as someone who exhibits the following leadership characteristics: be humble, be an active listener, lead by example, be spiritual, and be moral. This case study will examine empirical research updates to the Greenleaf (1970) servant leadership model and show Jesus' influence from the Bible on today's servant leaders using these corresponding leadership characteristics.

Recent research shows how effective or exceptional leadership is linked to the qualities of humility, actively listening, leading by example, being spiritual, and being moral and how the Greenleaf (1970) theory of servant leadership is supported with empirical studies. While servant leadership is applicable to successful leadership in the for profit, not for profit, nonprofit, and public administration sectors, this chapter will focus on nonprofit organizations (NPOs). The secular, servant leadership worldview will be balanced with a biblical, servant leadership worldview based on key elements of relevant Bible passages from the New Testament section of The New King James Version (NKJV).

Definition of Terms

There are two concepts that require a baseline definition for the purposes of this discussion. The concepts are servant and leader. While there is no singularly agreed upon definition for either, definitions for both are provided to establish a common level of understanding.

Servant

The "servant" portion of servant leadership "focuses on serving [other] people" first (Coetzer, Bussin, & Geldenhuys, 2017, p. 2). Servant leaders show their organizational teammates genuine care and concern before thinking about themselves. The intent is to demonstrate the servant behavior with the expectation that other leaders within the group or organization will emulate this approach until it ideally permeates the entire culture of the organization.

There is a biblical commission for leaders to think about others first. "As leaders grounded in our faith, we are called to serve and to put serving others first in our daily lives" (Campbell, Strawser, & Sellnow, 2017, p. 2). Jesus described servant leadership to his disciples or students after two of his students, the brothers James and John, began squabbling about who will be the greater disciple:

> You know that the rulers of the Gentiles [Romans] lord it over them, and those who are great exercise authority over them. Yet it shall not be so among you; but whoever desires to become great among you, let him be your servant. And whoever desires to be first among you, let him be your slave—just as the Son of Man [Jesus] did not come to be served, but to serve, and to give His life a ransom for many. (Matthew 20:25–28, NKJV)

The same biblical perspective on servant leadership is corroborated in Mark 10:42–45 and Luke 22:24–27.

It is also important to keep in mind what the plight of the Jewish people was at this time in history. Israel was a part of the Roman Empire. The Jewish people were made subservient to the Romans based on Roman laws and Roman rule. Despite the daily challenges of living in an occupied country as a Jewish man, Jesus encouraged his disciples to "love one another" (John 13:34). "Be kind to one another, tenderhearted, forgiving one another" (Ephesians 4:32). He then took the radical step of encouraging his disciples to "love your enemies, do good to those who hate you" (Luke 6:27). "Bless those who persecute you; bless and do not curse ... repay no one evil for evil ... do not be overcome by evil, but overcome evil with good" (Romans 12:14–21).

In The Gospel of John (13:1–11), Jesus washes his disciples' feet to show his servant heart. This is significant because the roads in Jerusalem were dirty and dusty. Men wore sandals or went barefoot. The washing of feet was a cultural custom accomplished by all of the meal participants before eating an evening meal together with the assistance of a servant. Jesus did this the night before he was betrayed by one of his disciples and nailed to a cross when he said, "most assuredly, I say to you, a servant is not greater than his master; nor is he who is sent greater than he who sent him" (John 13:16).

Leadership

A single, mutually agreed upon definition for servant leadership is nonexistent in the literature (Focht & Ponton, 2015, p. 48). For this chapter, the Paglis and Green (2002) definition of leadership will apply throughout its entirety. Paglis and Green define leadership as

> the process of diagnosing where the work group is now and where it needs to be in the future and formulating a strategy for getting there. Leadership also involves implementing change through developing a base of influence with followers, motivating them to commit to and work hard in pursuit of change goals, and working with them to overcome obstacles to change. (p. 217)

Kouzes and Posner (2003) remind researchers that the essence of leadership is defined in the quality of the relationship between the leader and the followers (p. 251). Thus, the Coetzer, Bussin, and Geldenhuys (2017) definition of "servant" combined with the Paglis and Green (2002) definition of "leadership" to give an academic, consolidated definition of "servant leadership." However, servant leadership has a more basic definition. "Servant leadership is love in action" (Blanchard, 2017, p. 21).

Humility

Greenleaf (1970) predicates his servant leadership style on a leader who is humble and caring enough to put others first as a leadership philosophy and way of life (Schneider & George, 2011). In Greenleaf's model, the servant leader is free from ego, can communicate a message by just doing something for followers to emulate, and the servant leader is a humble person who strives to keep any ego to the side (Greenleaf, 2003; Spears, 1996). Parolini, Patterson, and Winston (2009) note that the servant leader can accomplish the same leadership results as transformational leaders by example alone without saying anything. Kouzes and Posner (2003) provide an example of a servant leader who is humble via:

> Max De Pree, chairman of Herman Miller, one of America's most admired companies, [who] has written, "The first responsibility of a leader is to define reality. The last is to say thank you. In between the two, the leader must become a servant and a debtor. That sums up the progress of an artful leader." (p. 262)

This philosophy of humility is summed up by Lao-tzu who said:

> A leader is best
> When people barely know that he exists,
> Not so good when people obey and acclaim him,
> Worst when they despise him.
> 'Fail to honor people,
> They fail to honor you;'
> But of a good leader, who talks little,
> When his work is done, his aim fulfilled,
> They will say, "We did this ourselves."
> (O'Toole, 2003, p. 304)

Servant leadership is viewed as a natural fit with nonprofit organizations that have vocational, social justice missions (Schneider & George, 2011). Greenleaf advocates for servant leaders to think of and improve the plight of "the least privileged in society" without care for themselves (Wren, 1995, p. 22). The emphasis for a servant leader, then, is aimed at bringing social justice through unconditional equality and humility (Hummel, 2013). This is the ultimate challenge for leaders.

Jesus accepted and excelled at bringing peace with humility. He started his leadership training with a "lowly heart," and encouraged his followers to "take my yoke upon you and learn from me, for I am gentle and lowly in heart..." (Matthew 11:29). This is the only time in the Gospels [Matthew, Mark, Luke, and John] where Jesus refers to himself as "himself *tapeinos têi kardiai*, which we can translate as 'humble'" (Feldmeier, 2014, p. 63).

Jesus also went against the cultural norms of his time by associating with tax collectors, prostitutes, and other social pariahs within the Jewish community. In Matthew 9:10–13, Jesus explains his rationale for what the religious leaders (Pharisees) felt were odd relationships. "Jesus was hanging out with people that no religious leader in his right mind would be caught dead with" (Hale, 2015). As the Pharisees continued to question him about the outcasts with whom he was friends, Jesus said, "Those who are well have no need of a physician, but those who are sick [do]."

Paul reminds the Christians in Macedonia at Phillipi to be servant leaders following in Jesus' footsteps:

> Let nothing be done through selfish ambition or conceit, but in lowliness of mind let each esteem others better than himself. Let each of you look out not only for his own interests, but also for the interests of others. (Philippians 2:3–4)

The apostle, Paul, encapsulates Jesus' directions to his disciples to "walk worthy of the calling with which you were called, with all lowliness and gentleness, with longsuffering, bearing with one another in love" (Ephesians 4:1–2). Jesus "humbled himself and became obedient to the point of death, even the death of the cross" (Philippians 2:8). His encouragement for Jesus' disciples to stick together and maintain their commitment was an extremely difficult leadership challenge for them after his death. With the threat of being killed for their beliefs, Jesus' disciples carried out Jesus' vision by teaching his lessons to their congregants. Eventually, all of Jesus' apostles, except John, were martyred for teaching their beliefs. The same fate was extended to other Christians after them as well. "The Roman governor of Bithynia (on the Black Sea) had no hesitation in sending to immediate execution those who had been denounced as being Christians" (Ferguson, 1990).

Active Listener

The focus is on the servant who seeks to listen to what others are saying and to understand what they are saying. The servant leader is an active listener who does more listening than talking (Cohen & Warwick, 2006; Greenleaf, 2003). An active listener is engaged with and genuinely concerned with hearing what others have to say.

Leaders communicate with followers through verbal and nonverbal communication methods (Tramel, 1981). Both of these communication methods are essential to communicating effectively to the various echelons of followers in an organization (Smith, 1997; Tramel, 1981). Leaders are expected to constantly scan their environment by listening, observing, speaking, and taking action (Hummel, 2013). This requires leaders to be aware of what is happening in the organization at all times and ensure that the right message is conveyed either verbally or nonverbally (Schein, 1999).

Verbal communication is best accomplished via two-way communication between the leader and the leader's followers (Schein, 1999; Schein, 2004; Schein, 2009; Tramel, 1981). This form of verbal communication encourages dialogue between the two parties. It enables the leader and the follower to communicate with one another in a relatively relaxed environment where each person values the other's opinion. Based on what the leader learns in the conversation, the leader will contemplate how to best respond in light of the information.

Positive leaders seek to be helpful and humane to others. "When we help others to value and believe in themselves, when we help them to feel supported in their outcomes no matter what the outcomes may be, we help them to grow into their greatness" (Tice, 2010, p. 172). "What employees want (and need) the most is to be treated with dignity and respect as intelligent human beings capable of making their own contributions to the success of the company. They crave appreciation and recognition" (Cohen & Warwick, 2006, p. 53).

"Jesus was probably the most effective communicator who ever lived...we're still quoting him" (Loftus, 2014). He was an active listener who was able to effortlessly speak well with, relate to, and, in some instances, match wits with a disparate group of folks ranging from the common fisherman to the Roman governor (Hughes, 2014). In Luke 10:38–42, Jesus is visiting with Martha who is so busy trying to be a hospitable host that she fails to stop and listen to what Jesus is saying. Jesus, a practitioner of active listening, asks Martha to pause and quickly teaches her what it means to be an active listener.

The toughest group that Jesus communicated with was his disciples. He chose 12 men to be his students. While all of the occupations of the 12 apostles are unknown or unmentioned, we do know there were four fishermen, a tax collector, a doubter, a zealot, a skeptic, and a traitor. He called them to be his disciples in three stages: conversion, ministry, and apostleship (MacArthur, 2002, pp. 3–4). Jesus' disciples, like Jesus, were raised in the Jewish faith. They became the first Christians by learning and accepting Jesus' teachings.

Jesus then taught them as apprentices in his initial ministry team. His disciples gained experiential, on-the-job learning that was common at this time. Jesus taught them as they traveled from town to town often on foot. Once he was in a town, Jesus shared his teaching with up to 5,000 people at once (Matthew 14:13–21). "Jesus went all about Galilee, teaching in their synagogues... then his fame went throughout Syria... great multitudes followed him—from Galilee, and from Decapolis, Jerusalem, Judea, and beyond the Jordan [river]" (Matthew 23–25). He often taught using parables that are retold in Luke.

Jesus used a parable, "a usually short fictitious story that illustrates a moral attitude or a religious principle," to teach his followers (Merriam-Webster, n.d.). Jesus explained that he spoke in parables because "seeing they do not see, and hearing they do not hear nor do they understand" (Matthew 13:13). One of the more recognized parables is the Good Samaritan parable from Luke 10:25–37 whereby a Samaritan, an outcast, shows compassion for a stranded traveler on the side of the road who has been robbed, beaten, and left for dead by treating his wounds, transporting him to an inn, and paying for a room at an inn out of his own pocket. Jesus used this parable to teach his disciples to be merciful neighbors to one another regardless of social position.

Once their apprenticeship was complete, Jesus' disciples were then apostles—or those who were sent out—to teach as Jesus did (House Church Network Association, 2005). In an era where access to books or papyrus scrolls and the ability to read were limited to scholars and scribes, it was incumbent upon Jesus and his apostles to be captivating storytellers (White, 1998). Jesus' disciples had spent about three and a half years with him before becoming apostles. They began to teach two by two on their own in Europe, the Middle East, and as far east as India (Luke 10; MacArthur, 2002).

Some of Jesus' verbal skills involved verbal sparring with the Jewish leaders. Jesus had several encounters with the Pharisees who were responsible for teaching and enforcing the Jewish law. The Pharisees felt threatened by Jesus and the power he'd gained over the Jewish people in such a short period of time. The Pharisees sought to trick Jesus with questions that only had answers that violated the Jewish law. One encounter was captured in Matthew 23:1–36:

> Jesus spoke to the multitudes and to his disciples saying: the scribes and the Pharisees sit in Moses' seat. Therefore, whatever they tell you to observe, *that* observe and do, but do not do according to their works; for they say, and do not do... (verse 2–3, emphasis in original)

Jesus called them hypocrites with his eloquent use of the vernacular.

After Jesus' betrayal by Judas Iscariot, the Pharisees charged Jesus with blasphemy and had him taken to the Sanhedrin: a Jewish religious council consisting of Caiaphas, the high priest, the chief priests, the scribes, and the elders (Matthew 26:57–68). The next day, the Sanhedrin took Jesus to Pontius Pilate, the Roman governor, for sentencing. Pilate asked Jesus "are you the King of the Jews? Jesus said to him, it is as you say" (Matthew 27:11). After that Jesus stopped answering questions because his mission would soon be complete.

Leadership by Example

Encouragement

Tice (2010) urges leaders to mentor and encourage their followers. Govindarajan (2010) relayed a story about how his grandfather spent every weekend teaching impoverished children from the "untouchables" caste (pp. 191–192). While he failed to understand why his grandfather would spend so much time with these children, it was later in life that Govindarajan (2010) realized that his grandfather's encouragement helped significantly change these children's lives despite their social class. These children became leaders in their community because they were esteemed and inspired by his grandfather to excel.

Leaders also serve to build the confidence of their followers through a mentor–protégé relationship (Egeni, 2011). Thomas (2010) emphasizes that leaders or "change agents must help individuals and organizations through paradigm shifts and related clashes and shocks" (p. 133). It is the leaders' responsibility to guide followers (Tramel, 1981). Successful leaders empower followers by helping build followers' confidence in the leader and their own self-confidence (Wren, 1995). Leaders coach followers on how to do something, and then entrust the followers to handle a similar situation on their own (Egeni, 2011; Goldsmith, Kaye, & Shelton, 2010; Tramel, 1981; Wren, 1995).

Motivation

Ramaswamy and Gouillart (2010) advocate for leaders and followers to be motivated as co-creators who work together collaboratively. In the Burns (1978) formula, motive and resources are the two halves of his power equation. In order for a leader to have power, it requires the leader to have the ability (resources) and motive to accomplish the organization's goals. There are two academic perspectives for motive (Burns, 1978).

In the first perspective, motives are based on inherently, personal values. Motivation is a quality that is present with a person from birth. It is an ethical imperative that is built into the leader's character whereby the leader seeks to do the right thing (Ciulla, Knights, Mabey, & Tomkins, 2018; Hosmer, 1994; Wren, 1995). This view is diametrically opposed by authors who argue that motivation can be learned.

With the second perspective, these motives and values are taught through experience (Smith, 1997). With his hierarchy of needs, Maslow (1998) describes this as the leader's eternal quest for self-actualization that builds from and goes beyond self-esteem (Tramel, 1981). Achieving this point of self-actualization—where the leader selflessly focuses on doing things to constantly improve the organization based on a desire to provide the leader's followers with the best work experience possible—is what motivates the leader (Maslow, 1998, p. 9). In Maslow's perspective, the leader is motivated by inspiration to continuously innovate based on the changing scenarios (Greenleaf, 1970).

Foresight (Vision)

A leader's vision of the organization's development includes its members' personal growth through self-confidence (Smith, 1997). Leaders push members to achieve greatness because they can see the future possibilities through foresight for members based on their current capabilities (Tice, 2010, p. 170). Kouzes (2003) states that "while credibility is the foundation [for leadership], the capacity to paint an uplifting and ennobling picture of the future is that special something that truly sets leaders apart" (p. xx). The leader is expected to have a shared vision with the organization's followers through the strength of the leader's relationship with the organization's followers (Smith, 1997). Greenleaf (2003) describes "prescience, or foresight, [as] a better than average guess about *what* is going to happen *when* in the future" (p. 125). Foresight is what distinguishes a leader from a manager.

Self-Efficacy

Bandura (1986) presents his theory on self-efficacy from a psychological perspective as he recognizes that the degree of effectiveness is based on the leader's subjective review of the intended change results (if planned) and the actual change results. Bandura (2007) also notes that "perceived self-efficacy is conceptualized as *perceived operative capability*. It is concerned not with what one *has* but with belief in what one *can do* with whatever resources one can muster" (p. 646). Fitzgerald and Schutte (2010, p. 497) identify four factors from Bandura (1986) that "determine the level of an individual's self-efficacy beliefs in a given realm of life:

1. personal mastery experiences,
2. vicarious mastery experiences,
3. verbal persuasion, and
4. physiological and affective states.

McCann, Langford, and Rawlings (2006, p. 243) simply label this trait as "self-assurance." Seijts and Roberts (2011, p. 193) refer to it as a "perceived sense of competence." Paglis and Green (2002, p. 218) ensure that self-esteem remains outside of this model because Bandura (1986) emphasizes that self-esteem—one's personal view of one's self-worth—is only one of many traits that contribute to the overall level of self-efficacy.

Since Bandura (1986) defined the concept of leadership self-efficacy, other researchers have sought ways to advance his concept. Baron and Marin (2010) examined the impact of executive coaching on leadership self-efficacy. Machida and Schaubroeck (2011, p. 461) added preparatory self-efficacy, efficacy spirals, learning self-efficacy, and resilient self-efficacy in their study. Pidgeon, Jr. (2004) and McDaniel and DiBella-McCarthy (2012) advocate for leaders to use reflection to improve their leadership self-efficacy. All of these authors' study results point to more positive results through an appreciative learning approach to leadership self-efficacy.

Van Velsor and Guthrie (2003) warn that "research has shown that *stability* of self-esteem [for self-efficacy] may be even more important than its level" (p. 231). An emotionally stable leader allows the leader's followers to gain and have confidence in the leader when the organization hits tumultuous times (Wren, 1995). Like the captain of a ship, this type of leader remains calm and steers the organization to safety.

Jesus set the example for his disciples to follow (Atkinson, 2014). He encouraged, motivated, shared his vision for the future, and taught self-efficacy to his apostles. Jesus displayed these servant leadership traits when he encouraged them to be free of worry (Matthew 6:25–34), "Ask, and it will be given to you; seek, and you will find; knock, and it will be opened to you" (Matthew 7:7) and build a house on a rock foundation metaphor (Matthew 7:24–29). He did the same with his parables. Jesus also taught his disciples to critically reflect, pray, and meditate before taking action.

John 12–19 shows how Jesus made the ultimate sacrifice as he died, labeled as a criminal, because he refused to compromise his beliefs. During the Passover feast, Jesus entered Jerusalem to fanfare on a donkey as the people lined the streets and fanned him with palm fronds. Some of his followers felt that Jesus, as the Messiah, would remove the oppressive Roman government. When Jesus revealed that his mission omitted the peoples' desire to overthrow the Romans, they turned on him and wanted him crucified. Yet, he remained undaunted by taunts, name-calling, and physical beatings. He simply carried out his mission.

Spirituality

As a leadership style, servant leadership includes a spiritual aspect (Parolini, Patterson, & Winston, 2009). Freeman (2011) identified a similar linkage to a previous model used by Fry (2003), whereby "spirituality includes two essential elements in a person's life:

(a) transcendence of self, manifesting in a sense of calling or destiny, and

(b) belief that one's activities have meaning and value beyond economic benefits or self-gratification" (p. 121).

Servant leaders experience a "transcendence of self" whereby they feel called to a vocation. Also, servant leaders see how their contributions to a leadership position exceed measure as a form of goodwill that far exceeds any economic goodwill.

"Christian spirituality, in contrast to other ideologically-based spiritualities, is theological-based Spirituality" (Melé & Fontrodona, 2017, p. 673). Jesus encouraged his disciples to be peacemakers and "love your enemies, bless those who curse you, do good to those who hate you, and pray for those who spitefully use you and persecute you" (Matthew 5:44). Jesus prayed for peace and guidance during the turbulent times surrounding his ministry. Jesus felt called to teach his disciples "the way, the truth, and the light" (John 14:6). He made this his life's work.

Jesus prayed to refresh his mind after teaching, "When he had sent the multitudes away, he went up on the mountain by himself to pray" (Matthew 14:23). This same theme is echoed in Mark 6:46, Luke 5:16, and Luke 6:12. In Matthew 26:36–46, Jesus went up to the garden at Gethsemane the night before his crucifixion with Peter, John, and James and asked them to stay awake and wait for him. "He went a little farther and fell on his face, and prayed" (Mark 14:32, Luke 22:39–46). Mark and Luke recounted the same events at Gethsemane or the Mount of Olives. Luke 22:44 provides additional detail that "being in agony, he prayed more earnestly."

Morality

The servant leader is a leadership style based on a moral imperative rather than an efficient way to get things done through a response to a vocation or calling (Greenleaf, 1970; O'Toole, 2003, p. 294; Wren, 1995). Goldsmith, Kaye, and Shelton (2010) present a collection of leadership works. Two of the first three works directly address the leader's need to be trustworthy. Solomon (2004) describes "leadership [as] an emotional relationship of trust" (p. 94) between a leader and the leader's followers. Johnson (2010, p. 99) equivocates being trustworthy to having integrity with one's self and honesty with others. Trustworthy can also describe a leader's credibility (Grint, 1997; Wren, 1995). Kouzes (2003) states that "*Credibility is the foundation of leadership*... values and beliefs are at the core of personal credibility. To be credible, leaders must know who they are and what they stand for" (p. xix). When a leader displays integrity and honesty, the leader builds trust from followers through respect for followers' core beliefs (Cohen & Warwick, 2006; O'Toole, 2003; Wren, 1995).

Two things that successful leaders do in leading their followers are: relay the leader's vision in a manner that is personally tailored to appeal to the core beliefs of the member's present and take a participative approach to implementing the leader's vision in order to ensure all voices are represented and heard (Kotter, 2003, p. 38). McCall (2003) warns leaders that each leadership trait can be problematic if the leader goes to a negative extreme. The author provides contrasting examples captured in Figure 7.1 (McCall, 2003, p. 192, Exhibit 13.2). James C. Collins and Jerry I. Porras in Kouzes (2003) contend that a visionary leader can be successful without being charismatic (Ciulla, 2004).

"A high-profile, charismatic style is absolutely not required to successfully shape a visionary company" (Collins & Porras, 2003, p. 387). A leader can take a successful, low key approach similar to the servant leader provided that the leader is ethical and acts with the group's best interests in mind (Ciulla, 2004).

From a biblical perspective, a "Christ-centered ethical leadership speaks to the heart of the way contemporary firms, enterprises and networks organize themselves" (Mabey, Conroy, Blakely, & de Marco, 2017, p. 9). "Heart is not easily defined—nor is it obvious to everyone" (Krzyzewski, 2004, p. 31). Jesus advised his disciples that "for within, out of the heart of men, proceed evil thoughts, adulteries, fornications, murders, thefts, covetousness, wickedness, deceit, lewdness, an evil eye, blasphemy, pride, foolishness. All these things come from within and defile a man" (Mark 7:21–23).

Jesus was the epitome of a moral, servant leader. He had gained the trust of his disciples and proved himself trustworthy through his unwavering integrity. Klenke (2007) describes this as authentic leadership based on leaders' views of self-identity, leader identity, and spiritual identity (p. 70).

Competency	Potential Dark Side
Is a team player	Not a risk taker, indecisive, lacks independent judgment
Is customer-focused	Can't create breakthroughs, can't control costs, unrealistic, too conservative
Is biased toward action	Reckless, dictatorial
Is an analytical thinker	Prone to analysis paralysis, afraid to act, inclined to create larger staffs
Has integrity	Holier-than-thou, rigid, imposes personal standards on others, zealot
Is innovative	Unrealistic, impractical, wastes time and money
Has global vision	Misses local markets, over-extended, unfocused
Is good with people	Soft, can't make tough decisions, too easy on people

Figure 7.1 Competencies and their dark sides. *Source:* McCall, 2003, p. 192, Exhibit 13.2.

Jesus knew what His leader's vision was and He implemented it. He was an active, participative, collaborative leader who led from the front versus the rear. Two examples of this are seen in Luke 2:13–16 and Matthew 5:38–40.

During Passover, Jesus was incensed to find people selling merchandise in the temple (Luke 2:13–16). The Jewish temple was originally established as a sanctified, reserved place of worship that had become corrupt over time. Jesus attempted to right this religious wrong that railed against his moral fiber. Thus, he forced the money changers and salesmen out of the sanctuary.

As part of the Sermon on the Mount, Jesus encouraged his followers to "not resist an evil person. But whoever slaps you on your right cheek, turn the other to him also. If anyone wants to sue you and take away your tunic, let him have *your* cloak also" (Matthew 5:39–40). Jesus fed the hungry and homeless. He took care of widows and orphans. He befriended those who were friendless.

MEASURING THE QUALITIES OF SERVANT LEADERS THROUGH EMPIRICAL STUDIES

Currently, there is no singularly agreed upon method to routinely, consistently measure the qualities of servant leaders and validate them with empirical research. However, progress has been made in the last 12 years to begin to bridge the gap between qualitative servant leader studies and quantitative, empirical servant leadership studies. Barbuto and Wheeler (2006); Melchar and Bosco (2010); Walumbwa, Hartnell, and Oke (2010); Parris and Peachey (2013); and Coetzer, Bussin, and Geldenhuys (2017) are examples of researchers who have begun to help correct the disparate imbalance between these two servant leadership research methods.

Barbuto and Wheeler (2006) attempted to create the first empirical model for repeating and accurately measuring servant leadership based on previous work by Hinkin and Schriesheim (1989) and Devellis (1991). The Barbuto and Wheeler (2006) model consisted of an 11-item servant leader questionnaire that they felt had a sampling procedure limitation due to a lack of random sampling. In addition, the authors also noted that the politicians in their study were allowed to self-select who from their respective staffs filled out a questionnaire and participated in the study.

Melchar and Bosco (2010) used the Barbuto and Wheeler (2006) servant leader questionnaire and applied it to employees in the luxury car industry. Melchar and Bosco recognized limitations in their study associated with only looking at one industry with a small sample size in a for-profit industry (p. 85). Later that same year, Walumbwa, Hartnell, and Oke (2010) used the Ehrhart (2004) 14-item servant leadership scale to examine data gathered from 815 employees and 123 supervisors "from seven multinational companies operating in Kenya" (Walumbwa, Hartnell, & Oke, 2010, p. 522). These researchers, like Melchar and Bosco (2010), recognized limitations in their study associated with survey design, the sole focus on one country, inability to determine behavioral cause and effect, and the shortcomings of employees who evaluate themselves. Walumbwa, Hartnell, and Oke (2010) suggested that a longitudinal study such as the Global Leadership and Organizational Behavior Effectiveness (GLOBE) project be used to better moderate "followers' reactions to servant leadership" (p. 527) Den Hartog, House, Hanges, Ruiz-Quintanilla, and Dorfman (1999) conducted a two-part, universal GLOBE study that attempted to identify specific leadership traits that every "outstanding" transformational leader has (p. 250). The authors' longitudinal study spanned 59 countries from 1991 to 1999 with pilot tests conducted in each country. The GLOBE authors cited "motive arouser, foresight, encouraging, communicative, trustworthy, dynamic, positive, confidence builder, and motivational" as these key traits (Den Hartog et al., 1999, p. 250).

By 2013, there still was no agreed upon measurement instrument of the theoretical construct of servant leadership. Parris and Peachey (2013) determined that there were only 39 empirically based studies that examined servant leadership. The authors noted that the synthesis of these empirical studies revealed

- there is no consensus on the definition of servant leadership;
- servant leadership theory is being investigated across a variety of contexts, cultures, and themes;
- researchers are using multiple measures to explore servant leadership; and
- servant leadership is a viable leadership theory that helps organizations and improves the well-being of followers. (p. 377)

Four years later, Coetzer, Bussin, and Geldenhuys (2017) conducted an internet-based, search engine review of the word "servant leadership" using scholarly databases with a time range from 2000–2015. About 63% (55/87) of the servant leadership articles they found were classified as quantitative (versus qualitative or mixed method). Additionally, 87% (48/55) of the quantitative servant leadership studies were rated as "high quality" (p. 5). Thus, researchers have listened to their predecessors over the course of the last 20 years as they have focused on quantitatively analyzing servant leadership through empirical studies.

The focus of each empirical study differs by industry; the variables examined; the nomenclature assigned to variables; and the method. Researchers may be searching for the "Holy Grail" of leadership studies in their quest to universally define servant leadership with a multi-variable, multi-national, multicultural, and multi-industry, common empirical construct. Perhaps they are searching for something that is unquantifiable.

APPLICABILITY OF BIBLICAL PERSPECTIVE OF SERVANT LEADERSHIP TO NPOS

"A nonprofit corporation is an organization formed for the purpose of serving a purpose of public or mutual benefit other than the pursuit or accumulation of profits" (Nonprofit Resource Center, 2001). A nonprofit organization is also defined as a nongovernmental entity that possesses special legal status under state and federal law and possesses a public service mission (Wolf, 1999; Peter Drucker as cited in Kouzes, 2003). NPOs are service-oriented organizations that rely on a small, core staff augmented predominantly by volunteers from the surrounding community.

In contrast to for-profit organizations, NPOs maintain an organizational structure that does not promote private, financial gain (Wolf, 1999). The voluntary nature of NPOs also places a large emphasis on recruiting and retaining a volunteer workforce (Coolsen & Wintz, 1998; Hinds, 2002). Knox and Gruar (2006) noted that NPOs have their own unique hurdles in maintaining management and employee group dynamics during turbulent times of change. Drucker (1989) suggests these challenges can be managed in NPOs as long as the nonprofit organization maintains a clear mission statement and has a strong board of directors (Axelrod, 1994; Forbes & Miliken, 1999).

There are six characteristics of NPOs:

1. formally constituted,
2. private,
3. nonprofit distributing,
4. self-governing,
5. voluntary, and
6. offer public benefit (Hinds, 2002; Salamon, 1999).

The most notable difference between for-profit organizations and NPOs is that for-profit organizations are focused on generating and distributing profit to members or employees of the organization whereas NPOs are focused on maintaining and sustaining the organization's operations through grants and donations (Tolbert, Moore, & Wood, 2010). NPOs can be classified into the following categories: funding intermediaries organized to provide funds to other organizations, religious congregations organized to engage in religious practices, service-providing organizations organized to provide a social service or advocate for a particular cause, and public benefit/political associates organized primarily for political purposes (Salamon, 1999).

While there may be adequate concern with NPOs becoming too corporate, there are positive aspects of the nonprofit instituting for-profit rigor in its organizational processes. An emphasis has been placed by nonprofit CEOs on balancing their nonprofit culture with the for-profit processes of conducting strategy, planning, and operations. This practical application of corporate practices by the nonprofit sector CEOs is in line with the best business practices within the United States regardless of the sector (Bromberger, 2011; Clark, 2012; Enright, 2014). Nonprofit CEOs adapt their organizations to continue to achieve their organizations' missions.

McMurray, Islam, Sarros, and Pirola-Merlo (2013) describe NPO leaders as "transformational leaders [who] stimulate their followers to think about old problems in new ways without fear of punishment or ridicule and encourage them to challenge their own values, traditions, and beliefs" (p. 381). Nonprofit CEOs' success is incumbent upon building strong relationships with the members of their organizations; this enables the CEOs and the members to build trust in one another as the organization changes with its environment (Butler, 2014; Jaskyte, Byerly, Bryant, & Koksarova, 2010, p. 90; Lansford, Clements, Falzon, Aish, & Rogers, 2010).

Salamon (1999) also asserts that NPOs have been the catalyst for most civil reforms in American history (e.g., women's right, environmental protection, civil rights, etc.). Despite the growth of the government and expansion of government-sponsored social programs in the United States over the past several decades, the number of NPOs has also grown dramatically (Axelrod, 1994; Hinds, 2002; Salamon, 1999). The foundations of NPOs are not only rooted in American culture but also reflect the fundamental values of American culture. NPOs have supported the American desire to solve social problems such as homelessness, hunger, alcohol and drug abuse, and domestic abuse (Kelley & Lewis, 2010; Salamon, 1999). These organizations continue to reflect a democratic, market-based culture that tries to solve social problems independent of centralized government to solve social problems (Hinds, 2002).

NPOs have also been used to combat the downturns in the nation's market-based economy by providing social services that aim to improve society by addressing social problems (Salamon, 1999). These organizations function as catalysts as they help augment the government's limited ability to provide critical, social services. Nonprofits provide a means for citizens to pool their resources and act collectively (Hinds, 2002; Salamon, 1999). NPOs can augment government services and programs by providing critical services to a wider population of Americans. As a result, NPOs focus on providing services to people in a local community where resources are scarce (Chapman, 1998). Despite their not-for-profit business models, many nonprofits face the same set of leadership challenges that for-profit organizations face: employee retention, marketing, and planning (Hagar, Galaskiewicz, & Larson, 2004; Villinger, 2009).

Based on the description of NPOs, there appears to be a natural connection between Jesus' qualities of servant leadership and the desired qualities of NPO leaders. NPO leaders must lead with love for their teammates (Karmo, 2017; Van Dierendonck & Patterson, 2015). Many serve clientele within their community who are on the fringes of societal support—drug users, prostitutes, runaways, homeless, alcoholics, and so forth. Tender-hearted leaders at NPOs are the face of the organization that is chartered to help these members of their community overcome their current circumstances.

NPO leaders and intake specialists begin the process by actively listening to their clients. From their clients' description of their needs, a plan of action is formulated. The plan includes actions that the client and the NPO team must take in order to help the client achieve a successful outcome. This may include education and training sessions or community service projects. If either party falters then the plan will crumble. NPO leaders may have to set the example for the client to follow.

Servant leadership within public NPOs may challenge NPO leaders to overtly express or share their spirituality within their day-to-day activities. Servant leaders who are answering a transcendent call to serve will find a way to share their spirituality in how they interact with and lead their NPOs within the bounds and constraints of their civic duties as public officials. Their actions as servant leaders in their NPOs will be clearly aligned with their spiritual and moral beliefs.

Trust and credibility are the moral elements that servant leaders in NPOs will build with their staff and their clients over time. These foundational attributes help create an environment where an organizational team lives to serve the community. Each team member is there to support one another in this endeavor.

SUMMARY

The terms servant and leadership were defined using a combination of literature from the Greenleaf (1970) servant leadership body of work and Jesus' embodiment of servant leadership as described in the New King James version of the Bible. Key elements of servant leadership—humility, active listener, leadership by example, spirituality, and morality—were discussed based on a secular worldview and a biblical worldview with augmentation from relevant authors and references for each element. A literature review synopsis of servant leadership empirical research was provided as part of the case study. Finally, the biblical perspective of servant leadership was applied to leaders of NPOs.

RECOMMENDATIONS

Four recommendations are identified for servant leadership researchers. First, ensure you acknowledge that servant leadership is rooted in and drawn from a biblical worldview with thousands of years of leadership lessons from Jesus. "Greenleaf credits Jesus of Nazareth for teaching the importance of leaders having a servant's heart" (Carroll, 2005, p. 18). The connection to Jesus appears to have been downplayed more and more over the last 48 years in favor of the more socially palatable Herman Hesse *Journey to the East* narrative (Greenleaf, 1970, p. 9). Boje (2015) defines this as an antenarrative or not yet fully-formed narrative based on the stakeholders' involved in organizational change. If the intent is to erase Jesus from servant leadership literature and narrative, then anticipate resistance to this change.

Second, remember that servant leadership was a way of life for Jesus versus a leadership philosophy associated with an executive level job. The Modern Servant Leader (Lichtenwalner, 2010) website identifies over 100 corporate companies and military organizations on its servant leadership companies list but has methodically disqualified "churches and religious organizations whose primary mission is progressing their faith. There are simply too many to list" (para. 4). The main qualification is that "there must be at least one, publicly documented reference to the organization and its view of, support for, or belief in servant leadership principles. This may be in job descriptions, news articles, employee posts or other publicly available sources" (para. 5). An approach like this dilutes the meaning of servant leadership and precludes faith-based organizations from being recognized for organization excellence in servant leadership.

Third, before researchers focus on validity and reliability of questionnaires for empirical research, it's recommended that researchers start with the small bite of a globally-accepted definition of servant leadership and its characteristics before tackling the dissection and consumption of the entire elephant (Brown & Bryant, 2015). The lexicon associated with servant leadership appears to vary from industry to industry. Invalid methods with unreliable data will continue to be a challenge for researchers who desire to conduct reproducible empirical studies.

Fourth, servant leadership can be difficult for NPO leaders to practice when they are resource-constrained for manpower and budget yet expected to meet higher demands for organizational services by board members and stakeholders (Dimock, 2016). "To be effective in leadership you need to have a heart for it and a connection bigger than we are...that makes it easier to have a passion and energy for the causes you work for [Brewester Hamm]" (Kopenkoskey, 2014, p. 6). NPO leaders are encouraged to start with Jesus' example of unconditional, agape love.

CONCLUSION

Servant leadership remains an organizational management and leadership hot topic that causes polarized reactions when a biblical worldview is presented with a secular world view. The inclusion of multiple perspectives can help better refine what servant leadership is. Researchers with differing opinions will have to agree to disagree in order for real progress to be made in baselining and conducting empirical research studies in the future.

REFERENCES

Atkinson, W. (2014). The trinity and servant-leadership. *Evangelical Review of Theology, 38*(2), 138–150.

Axelrod, N. R. (1994). *Board leadership and board development* (3rd Ed.). San Francisco, CA: Jossey-Bass.

Bandura, A. (1986). The explanatory and predictive scope of self-efficacy theory. *Journal of Social and Clinical Psychology, 4*(3), 359–373. https://doi.org/10.1521/jscp.1986.4.3.359

Bandura, A. (2007). Much ado over a faulty conception of perceived self-efficacy grounded in faulty experimentation. *Journal of Social and Clinical Psychology, 26*(6), 641–658. Retrieved from http://search.proquest.com/docview/224864588?accountid=26967

Baron, L., & Morin, L. (2010). The impact of executive coaching on self-efficacy related to management soft-skills. *Leadership & Organization Development Journal, 31*(1), 18–38. https://doi.org/10.1108/01437731011010362

Barbuto, J. E., Jr., & Wheeler, D. W. (2006). Scale development and construct clarification of servant leadership. *Group & Organization Management, 31*(3), 300–326.

Blanchard, K. (2017). Servant leadership in action. *Chief Learning Officer, 16*(9), 18–21.

Boje, D. M. (Ed.). (2011). *Storytelling and the future of organizations: An antenarrative handbook*. New York, NY: Routledge.

Bromberger, A. R. (2011). A new type of hybrid. *Stanford Social Innovation Review, 9*(2), 49–53.

Brown, S., & Bryant, P. (2015). Getting to know the elephant: A call to advance servant leadership through construct consensus, empirical evidence, and multilevel theoretical development. *Servant Leadership: Theory & Practice, 2*(1), 10–35.

Burns, J. (1978). *Leadership*. New York, NY: Harper & Row.

Butler, L. (2014). Top tips for improved leadership. *Nonprofit World, 32*(1), 26–28.

Campbell, H., Strawser, M. G., & Sellnow, D. D. (2017). Addressing the leadership crisis through servant-infused pedagogy in the college classroom. *Journal of Communication & Religion, 40*(2), 43–60.

Carroll, A. (2005). Do you have what it takes to be a servant-leader? *Nonprofit World, 23*(3), 18–20.

Chapman, J. (1998). Do process consultants need different skills when working with nonprofits? *Leadership & Organization Development Journal, 19*(4), 211–215.

Ciulla, J. (Ed.). (2004). *Ethics, the heart of leadership* (2nd ed.). Westport, CT: Praeger.

Ciulla, J. B., Knights, D., Mabey, C., & Tomkins, L. (2018). Philosophical contributions to leadership ethics. *Business Ethics Quarterly, 28*(1), 1–14. https://doi.org/10.1017/beq.2017.48

Clark, W. (2012). Introducing strategic thinking into a non-profit organization to develop alternative income streams. *Journal of Practical Consulting, 4*(1), 32–42.

Coetzer, M. F., Bussin, M., & Geldenhuys, M. (2017). The functions of a servant leader. *Administrative Sciences, 7*(1), 1–32. https://doi.org/10.3390/admsci7010005

Cohen, B., & Warwick, M. (2006). *Values-driven business: How to change the world, make money, and have fun.* San Francisco, CA: Berrett-Koehler.

Collins, J., & Porras, J. (2003). Clock building, not time telling. In J. Kouzes (Ed.), *Business leadership* (pp. 373–403). San Francisco, CA: Jossey-Bass

Coolsen, P., & Wintz, L. (1998). Learn, grow, & change: Adapting service organizations to a changing world. *Nonprofit World, 16*(1), 44–48.

Den Hartog, D., House, R., Hanges, P. Ruiz-Quintanilla, S., & Dorfman, P. (1999). Culture specific and cross-culturally generalizable implicit leadership theories: Are attributes of charismatic/transformational leadership universally endorsed? *The Leadership Quarterly, 10*(2), 219–256.

Devellis, R. (1991). *Scale development: Theory and applications.* London, England: SAGE.

Dimock, A. (2016, March 21). Servant leadership: a better approach for nonprofits? [Blog post]. Retrieved from http://www.beaconfire-red.com/epic-stuff/servant-leadership-better-approach-nonprofits

Drucker, P. (1989). What business can learn from nonprofits. *Harvard Business Review, 67*(4), 88–93.

Egeni, C. C. (2011). *The anatomy of leadership: A conceptual analytical approach.* Bloomington, IN: AuthorHouse.

Enright, K. P. (2014, Spring). What would it take? *Stanford Social Innovation Review.* Retrieved from https://ssir.org/articles/entry/what_would_it_take

Ehrhart, M. G. (2004). Leadership and procedural justice climate as antecedents of unit-level organizational citizenship behavior. *Personnel Psychology, 57*(1), 61–94.

Feldmeier, R. (2014). *Power, service, humility: A new testament ethic.* Waco, TX: Baylor University Press.

Ferguson, E. (1990). Persecution in the early church: Did you know? *Christian History.* Retrieved from https://www.christianitytoday.com/history/issues/issue-27/persecution-in-early-church-did-you-know.html

Fitzgerald, S., & Schutte, N. S. (2010). Increasing transformational leadership through enhancing self-efficacy. *The Journal of Management Development, 29*(5), 495–505. https://doi.org/10.1108/02621711011039240

Focht, A., & Ponton, M. (2015). Identifying primary characteristics of servant leadership: Delphi study. *International Journal of Leadership Studies, 9*(1), 44–61.

Forbes, D. P., & Miliken, F. J. (1999). Cognition and corporate governance: Understanding boards of directors as strategic decision-making groups. *Academy of Management Review, 24*(3), 489–505.

Freeman, G. T. (2011). Spirituality and servant leadership: A conceptual model and research proposal. *Emerging Leadership Journeys, 4*(1), 120–140.

Fry, L. W. (2003). Toward a theory of spiritual leadership. *The Leadership Quarterly, 14*(6), 693–727.

Goldsmith, M., Kaye, B., & Shelton, K. (Eds.). (2010). *Learn like a leader*. Boston, MA: Nicholas Brealey.

Govindarajan, V. (2010). Contagious influence is a wonderful teacher. In M. Goldsmith, B. Kaye, & K. Shelton (Eds.), *Learn like a leader* (pp. 189–192). Boston, MA: Nicholas Brealey.

Greenleaf, R. (1970). *The servant as leader*. Indianapolis, IN: The Robert K. Greenleaf Center.

Greenleaf, R. (2003). The servant as leader. In J. Kouzes (Ed.), *Business leadership* (pp. 117–136). San Francisco, CA: Jossey-Bass.

Grint, K. (1997). *Fuzzy management: Contemporary ideas and practices at work*. New York, NY: Oxford University Press.

Hagar, M., Galaskiewicz, J., & Larson, J. (2004). Structural embeddedness and the liability of newness among nonprofit organizations, *Public Management Review, 6*(2), 159–188.

Hale, C. (2015, July 20). Why tax collectors and prostitutes hung out with Jesus [Blog post]. Retrieved from http://ironcity.org/blog/dine-with-sinners

Hinds, M. (2002). *Reengaging America's nonprofit organizations* (Unpublished doctoral dissertation). Hamline University, Saint Paul, MN.

Hinkin, T. R., & Schriesheim, C. A. (1989). Development and application of new scales to measure the French and Raven (1959) bases of social power. *Journal of Applied Psychology, 74*(4), 561–567.

Hosmer, L. T. (1994). *Moral leadership in business*. Burr Ridge, IL: Richard D. Irwin.

House Church Network Association. (2005). What's the difference between a disciple and an apostle? [Blog post]. Retrieved from http://www.hcna.us/columns/apostle-disciple.htm

Hughes, A. (2014, September 28). Jesus, the active listener [Video file]. Retrieved from http://stmaryorthodoxchurch.org/orthodoxy/sermons/2014/jesus-active-listener

Hummel, M. (2013, April). *Synergistic leadership: Group discussion*. Symposium conducted at the meeting of Colorado Technical University Doctorate of Management, Colorado Springs, CO.

Jaskyte, K., Byerly, C., Bryant, A., & Koksarova, J. (2010). Transforming a nonprofit work environment for creativity. *Nonprofit Management & Leadership, 21*(1), 77–92. https://doi.org/10.1002/nml.20013

Johnson, S. (2010). Integrity or out of Tegrity? In M. Goldsmith, B. Kaye, & K. Shelton (Eds.), *Learn like a leader* (pp. 97–101). Boston, MA: Nicholas Brealey.
Karmo, M. (2017, October 31). The no. 1 characteristic every nonprofit leader needs to be successful. *Forbes*. Retrieved from https://www.forbes.com/sites/forbesnonprofitcouncil/2017/10/31/the-no-1-characteristic-every-nonprofit-leader-needs-to-be-successful/?sh=9e0b273b886d
Kelley, D., & Lewis, A. (2010). Funding of human service sector nonprofit organizations. *Business Strategy Series, 11*(3), 192–199.
Klenke, K. (2007). Authentic leadership: A self, leader, and spiritual identity perspective. *International Journal of Leadership Studies, 3*(1), 68–97.
Knox, S., & Gruar, C. (2007). The application of stakeholder theory to relationship marketing strategy development in a non-profit organization. *Journal of Business Ethics, 75*(2), 115–135. https://doi.org/10.1007/s10551-006-9258-3
Kopenkoskey, P. (2014). A heart for leadership and helping the hungry. *Grand Rapids Business Journal, 32*(14), 6.
Kotter, J. (2003). What leaders really do. In J. Kouzes (Ed.), *Business leadership* (pp. 29–43). San Francisco, CA: Jossey-Bass.
Kouzes, J. (Ed.). (2003). *Business leadership*. San Francisco, CA: Jossey-Bass.
Kouzes, J., & Posner, B. (2003). Leadership is a relationship. In J. Kouzes (Ed.), *Business leadership* (pp. 251–267). San Francisco, CA: Jossey-Bass.
Krzyzewski, M. (2004). *Leading with the heart*. New York, NY: Time Warner Book Group.
Lansford, M., Clements, V., Falzon, T., Aish, D., & Rogers, R. (2010). Essential leadership traits of female executives in the non-profit sector. *The Journal of Human Resource and Adult Learning, 6*(1), 51–62.
Lichtenwalner, B. (2010, August 21). *Servant leadership companies list* [Web log post]. Retrieved from https://www.modernservantleader.com/featured/servant-leadership-companies-list/
Loftus, G. (2014, April 2). The greatest leader of all. *Forbes*. Retrieved from https://www.forbes.com/sites/geoffloftus/2014/04/02/lead-like-jesus/#2044b5a663b9
Mabey, C., Conroy, M., Blakely, K., & de Marco, S. (2017). Having burned the straw man of Christian spiritual leadership, what can we learn from Jesus about leading ethically? *Journal of Business Ethics, 145*, 757–769. https://doi.org/10.1007/s10551-016-3054-5
MacArthur, J. (2002). *Twelve ordinary men: How the master shaped his disciples for greatness, and what he wants to do with you*. Nashville, TN: Thomas Nelson.
Machida, M., & Schaubroeck, J. (2011). The role of self-efficacy beliefs in leader development. *Journal of Leadership & Organizational Studies, 18*(4), 459–468. https://doi.org/10.1177/1548051811404419
Maslow, A. (1998). *Maslow on management*. New York, NY: Wiley.
McCall, M. (2003). The derailment conspiracy. In J. Kouzes (Ed.), *Business leadership* (pp. 189–212). San Francisco, CA: Jossey-Bass.
McCann, J. A. J., Langford, P. H., & Rawlings, R. M. (2006). Testing Behling and McFillens syncretical model of charismatic transformational leadership. *Group & Organization Management, 31*(2), 237–263.

McDaniel, E., & DiBella-McCarthy, H. (2012). Reflective leaders become causal agents of change. *Journal of Management Development, 31*(7), 663–671. https://doi.org/10.1108/02621711211243863

McMurray, A. J., Islam, M., Sarros, J. C., & Pirola-Merlo, A. (2013). Workplace innovation in a nonprofit organization. *Nonprofit Management & Leadership, 23*(3), 367–388. https://doi.org/10.1002/nml.21066

Melchar, D. E., & Bosco, S. M. (2010). Achieving high organization performance through servant leadership. *The Journal of Business Inquiry, 9*(1), 74–88.

Melé, D., & Fontrodona, J. (2017). Christian ethics and spirituality in leading business organizations: Editorial introduction. *Journal of Business Ethics, 145*(4), 671–679. https://doi.org/10.1007/s10551-016-3323-3

Nonprofit Resource Center. (2011). *What is a nonprofit organization?* Retrieved from www.not-for-profit.org

O'Toole, J. (2003). Why amoral leadership doesn't work. In J. Kouzes (Ed.), *Business leadership* (pp. 279–306). San Francisco, CA: Jossey-Bass.

Paglis, L. L., & Green, S. G. (2002). Leadership self-efficacy and managers motivation for leading change. *Journal of Organizational Behavior, 23*(2), 215–235. https://doi.org/10.1002/job.137

Parable. (n.d.). In *Merriam-Webster's online dictionary*. Retrieved from https://www.merriam-webster.com/dictionary/parable

Parolini, J., Patterson, K., & Winston, B. (2009). Distinguishing between transformational and servant leadership. *Leadership & Organization Development Journal, 30*(3), 274–291.

Parris, D., & Peachey, J. (2013). A systematic literature review of servant leadership theory in organizational contexts. *Journal of Business Ethics, 113*(3), 377–393. https://doi.org/10.1007/s10551-012-1322-6

Pidgeon, W. (2004). *The not-for-profit CEO: How to attain & retain the corner office.* Hoboken, NJ: Wiley.

Ramaswamy, V., & Gouillart, F. (2010). *The power of co-creation: Build it with them to boost growth, productivity, and profits.* New York, NY: Free Press.

Salamon, L. M. (1999). *America's nonprofit sector: A primer.* New York, NY: Foundation Center.

Schein, E. (1999). *The corporate culture survival guide* (2nd ed.). San Francisco, CA: Jossey-Bass.

Schein, E. (2004). *Organizational culture and leadership* (3rd ed.). San Francisco, CA: Jossey-Bass.

Schein, E. (2009). *Helping: How to offer, give, and receive help: Understanding effective dynamics in one-to-one, group, and organizational relationships.* San Francisco, CA: Berrett-Koehler.

Schneider, S., & George, W. (2011). Servant leadership versus transformational leadership in voluntary service organizations. *Leadership & Organization Development Journal, 32*(1), 60–77. https://doi.org/10.1108/01437731111099283

Seijts, G. H., & Roberts, M. (2011). The impact of employee perceptions on change in a municipal government. *Leadership & Organization Development Journal, 32*(2), 190–213. https://doi.org/10.1108/01437731111113006

Smith, D. (1997). *The practical executive and leadership.* Lincolnwood, IL: NTC.

Solomon, R. (2004). Ethical leadership, emotions, and trust: Beyond "charisma." In J. Ciulla (Ed.), *Ethics, the heart of leadership* (2nd ed., pp. 83–102). Westport, CT: Praeger.

Spears, L. (1996). Reflections on Robert K. Greenleaf and servant-leadership. *Leadership & Organization Development Journal, 17*(7), 33–35.

The Robert K. Greenleaf Center For Servant Leadership. (2018). *The servant as leader*. Retrieved from https://www.greenleaf.org/what-is-servant-leadership/

Thomas, R. R. (2010). The impact of paradigms on change. In M. Goldsmith, B. Kaye, & K. Shelton (Eds.), *Learn like a leader* (pp. 127–135). Boston, MA: Nicholas Brealey.

Tice, L. (2010). Mentoring for untapped potential. In M. Goldsmith, B. Kaye, & K. Shelton (Eds.), *Learn like a leader* (pp. 170–173). Boston, MA: Nicholas Brealey.

Tolbert, T. H., Moore, G. D., & Wood, C. P. (2010). Not-for-profit organizations and for-profit businesses: Perceptions and reality. *Journal of Business Economics Research, 8*(5), 141–153.

Tramel, M. (1981). *Executive leadership*. Englewood Cliffs, NJ: Prentice-Hall.

Van Dierendonck, D., & Patterson, K. (2015). Compassionate love as a cornerstone of servant leadership: An integration of previous theorizing and research. *Journal Of Business Ethics, 128*(1), 119–131. https://doi.org/10.1007/s10551-014-2085-z

Van Velsor, E., & Guthrie, V. A. (2003). Enhancing the ability to learn from experience. In J. Kouzes (Ed.), *Business leadership* (pp. 223–247). San Francisco, CA: Jossey-Bass.

Villinger, N. D. (2009). Analyzing NPOs: Managerial frameworks and evaluation. *Journal of Global Business Issues, 3*(1), 61–66.

Walumbwa, F. O., Hartnell, C. A., & Oke, A. (2010). Servant leadership, procedural justice climate, service climate, employee attitudes, and organizational citizenship behavior: A cross-level investigation. *Journal of Applied Psychology, 95*(3), 517–529. https://doi.org/10.1037/a0018867

White, L. M. (1998, April). Importance of oral tradition [Blog post]. Retrieved from https://www.pbs.org/wgbh/pages/frontline/shows/religion/story/oral.html

Wolf, T. (1999). *Managing a nonprofit organization in the twenty-first century*. New York, NY: Simon & Schuster.

Wren, J. (1995). *The leaders companion: Insights on leadership through the ages*. New York, NY: The Free Press.

CHAPTER 8

THE STRATEGY OF SPIRITUALITY

How Best Can Spiritual Leadership and Spirituality at Work Support and Sustain Organizational Strategy? A Christian Perspective

Richard Peters and Joe Ricks
Xavier University of Louisiana

Spiritual leadership (SL) and spirituality in the workplace (SAW) are significant themes of contemporary business literature that offer an alternative approach to doing business. As organizations have increasingly turned to morality and social responsibility to guide both principles and policies, traditional taboo themes such as religion, righteousness, and reverence are increasingly intersecting with issues of relevance (with respect to work and/or authority) and reward (financial and otherwise). Arguably, both academics and practitioners, are open and often welcoming of an organizational perspective that promotes spirituality and its complements. Workers seeking a sovereign's calling, managers striving for servanthood-type leadership,

Blessed are Those Who Ask the Questions, pages 163–185
Copyright © 2021 by Information Age Publishing
All rights of reproduction in any form reserved.

and organizations supplying supportive environments all suggest that firms can harmoniously integrate purpose and profit.

Ideally, this sounds ambitious but advantageous. A more empowered workforce, enlightened management and an embracing workplace should lead to conventional ingredients of success: efficiency and effectiveness. However, inevitably many firms find it both impractical and/or implausible to fully commit to the tenets of workplace spirituality. We posit that this unwillingness or inability stems from two conflicts inherent in our present treatment of spirituality in business. The first is that spirituality that "fits" with conventional business models and applications is not spiritual enough and compromises its religiosity for financial reward. The second is that perspectives that try to correct this, those that prioritize the normative over the instrumental, are irreconcilable with most strategic thinking and, therefore, unfeasible to implement. Ironically, both conflicts often lead to the same unfortunate consequence: the relegation of spirituality to the fringes or grassroots of business. Without resolution, this is where it is likely to stay, gaining little actual legitimacy and leverage from corporate decision-makers.

As difficult as it may seem, we believe it is critical for organizations to reconcile workplace spirituality with strategic thinking and business operations because religious identity is still very important in the United States. Data from the latest Pew Research Center shows 77% of Americans self-identify with an established faith (Pew Research Center, n.d.). Identity is formed by the interaction of two components: structure and agency (Cinoğlu & Ankan, 2012). Structure involves the external factors that influence identity while agency involves one's freedom of choice. Even if organizations try to create religious free zone structures where work is work and not a place for personal beliefs, this will, at minimum, create conflict with the individual agent or employee that has chosen to identify as a Christian. Evidence suggests that the conflict between individual faith and the workplace is already taking place and finding its way to the judicial system. Employment discrimination claims based on religion rose 82% between 1992 and 2003. These claims have come from a broad spectrum of faith groups, from small poorly understood faiths as well as Catholics and Evangelicals (Foltin & Standish, 2004).

Using as evidence, Jesus' references to work roles and work-related activity, we can conclude that work and the workplace was very important to Jesus. Issler (2014) explored work related references in the parables Jesus used to communicate to his followers. According to Issler (2014), 32 parables mention some form of labor related activity, and the estimated number of parables Jesus uses will vary from 37 to 75 depending on how one defines a parable. Using this range, Jesus references work in somewhere between 42 and 86% of his parables.

To address this issue, we argue for a pivotal balance that values and utilizes the benefits of spirituality while simultaneously advocating for its co-existence and complementation of existing strategic thinking. Unlike the two opposing perspectives previously identified, we do not suggest that either (strategy or spirituality) must be prioritized or, conversely, made subservient. Instead, we outline and discuss alternative principles that aim to reconcile the "differences" and effectively merge these together and essentially build the bridge between Christianity and capitalism. As we make our arguments, it will be obvious that our empirical and conceptual arguments are based on ethics and corporate social responsibility (CSR). We recognize that all ethical and socially responsible concepts are not Christian; ethics and social consciousness are necessary but insufficient for Christianity. However, we do rely on the premise that organizations with these foundational concepts are those where Christian faith and business strategy is likely to thrive.

In this chapter, we start by reviewing the evolution of SAW/SL generally and the literature that examines these concepts from a Christian perspective. During the review, we identify significant obstacles that have thus far kept these concepts on the fringes of general management thinking and practices. While purportedly prioritizing personal value and Christ-like attributes, they however present challenges to managing organizations, especially those which adopt a religious and/or moral approach to business enterprise. After identifying the challenges associated with a Christian approach to SAW/SL, we offer principles based on Christian perspective and biblical interpretations that also offer the requisite pragmatism for strategic thinking and implementation.

SAW/SL and Christianity: Commonality and Contention

A portion of the motto of the Sisters of the Blessed Sacrament, a Catholic order which was highly influential in the American educational landscape, reads "Man's master art is the leading of man to God" ("Faith & Leadership," n.d., para. 2). This statement echoes the importance of faith, religion, and spirituality in professional development and delivery. Humans have arguably found it both impractical and imprudent to separate the spiritual from the secular related to vocational activity. Thus, the emergence of academic and practitioner discourse focused on SAW and SL is essentially a testament, rather than a legitimization, of a reality that has always existed at the individual, group, and organizational level (Brown, 2003; Lewis & Geroy, 2000; Mirvis, 1997; Neal & Bennett, 2000).

Additionally, as the preceding statistics suggest, religious belief is still valued by many working Americans, and thus this focus SAW on SL is only likely to grow in richness and rigor.

From its inception, authoritative advocates of work spirituality and/or leadership have touted the mutual and synergistic benefits that both employees and their organizations derive from bringing higher order meaning into work (Mitroff & Denton, 1999; Mitroff, 2003). The enhanced sense of comfort and community that individuals enjoy by pursuing work (both content and context) in a manner consistent with spiritual values translates into positive employee attitudes and behaviors such as job satisfaction, organizational commitment and job involvement, motivation, creativity and productivity (Collins & Porras, 1994; Hawley, 1993; Kraimer, 1997; Neck & Milliman, 1994) that ultimately affects the performance and holistic well-being of the entire firm (Bell, 2008; Milliman, Czaplewski, & Ferguson, 2003).

While spirituality and religion are not necessarily interchangeable terms in the SAW and SL literature and previous authors have argued for nonreligious approaches to both constructs (Hyland, Lee, & Mills, 2015; Mitroff & Denton, 1999; Neck & Milliman, 1994), the implicit bond between spirituality and religion has and continues to be evident in both writing and application. Further, considering the prominence and prioritization of Christianity in the United States, there has been a small but informative body of work that has exclusively posited Christian teachings and doctrine in its treatment of SAW and SL (c.f. Cavanagh, 1999; Mabey, Conroy, Blakely, & de Marco, 2016; Reave, 2005).

These works have been complemented by high profile corporate examples like Chick-fil-A and Hobby Lobby that have vehemently defended their faith while demonstrating their financial viability. These "success stories" thus seemingly refute assertions that "religion and business don't mix," and instead add credence to the notion that spirituality, even one based on a particular religious affiliation, can enhance traditional firm outcomes.

Ironically this suggestion, that the sacred can support the secular, has perhaps brought the greatest level of scrutiny and suspicion to bear on these concepts. Aside from definitional ambiguity, SAW and SL have been primarily criticized for a perceived exaggeration of financial gain and a coinciding sacrifice of the purity of spiritual pursuit. For example, Tourish and Tourish (2010) chastise SL as a tool predicated on manipulation and subservience of employee individuality and will. Essentially, they argue, managers use spirituality to quench free thought, quell rebellion and quiet anything and anyone that offers a contradictory message to that of leadership. This warped approach to spirituality may masquerade as emancipatory but in actuality, by mystifying leader actions and "coercing" consensus, subjugates the views of the many to the goals of the one (i.e., the organization).

Tourish and Tourish (2010) blame the power asymmetry in most organizations for the abuse of SL and SAW. This imbalance, in their opinion, impinges on the intended individualism and diversity of spirituality and replaces this personal pursuit with managerial missions that are heavily tainted by the spiritual leanings of owners and creators of corporate culture. Chick-fil-A and Hobby Lobby are both family owned enterprises, with owners with strong Christian convictions. Christianity plays a pivotal role in both the centric values and the operations of these firms. At Chick-fil-A there is Christian themed music; at Hobby Lobby there is Christian themed décor, and both operations, through their ownership, have opposed legal changes that are perceived as conflicting to biblical teachings.

While neither organization requires their potential and current employees to ascribe or adopt Christianity, such personal affiliation would most likely lead to greater organizational congruence. Conversely, holding differing or no religious affiliation may promote ostracism, even if this is unintended (Burlingham, 2007; Tourish & Tourish, 2010).

Christian authors have also criticized previous perspectives and practices of SAW/SL for its power perpetuation. Mabey et al. (2016) for example concur with Tourish and Tourish (2010) that the motive of organizational spirituality may be more instrumental than normative, and interestingly suggest that becoming more Jesus-centered would reposition SL and spirituality such that it aligned vocational activity with obedience and worship to God. They, therefore, blame the failing of SAW/SL, even Christian iterations, on a misrepresentation of Christianity and Christ's leadership that encourages not only manipulation, but monoculturalism and materialism. All three are interrelated, but the last, materialism, specifically condemns the enlistment of spirituality in an organization's drive towards financial prosperity. They do not consider success and spirituality but, as Mabey et al. (2016) note when speaking about biblical values "they are immediately diminished when instrumentally and exclusively conscripted to this cause" (p. 5). Further, they, like Driscoll and Wiebe (2007), agree that morality must be the master of money and never the other way around.

This normative approach is relatively appealing but stirs significant wariness and reservations. These reservations are birthed and bolstered by the historical lessons and experiences related to altruistic CSR, which, though conceptually is the purest and most evolved form of firm-social involvement (Carroll, 1979), has faced the widest criticism and most resistance.

We must firmly state that we do not believe or argue that a normative approach to SAW/SL and altruistic CSR are identical constructs. However, admittedly there are strong parallels between the two that strongly suggest that the obstacles faced by the latter will plague the former, and, more importantly, that they can be resolved in a similar fashion.

To illustrate our comparison, we consider five dimensions as displayed in Table 8.1. While, as noted, each construct has its own focus and discipline, dogmatically they share many consistencies. For example, considering *motivation*, a normative SAW/SL perspective views employees as potential disciples pursuing a calling, rather than a career. Altruistic CSR, although not

TABLE 8.1	Comparison of JCL and Altruistic CSR	
	Normative SAW/SL	**Altruistic CSR**
Management	Employee involvement and opposition necessary, especially where leadership behavior is ethically questionable.	Organizational leaders and members work cooperatively to pursue social ideals.
Motivation	Organizational work helps fulfill a larger life mission and should be viewed as a "calling."	Organizations are created by society to add value to society and are thus obligated to this philanthropic pursuit.
Materialism	Value is derived from fulfillment of higher purpose rather than financial growth.	Profit is secondary to social need and should be sacrificed if and when necessary to achieve greater social good.
Markets	Organizations and leaders should remain focused on ethical pursuit, irrespective of market-driven demands.	Social justice and equity, not market forces, should dictate firm behavior.
Monitoring	Organizations should not be coerced into acting ethically, but embrace it internally and wholeheartedly.	Social investment is discretionary and is therefore always intimate and voluntary.

from an individual perspective, does similarly position firms as social and moral agents (Bowen, 1953), vested with an obligation to cure critical ills in society, thus allowing for and even prioritizing social justice in normal organizational operations (Lantos, 2002).

Also, there is great congruency in the dimension of materialism. Mabey et al. (2016) propose that the measure of organizational value should not ultimately be based on financial cost or contribution, but rather on using God-given talent to enrich the lives of stakeholders. Congruently, altruistic CSR supports, vehemently, the mantra of people and planet before profit, requiring firms to sacrifice for the greater and common good (Lantos, 2001).

Clearly, the core social precept is an intimate and fundamental theme of both normative SAW/SL and altruistic CSR. They strive to bring a moral efficacy to what their proponents often surmise to be an immoral or, at best, amoral capitalist system. They both sell a system that triangulates vows, virtue, and value, arguing that it is more important to be righteous than to be rich, even or especially in a hyper-competitive landscape.

Though well-meaning, altruistic CSR has not had many converts, not because of what it professes, but for what it fails to propose. As its critics have previously proffered, the level of ambiguity, especially with respect to its licensure and limits, leaves too much room for contention and confusion (Lantos, 2001, 2002; Jamali, 2007).

It is not just the clarity of communication that is problematic, but the general disregard for the benefits of traditional business that is likely to impede the growth of normative SAW/SL, as it has for altruistic CSR. As noted earlier, the advocates of the latter have found little success converting corporations into churches, reluctantly and recalcitrantly recognizing that morality must merge with, and not submerge financial obligations (Lantos, 2002). Similarly, identifying and addressing opportunities for SAW and SL to contribute to the bottom line is, we argue, a necessary step in its evolution.

As models seek to demonstrate a more Christian approach to leadership by placing a higher priority on morality, we argue that application of such models will lead to considerable challenges with interruption, identity, instrumentality, idealism, and internalization. These five, we posit, make the reconciliation of workplace spirituality and leadership, and more precisely Christian workplace spirituality and leadership, with conventional strategic goals and organizational approaches problematic and contentious.

Interruption[1]

Christian leadership must be willing and able to question or disrupt status quo thinking and behavior, especially when these are perceived as immoral. This idea of independent thought and empowerment sounds reasonably appealing to contemporary management. Anecdotally and empirically, evidence can be provided that elucidates a tangible bond between ethical decision-making/leadership (Groves & LaRocca, 2011; Waldman, Siegel, & Javidan, 2006), whistle-blowing (Zhang, Chiu, & Wei, 2009), and even employee empowerment (Yu, 2009). However, a closer investigation of this approach suggests that some worrisome obstacles may contrive to undermine the benefit and even operationalization of these activities within the boundaries of existing organizations.

The first impediment is control, which is directly tied to the corresponding leadership behavior. Multiple studies have empirically demonstrated that dominant leaders, that is, those who are most able and likely to influence their employee's attitudes and behavior, are often in charge of firms which are most likely to prioritize ethical decision-making and social activity. For example, Waldman et al. (2006) demonstrate that CEO intellectual stimulation, a component of transformational leadership, is positively related to CSR. Similarly, Waldman et al. finds evidence that visionary leaders, those that inspire and influence followers, impact followers' opinion on CSR and ethics. Further, Angus-Leppan, Metcalf, and Benn (2010) find that autocratic leadership corresponded directly to explicit CSR, that is, social responsibility that was motivated by strategic interests and firm well-being (Carson, Hagen, & Sethi, 2015). Additionally, Groves and LaRocca (2011) indicate that transformational leaders promote follower attitudes congruent with a belief that effective CSR leads to better organizational outcomes. Interestingly these studies collectively bolster the argument that (a) influential leaders can and often do "sell" subordinates on ethics and CSR and (b) this influence is most effective when ethics and CSR are oriented through a strategic lens. Thus, this ability to both inspire, as well as direct subordinates towards a specific agenda and corresponding goal set, seems critical to empowering and promoting the behavior consistent with Christian leadership.

The second aspect that "inhibits" subordinate interruption is the concept of collectivity and in particular, organizational identity. Dutton and Dukerich (1991) illustrate collective identity through the example of the Port Authority's response to homelessness in the 1980s. Interestingly, the authors note that not only does this phenomena frame how organizational members should respond to issues, it also importantly helps determine the boundaries of acceptable activity. For example, while upper management was vehement that homeless persons in the Port Authority facilities should not be put out into the cold, they were equally adamant that the organization does not provide social services itself, deeming that outside both its scope and sphere. This focus on selectivity with respect to social involvement is a defining characteristic of a strategic approach to ethical leadership and social responsibility. As Porter and Kramer (2002) posit, this propensity to limit social investment to areas where organizational and social outcomes are aligned and to which the firm's technical skills are best suited helps define the boundaries of engagement. It also reduces the organizational ambiguity that has challenged past normative approaches like altruistic CSR and that will likely challenge Christian leadership models with a primary focus on morality.

Finally, and relatedly, consistency of behavior is argued to be an inhibitor of interruption. Extending the definition of Porter and Kramer (2002), Ricks (2005) proposes that a strategic approach to ethics and social responsibility must also be measurable. Measurement, while not mandatory for consistency, is often supported by repetition and routinization. Leaders view routines as operational means to visionary ends, and they (routines) become integral components of organizational identity. Maverick and independent stances may sound idealistic and constructive but are likely to hurt the coherence and community necessary to engage and sustain Christian leadership in a systematic, rather than haphazard way.

Identity

Employees view jobs and professions more as spiritual pathways rather than vocational outlets. Arguably, millennials are increasingly seeking fulfillment in work activity, seeking meaning, purpose, and personal development from their professional roles (Richardson, 2016). Additionally, the literature connects ethics and social responsibility to employee values (c.f.

Branco & Rodrigues, 2006; Greening & Turban, 2000; Orlitzky, 2008; Turban & Cable, 2003; Turban & Greening, 1997). However, while confirming that employees do care about social involvement and fusing their professional lives with personal values, previous literature does not suggest that an apostolic attitude to work is attractive, or even acceptable (Orlitzky, 2008). One reason for this lies in employee expectations. We propose that employees who view themselves as following God's calling may aspire to more holistic social agendas, which are likely to be much broader than the focused initiatives pursued by their organizations. We argue that this mismatch in ambition may result in feelings of restraint, frustration, and despondence, even in instances where organizations are forthright about their level of social involvement, this may undermine both motivation and commitment. As Rupp, Ganapathi, Aguilera, and Williams (2006) contend, the influence of firm social responsibility on employee attitude and behavior is mediated by individual need for meaningfulness, and thus an organization's failure to meet this need, may negatively influence employee outcomes. Further, while admittedly speculative, the fact that millennials often eschew company loyalty in the pursuit of personal fulfillment suggests that any cause for disillusion, including unmet spiritual expectations, may encourage employee disengagement and/or turnover.

Another reason is the possibility for the misdirection of employee effort. As Branco and Rodrigues (2006) explicate, the human capital competitive advantage derived from social engagement is predicated on greater access to qualified and quality talent. This talent, while supporting ethics and morality, is more critically expected by managers to contribute to the strategic outcomes of the firm through normal work. If social and operational goals coincide, then organizations reap the benefits of a win-win scenario, but if "calling-oriented" employees sacrifice normal work on the altar of their calling, firms are unlikely to maximize the return of their human investment. Thus, extensive and altruistic social involvement, which taxes and depletes finite employee resources, are likely to be discouraged, even by firms that ascribe to social responsibility and an ethical mandate (Lantos, 2001). As Vogel (2005) asserts, and empirical studies suggest (c.f. Barnett & Salomon, 2012; McWilliams & Siegel, 2001), the impact of social responsibility on financial performance is relatively modest and often outweighed by more traditional factors such as innovation and efficiency.

Thirdly, we propose that this scale of involvement may diminish employee engagement. Although previous research has demonstrated that social engagement can positively impact organizational commitment and identity (Dutton & Dukerich, 1991; Orlitzky, 2008), the fact that a spiritual calling "is not confined to an organization or even a profession" (Mabey et al., 2016, p. 764) may increase employees' urging to leave, even when they are invested and/or incentivized to stay. Thus we term this as the "demand of duty," characterized by a need to pursue a higher level calling at the expense of comfort and/or commitment. Paul's apostolic ministry exemplifies such a demand, which "required" him to press on purposefully, despite his personal desires.

Instrumentality

This challenge deals specifically with the problematic nature of materialism. As Christians, we agree that a strategy solely focused on profit and ignoring spirituality is worrisome. However, we submit for business, spirituality in the absence of profitable strategy is also problematic. Thinking theologically while planning materially, is both preferential and necessary. Schwartz (2006) provides an interesting perspective, suggesting that God should be treated as a stakeholder in managerial decision-making, and thus integrated directly into the traditional financial affairs of the firm.

We posit that considering the financial implications of spiritual/Christian leadership encourages decision-makers to more effectively integrate social behavior and attitudes into normal business operations and supports the seamless intertwining of work and social purpose. This is essentially the virtue of a shared valued approach, to merge matters of society with matters of the firm and, thereby, minimize the schism between obligation and operation (Porter & Kramer, 2011).

Arguably, material thinking is consistent with an ethical mindset, and more importantly, a Christian mindset. Jesus spoke of money, wealth, and possession on numerous occasions, many of which were not derogatory. In fact, the often misquoted verse about the love of money and its connection to evil suggest that it is not a focus on the financials, but an exaggerated emphasis on it, to the detriment of legal, ethical, and social obligations, that is essentially problematic. Thus, from a strategic perspective, material consideration is inherently critical. While we think socially we must act sensibly, especially concerning financial performance (Ricks & Peters, 2013).

Investment

Christian leaders should not "bow to market pressures" and Jesus-centered managers should seek to protect those under their charge from market forces (Mabey et al., 2016). While we agree that market forces are relatively imperfect and can reinforce or create inequalities, we argue that it is a necessary and critical component of organizational and environmental evolution. More relevant to our examination is the importance of institutional forces to discussions of ethics and CSR (Brammer, Jackson, & Matten, 2012; Matten & Moon, 2008). Arguably, the demand for ethics and CSR in contemporary business circles has largely been fueled by stakeholders in the market, including consumers, employees, stockholders, and other involved and interested parties (Carroll, 2001; Freeman, 1984).

Market forces have and continue to place pressure on firms to shift and transform the dynamic demands of their situations (DiMaggio & Powell, 1983; Hannan & Freeman, 1977). But rather than producing obstacles, we suggest that these forces may help firms to identify and manage the interconnectedness most organizations share with a myriad of stakeholders (Peters & Golden, 2013). These stakeholders communicate their diverse interest through multiple channels, including market forces. Failure to adequately acknowledge these messages, or perceive them as combative, may not only alienate existing stakeholder constituents but potentially eliminate new market engagements.

A strategic approach to social engagement does not discount or disavow Christian leadership. Indeed, one of its most prominent characteristics is that it requires the firm to cultivate and consistently maintain a specific social identity (Porter & Kramer, 2002). However, a strategic approach to social engagement substantially leverages market forces to assist the firm in determining both the social climate as well as the individual requirements of its stakeholders and adapting responses to fit these realities. It works with rather than against the market to create shared value between the firm and society (Porter & Kramer, 2011) thereby promoting both ethical and financial outcomes.

Internalization

This principle addresses the motivation for ethical behavior. It could be argued that leaders use conduct codes and benchmarks as public relations tools. Instrumental and auditing approaches, both external and internal, are easily manipulated for unmerited gain. Ironically, these approaches hamper, rather than invigorate, the pursuit of righteousness (Mabey et al., 2016). Much like Jesus chastised the scribes and Pharisees for embracing the letter of the law while ignoring its true intent, it is easy to conceptually criticize instrumental approaches and the leaders that rely on them.

Alternatively, we propose that guidelines, principles, codes, audits, and so forth can be vital resources in an organization's quest to cultivate and/or promote ethical and socially responsible orientations. While we appreciate that some such approaches may be deemed as rudimentary or regulatory, we propose that they offer significant utility to organizations and leaders which aspire to the type of social/servant leadership consistent with Christianity.

The first such benefit resides in acknowledgment. As Peters, Waples, and Golden (2014) note, ethics and social responsibility are vying with numerous other stimuli for management attention and can easily be lost in the clutter if not operationalized and measured. Further, as Ricks and Peters (2013) suggest, it is a measurement of ethical and philanthropic policies and processes that qualifies these endeavors as strategic and central to organizational decision-making.

Beyond acknowledgment, control processes offer informational access to firms that are relatively new to an ethical leader and CSR adoption, or to organizations seeking to improve their performance in this arena. Guidelines provided by political entities, industry groups, or even individual firms are often the purveyors and teachers of best practices, especially in areas where these concepts are embryonic (Matten & Moon, 2008). For example, in Denmark, legislation requiring social and environmental auditing/reporting has helped firms accept and account for social obligations and transformed the business climate of the nation and the region (Brown & Knudsen, 2015).

Finally, the accountability associated with proper implementation and measurement of social standards provides both firms and their stakeholders with the ability to monitor and assess performance. Much like conventional financial statements, external social and ethical reports tie firms to specific mandates and promote transparency necessary to objectively determine the extent of social and ethical engagement (Campbell, 2007). External codes and guidelines may therefore help codify and clarify the "essentials" to effective ethical and/or socially responsible leadership.

Based on the preceding review and our discussion of the challenges associated with a traditional Christian approach to SL/SAW, we next offer some principles which we propose help reconcile the autonomy and personal conviction of morality with the consensus and control necessary for sustainable strategic management. These principles are based on Christian perspectives and interpretations and embrace ideals consistent with a religious approach to spirituality. But their pragmatism and holism endorse their utility in diverse settings and contexts and offer organizations implementable approaches to mutually supporting spirituality and strategy.

Principles of Strategic Spirituality

Subsidiarity With Solidarity

We believe that followership should never be a passive response to a dictatorial demand, especially in circumstances where leaders fail to uphold their vested mandate to their organization as well as general society. Yet, as we have previously argued, there is a prevailing "danger" that this spirit of independence and interruption might unduly/unintentionally create within an organization a climate of both subversion and suspicion between employees and their bosses. Workers emboldened to "fight the good fight of faith," might unnecessarily undermine or even usurp established leadership in an effort to uphold their notion of righteousness.

Therefore, what seems necessary is a feasible approach that protects the power of the individual while simultaneously fostering coherence among all members in the organizational structure. For this, we turn to the concept of subsidiarity. Subsidiarity, in its simplest form, can be defined as a principle of decentralization whereby operational involvement and decision-making are accomplished by the organizational unit with greatest immediacy, familiarity, and/or competency with the subject matter (Daly, 2009). This diffusion of responsibility then positions the system's centralized authority as a subsidiary, acting as a complementing entity rather than a directorial presence, thereby supporting the diffusion of work throughout the entire system (Byron, 2006; Handy, 1994).

Subsidiarity promotes and prioritizes the value of organizational members, not just as objective contributors to economic output, but as gifted human beings with talents and pursuits far greater than their professional obligations (Alford & Naughton, 2001). It advocates for decentralization, but not through subordination or supplementation (Drucker, 2006; Handy, 1994; Naughton, Buckeye, Goodpaster, & Maines, 2015). Instead, it urges leaders to identify, encourage, cultivate, and leverage the uniqueness of its charges, to benefit both employee and firm, independently but also interdependently (Chamberlain & Dickson, 2004; Drucker & Collins, 2008). Subsidiarity embraces a "constructive" level of individualism and self-authorship. However, it also recognizes that allowing independent thought and action can be a risky proposition if not managed effectively and intimately (Naughton et al., 2015).

To avert or mitigate this risk, Naughton et al. (2015) have introduced the concept of solidarity, defined as the "unity of a common good" (p. 27). They argue poignantly that solidarity is a necessary complement to subsidiarity and discuss how the latter without the former can lead to troublesome issues. For example, they suggest that an approach that focuses on self rather than system (subsidiarity without solidarity) is likely to motivate "employees who are isolated from the market and the larger community" (p. 28). This preoccupation with self-reference, they further argue, may shift consideration away from collective obligations to individual rights, thereby discouraging shared identity and, ultimately, the common good. Rather than "undisciplined empowerment" (Naughton et al., 2015, p. 28), this approach, we propose, will foster individual employee engagement and discretion, but through the channels of a coherent commitment to a common cause.

Nowhere biblically is this more illustrated than in 1 Corinthians, 12:12–27. Here, Paul, in describing the structure and operations of the church, likens it to the anatomy of the body. He vividly notes, congruent subsidiarity, that all parts have independent, functional value and discounts any notion of superiority among these parts. However, importantly, he maintains the idea of subsidiarity and solidarity throughout by reminding his readers of the importance and primacy of support and unity. Theological scholars suggest Paul's use of oneness could be allocated for social as well as theological purposes (Byers, 2016). We argue that this oneness should be allocated for organizational purposes also. According to the Gospel of John, this idea of unity is echoed by Jesus himself in his pleas to heaven that all his disciples and followers "that all of them may be one, Father, just as you are in me and I am in you. May they also be in us so that the world may believe that you have sent me." (John 17:21, NIV). Theologian Gert Breed (2014) in his article examining the use of the word daikon in the Bible puts it this way:

> The diakonos of Jesus is therefore also an agent who communicates the words of Christ—which are the Words of the Father—to others. The aim of the communication is that the others should accept the words in faith and believe them and that they would be drawn to Christ by the words. Whoever believes and follows Jesus serves him, and whoever serves Jesus will be with him. It is clear from John 15 and 17 that being with Jesus entails that believers become part of the community between the Father and the Son and that believers are one with each other. When this unity becomes visible, it makes the testimony of the believers effective so that others will also come to the faith (see 17:20–23; Kysar 2001, p. 372). (Breed, 2014, p. 5)

The sometimes-competing concepts of unity and individuality are clearly critical to organizational and theological contexts. The concept of subsidiarity with solidarity provides the framework to strike that balance.

Stewardship

In what is colloquially described as the Parable of the Talents, Jesus discusses the attitude and approach of three servants to the management of their master's wealth (Matthew 25:14–30). Two servants were lauded for their willingness and ability to grow their initial investment while the other was heavily chided for both his risk aversion and wastefulness of opportunity. Through this story, Jesus introduces his audience to the concept of stewardship (i.e., the ethic of responsibility). Stewardship requires individuals to view resources and opportunities as charges requiring dutiful management and preservation, in order to promote sustainability and social well-being. It encourages other centricity, but via the prudent use and growth of material assets.

When addressing what could be competing priorities like other centricity and growth of material assets, organizational leaders need frameworks to strike a proper balance. Scholars like Mabey et al. (2016) dictate that profit be subordinate to perceived social purposes. In fact, their appeal to "think theologically not materially" seemingly presumes that true Christianity and pure capitalism cannot be pursued, at least cognitively, simultaneously. We contend this confluence is not necessarily incorrect. Inherently, one cannot practice true stewardship without to some extent adopting a selfless and servanthood orientation. But rather than conflicting with the precept of profit maximization, we argue that effective stewardship advocates the marriage of morality and money. Independently, each view suffers from incompleteness and ignorance. Money, sans morality, engenders avarice that would never be acceptable to Christians or any people of faith. However, morality without explicit consideration of profit can be equally dangerous, by undermining sustainability (Lantos, 2002).

Theoretically and empirically, a viable integration of both has proven to be palatable and prescriptive (Orlitzky, Seigel, & Waldman, 2011). The concept of mutually matching firm strengths with community service (Porter & Kramer, 2002; Ricks, 2005) has bridged any gaps/contradictions among profit, people, and planet. Firms are also finding novel ways to integrate conventional business goals with additional social support as attested to by bottom of the pyramid strategies and other such social entrepreneurship (Prahalad, 2012). Consistent with these scholars, Hunt and Morgan (1995), in their presentation of comparative advantage theory as an alternative to neoclassical theory, argue that firms operate under constrained self-interest and not profit or wealth maximization. They argue that both consumers and managers are constrained in their self-interest seeking by considerations of what is right, proper, ethical, moral, or appropriate.

But, while such integration is strategically sensible, we suggest that is also biblically based. The Parable of the Talents itself is a testament to Jesus's belief that material gain is not offensive, but potentially constructive if managed and motivated appropriately. Paul, similarly, is not antagonistic towards wealth but proposes that Christians should use these material gains philanthropically (1 Timothy 6:17–19). Eubank (2011) argues the commandment found in verse 14 in the Good Confession (1 Timothy 6:11–14) is almsgiving. To follow this commandment there must be people with material means to give to the poor, which positions organizational profit as advantageous in the pursuit of doing God's work.

Support and Empowerment

Redefining work as a purposeful life choice is a defining characteristic of many spiritual approaches to leadership and business. Employees and their efforts should have greater meaning than the product and services they help deliver. The challenge for Christian leaders is creating this type of environment without creating either a closed organizational community or disenchanted, nomadic members. In his book *Small Giants*, Bo Burlingham (2007) provides an example of an organization, Reell Precision Manufacturing, that illustrates the operational challenges faced by firms attempting to be more "Christian like," by replacing the corporation with the church. As Burlingham, discussing Reell, notes:

They instituted an optional weekly Bible class that employees could attend on company time, but they asked only that employees support the company's values, not the founders' religious beliefs, and they went out of their way to welcome employees of other faiths as well as nonbelievers. Nevertheless, Reell inevitably attracted a significant number of born-again employees, and they were not as sensitive as the partners to others who might not share their beliefs. When it appeared that the Bible-study meetings were creating divisions in the company rather than fostering unity and mutual commitment, they were canceled. (p. 126)

When Jesus chose his disciples, he ignored the existing religious leaders. Instead, he admitted fishermen, tax collectors, doctors, and other ordinary, secular people to further his mission on earth. Interestingly, Jesus's method of recruitment was less about enlistment and more about engagement. None of his followers initially were motivated by meeting the mandate of God, but were drawn to and empowered by the man and the message. Jesus' ability to empower his disciples is documented in John 21. Hoehl (2008) provides a comprehensive exploration of the empowerment style of Jesus found in John 21:1–25, providing an understanding of effective Christian leadership principles through support and empowerment.

We propose that, much like Jesus, Christian business orientations should be careful to be supportive rather than selective in their approach to "catching" and cultivating employees. This implies that organizations may provide access and opportunity for spiritual enlightenment and/or development, but all attempts must be made so that these efforts are inclusive as well as beneficial to the good of the organization. Christian business leaders should be mindful to protect the integrity of the work environment from all subversive elements, especially those that confuse conversion and collegiality.

Further, while we recognize the significant contribution a renewed spirituality to the workplace can have on employee productivity and general well-being (Case & Gosling, 2010; Goffee & Jones, 2013), there is a substantial difference and continuum between employees viewing work as torturous and those perceiving it as a righteous role. We contend that many of the benefits and outcomes of workplace spirituality may be derived without firms and employees unequivocally embracing organizational activity as the pursuit of God's kingdom and that, ironically, stressing calling vs. career may unduly impose pressure on workers to meet even greater expectations, thereby making work more burdensome and unfulfilling.

Therefore, similar to solidarity acting as a rudder to subsidiarity, workplace spirituality must be tempered with an explicit appreciation that employees are spiritual beings with vocational responsibilities. And while these two may be integrated and intertwined, organizations and employees must ensure that spirituality helps rather than hurts; it is not disruptive, distractive, or divisive.

Synergy

In the wake of the horrific terror attack in Orlando, Florida, many business organizations were quick to offer to the victims and official responders both vocal support as well as tangible assistance. One such organization was Chick-fil-A. The restaurant chain made and delivered food to those waiting in line to donate blood to victims as well as medical and police officials working in the aftermath of the attacks (Richardson, 2016).

These actions were relatively conspicuous, considering that employees of the firm were working on a Sunday, a day that the organization has traditionally closed its doors in the commemoration of the "Christian Sabbath." Further, and perhaps more surprisingly was that the violent events targeted the LGBTQ community, a demographic that had previously been critical of Chick-fil-A and its outspoken owner, Dan Cathay, for his stand on same-sex marriage (McGregor, 2012).

However, these most recent efforts are relatively consistent with Chick-fil-A's contemporary engagement with the LGBTQ market. Since Cathay's highly publicized comments, the restaurant and Cathay himself have tried purposely to remove the rift between themselves and their critics. Cathay, without retracting his statements, admitted that he had erred by subscribing his personal viewpoints to his professional enterprise, and in so doing had injudiciously alienated significant segments of the consumer market (Stafford, 2014). The organization also sought to distance itself from previous partners that were viewed as discriminatory and internally recognized its responsibility to respect all individuals, irrespective of sexual orientation.

While some may view Chick-fil-A's actions as an insincere ploy or even a cowardly capitulation, we perceive it as both strategic and spiritual. The company's willingness to forego stringency with respect to a mindset and adopt synergy with respect to a market is aligned with the attitudes and actions of Christ. Jesus on numerous occasions courted controversy by contravening custom, including healing and gathering food on the Sabbath (Matthew 12:9–14; Mark 3:1–6; Luke 6:6–11), and interacting intimately with those considered "unclean" (John 4:7; Mark 2:15). In Ringe (2005) examination of Sabbath observance, the healing controversies bring attention to the debate regarding keeping specific Sabbath rules, versus how to make the day holy, which is what those rules were meant to assure. While Ringe's (2005) examination demonstrates the complexity of this debate, one thing relevant to our discussion is quite clear. No matter how clear or well-meaning rules are there will be a need for exceptions. The complexity comes in determining boundaries for those exceptions. Jesus set broad boundaries by focusing on the purpose of Sabbath observance rather than the specifics. Jesus' aim through these contraventions was not to advocate for compromise but to appeal for community, a goal Chick-fil-A has seemingly favored in its contemporary beliefs and behaviors.

The concept of synergy allows organizations to remain focused on their ideals but flexible in their implementation. As we have demonstrated through this discourse, it is possible, and often practical to be spiritually purposeful and strategically prudent, and that immovable precepts and policies may actually endanger the outcome of virtuous leadership. Alternatively, we suggest that systematically synergizing with market movements is likely to be more effective in upholding the tenets of Christian leadership but also in sharing these tenets with a wider, more diverse audience.

CONCLUSION

The purpose of this chapter is not to criticize the foundations of SAW and SL, or even recent Christian reinterpretations of these convictions. These perspectives never intentionally demonize fiduciary responsibilities but by positional spirituality as adversarial to management/organizational objectives they have emboldened the potential tension between Christianity and capitalism. This tension is notably evident in the common misquoting and misconceptions surrounding 1 Timothy 6:10. In this verse Paul states, "For the love of money is a root of all kinds of evil. Some people, eager for money, have wandered from the faith and pierced themselves with many griefs" (1 Timothy 6:10, NIV). It is obvious that Paul's warning concerns motive rather than money, but our willingness to erringly contract this verse to the surmise that "money is evil" inadvertently and unfortunately pits spirituality against strategic success.

This contention, we propose, was never the intent of Christ, and further characterizing spirituality as incompatible with general strategic principles leaves it susceptible to ambiguity, ambivalence, or worse, avoidance.

The onus is therefore on academics and practitioners alike to become more practical in their premises and policies and thereby become more attractive to organizations that want to implement spiritual values in management, but also sustain and surpass profitability objectives. The reinterpretations and reorientations we discuss could allow for greater implementation, and thereby incentivize more widespread acceptance of the values these perspectives prioritize.

We therefore have a mandate to embrace flexibility and encourage open mindedness, if it is to fully emulate the life of Jesus. This will not only help in fulfilling its Christian calling, but also provide the greatest likelihood of growth beyond the grassroots.

NOTE

1. The following section is adapted from a manuscript "Jesus-Centered Leadership: An Alternative Approach" published in *Business & Society Review* (Peters, Ricks, & Doval, 2017).

REFERENCES

Alford, H. J., & Naughton, M. (2001). *Managing as if faith mattered: Christian social principles in the modern organization.* Notre Dame, IN: University of Notre Dame Press.

Angus-Leppan, T., Metcalf, L., & Benn, S. (2010). Leadership styles and CSR practice: An examination of sensemaking, institutional drivers and CSR leadership. *Journal of Business Ethics, 93*(2), 189–221.

Barnett, M. L., & Salomon, R. M. (2012). Does it pay to be really good? Addressing the shape of the relationship between social and financial performance. *Strategic Management Journal, 33*(11), 1304–1320.

Bell, E. (2008). Towards a critical spirituality of organization. *Culture and Organization, 3*, 293–307.

Bowen, H. R. (1953). *Social responsibilities of the businessman.* New York, NY: Harper & Row.

Brammer, S., Jackson, G., & Matten, D. (2012). Corporate social responsibility and institutional theory: New perspectives on private governance. *Socio-Economic Review, 10*(1), 3–28.

Branco, M. C., & Rodrigues, L. L. (2006). Corporate social responsibility and resource-based perspectives. *Journal of business Ethics, 69*(2), 111–132.

Breed, G., (2014). The meaning of the diakon word group in John 12:26 applied to the ministry in congregations. *Verbum et Ecclesi, 35*(1), 1–8.

Brown, D., & Knudsen, J. S. (2015). Domestic institutions and market pressures as drivers of corporate social responsibility: Company initiatives in Denmark and the UK. *Political Studies, 63*(1), 181–201.

Brown, R. B. (2003). Organizational spirituality: The sceptic's version. *Organization, 10*(2), 393–400.

Burlingham, B. (2007). *Small giants: Companies that choose to be great instead of big.* New York, NY: Penguin.

Byers, A. (2016). The one body of the Shema in 1 Corinthians: An ecclesiology of Christological monotheism. *New Testament Studies, 62*(4), 517–532.

Byron, W. J. (2006). *The power of principles: Ethics for the new corporate culture.* Maryknoll, NY: Orbis Books.

Campbell, J. L. (2007). Why would corporations behave in socially responsible ways? An institutional theory of corporate social responsibility. *Academy of Management Review, 32*(3), 946–967.

Carroll, A. B. (1979). A three-dimensional conceptual model of corporate performance. *Academy of Management Review, 4*(4), 497–505.

Carroll, A. B. (2001). Models of management morality for the new millennium. *Business Ethics Quarterly, 11*(02), 365–371.

Carson, S. G., Hagen, Ø., & Sethi, S. P. (2015). From implicit to explicit CSR in a Scandinavian context: The cases of HÅG and Hydro. *Journal of Business Ethics, 127*(1), 17–31.

Case, P., & Gosling, J. (2010). The spiritual organization: critical reflections on the instrumentality of workplace spirituality. *Journal of Management, spirituality and Religion, 7*(4), 257–282.

Cavanagh, G. F. (1999). Spirituality for managers: Context and critique. *Journal of Organizational Change Management, 12*(3), 186–199.

Chamberlain, G. L., & Dickins, D. (2004). The evolution of business as a Christian calling. *Review of Business, Special Issue: Catholic Social Thought and Management Education, 25*(1), 27–36.

Cinoğlu, H., & Arıkan, Y. (2012). Self, identity and identity formation: From the perspectives of three major theories. *International Journal of Human Sciences, 9*(2), 1114–1131.

Collins, J. C., & Porras, J. I. (1994). *Built to last: Successful habits of visionary companies.* New York, NY: Harper Business.

Daly, L. (2009). *God's economy: Faith-based initiatives and the caring state.* Chicago, IL: University of Chicago Press.

DiMaggio, P. J., & Powell, W. W. (1983). The iron cage revisited: Institutional isomorphism and collective rationality in organizational fields. *American Sociological Review, 48*(2), 147–160.

Driscoll, C., & Wiebe, E. (2007, August). *Technical spirituality at work: Jacques Ellul on workplace spirituality.* Paper presented at the annual meeting of the Academy of Management, Philadelphia, PA.

Drucker, P. F. (2006). *Classic drucker: Essential wisdom of peter drucker from the pages of Harvard Business Review.* Boston, MA: Harvard Business Review Book.

Drucker, P. F., & Collins. J. C. (2008). *The five most important questions you will ever ask about your organization.* New York, NY: Leader to Leader Institute.

Dutton, J. E., & Dukerich, J. M. (1991). Keeping an eye on the mirror: Image and identity in organizational adaptation. *Academy of management journal, 34*(3), 517–554.

Eubank, N. (2011). Almsgiving is 'the commandment: A note on 1 Timothy 6:6–19. *New Testament Studies, 58,* 144–150.

Faith & Leadership: Catholic Mission & Ministry. (n.d.) Retrieved from the website of Xavier University of Louisiana, https://www.xula.edu/faithandleadership

Foltin, R., & Standish, J. (2004). Reconciling faith and livelihood: Religion in the workplace and Title VII. *Human Rights, 31,* 19–24.

Freeman, R. (1984). *Strategic management: A stakeholder approach.* New York, NY: Harper Collins.

Goffee, R., & Jones, G. (2013). Creating the best workplace on earth. *Harvard Business Review, 91*(5), 98–106.

Greening, D. W., & Turban, D. B. (2000). Corporate social performance as a competitive advantage in attracting a quality workforce. *Business & Society, 39*(3), 254–280.

Groves, K. S., & LaRocca, M. A. (2011). An empirical study of leader ethical values, transformational and transactional leadership, and follower attitudes toward corporate social responsibility. *Journal of Business Ethics, 103*(4), 511–528.

Handy, C. B. (1994). *The age of paradox*. Boston, MA: Harvard Business School Press.
Hannan, M. T., & Freeman, J. (1977). The population ecology of organizations. *American Journal of Sociology, 82*(5), 929–964.
Hawley, J. (1993). *Reawaking the spirit in work: The power of dharmic management*. San Francisco, CA: Berret-Koehler.
Hoehl, S. (2008). Empowered by Jesus: A research proposal for an exploration of Jesus' empowerment approach in John 21:1–25. *The Journal of Applied Christian Leadership; Berrien Springs, 2*, 6–18.
Hunt, S. D., & Morgan, R. M. (1995). The comparative advantage theory of competition. *The Journal of Marketing, 59*(2), 1–15.
Hyland, P. K., Lee, R. A., & Mills, M. J. (2015). Mindfulness at work: A new approach to improving individual and organizational performance. *Industrial and Organizational Psychology: Perspectives on Science and Practice, 8*(4), 576–602.
Issler, K. (2014). Exploring the pervasive references to Jesus' parables. *Journal of Theological Society, 57*(2), 323–339.
Jamali, D. (2007). The case for strategic corporate social responsibility in developing countries. *Business and Society Review, 112*(1), 1–27.
Kraimer, M. L. (1997). Organization goals and values: A socialization model. *Human Resource Management Review, 7*(4), 425–448.
Lantos, G. P. (2001). The boundaries of strategic corporate social responsibility. *Journal of consumer marketing, 18*(7), 595–632.
Lantos, G. P. (2002). The ethicality of altruistic corporate social responsibility. *Journal of Consumer Marketing, 19*(3), 205–232.
Lewis, J. S., & Geroy, G. D. (2000). Employee spirituality in the workplace: A cross-cultural view for the management of spiritual employees. *Journal of Management Education, 24*(5), 682–694.
Mabey, C., Conroy, M., Blakeley, K, & de Marco, S. (2016). Having burned the straw man of Christian spiritual leadership, what can we learn from Jesus about leading ethically? *Journal of Business Ethics, 145*, 757–769. https://doi.org/10.1007/s10551-016-3054-5
Matten, D., & Moon, J. (2008). "Implicit" and "explicit" CSR: A conceptual framework for a comparative understanding of corporate social responsibility. *Academy of management Review, 33*(2), 404–424.
McGregor, J. (2012, July 19). Chick-fil-A CEO Dan Cathy steps into gay-marriage debate. *The Washington Post*. Retrieved from https://www.washingtonpost.com/blogs/post-leadership/post/chick-fil-a-president-dan-cathy-bites-into-gay-marriage-debate/2012/07/19/gJQACrvzvW_blog.html
McWilliams, A., & Siegel, D. (2001). Corporate social responsibility: A theory of the firm perspective. *Academy of management review, 26*(1), 117–127.
Milliman, J., Czaplewski, A. J., & Ferguson, J. (2003). Workplace spirituality and employee work attitudes: An exploratory empirical assessment. *Journal of Organizational Change Management, 16*(4), 426–447.
Mirvis, P. (1997). "Soul work" in organizations. *Organization Science, 8*(2), 193–206.
Mitroff, I. A. (2003). Do not promote religion under the guise of spirituality. *Organization, 10*(2), 375–382.
Mitroff, I. A., & Denton, E. A. (1999). *A spiritual audit of corporate america: a hard look at spirituality, religion, and values in the workplace*. San Francisco, CA: Jossey-Bass.

Naughton, M., Buckeye, J., Goodpaster, K., & Maines T. D. (2015). *Respect in action: Applying subsidiarity in business.* Saint Paul, MN: UNIAPAC, St. Thomas University.

Neal, J. A., & Bennett, J. (2000). Examining multi-level or holistic spiritual phenomena in the work place. *Management, Spirituality, & Religion Newsletter, Academy of Management, 1,* 1–2.

Neck, C. P., & Milliman, J. F. (1994). Thought self-leadership: finding spiritual fulfillment in organizational life. *Journal of Managerial Psychology, 9*(6), 9–16.

Orlitzky, M. (2008). Corporate social performance and financial performance: A research synthesis. In A. Crane, A. McWilliams, D. Matten, J. Moon, & D. Seigel (Eds), *The Oxford handbook on corporate social responsibility* (pp. 113–136). Oxford, England: Oxford University Press.

Orlitzky, M., Siegel, D. S., & Waldman, D. A. (2011). Strategic corporate social responsibility and environmental sustainability. *Business & society, 50*(1), 6–27.

Peters, R., & Golden, P. (2013). Stakeholder networks and strategy: The influence of network consistency and network diversity on firm performance. *Journal of Business Strategies, 30*(2), 120–144.

Peters, R., Ricks, J., & Doval, C. (2017). Jesus-centered leadership: An alternative approach. *Business and Society Review, 122*(4), 589–612.

Peters, R., Waples, E., & Golden, P. (2014). A real options reasoning approach to corporate social responsibility (CSR): Integrating real option sensemaking and CSR orientation. *Business and Society Review, 119*(1), 61–93.

Pew Research Center. (n.d.). *Religious landscape study.* Retrieved from http://www.pewforum.org/religious-landscape-study/

Porter, M. E., & Kramer, M. R. (2002). The competitive advantage of corporate philanthropy. *Harvard business review, 80*(12), 56–68.

Porter, M., & Kramer, M.R. (2011). Creating shared value. *Harvard Business Review, 89*(1), 32–49.

Prahalad, C. K. (2012). Bottom of the pyramid as a source of breakthrough innovations. *Journal of Product Innovation Management, 29*(1), 6–12.

Reave, L. (2005). Spiritual values and practices related to leadership effectiveness. *The Leadership Quarterly, 16*(5), 655–687.

Richardson, B. (2016, June 13). Chick-fil-A restaurants respond to Orlando massacre with free food at blood drives. *The Washington Times.* Retrieved from https://www.washingtontimes.com/news/2016/jun/13/chick-fil-responds-orlando-massacre-free-food-bloo/

Ricks, J. M., Jr. (2005). An assessment of strategic corporate philanthropy on perceptions of brand equity variables. *Journal of Consumer Marketing, 22*(3), 121–134.

Ricks, J. M., & Peters, R. C. (2013). Motives, timing, and targets of corporate philanthropy: A tripartite classification scheme of charitable giving. *Business and Society Review, 118*(3), 413–436.

Ringe, S., H. (2005). Holy, as the Lord your God commanded you: Sabbath in the New Testament. *Interpretation: A Journal of Bible and Theology, 59*(1), 17–24.

Rupp, D. E., Ganapathi, J., Aguilera R. V., & Williams, C. A. (2006). Employee reactions to corporate social responsibility: An organizational justice framework. *Journal of Organizational Behavior, 27*(4), 537–543.

Schwartz, M. S. (2006). God as a managerial stakeholder? *Journal of Business Ethics, 66,* 291–306.

Stafford, L. (2014, March 14). Cathy seeks to put gay marriage flap behind Chick-fil-A. *The Atlanta Journal-Constitution.*

Tourish, D., & Tourish, N. (2010). Spirituality at work and its implications for leadership and followership. *Leadership, 6*(2), 207–224.

Turban, D. B., & Cable, D. M. (2003). Firm reputation and applicant pool characteristics. *Journal of Organizational Behavior, 24*(6), 733–751.

Turban, D. B., & Greening, D. W. (1997). Corporate social performance and organizational attractiveness to prospective employees. *Academy of management journal, 40*(3), 658–672.

Vogel, D. (2005). Is there a market for virtue? *California Management Review, 47*(4), 19–45.

Waldman, D. A., Siegel, D. S., & Javidan, M. (2006). Components of CEO transformational leadership and corporate social responsibility. *Journal of management studies, 43*(8), 1703–1725.

Yu, X. (2009). From passive beneficiary to active stakeholder: Workers' participation in CSR movement against labor abuses. *Journal of Business Ethics, 87*(1), 233–249.

Zhang, J., Chiu, R., & Wei, L. Q. (2009). On whistleblowing judgment and intention: The roles of positive mood and organizational ethical culture. *Journal of Managerial Psychology, 24*(7), 627–649.

CHAPTER 9

MOTIVATION OR JUSTIFICATION

How Is Religiosity Used in the Decision to Engage in Environmental Sustainability Practices?

Shalei V. K. Simms
SUNY Old Westbury

Dorothy M. Kirkman
University of Houston, Clear Lake

Scholarly research has highlighted multiple factors that have influenced decisions made by organizations to implement environmental sustainability practices. These factors range from the motivations of the top management team (Bamberg & Moser, 2007) to the encouragement of an organization's employees (Benn, Teo, & Martin, 2015; Cirnu & Kuralt, 2013; Johannsdottir, Olafsson, & Davidsdottir, 2015; Merriman, Sen, Felo, & Litzky, 2016). Because the costs of environmental practices can be substantial and the benefits are not always immediate (Eccles, Perkins, & Serafeim, 2012), managers continue to search for factors that justify the need to enlist these practices, particularly in this regulatory climate.

Based on this continued search, the last decade has been witness to swings in Western society's focus on environmental sustainability policies and practices. While political and social perspectives previously placed an emphasis on incentivizing businesses to engage in environmental sustainability, there are now questions on the validity of global warming and a reduction in support of these incentives. For example, one of the United Nations primary goals was to transition consumers to clean energy by the year 2030 (UN General Assembly Resolution, 2015). However, there have been changes made in the mid-2010s that have reduced the regulatory oversight of organizations and encourage an open market focus on energy consumption, including the return to the use of coal and other fossil fuels (Parker & Davenport, 2016). With less governmental oversight, one must ask what other mechanisms will influence organizations' sustainability decisions?

The goal of this chapter is to further discuss the role religiosity plays in the decision to enlist an environmentally sustainable, or green strategy. It was previously found that Christian religiosity in particular was related to lower levels of environmental sustainability engagement by organizations considering these intentions (Cui, Jo, & Velasquez, 2015). Although they controlled for a number of firm level factors (i.e., growth potential, total assets, market value of equity, etc.) they do not take into consideration how other elements in the external environment integrate with religiosity to influence how top executives make the determination to "go green." This work will attempt to identify conditions under which there is either a reduced emphasis on environmental sustainability or increased encouragement to implement these practices. Specifically, when is religion used to motivate action or justify inaction?

WHY ENVIRONMENTAL SUSTAINABILITY?

Environmental sustainability is an element of an organization's corporate social responsibility strategy that determines how an organization will approach green initiatives. These initiatives have gained significant traction in recent years as attention to environmental deterioration has come to light. This is especially true as news of extreme weather events experienced in Western nations have gained national coverage. In most instances these events have been linked to matters of global warming and the role our business practices have played in its further development. These changes may have prompted some organizations to re-examine their corporate social responsibility strategy in general, and green strategy in particular.

A number of factors have been found to influence the decision to implement a green strategy. At the organizational level, financial indicators such as firm size, levels of debt, financial performance, and liquidity measures have been found to influence environmental decision-making (Clarkson, Richardson, & Vasvariet, 2011). Firm visibility is also said to have an impact on environmental strategies, particularly in industries where environmental initiatives are becoming an industry standard (Rowley & Berman, 2000). In addition, external stakeholders have also been found to influence this decision, including customers, regulators, and local communities (Anton, Deltas, & Khanna, 2004; Christmann & Taylor, 2001; Delmas & Terlaak, 2002; Kassinis & Vafeas, 2006). Where is religiosity in the decision to employ a green strategy?

RELIGIOSITY AND DECISION-MAKING

Research on religiosity in the business context has developed significantly in the last two decades. Religiosity is "an organized system of beliefs, practices, rituals and symbols designed to (a) facilitate closeness to the sacred (God, higher power, or ultimate truth/reality), and (b) foster an understanding of one's relation and responsibility to others living together in a community" (Koenig, 2000, p. 18). This construct has been found to influence the decision-making of both employees (Davidson & Cadell, 1994) and managers (Dyreng, Mayew, & Williams, 2012; McGuire, Omer, & Sharp, 2012). For example, CEOs consider their religious values when making strategic decisions (Phipps, 2012), while executives would look to connect with a transcendent power in their work capacity, especially when dealing with particularly difficult situations (Fernando & Jackson, 2006). For these managers, relying on a rational decision process was insufficient to deal with complex scenarios. Fernando and Burrows (2005) note that "linkage with a transcendent dimension of power could provide inspiration and guidance to business leaders to make the right decisions" (p. 3).

It is important to understand the role religiosity plays in decision-making in general because of the nature of decision-making in complex organizational environments. Allport's (1960) work identifies religiosity as an element that can motivate behavior, whether it is used for selfish ends or for more benevolent intentions. Because religiosity is part of the daily life of many (Vitell, Keith, & Mathuret, 2011), it may be expected that it would play a role in organizational decision-making. With that in mind, religiosity may also be a determining factor in deciding whether or not to enlist environmentally sustainable measures as part of an organization's overall strategy.

The decision to implement environmental strategies is considered an element of corporate social responsibility decisions and, as such, reflect the ethical orientation of an organization's leaders (Matten & Crane, 2005). Building sustainable organizations requires leaders to have a long-term vision, an ability to tolerate risks, and the motivation to incorporate measures of sustainability into basic operational decisions (Eccles et al., 2012). As was previously stated, the complexity of these decisions may push organizational leaders to use a combination of measures, including religiosity, to aid in this decision-making. However, it is not clear whether or not the inclusion of religiosity will result in the decision to implement green strategies.

While green strategies can require a substantial investment (Hart, 1995; Hart & Dowel, 2011), the focus on the costs of these practices may not fully explain an organization's decision to engage in such measures. There are also elements of religiosity that may influence an organization's strategic decisions regarding sustainability. For example, early work in this line of research note, some interpretations of Christian values assert that believers have "dominion" over the environment and, therefore, may selectively determine how they chose to use elements of the environment (White, 1967). Cui et al. (2015) found that high levels of religiosity were related to lower incidents of support to protect the environment based on this dominion argument; specifically, individuals interpreted regulations around sustainability as an infringement on their right to use the elements of their physical environment as they deem necessary. As such, they were less likely to support the pursuit of sustainability initiatives.

There are also differences in moral perspectives based on religiosity. For example, Brammer, Williams, and Zinkin (2007) argue that Christians, Muslims, and Hindus found economic responsibility more important than did Jews and Buddhists. In addition, Buddhists also felt that ethical behavior is the responsibility of the individual and not the organization. When examining the relationship between religiosity and engaging in sustainability practices, we begin to understand that religiosity can influence managers' decision-making regarding green strategies, as they must consider economic impact as well as organizational responsibility. Ultimately, religiosity has been found to impact ethical judgement (Vitell et al., 2011), make individuals more sensitive to ethical issues (Siu, Dickinson, & Lee, 2000), as well as more likely to have ethical intentions (Vitell et al., 2011). With this in mind, this chapter explores how religiosity operates in the decision to facilitate the implementation of green strategies.

Environmentally sustainable, or green, strategies can be beneficial to overall firm performance (Eccles et al., 2012), but they are often pursued under conditions of uncertainty. As such, it may be difficult for top executives to decide to incorporate green strategies in the overall organizational operation. Although scholars noted that top executives were expected to have the ability to tolerate risks to build a green strategy (Eccles et al., 2012), there is an equivocal relationship between risk and religiosity. While Miller and Hoffman (1995) found a negative relationship between religiosity and attitudes towards risk, and Shu, Sulaeman, and Yeung (2012) demonstrate that individuals that scored low on Protestant values also demonstrated higher levels of risk-taking, Hilary and Hui (2009) found individuals who measured higher in religiosity were also more risk averse. This becomes apparent when examining the varied approach to environmental initiatives across an industry. If organizations that operate in high-religiosity contexts present lower levels of risk in their decision-making (Kanagaretnam, Lobo, Wang, & Whalen, 2015), and interpret biblical expressions of environmental responsibility as "dominion," under what conditions will religious interpretations result in environmental sustainability engagement?

We extend Cui et al. (2015) findings regarding religiosity and managerial decision-making by arguing that the effect of leaders' religiosity on decision-making, particularly regarding green strategies, is contingent upon their interpretation of institutional pressures in the external environment. Hoffman (2001) stated that a "form of organizational response is as much a reflection of the institutional pressures that emerge from outside the organization as it is the form of organizational structure and culture that exist inside the organization" (pp. 136–137). That is to say, some determinants of environmental decisions can come from customers (Christmann & Taylor, 2001); and external regulators (Delamas & Teraak, 2002; Delmas & Toffel, 2004, 2008); in addition to corporate stakeholders (Crane, Matten, & Moon, 2004). It is our position that religiosity will be expressed based on the nature of these institutional pressures. Specifically, we argue that executives operating in high-religiosity environments will interpret the decision to avoid green strategy implementation through the "dominion" lens if there is no institutional pressure to "go green." We contend that in these instances religiosity is not necessarily influencing the decision, but providing a socially acceptable means to justify inaction. That is to say, if there is no institutional logic within a given industry to prompt green engagement, religiosity may have greater influence on this decision, particularly in high-religiosity environments.

On the other hand, if the climate to participate in environmentally sustainable initiatives is strengthened by institutional pressures, executives may integrate religiosity with their institutional logic to determine their strategic direction. As was previously stated, the decision to enlist green strategic initiatives requires significant investment of organizational resources, even though the decision is often made under conditions of uncertainty. It is at times of uncertainty where these institutional pressures may have greater influence (Goodrick & Salancik, 1996). We argue that even if organizations are operating in a high-religiosity environment with a "dominion" perspective, they are more likely to enlist green strategies where institutional pressures are strong. First, firms gain legitimacy by following industry practices (DiMaggio & Powell, 1983), essentially removing the semblance of choice from the scenario. Second, organizations often comply with environmental initiatives to appease external stakeholders (Delmas & Toffel, 2008). We contend that although institutional logics significantly influence the strategic direction a company may take, executives in high-religiosity contexts may use religious perspective to publicly justify compliance in green strategies. Specifically, the decision to engage in sustainable practices may be framed as an exercise of "dominion," where personal choice based on religiosity is the primary motivation.

Finally, it is our estimation that the green strategy decision may be motivated by the spirituality of top executives in environments with low measures of religiosity and low institutional pressure. Whereas religiosity reflects an organized set of beliefs, spirituality is the "personal quest for understanding" (Koenig, 2000, p. 18.). Spirituality reflects the individual pursuit of a relationship with a higher being, regardless of the presence of a religious community (King & Crowther, 2004). Without boundaries imposed by the external pressure of institutional logics, the pursuit of green strategies may come from the degree of spirituality possessed by the top executives. According to Sharma (2000), organizations either comply with institutional pressures or voluntarily engage in environmental strategies, dependent upon organizational motivations. If some religions attest that ethical behavior is the responsibility of the individual and not the community (Brammer et al., 2007), then the leader's level of spirituality becomes increasingly important in motivating green decision-making and a factor that pushes an organization beyond compliance (Sharma & Henriques, 2005; Tombaugh & Tombaugh, 2009).

CONCLUSION

Scholars have been hesitant to include God and religion in discussions of managerial behavior in early management literature. However, since 2000 we have seen an increase in the recognition that religiosity has significant presence in managerial decision-making. Top leaders have noted that including religion in their decision-making process has allowed them to manage complex decisions, has helped reduce their levels of stress, and has facilitated more creativity and proficiency in the decisions they have made. Maybe of greatest import, including religiosity in their decision-making has had a great impact on making ethical decisions. One of the most pressing forms of ethical decision-making as an organizational leader is incorporating green strategies in the overall operation of an organization.

An environmentally sustainable, or green, strategy is an essential element of organizational strategic decision-making, but it is not an easy or even obvious decision to make. While the evidence shows that environmental strategies have a significant and positive impact on organizational performance (Eccles et al., 2012), they are costly to implement and require buy-in from all levels of the organization to be implemented successfully. Based on the complexity of this decision, it makes sense to identify the role God plays in an executive's ability to make and continue to support the pursuit of a green strategy.

For some, religious beliefs are reflected in the decision to refrain from engaging in environmental strategies. As a reflection of God, the position one holds in society is based on the premise of hierarchy, with humans at the top of the organization. As such, their religious beliefs support the notion that they are an earthly representation of God and, therefore, have been given dominion over all other creatures (Cui et al., 2015). Based on this perspective, the motivation to take personal actions to sustain the environment is less prevalent than the belief that the world is operating in its natural order as dictated by God. Without the external pressures to implement and support green strategies, religiosity may be used to validate decisions to forego such implementation.

For others, the established order of organized religion has less influence on their decision-making than does the individual pursuit of a connection to the transcendent. In these cases, there is a belief that ability to achieve a connection to a higher being is open to many possibilities. As a result, executives enlisted in this individual pursuit may be more inclined to pursue green strategies than those who are less interested in seeking this connection. This may be particularly true in instances where there is pressure from neither internal nor external stakeholders to "go green." In these instances, environmental sustainability may be seen as a spiritual responsibility and a mechanism by which the connection to a higher being is made.

It is important to note that this research has a specifically Western perspective. The attestations made by the authors may be based distinctly on Judeo-Christian principles. For example, spiritual beliefs shared by indigenous communities in North America are based on the connection to the four primary elements: fire, water, land, air. The premise argued in this chapter, that religiosity and spirituality are distinct from environmental strategies, may not be the basis on which these arguments are built if taken from the indigenous perspective.

REFERENCES

Allport, G. W. (1960). *The individual and his religion* (2nd ed.). New York, NY: MacMillan.
Anton, W. R. Q., Deltas, G., & Khanna, M. (2004). Incentives for environmental self-regulation and implications for environmental performance. *Journal of Environmental Economics and Management, 48*(1), 632–654.

Bamberg, S., & Möser, G. (2007). Twenty years after Hines, Hungerford, and Tomera: A new meta-analysis of psycho-social determinants of pro-environmental behaviour. *Journal of Environmental Psychology, 27*(1), 14–25.

Benn, S., Teo, S. T. T., & Martin, A. (2015). Employee participation and engagement in working for the environment. *Personnel Review, 44*(4), 492–510.

Brammer, S., Williams, G., & Zinkin, J. (2007). Religion and attitudes to corporate social responsibility in a large cross-country sample. *Journal of Business Ethics, 71*(3), 229–243.

Christmann, P., & Taylor, G. (2001). Globalization and the environment: Determinants of firm self-regulation in china. *Journal of International Business Studies, 32*(3), 439–458.

Cirnu, C. E., & Kuralt, B. (2013). The impact of employees' personal values on their attitudes toward sustainable development: Cases of Slovenia and Romania. *Management: Journal of Contemporary Management Issues, 18*(2), 1–20.

Clarkson, P. M., Li, Y., Richardson, G. D., & Vasvari, F. P. (2011). Does it really pay to be green? determinants and consequences of proactive environmental strategies. *Journal of Accounting and Public Policy, 30*(2), 122–144.

Crane, A., Matten, D., & Moon, J. (2004). Stakeholders as citizens? Rethinking rights, participation, and democracy. *Journal of Business Ethics, 53*(1/2), 107–122.

Cui, J., Jo, H., & Velasquez, M. (2015). The influence of Christian religiosity on managerial decisions concerning the environment. *Journal of Business Ethics, 132*(1), 203–231.

Davidson, J. C., & Caddell, D. P. (1994). Religion and the meaning of work. *Journal for the Scientific Study of Religion, 33*(2), 135–147.

Delmas, M., & Terlaak, A. (2002). Regulatory commitment to negotiated agreements: Evidence from the United States, Germany, the Netherlands, and France. *Journal of Comparative Policy Analysis, 4*(1), 5–29.

Delmas, M., & Toffel, M. W. (2004). Stakeholders and environmental management practices: An institutional framework. *Business Strategy and the Environment, 13*(4), 209–222.

Delmas, M. A., & Toffel, M. W. (2008). Organizational responses to environmental demands: Opening the black box. *Strategic Management Journal, 29*(10), 1027–1055.

Dyreng, S. D., Mayew, W. J., & Williams, C. D. (2012). Religious social norms and corporate financial reporting. *Journal of Business Finance and Accounting, 39*(7/8), 845–875.

DiMaggio, P., & Powell, W. (1983). The iron cage revisited: Institutional isomorphism and collective rationality in organizational fields. *American Sociological Review. 48*(2), 147–160.

Eccles, R. G., Perkins, K. M., & Serafeim, G. (2012). How to become a sustainable company. *MIT Sloan Management Review, 53*(4), 43–50.

Fernando, M., & Burrows, S. (2005, December). *Unbounded rationality: The role of connectedness in right decision-making.* Paper presented at the Australia and New Zealand Academy of Management (ANZAM) Conference, Canberra, Australia.

Fernando, M., & Jackson, B. (2006). The influence of religion-based workplace spirituality on business leaders' decision-making: An inter-faith study. *Journal of Management and Organization, 12*(1), 23–39.

Goodrick, E., & Salancik, G. R. (1996). Organizational discretion in responding to institutional practices: Hospitals and cesarean births. *Administrative Science Quarterly, 41*(1), 1–28.

Hart, S. L. (1995). A natural-resource-based view of the firm. *Academy of Management. The Academy of Management Review, 20*(4), 986–1014.

Hart, S. L., & Dowell, G. (2011). A natural-resource-based view of the firm: Fifteen years after. *Journal of Management, 37*(5), 1464–1479.

Hilary, G., & Hui, K. W. (2009). Does religion matter in corporate decision making in America? *Journal of Financial Economics, 93*(3), 455–473.

Hoffman, A. J. (2001). Linking organizational and field-level analyses: The diffusion of corporate environmental practice. *Organization & Environment, 14*(2), 133–156.

Johannsdottir, L., Olafsson, S., & Davidsdottir, B. (2015). Leadership role and employee acceptance of change. *Journal of Organizational Change Management, 28*(1), 72–96.

Kanagaretnam, K., Lobo, G. J., Wang, C., Whalen, D. J. (2015). Religiosity and risk-taking in international banking. *Journal of Behavioral and Experimental Finance, 7,* 42–59.

Kassinis, G., & Vafeas, N. (2006). Stakeholder pressures and environmental performance. *Academy of Management Journal, 49*(1), 145–159.

King, J. E., & Crowther, M. R. (2004). The measurement of religiosity and spirituality: Examples and issues from psychology. *Journal of Organizational Change Management, 17*(1), 83–101.

Koenig, H. G. (2000). Religion, spirituality, and medicine: Application to clinical practice. *JAMA, 284*(13), 1708.

Matten, D., & Crane, A. (2005). Corporate citizenship: Toward an extended theoretical conceptualization. *The Academy of Management Review, 30*(1), 166–179.

McGuire, S. T., Omer, T. C., & Sharp, N. Y. (2012). The impact of religion on financial reporting irregularities. *The Accounting Review, 87*(2), 645–673.

Merriman, K. K., Sen, S., Felo, A. J., & Litzky, B. E. (2016). Employees and sustainability: The role of incentives. *Journal of Managerial Psychology, 31*(4), 820–836.

Miller, A. S., & Hoffman, J. P. (1995). An exploration of gender differences in religiosity. *Journal for the Scientific Study of Religon, 34*(1), 63–75.

Parker, A., & Davenport, C. (2016, May 26). Donald Trump's energy plan: More fossil fuels, fewer rules. *The New York Times.* Retrieved from https://www.nytimes.com/2016/05/27/us/politics/donald-trump-global-warming-energy-policy.html

Phipps, K. A. (2012). Spirituality and strategic leadership: The influence of spiritual beliefs on strategic decision making. *Journal of Business Ethics, 106*(2), 177–189.

Rowley, T., & Berman, S. (2000). A brand new brand of corporate social performance. *Business & Society, 39*(4), 397–418.

Sharma, S. (2000). Managerial interpretations and organizational context as predictors of corporate choice of environmental strategy. *Academy of Management Journal, 43*(4), 681–697.

Sharma, S., & Henriques, I. (2005). Stakeholder influences on sustainability practices in the Canadian forest products industry. *Strategic Management Journal, 26*(2), 159–180.

Shu, T., Sulaeman, J., & Yeung, P. E. (2012). Local religious beliefs and mutual fund risk-taking behaviors. *Management Science, 58*(10), 1779–1796.

Siu, N. Y. M., Dickinson, J. R., & Lee, B. Y. Y. (2000). Ethical evaluations of business activities and personal religiousness. *Teaching Business Ethics, 4*(3), 239–256.

Tombaugh, J. R., & Tombaugh, E. F. (2009). Can spiritual leadership lead us not into temptation? *Business & Professional Ethics Journal, 28*(1/4), 95–119.

United Nations General Assembly Resolution. (2015). *Transforming our world: The 2030 agenda for sustainable development.* Retrieved from https://www.un.org/en/development/desa/population/migration/generalassembly/docs/globalcompact/A_RES_70_1_E.pdf

Vitell, S. J., Keith, M., & Mathur, M. (2011). Antecedents to the justification of norm violating behavior among business practitioners. *Journal of Business Ethics, 101*(1), 163–173.

White, L., Jr. (1967). The historical roots of our ecologic crisis. *Science, 155*(3767), 1203–1206.

CHAPTER 10

IS TODAY'S FOCUS ON INNOVATION ENTICING GLOBAL MANAGERS AWAY FROM RELIGIOUS AND SPIRITUAL PRINCIPLES?

Matthew Guah
South Carolina State University

> *The Golden Rule, a cornerstone of all religious understanding f or all their individual believers, can be summarized into this phrase: "Do unto others what you would have them do unto you."*
>
> —Oppelt, 2012

This chapter is based on a qualitative research conducted by the author to lay out certain religious and spiritual qualities of a global leader. Findings from the research also point out how managers in different parts of the globe are trying to obtain these qualities. The chapter explains how such qualities can be attained in conjunction with the manager's intimate relationship with religious belief.

The author wants readers to understand why most global managers put so much emphasis on innovation. Thus, this chapter begins with a clear definition of change management. A detailed justification for change management offers specific and practical tools that business managers, around the globe, apply in leading people within the context of Golden Rule principles. The author delves deeper into the realm of leadership—although these points are elevated to higher integrity—not only addressing pitfalls with major religions practiced by managers in different regions of the globe, but also tackling topics such as the global manager's ability to engage with employees, and customers. Readers would experience a demonstration of shift in interpretation of the Golden Rule principles, by the progression of religious practices over time. This illustrates how global managers frequently apply certain elements of management practices effectively to ensure project success, avoid valuable losses, and minimize the negative impact of change on productivity and customers' loyalty (Specht, Kuonoath, Pachler, Weisweler, & Frey, 2017).

The chapter also explains why it has become imperative that global managers fully understand various areas of the Golden Rule principles. The aim here is to draw attention to the dominant values that have shaped modern managerial goals, not only to the differences between broad and narrow definitions of Golden Rule in management, but also to some holistic values for equal treatment that need to be promoted, as well as an ethic that considers all human beings to have equal value, similar to the foundations of our faith and our beliefs in God.

The chapter concludes with keys for gaining inner cooperation between managers and employees, that is currently changing leadership habits through the use of Golden Rule.

MANAGEMENT PRACTICES IN THE 21ST CENTURY

The primary focus of global management in the 21st Century is the ability to lead a team of employees in the mist of constant change around the world (Guah, 2011). In essence, global managers must continuously deal with change management as the world around them goes through daily adjustments. In a longitudinal field study, Specht and colleagues (2017) identified an indirect effect of motivation to benefit others on change in teaching climate through organizational identification. Their results highlight the role of different facets in change agents' motivation to successfully implement changes and provide insights for the design of change programs in organizations. The elements below comprise such areas that can be used by global managers to create an edifice for managing change:

- change management process;
- identifying change;

- readiness assessments;
- communicating and planning for change management;
- coaching and training change agents;
- change roadmap;
- managing resistance;
- data collection, feedback analysis, and corrective action; and
- celebrating and recognizing successful changes.

Global managers frequently apply certain elements of management practices effectively to ensure project success, avoid valuable losses and minimize the negative impact of change on productivity and customers' loyalty (Specht et al., 2017). The rest of this section explains why it has become imperative that global managers fully understand the following areas to obtain adequate tools for the job.

Change Management Process

The change management process (see Figure 10.1) is the sequence of steps or activities that a change management team or project leader can

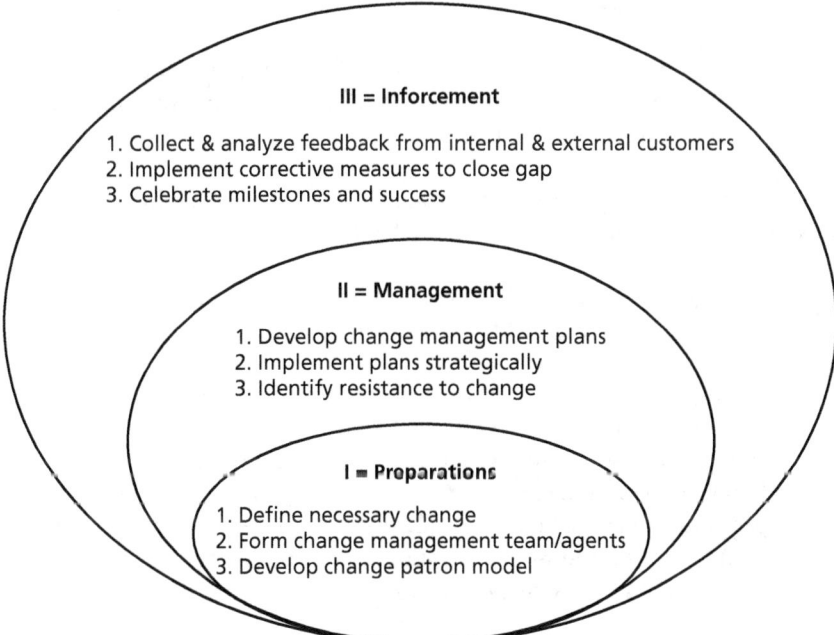

Figure 10.1 Change management process model.

follow to apply change management to a project. Guah (2011) suggests the following three steps for the most effective and commonly applied change management process for any large projects:

- *Step 1: Preparing for Change* (preparation, assessment, and strategy development)
- *Step 2: Managing Change* (detailed planning and change management implementation)
- *Step 3: Reinforcing Change* (data gathering, corrective action, and recognition)

Identifying Change

Change management has been defined as the application of a structured process and set of tools for leading a group of people during a series of activities to achieve a desired outcome (Michel, Stegmaier, & Sonntag, 2010). Global managers must have the ability to recognize what change management actually is. We begin by starting a number of things that change management is not:

- Change management *is not* a stand-alone process used to design a business solution.
- Change management *is not* a process improvement method.
- Change management *is not* a stand-alone technique for improving organizational performance.

Here are what global managers actually do when undertaking innovation through change management (Guah, 2009):

- Change management *is* a method for reducing and managing resistance to change when implementing process, technology, or organizational change.
- Change management *is* the processes, tools, and techniques for managing people when change is actually taking place.
- Change management *is* a necessary component for any organizational performance improvement process to succeed, including programs like: Six Sigma, business process re-engineering, total quality management, organizational development, restructuring and continuous process improvement.

Change management *is* how managers drive the adoption and usage they need to realize business results.

Readiness Assessments

Assessments are tools used by global managers to assess the organization's readiness to change. Readiness assessments can include organizational assessments, culture and history assessments, employee assessments, sponsor assessments, and change assessments (Cohen, Glaser, Calhoun, Bradshaw, & Petrocelli, 2017). Each tool provides the project team with insights into the challenges and opportunities they may face during the change process (Ariño & Ring, 2010; Guah, 2011).

- Assessing the scope of the change provides the manager with answers to the following questions:
  - How big is this change?
  - How many different regions/countries/people are affected?
  - Is it a gradual or radical change?
- Assessing the readiness of the organization impacted by the change provides the manager with answers to the following questions:
  - What is the value of the cultures and languages of the impacted groups?
  - How much change is already going on?
  - What type of resistance can be expected?
- Assessing the scope of the change provides the manager with answers to the following questions:
  - How big is this change?
  - How many countries or legal regulations and policies are affected?
  - Is it a gradual or radical change?
- Assessing the readiness of the organization impacted by the change provides the manager with answers to the following questions:
  - What is the value system and religious practices of the impacted population?
  - How much change is already going on?
  - What type of resistance can be expected?
- Assessing the strengths of your change management team in terms of education background, religious affiliation, ethnicity, and so forth.
- Assessing the change agents and taking the first steps to enable them to effectively lead the change process in different countries and regions.

Communication and Communication Planning

Global managers cannot assume that by giving a speech in one country to only one set of employees, the job will be fully accomplished. However, there are many reasons why employees may not have heard or understood what a global manager is saying the first time around. Even if the employee did hear the manager clearly, that message needs to be repeated six to seven times before the essence of the message is cemented into the minds of employees. Lee and colleagues (2006) suggest that each employee's readiness to hear depends on many factors. Thus, effective communicators have to carefully consider these three components: the audience, what is said, and when it is said.

For example, the first step in change management is building awareness around the need for change and creating a desire among employees for such change. The initial communications are typically designed to create awareness around the business reasons for change and the risk of not changing. Likewise, at each step in the process, communications should be designed to share the right messages at the right time.

To account for the Golden Rule in change management, communication planning must begin with careful analysis of the audiences, composition of key messages, and the timing for those messages. The change management team or project leaders must design a communication plan that addresses the needs of front-line employees, supervisors, and executives. Each audience has particular needs for information based on their role in the implementation of the change.

Roadmap for Change

Extent literature has concluded that managers play a critical patronizing role in change management around the globe (Abbasi, Vassilopoulou, & Stergioulas, 2017; Lee et al., 2006). The change agent must develop a plan for patronizing activities by the global manager to help key business leaders carry out these plans. Patronage by the global manager should be viewed as the most important success factor for any change within a global organization. Global managers cannot confuse the notion of patronizing change with supporting change. The CEO of an international company may support a project, but that is not the same as the CEO patronizing that particular initiative.

Patronage involves active and visible participation by a global manager throughout the change management process. Unfortunately, many executives do not know what this type of patronage looks like. A change agent's role includes helping the global manager do the right things to patronize the project.

Lee and colleagues (2006) suggest that a new product development project is a challenging task in management practice. In project planning, the manager's approach to each individual on the project is a fundamental tool. However, the frequent use of terms like "*product*" and "*activity*" often prove to be confusing and results in inefficiency when managing project tasks. Technology roadmap is used to transform the way managers assign various parts of the project to each employee (Lee et al., 2006). By using the Golden Rule principles, a global manager can align strategic management to project management.

Coaching and Manager Training for Change Management

Global managers always play a key role in managing change. Ultimately, the direct supervisors locally have more influence over the employees' motivation to change than anybody in a global organization. Unfortunately, local supervisors, as a particular category of managers, can be the most difficult to convince of the need for change and can be a source of resistance. It is vital for the change agents, and other important patrons, to gain the support of local supervisors and to build change leadership. Individual change management activities should be used to help these supervisors through the change process (Guah, 2014).

Once global managers and patrons are on board, the change agent should prepare a coaching strategy. They will need to provide training for supervisors including how to use individual change management tools with their employees.

Training and Training Development

Training is the cornerstone for building knowledge about any type of change and the required skills for such change. Change agents and project team members should develop training requirements based on the skills, knowledge, and behaviors necessary to implement the change (Guah, 2011; Woodley, 2014). Global managers must insist on having training requirements as the starting point for the training group or the project team to develop training programs throughout the organization.

Resistance Management

Global managers face resistance from employees and individual supervisors as a normal part of their jobs, as a normal occurrence during a change process. Persistent resistance, however, can threaten the entire project. The change management team needs to identify, understand, and manage resistance throughout the organization. Resistance management is the processes and tools used by global managers with the support of the change agent and patron to manage employee resistance.

Data Collection, Feedback, Analysis, and Corrective Action

Employee involvement is a necessary and integral part of managing changes within a global organization. Considering change management is not a one-way street, feedback from employees is a key element of the change management process. Analysis and corrective action based on this feedback provides a robust cycle for implementing change. The art of receiving this feedback from local employees creates feelings of equality and appreciation—both are important factors of the Golden Rule principles.

Celebrating and Recognizing Success

Various milestones or early successes and long-term wins must be recognized and celebrated publicly for all employees to see. Individual and group recognition are also necessary components of change management in order to cement and reinforce the change in global organizations.

After-action review is always the final and a necessary step in any change management process. This step is the point at which the global manager can stand back from the entire program, evaluate successes and failures, and identify process changes for the next project. This should be viewed as a part of the ongoing, continuous improvement of change management for global organizations and ultimately leads to change competency.

Management practices around the world have advanced beyond basic thinking to include leading God's people in God's way. Some readers may consider this style of management deep because it is structured around the Golden Rule and involves all aspects of leadership. Management by Golden Rule means having a high regard for spiritual influence as you allow God to work through your abilities and capabilities to undertake various management tasks. Through this style of leadership, global managers are demonstrating the propensity to be used by God to transform this world into a modern earth with the principles of the Golden Rule.

The clarity of this framework of management is less precise, not only making new leaders work harder in understanding and meeting their goals, but also having the possibility of creating confusion in some academic disciplines (Guah, 2014). For example, a young manager faced with implementing change at a grocery store and being required to follow the Golden Rule, may express the opinion that it seems as though God only allows changes based on how people are. In order words, this young manager is concluding that God changes how God deals with people based on their needs. It is safe to say that this young manager is not totally wrong. However, a better explanation of implementing changes in a business, based on the Golden Rule, involves the way human's character traits interact with one another during times of change within an organization.

Spiritual principles, also known as *universal laws*, are the basis of success in all areas of life, including business. That's because most problems in life relate to deviations from spiritually principled behavior as opposed to *participation* in the "wrong" things. Being guided by the Golden Rule or religious belief system is an increasingly common practice amongst managers of business all over the globe. However, it remains controversial in some business circles in Western society. As modern society becomes increasingly consumed by reported immoralities amongst top management, it has become imperative for higher education to promote just such a view, partly in support of broad missions of well-known people like the Dalai Lama, Nelson Mandela, and Pope Francis (Dalai Lama, 2011). These leaders have effectively demonstrated that it is possible to place spiritually principled thoughts and actions over belief in rigid doctrine.

REFERENCES TO GOLDEN RULE BY DIFFERENT RELIGIONS?

Research on the study of religions has not always applied the correct attitude to the Golden Rule (Wild & Wild, 2019). Simply put, any researcher studying another religion (other than his/hers) should first try to understand the other's faith as he/she would like his/her own faith to be understood. By implication, the researcher wants people approaching his/her faith, to:

- be prepared to listen carefully, be fair, show respect, and not distort the faith you are trying to study;
- not generalize from a few bad cases (i.e., because one Jew insulted a Hindu does not mean all Jews are bad people);
- not compare the best part of your faith with the worst of another;
- give the faith you are trying to study the benefit of the doubt and not give literal meaning to religious writings (i.e., "It is more difficult for a camel to pass through the eye of needle than for a rich man to enter heaven"; the Bible doesn't literally mean Christians must be very poor); and
- never deny nor exaggerate differences between your faith and the faith you are trying to study.

TABLE 10.1 References to Golden Rule in Global Religions

Religions	Golden Rule Slogans	Dedicated Verses
Buddhism	"Hurt not others in ways that you yourself would find hurtful."	Udana-Varga 5,1
Christianity	"All things whatsoever ye would that men should do to you, do ye so to them; for this is the law and the prophets."	Matthew 7:1
Confucianism	"Do not do to others what you would not like yourself. Then there will be no resentment against you, either in the family or in the state."	Analects 12:2
Hinduism	"This is the sum of duty; do naught onto others what you would not have them do unto you."	Mahabharata 5,1517
Islam	"No one of you is a believer until he desires for his brother that which he desires for himself."	Sunnah
Judaism	"What is hateful to you, do not do to your fellowman. This is the entire Law; all the rest is commentary."	Talmud, Shabbat 3id
Taoism	"Regard your neighbor's gain as your gain, and your neighbor's loss as your own loss."	Tai Shang Kan Yin P'ien
Zoroastrianism	"That nature alone is good which refrains from doing another whatsoever is not good for itself."	Dadisten-I-dinik, 94,5

Source: Christopher Newsletter, 2019.

Despite the conciseness of details about major religions in this chapter (Table 10.1), the reader is invited to reflect on several deeper points that are clearly made and the logical path of managers to ponder all aspects of applying the Golden Rule to leadership. A good leader is someone whose primary responsibility is leading God's people in moving the business world forward, as a valuable part of God's creation. Ariño and Ring (2010) describe this type of leadership style as being:

- guided by Golden Rule which is beyond basic leadership thinking;
- socially responsible management that avoids pitfalls for extreme profitability; and
- rightful management, with the abilities to deliver spiritual qualities such as prayer and moral support.

Business managers are often astonished that something as beautiful as religion quite often brings so much peace to its adherents and can equally be used to fuel hatred and conflict. Common examples of these situations are:

- the situations with Sunnis and Shias in Iraq,
- Buddhists and Muslims in Myanmar,

- the rise of anti-Muslim political parties in Europe, and
- the bastions of liberalism in Denmark.

An Indian businessman once said:

> While we can never stop religious violence, we can prevent it in our businesses and among our employees by remembering and instilling into this organization, the basic ethical principles that are held by all religious traditions—the Golden Rule.

The businessman found religions to be blinded by lust for power, materialism, prestige, and individualism, making it difficult for people of faith to stand together for the purpose of defending and promoting what all religious traditions hold as the highest human and divine values—Golden Rule. But business managers, all around the globe, are initiating and leading dialogues and encounters within and between their employees from different faith communities—helping to build on common values and communicate to a world in desperate need of reestablishing its moral compass, based on the Golden Rule.

One principle found in all religious traditions that each manager wants to obey is the Golden Rule—that people should treat others as they themselves would like to be treated. Each employee wants others to respect his/her life and dignity. Thus, he/she is prepared to respect and protect the life and dignity of others. A global manager aims to have an environment where each employee understands that if others are to respect our freedoms of religion, conscience, thought, and expression, we must respect and defend these freedoms for others. While it is proving impossible for religious leaders to unite in preaching this ethic of reciprocity, business managers can individually work towards implementing the Golden Rule—at the very heart of religion.

Regardless of which religion a business manager belongs to, he/she must set as a primary aim the excellence of human character, the development of human beings who from the depth of themselves, manifest kindness, compassion, truthfulness, courage, and all the virtues associated with the best of humanity—Golden Rule.

All the nonreligious, business managers we encountered during our research, affirmed these principles. They were not only unaware of the foundational principles for all the world's religions but also that all religious traditions provide a strong intellectual, spiritual, and emotional foundation for the Golden Rule. Yet, our research concluded that communicating this reality to the world is an urgent task of all business managers globally.

Research shows that most people grew up encountering only our homogeneous neighborhoods, experiencing only their local cultures and religious traditions, as well as learning what's right and what's wrong from their parents or close family members (Cohen et al., 2017). Meanwhile, the 21st century has ushered in remarkable changes in technology. This has resulted in major advances in the areas of transportation, communication, and the Internet—responsible for the inevitable shrink to the globe. Needless to mention that immigration and multinational companies have produced an unprecedented introduction/mixing of peoples and cultures. One reality of our time is that most neighborhoods have two people living next door to each other from diverse races, religions, ethnic groups, or sexual orientations. Yet people are still finding it very difficult to accept the fact that diversity has replaced homogeneity.

Global managers have to operate in such an environment, forcing them to invent their own individual answers to these three questions:

- How can diverse people learn to work together?
- How can employees living in our multicultural world find common values?
- How can employees living in our multinational world achieve a single goal?

The search for answers to the above question leads to most global managers realizing that despite some sharp differences (e.g., a Catholic woman working on the same team as a Muslim man who is legally married to three wives at the same time), good people from diverse groups tend to have some deep values in common. As long as a global manager can get his/her employees to understand the single shared value of the Golden Rule, and all agree to put this agreement into practice, both the Catholic woman and the Muslim man have a good chance of learning to live together harmoniously. The first responsibility of a global manager is to get all employees to realize the need to understand, celebrate, and practice this common value—Golden Rule—despite their recognizable diversity.

Golden Rule cannot avoid deeper religious and philosophical questions. The global manager must ask him/herself these questions and find answers that make sense to him/her. Managers need to make the Golden Rule a part of their larger framework of business management. The next section demonstrates how the Golden Rule fits quite well into many different business management frameworks. It discusses what the world's religions say about the Golden Rule, including concerns for other people, which the Golden Rule deals within a specific way with certain business management philosophies.

Applying Golden Rule With Possible Diversions

Managers all over the globe have high regard for the influence of religious practices in their organization. Any manager who displays an intentional disregard for the local religious practices, does it at the risk of business productivity, efficiency, and profitability. Businesses exist in a community where the people's behaviors are dictated by the local religious practices; so, ignoring such practices comes with great costs of energy, patience, pride, and so forth. However, a global manager does not necessarily have to be religious. He/she just needs to apply the Golden Rule.

Such managers are considered to be living rather mindlessly—on "autopilot" most of the time. The more mindful global managers become, the more aware they are of higher truths, as they "do business" with the entire world. This also results in better local support, more business growth, and more meaningful life.

Our research also noted the following attitudes of global managers, broken down into different regions of the world. Figure 10.2 (CIA World Factbook, 2010; WorldPress, 2012a; WorldPress, 2012b) shows a Golden Rule framework for global managers with different principles that are common in different regions. Some global managers call this obeying the spiritual laws, personal spiritual principles, spiritual truths, or spiritual management strategies. It should be a part of the manager's approach to life—ways of being, doing, thinking, believing, behaving, and engaging with life that can

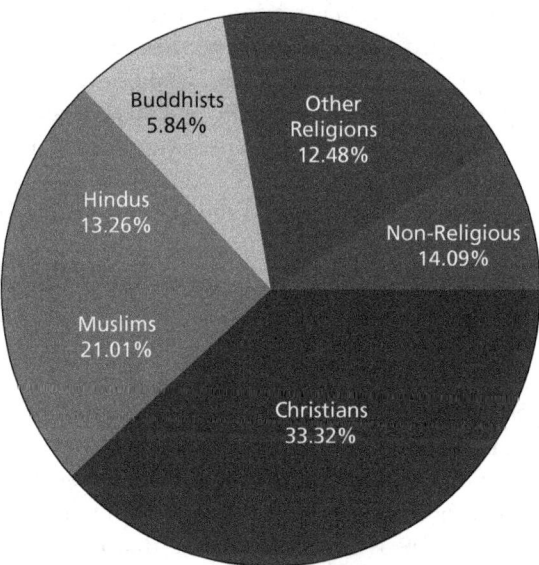

Figure 10.2 World religions by percentage (WordPress, 2012a).

enable him/her to live toward his/her highest potential. Some global managers call this "rules of engagement," considering they are not "religious" in any particular sense. A brief explanation of each principle follows with suitable examples.

In a world where religion is practiced in every region, why can't global managers practice the Golden Rule? The answer to this question is found in the major obstacle to unity in our communities—with divisive people. These are people found in every region in the world, who are willing to consciously ignore what their religions say about the Golden Rule. Instead, they prefer to practice hatred towards others usually because they do not belong to the same religion, race, nationality, or tribe. Any manager who is not prepared to treat his/her employees and customers the same as him/herself, is promoting divisiveness in the business, whether that manager is Christian, Muslim, Jewish, Hindu, or of another religion. Because most managers belong to one religion or another, the solution to having the Golden Rule successfully practiced in every business in the world requires a certain type of harmony between religions around the world. A number of religions have been known to teach a positive application of the Golden Rule (WorldPress, 2012b). For example: What you want done to yourself, should also be done to others. There are other religions that have been known to teach a negative application of the Golden Rule. An example of this is what you do not want done to yourself, should not be done to others. While these two forms of Golden Rule examples may appear different. They are logically equivalent, have identical logical implications, and both lead to the same objective. Some managers consider the latter rather negative because it emphasizes what not to do, while other managers feel it is flawed. The important thing to remember in these examples is that they both have the moral agreement that Golden Rule means treating every human being the same as yourself.

Let's look at a few differences in ways the various world religions refer to the Golden Rules. The Christians, for example, emphasize that a manager should "treat others as he/she wants to be treated." This is about taking positive actions. The Muslim, on the other hand, would emphasize that the manager "desire for others the same as what the manager desires for him/herself." One can see that the former is about action, while the latter is about desires. Obviously, actions are definitely different from desires. Though action and desire have different objectives, a global manager can agree that they are both complementary. Global managers understand morality as being about both actions and desires. Taking into account the various interpretations, there is no single phrase that can ultimately exhaust the Golden Rule. It is therefore possible to describe the Golden Rule far beyond a single principle because it is a family of related principles.

Africa: The Principle of Forgiveness

1. Mr. Kibikuu, a business manager in Tanzania, considered the Golden Rule as forgiveness. For her, it meant forgiving others when they are wronged. Understanding that spiritual and/or religious paths are not excuses for fighting, killing, or war; this is how we forgive ourselves. This is how we are forgiven.
2. Ms. Gbeyon, an executive in Liberia, believed the Golden Rule demands that a manager remains unattached/not permanently bound to present views in order to be open to others' insights and experiences, superseding discoveries, new/deeper realizations, and so forth.
3. Mr. Mohammed in Sudan saw the Golden Rule to be mindful of the present moment; not worrying about the future, not dwelling upon past events.
4. Ms. Nadelah in South Africa considered the Golden Rule as employing perseverance and discipline in the face of obstacles, the biggest of which is self; doing what you know you need to do, when you need to do it, whether you feel like it or not.
5. Ms. Whern, from Republic of Congo, felt the Golden Rule can be achieved through nonattachment to things, people, places, ideas, habits, money, lifestyle, beliefs, and so forth; one must be able to walk away from it all, if necessary, as required by traditional religion and Christianity.

America (North): The Principle of Expectation

1. Mr. Johnson, a retired General in the U.S. Army, found the Golden Rule when seeking opportunities to improve the world by asking, *"How may I serve?"*
2. Ms. Perry, in Canada, believed the Golden Rule was the understanding that hatred and revenge never cease through returned hatred and vengeful intent. Thus, it is about facing hatred with compassion, loving one's enemies, and overtly moving toward equanimity toward all.
3. Mr. Wilson, in the United States, applied the Golden Rule by practicing silence, restraint of tongue, pen, and electronic messaging.
4. Ms. Scott, an American, applied the Golden Rule through freedom of opinions and beliefs of others and by avoiding habitual conformity.
5. Mr. Alston, on the West Coast of America, applied the Golden Rule in his business by refraining from egotistical descriptions of one's own spirituality. This meant keeping his spiritual practices to himself when dealing with his employees and choosing to lead by example. He insisted it is not to discourage teaching spirituality

or spiritual practices to others, especially when feedback/advice/thoughts are requested.

America (South): The Principle of Generosity

1. Mr. Torres, a Columbian, felt that the Golden Rule is practicing mindfulness meditation on a daily basis to help you interact with others.
2. Mr. Rivera, a Mexican, felt the Golden Rule is practicing quiet contemplation to develop and deepen insight on other people's lives.
3. Ms. Carrillo, from Brazil, found the Golden Rule to be out of service orientation because our lives, including all business activity, should be focused on providing *real service* to others.
4. Mr. Tapia, from Venezuela, applied the Golden Rule in his business by practicing discernment, where he sincerely tries to consider the nature of reality in every situation and the way things really are when he interacts with his employees. He felt the world would improve if everyone should contemplate on moving from where they are toward freedom from attachments, fears, patterns, habits, and so forth.
5. Mr. Marquez, from Chile, suggested that the Golden Rule is deflating the ego, the result of spiritual practice over time and the development of self and others.

Asia: The Principle of Gratitude

1. Ms. Bandodkar, from India, saw the Golden Rule as a life with integrity which means being the same person no matter whom the manager is in the presence of.
2. Mr. Kahn, from Pakistan, presented the Golden Rule by expressing genuine compassion and wanting as much or more *for others* as you do for yourself.
3. Ms. Luim, from China, demonstrated the Golden Rule by expressing gratitude and appreciation at all times. He thinks people should remain grateful for everything and everyone that comes in their lives. Similarly, he chooses to be grateful for what *others* have in *their lives*.
4. Ms. Yasmine, from Singapore, showed the Golden Rule by extending goodwill and practicing the right action not only toward humanity, but to nature in its entirety.
5. Mr. Kim, from South Korea suggested the Golden Rule is the ability for a manager to demonstrate common-sense stewardship of nature/creation in its entirety. He explains this through the acknowledgment of a critical need to recognize, understand, and address the spiritual dynamics at the root of environmental degradation.

Australia: The Principle of Humility

1. Mr. Hawes, from Melbourne, used the Golden Rule to look deeply at her thought process, her actions, and other people with an eye of compassion.
2. Ms. Bennett, in Brisbane, has always treated others as she likes to be treated. She considered the Golden Rule as a way to extend kindness and love to others in both thought and deed.
3. Mr. Pratt, in Canberra, constantly practiced honesty as his interpretation of the Golden Rule. By telling the truth, and avoiding lies, giving your services to others, acting right, and helping people as anonymously as possible, he found a great way to practice humility.
4. Ms. Brittingham, from Sydney, practiced humility as her attempt of obeying the Golden Rule. It is a clear recognition of who and what she is, followed by a sincere attempt to become what she could be, avoiding the temptation of comparing herself to others.
5. Mr. Roger, in Perth, believed that following the Golden Rule avoids any rigid or fundamentalist worldviews that declare all others to be wrong. As a global manager, he is expected to avoid *us vs. them* thinking. He must avoid the belief that members of other race, religions, spiritual practices, culture, or political affiliation can never be right. A global manager who practices any type of elitism does so at his/her peril.

Europe (Eastern): The Principle of Optimism

1. Mr. Timakova, a Russian economist, used the Golden Rule to focus upon unity, oneness, and sharing rather than division, separateness, and differences. He looks at the similarities in people and focuses on the common ground each individual brings to the table.
2. Ms. Hershkovitz, from Poland, characterized the Golden Rule as promoting open-mindedness, flexibility, willingness to learn and be able to objectively explore and study, rather than blindly accepting whatever you are told you "should" do or "ought" to believe.
3. Mr. Gonslavka, from Croatia, considered the Golden Rule as expressing hope and maintaining a positive outlook to business, even in the face of personal despair. It empowers a global manager to deeply understand that there is no need to worry about little things going on around him/her because there is always a bigger picture to consider in the long run.
4. Ms. Kowalski, of Belarus, simply put the Golden Rule as the ability to practice what one preaches and that is the most critical aspect of having integrity.

5. Mr. Brizek, from Romania, suggested the principle of the Golden Rule is basically the common-sense application of critical thought to potentially consequential views and activities.

Europe (Western:) The Principle of Intention

1. Ms. Kwast, in The Netherlands, has seen the Golden Rule in practice several times in his life. It makes global managers aware of the anguish caused by intolerance and zealotry. That helps a global manager choose to remain open-minded and teachable, even pliable like clay, or like a child, as opposed to being rigid and closed-minded.
2. Mr. McCormack, in Ireland, used the Golden Rule so many times during the difficult years of political turmoil between the Irish Republic Army and the Unionist/British government. The Golden Rule guided few decent managers during that time to be peacemakers. The Golden Rule not only allowed him to be a giver to people on the other side of the political divide, but also encouraged pacifism and nonviolence. It facilitated him taking a dedicated stance against the war.
3. Mr. Williams, in Wales, believed that the Golden Rule may have formulated his understanding that coming to one's self and moving through increasingly deeper and meaningful spiritual experiences and awakenings is a completely *subjective experience* which cannot be directly taught or transferred to others. He is convinced that words themselves are only symbols which are like a finger pointing at the moon, though the finger is not the moon. Obeying the Golden Rule is always the result of direct experience of the God, not merely obeying the law of the land or following any specific religious principle.
4. Ms. Liasi, from Italy, interpreted the Golden Rule as deeply realizing that *everything is connected, and no one is truly separate* from others or from anything. Ms. Liasi thinks the Golden Rule is being aware of and being in control of our own deep connection to oneness, to "the Source," and not having a need to define or completely understand it, regardless of what one prefers to name that it (God, Allah, Tao, universal intelligence, spiritual connection, Creator, creative force, etc.) and consequently demonstrating this in both *thought* and *action*.
5. Mr. Hierra, from Spain, simply translated the Golden Rule as practicing love, tolerance, and acceptance. That is partly responsible for his power to refrain from criticizing, condemning, and complaining about the world around him.

Middle East: The Principle of Relevance

1. Mr. Farjadma, from Iran, felt global managers should think about the Golden Rule and be aware of the hardship caused by imposing his/her own views upon others, refraining from forcing others to adopt a set of beliefs through any means whatsoever, be it propaganda, indoctrination, money, authority, and so forth.
2. Mr. Eid, from Lebanon, utilized the Golden Rule to display courage in the face of fear, especially when he needs to act out of love rather than fear.
3. Ms. Nodine, in Israel, used the Golden Rule to refrain from gossip, when speaking of an individual that is not present. It guides her to speak about that person as though he/she was present.
4. Ms. Ryab, from Saudi Arabia, believed the Golden Rule helps a global manager to not consider anything personally, be it *any* statement or action of another person. Especially in an environment where many consider tribal, political, or sports chanting, historical saying, or even proverb are considered offensive.
5. Mr. Al-Rashed, from Kuwait, considered the Golden Rule as doing what one says and what one does. It is the act of being impeccable with one's word.

One common lesson from all these global managers is that the Golden Rule emphasizes that every day is a gift and every transaction in business or interaction with another individual or group of people is a gift. Therefore, a manager should take nothing for granted in the time that his/her business is in existence. The experience of feeling grateful—generally, generically, and specifically—seems to clear away much of the petty, day-to-day crankiness so many managers experience—the feelings of annoyance, impatience, resentment, anger, and indignation. There is something very uplifting about managing an organization with a sense of gratitude, when the manager first arrives in the office, leads the first meeting, signs the first contract, or submits the first tax return with a positive balance sheet. Gratitude for all the good things that happen in business resulting from the commitment of employees, and gratitude for all that *has not* gone in the way of the business during a particular period.

INNOVATION VERSUS OBEYING GOLDEN RULE

Research has shown a consistent struggle to meet up with all the true characteristics for fair leadership following the Golden Rule, though many are struggling to become that type of leader. True Godly character comes from spending time in the presence of God, not from struggling to attain that character. That's because it requires self-examination, which is good, but it also requires the leader to seek repentance and constant worshiping in the presence of God. Evidence from religions demonstrates that only in the presence of the greatest good that one's heart is transformed to be like God. This can give the manager required motivation and strength to be a good servant for God's people.

Most global managers live in countries where development and progress in the lives of its citizens have been seriously hampered by corruption. Damoah and colleagues (2018) conclude that corruption is a constant concern for countries that face economic problems. While the extant literature has been devoted to this topic, the repeated discussions have focused mainly on the relationship between corruption and variables, such as economic development, social effects, innovation, firm management quality, gross domestic product, returns on investment, increase in government budget, political discontent, instability, and violence, rule-violating intentions, democracy, and inequality (Damoah et al., 2018). To date, there has been no widely published work on the impact of corruption on the Golden Rule.

Not only does corruption undermine national development, and the implementation of very expensive government projects or programs, but also has a negative impact on all other parts of civil society in a given country (Sundstrom, 2016).

Locatelli et al. (2017) found that government officials go into leadership positions with the intention of not only making money for personal gain, but also to use the money to support their political party. That inevitably leads to inflating contract sums through connivance with contractors. The process of awarding government contracts also seems to breed corrupt practices. As a result of corruption, contract awards in most development countries involve a long process where contractors and government officials engage the services of unofficial middlemen who take a certain percentage—usually 10% of the contract sums. Needless to say, the contractors obviously add the additional cost on to the total project cost, making the taxpayer bear the costs of such corrupt practices.

People in developing countries constantly talk about corruption in projects because those projects are obvious and visible, although corruption affects every fabric of these countries' way of life.

The findings from Damoah et al. (2018) not only provide a theoretical framework for the assessment of the relationships that exist between corruption and government project failure with multiple failure criteria, but also convey the need for global managers to follow the Golden Rule to make both strategic and operational decisions. Every person, male and female, from every race and nationality is made as a precious image bearer of

God and is equal before God. This means primarily that humans are made by God to take dominion over the earth reflecting the rule of God on the earth. Leaders are therefore moral creatures, consciously knowing God's moral law, in ways that animals do not.

All the major religions in our world teach man not to "hate" anyone, rather, to be compelled by the love of God to love his/her fellowmen. The Christians continuously praise God for a leader, like Jesus, who managed to love and forgive those who killed him. Following his example, Christians strive to walk in a manner of love towards all, a classical demonstration of the Golden Rule.

CONCLUSION

Looking around the business world today, one truly acknowledges the extensive efforts required by global managers to overcome prejudices and insensitivities existing in business. These can also be overcome by acknowledging and accepting that each of us belongs to the same human race. A harmonious workplace can be accomplished by practicing the Golden Rule principles at our places of work. The simple fact is that global managers need to help their employees to imagine him/herself in the place of the other person, and then test whether he/she can accept the treatments received in return. If both parties follow this, everyone will learn to get along well—in essence, the Golden Rule principles.

This chapter has shown how the Golden Rule model, used by global managers around the world, comes with stylistic and cultural differences. Here is a famous African proverb commonly repeated by teenagers on backyard soccer fields: "Any person who plans to use a pointed stick to pinch a rat, should first try it on him/herself to know how it truly feels" (Author Unknown, though West Africans consider it as part of Yoruba African Tradition in Nigeria). This African proverb presents a vivid and concrete presentation of the Golden Rule in the workplace. There is nothing abstract or general about the meaning here. All global managers can take lessons from this African proverb. It is all about how to treat each person as a human being, through the way we treat other sentient beings. This is a great example of how the Golden Rule is rooted in some local cultures.

Another reason the Golden Rule differs significantly between religions around the world is how religious leaders have the habit of emphasizing subtle differences in wording between Golden Rule in their own individual traditions. Translations can vary significantly as most religions are in various languages.

Certain religions use parables and stories to express basic insights into the Golden Rule, providing greater technical precision due to leadership desires to withstand objections and to facilitate the application of the Golden Rule more easily to difficult situations. Regardless of variations in interpretation of Golden Rule practices, it is vital to accept that each religion emphasizes that people learn to live together in peace—the essence of the Golden Rule.

Five scientific reasons why managers have accepted to follow Golden Rules globally are:

- *Religious:* God implanted the Golden Rule in the hearts of each individual around the world.
- *Biological:* Evolutionary history explains that the Golden Rule has been hardwired into the genes and brains of human beings.
- *Psychological:* As the world goes through various stages of universal development, the heart of each person leads toward the Golden Rule, especially in the lives of individuals performing leadership roles.
- *Sociological:* History has documented many instances where societies have needed the Golden Rule to continue in existence.
- *Logical:* It has also been documented that most managers have cognitive dissonance to avoid inconsistency and of course the Golden Rule forbids an inconsistent environment for thriving business.

In this wake-up experience for managers globally, the author has provided both exhilarating and enlightening examples to aid in the discovery of a solution for hatred towards another religion and a light injection of some blissful international business leadership.

The author grew up under a theology that stressed holiness by human effort, and it is only after suicidal guilt that he finally began to understand how God transforms us through His grace. Identity must precede activity. The lesson in this chapter is that managing God's children, anywhere in the world, requires tapping into one's heart for the interpretation of the Golden Rule. That means putting GOD first in order to achieve success in business. A simple message that many people are struggling to follow from day to day in the business world.

REFERENCES

Abbasi, M., Vassilopoulou, P., & Stergioulas, L. (2017). Technology roadmap for the Creative Industries. *Creative Industries Journal, 10*(1), 40–58.

Ariño, A., & Ring, P. S. (2010). The role of fairness in alliance formation. *Strategic Management Journal, 31*(10), 1054–1087.

Cohen, P. J., Glaser, B. A., Calhoun, G. B., Bradshaw, C. P., & Petrocelli, J.V. (2017). Examining readiness for change: A preliminary evaluation of the University of Rhode Island change assessment with incarcerated adolescents. *Journal of Measurement and Evaluation in Counseling and Development, 38*(1), 45–62.

Christopher Newsletter in Teaching Values. (2019). *The universality of the golden rule in the world religions.* Retrieved from www.teachingvalues.com/goldenrule.html

CIA World Factbook. (2010). *The world factbook.* http://cia.gov/the-world-factbook/field/religions/

Dalai Lama. (2011). *Beyond eeligion: Ethics for a while world.* New York, NY: Houghton Mifflin Harcourt.

Damoah, I. S., Akwei, C. A., Amoako, I. O., & Botchie, D. (2018). Corruption as a source of government project failure in developing countries: Evidence from Ghana. *Project Management Journal, 49*(3), 17–33.

Guah, M. W. (2009). *Managing very large I.T. projects.* Hershey, PA: Information Systems Research.

Guah, M. W. (2011). Why doesn't Information Systems Vision exist in the Healthcare Sector? In S. A. Brown & M. Brown (Eds.), *Ethical issues and security monitoring trends in global healthcare: Technological advancements* (pp. 207–217). Hershey, PA: IGI Global.

Guah, M. W. (2014). *Enterprise information systems: Theory and real cases.* Los Angeles, CA: BVT.

Lee, H., Liu, C., & Lee, M (2006). Aligning the business roadmap to technology roadmap for managing the new product development project. *Journal of the Chinese Institute of Industrial Engineers, 23*(6), 449–457.

Locatelli, G., Mariani, G., Sainati, T., & Greco, M. (2017). Corruption in public projects and megaprojects: There is an elephant in the room! International. *Journal of Project Management, 35*(3), 252–268.

Michel, A., Stegmaier, R., & Sonntag, K. (2010). Scratch your back—you scratch mine: Do procedural justice and organizational identification matter for employees' cooperation during change? *Journal of Change Management, 10*(1), 41–59.

Oppelt, J. (2012, July 10). 15 great principles shared by all religions. *Integral Church.* https://integralchurch.wordpress.com/2012/07/10/15-great-principles-shared-by-all-religions/

Specht, J., Kuonath, A., Pachler, D., Weisweiler, S., & Frey, D. (2017). How change agents' motivation facilitates organizational change: Pathways through meaning and organizational identification. *Journal of Change Management, 18*(3),198–217.

Sundstrom, A. (2016). Corruption and violations of conservation rules: A survey experiment with resource users. *World Development, 85,* 73–83.

Wild, J. J., & Wild, K. L. (2019). *International business: The challenges of globalization.* London, England: Pearson.

Woodley, M. (2014). *Billy Graham: Leading with love: 5 timeless principles for effective leaders.* Grand Haven, MI: Waterfall Press.

WordPress. (2012a). *World of religions* [Photo]. Retrieved from https://integralchurch.files.wordpress.com/2012/07/worldofreligions_4edd4e8a5cf89.jpg

WordPress. (2012b). *Countries of global religions* [Photo]. Retrieved from https://integralchurch.files.wordpress.com/2012/07/world-religions-infographic.jpg

CHAPTER 11

(WHAT'S) THE MATTER WITH BABEL?

Daniel Q. Vass-Goosby

THE TOWER OF BABEL

In Judaism and consequently Christianity, the story of the Tower of Babel is presented. Though presented with no context and only containing nine verses, this short story has been recanted for thousands of years. Humans seek to describe the state of confusion (and unproductivity) that ensues when people are unable to communicate effectively. Genesis Chapter 11, verses 1–9 in the Jewish Torah and Christian Bible read as follows:

> Now the whole world had one language and a common speech. As people moved eastward, they found a plain in Shinar and settled there. They said to each other, "Come, let's make bricks and bake them thoroughly." They used brick instead of stone, and tar for mortar. Then they said, "Come, let us build ourselves a city, with a tower that reaches to the heavens, so that we may make a name for ourselves; otherwise we will be scattered over the face of the whole earth." But the Lord came down to see the city and the tower the people were building. The Lord said, "If as one people speaking the same language they have begun to do this, then nothing they plan to do will be impossible

for them. Come, let us go down and confuse their language so they will not understand each other." So the Lord scattered them from there over all the earth, and they stopped building the city. That is why it was called Babel—because there the Lord confused the language of the whole world. From there the Lord scattered them over the face of the whole earth. (Holy Bible, New International Version)

An essentially similar story occurs in the Holy Qur'an, the sacred scriptures of Islam. In the Holy Qur'an (28:38–40) the writer shares an order that Pharaoh gave one of his subjects:

38. Pharaoh said: O Chiefs! No god do I know for you but myself. Therefore, O Haman! Light me a (kiln to bake bricks) out of clay, and build me a lofty palace, that I may mount up to the God of Moses. But as far as I am concerned, I think (Moses) is a liar! 39. And he was arrogant and insolent in the land, beyond reason—He and his hosts. They thought that they would not have to return to Us! 40. So We seized him and his hosts, and We flung them into the sea. Now behold what was the end of those who did wrong! (Ali, 2016)

This chapter presents metaphor's importance for effective human communication about individually and collectively perceived realities by applying quantum mechanics to the communication process. Its eventual goal is to show that when matter or "reality" is seen accurately in its fluidity, instead of in an oversimplified state of static reality, our hopes for more effective communication and collaboration can be better realized.

> *An idea is a point of departure and no more. As soon as you elaborate it, it becomes transformed by thought.*
> —Pablo Picasso

Man perpetually searches for answers, which inevitably leads to more questions. Driven by ego, he holds tight to his ideas and ideals, resisting change at all cost. A primitive fear of chaos dictates the nature in which mankind has evolved to strive for stability. In demonstrating his certainty about reality, man forms perspective, structure, culture, and society. Although briefly capable of collaboration, man-made structures (conceptual, physical, societal) habitually disintegrate into stagnation, followed by disorder. While terrified at its prospect, chaos seems to be inevitable under the currently accepted frames of thought. Through a quantum framework and an integral lens, chaos is a context which can illuminate a deeper connectedness than previously thought to exist.

The state of the world is in disarray as it has been for centuries. This is evident in the seemingly inevitable rise and fall of civilizations throughout history. Due in part to the spectrum of languages, cultures, beliefs, and ideals, and so forth, humans struggle to understand each other at a fundamental level, thus confusing perception of individual and collective purpose. Spirituality and science are complementary modes of correlating meaning and reality; both of which mankind has fragmented in our attempts to conceptualize existence.

Indeed, humanity can attribute collective disorientation to this tendency toward fragmentation. Division and fragmentation seem to derive from man's desire to regard context in reality, through which the knowledge attained is employed in order to expedite processes. Fragmentation in and of itself, is not superfluous when applied to simple systems, whereby cause and effect are closely related in terms of time. Additionally, conceptual evaluation calls for an appropriate separation and understanding of the basic elements contained therein.

Man's designation as being separate from reality is perhaps the most fundamental presentation of such fragmentation. That is, the pattern of thought developed through which "I" am distinct from "you," and therefore exist independently of my environment confounds the totality of reality when experienced solely through said paradigm. If, then, unaware of the nature of his effect on reality, as Bohm (1980) expresses, "Man ceases to regard the resulting divisions as merely useful or convenient and begins to see and experience himself and his world as actually constituted of separately existent fragments" (p. 3).

The issue is not fragmentation itself, but the widespread acceptance of this methodology which is fundamental to existence at all levels (Bohm, 1980). From the genesis of creation, man has demonstrated the awareness of this fundamental attribution error, communicating such through religious and scientific texts. In other words, plenty of evidence exists which exhibits man's desire for wholeness and harmony (Bohm, 1980). The challenge is not in realizing the need for a major paradigm shift, but in employing practically viable solutions which emphasize scope and context.

The current worldview operates under a mechanistic paradigm, which is perpetuated by Western society's acceptance of mechanistic scientific principles. This reduction and analysis of "parts" within this machine denotes the existence of complex hierarchical relationships, and attributes error to faulty "parts," whereas, taking the dynamics and temporality of cause and effect into account, the systemic nature of occurrences becomes apparent. While hierarchies exist in nature, the order of which is determined through a dynamic, contextual process, reality is dynamic/quantum in nature, and the state of matter is determined by the method of observation.

Being that basic scientific ideology has led Western thought, and therefore society through its peaks and valleys since the Age of Enlightenment, it is evident that our fundamental view of matter and fields affects respective and collective views of reality. Because accepted paradigms cause us to view cause and effect as a linear process, and although much research exists on the topic, many who may be averse to change will view this connection as a stretch; however, physicists, such as David Bohm and organizational theorists, such as Margaret Wheatley assert that our view of reality affects our ideas of change.

By abandoning a perspective based solely in fragmentation, and to avoid taking a strictly holistic worldview, integral theory was born. A shift to an inclusive perspective is the first of many necessary actions, as our accepted view of reality (worldview) determines our metaphors, which are instrumental in verbal and written communication. Hence, Newtonian physics is the basis upon which we establish metaphorical communication through language. Emergent thinkers have used quantum mechanics to prove that our perception of problems and phenomena determine how they present themselves, and that although humans have a propensity to predetermine meaning for the sake of expediency, structure presents itself through observation of the connection between aspects of the quantum or chaotic state over a given time period.

Since the nature of reality is quantum, when properly observed, the connections that exist appear to exist throughout holonic systems. Wilbur's AQAL model can be used as a practical, perceptual kaleidoscope through which to view phenomena while considering the quantum, holonic view of reality. Similarly, Quinn's competing values framework gives various forms which organizational culture might present. With chaos manifesting as disorder within society's broken systems, authentic leadership is needed in order for humanity to further innovate toward change, and to build sustainable conceptual organizational and cultural systems. True leaders first look within and seek to resolve organizational and systemic issues through proper discernment, and contextual application of principles.

THE WESTERN MACHINE

Western society operates within a mechanistic worldview, through which processes and structures are equated to those qualities designating a machine as such. The acceptance of analysis as the dominant thought pattern has led the worldview into a paradigm wherein reality is mechanistic in nature. Therefore, work was mechanized as each task was broken down and analyzed according to its function and subsequently mechanized, bringing about the existence of assembly lines and factories. This perspective led to the mechanization of workers and the dehumanization of work, which is a paradigm divergent from systems thinking. The mechanization of workers has led to "lack of obligation, commitment, and motivation" within organizations, which has caused a decline in work productivity (Johanessen, OiAasen, & Olsen, 1999, p. 24). As it stands, work productivity has reached its limit within the current analytical, mechanistic, system which affects (and is affected by) economics and technology (Ackoff, 1994; Johanessen, Oiaisen, & Olsen,1999; Senge, 1991; Thurow, 1997).

Conversely, systems thinking relies on synthesis, in which it is necessary to (a) expand the system, (b) understand the larger system which the system in focus is a part of, and (c) disintegrate the entire system in order to understand the functioning of the individual systems. Synthesis begins with understanding the given system as a part of a larger system. Synthesis then calls for the understanding of the larger system, its parts and function, by "disintegrating" its communicative systems in order to disrupt the system. The purpose is to evoke authentic communication (Luhman, 1992). The systems approach focuses on understanding the organization based on the ability to explain it in relation to its environment, and its parts. Understanding as to why the system functions the way it does is also a major focus. The context of explaining an organization is outside and above itself as far as its relationship to the overarching system. Anasynthesis (analysis + synthesis) is the methodology upon which systems thinking is predicated and is the mechanism by which reductionism and expansionism are duly avoided (Johanessen, Olaisen, & Olsen, 1999).

Pragmatism and functionalism dominate the purview of Western thought. This mechanistic paradigm can be traced back to the Age of Enlightenment, which birthed an unprecedented level of technological and societal innovation. While functionality was put at the forefront of meaning during this time period, the conceptual fragmentation of cognition began with the Ancient Greeks. The genesis of conventional Western thought practices saw Plato and Aristotle's discussions regarding knowledge and nature evolve into dialogue concerning memory and thought. Philosophy would then present as two distinct ideologies wherein, according to Anderson (2010), "the two positions were *empiricism*, which held that all knowledge comes from experience, and *nativism*, which held that children come into the world with a great deal of innate knowledge" (p. 6, emphasis in original). Anderson also describes that this debate raged on throughout the centuries of Enlightenment in which empiricist philosophers including Berkeley, Hume, Locke, and Mill diverged from nativist thinkers Descartes and Kant, and "during this long period of philosophical debate, such sciences as astronomy, physics, chemistry, and biology developed markedly" (p. 6). Perhaps because scientists and philosophers exhibit the peak of humanity's intellectual capacity, practices employed in order to understand external reality were then applied internally, which manifested in societal perception and function.

In the wake of such evident benefit to a view of reality based primarily in functionality, mankind began to adhere to seemingly unbreakable laws of existence, and subsequently, as stated by Wheatley (1994) "Organized work and knowledge based on our beliefs about this predictable universe" (p. 28). Such a paradigm was extremely effective during a period of Western domination. Societies thrived, and various discoveries were made, upon which

Western civilization would base key processes. Similar to Greek philosophy, the Newtonian paradigm was extremely effective for centuries, but stagnated when applied to new realms, which called for new solutions. Unfamiliar circumstances created by unprecedented events inspired the theory of relativity, and quantum theory. Through context, it is apparent that human and societal adoption of ideologies shape and form knowledge (Bohm, 1980).

Traditional thought (mechanistic thinking, linear thought) relies on analysis in order to understand organizations and phenomena. Johanessen, Olaisen, and Olsen (1999) explain that, within analysis, one must: (a) split up the system, (b) examine each part separately, (c) aggregate the parts in order to understand the whole. Analysis calls for the researcher to split the "machine" into its individual parts, so as to observe, define, and understand them separately, via the relationship between parts; and then to combine the functions of the parts, in order to understand the entire system. This results in functional knowledge about the system, and its structure (p. 27).

The nature of boundaries becomes a focal point in a world depicted as a machine. Under such a paradigm, organizations, like machines, designate roles for people or "parts," which limit their responsibilities according to deeply authoritative principles (Wheatley, 1994, p. 30). Throughout history, with respect to society, man fragmented itself into classes predicated upon notions of authority. This relationship between oppressor and oppressed is the dominant theme in Western history. An already fragmented view of reality manifested in society as class systems, which were meant to promote order and efficiency. Marx and Engels (1848) explain that this perpetual conflict ends each time "either in a revolutionary reconstitution of society at large, or in the common ruin of the contending classes" (p. 15). History shows that the very same focus on boundaries, originally meant to promote order, are inevitably dissolved.

During the industrial revolution, as stated by Marx and Engels (1848), "Steam and machinery revolutionized industrial production. The place of manufacture was taken by the giant, Modern Industry, the place of the industrial middle class by industrial millionaires, the leaders of the whole industrial armies, the modern bourgeois" (p. 15). Originally meant to abolish the feudal caste system, bourgeois society simply gave rise to a new set of classes governed again by the nature of power and oppression. Increased trade between nations led to new markets. These new markets would increase the demand placed on industrial production, rendering the old feudal system, characterized by closed guilds, obsolete. Increased demand gave way to a manufacturing system, which then combined with proprietary technology to produce an industrial system the likes of which the word had not yet seen.

Western society progressed exponentially during the 20th century, a time that saw a shift from industry ruled by a feudal system of closed elite groups, to a market driven culture. The early 1900s was a period of vigorous growth and progress, leading to great affluence. This period was characterized by the rise of great individual industrial leaders: Henry Ford, Frederick Taylor. The first two management models were created... the rational goal model: productivity and profit are the ultimate criteria for the effectiveness of the organization. The goal–resources theory underlying this approach is based on the conviction that clear leadership produces productive results. The manager's task is to be a firm director and producer. (Robert E. Quinn's Competing Values Framework, n.d., n.p.)

The second, termed the internal process model, prioritized descriptive processes such as responsibility and measurement. Hierarchy and rigidity characterized organizational culture during this era. The Industrial Revolution and the years following shaped production for years to come. Although resulting in major wars, the ever-expanding market driven culture, along with the mechanization of work and workers facilitated Western economic and military dominance worldwide. Man's need to exhibit control over his environment is a hallmark of modern Western culture.

ENTROPY

Functional understanding of power derives from the notion that reality exists as a set of closed systems, which inevitably wear down and cease to operate. Machines are closed systems which produce work via energy, the nature of which is determined by the position and interaction of its parts.

If, in fact, life reflects the inner workings of a machine, eventuality maintains that production will, at some point, halt. Put scientifically, this state is termed in the second law of thermodynamics, as equilibrium. Stickland (2002), defines this eventuality in accordance with the second law of thermodynamics, in which

> the entropy of a closed system will increase with time. As a consequence, entropy will in part determine the direction of natural change in a closed system... Most changes require energy to move the system from one state to another and therefore low entropy is usually necessary if change is to be achieved—particularly when little external intervention and environmental change is possible. (p. 222)

Wheatley (1994) expounds that production will come to an end at

> the point at which the system has exhausted all of its capacity for change, done its work, and dissipated its productive capacity into useless entropy. (Entropy is an inverse measure of a system's capacity for change. The more entropy there is, the less the system is capable of changing). (p. 76)

Pragmatists view chaos as wholly undesirable, and view equilibrium as a means to maintaining systemic entropy. Through this perspective, the ultimate state of a machine which ceases to operate effectively is one of chaos. Change and entropy are conceptually opposed through a mechanistic paradigm, therefore change is viewed as a predictor of impending chaos, whereas entropy is then a result of behaviors that promote equilibrium. Life, when viewed as a closed system, is predicated upon a fear of change, and ultimately chaos. Ironically, futile human attempts at willfully controlling reality actually promote chaos, especially within systems that do not recognize its value.

Being that Newton's third law of motion is, "For every action (force) in nature there is an equal and opposite reaction," Western society, by and large, views cause and effect as maintaining a linear relationship in which the two elements are temporally adjacent. Accepted views of organization necessitate authority and control, facilitated through predesignated hierarchical systems that reduce people into roles, and responsibilities into functions. In conceptualizing organization, humans emulate their understanding of reality, hence Wheatley's (1994) concept that "the machine imagery of the cosmos was translated into organizations as an emphasis on material structure and multiple parts" (p. 29). This ontology is reflected in Western spiritual practices, as it is accepted that a divine entity constructed and operates this complex machine in which we exist. To summarize Wheatley (1994), the "creator," who exists separate from "His" creation, is rational, and operates in accordance with simple laws, by which cause and effect are simplified.

Reductionist viewpoints led to society's supposition that reality is controllable (p. 22). If then, cause and effect is linear, and reality is governed by rules, so too would be the relationships between all of its parts. In utilizing this functional philosophy, one would accept that authority is the structure by which collisions between different elements are directed into processes which promote equilibrium, as chaos is then an utterly undesirable state.

What appears as chaos are often dynamics too complex and widespread to predict. Due to sheer scope, simple systemic loops have overlapped throughout Western society and all of its networks that create unpredictable dynamics. Modern society functions systemically as a result of extended time delays between implementation of institutions or procedures meant to affect an inherent cause, and the appearance of evidence pertaining to the nature of the effects which have occurred. Dynamics occur within systems, due to the interaction between two types of feedback loops. Positive (or self-reinforcing) feedback loops amplify systemic occurrences, whereas negative (or self-correcting) feedback loops promote entropy. In context with society, although only positive and negative loops are at play, thousands of combinations of loops exist through a variety of time delays, nonlinearities, and accumulations. Strictly functional approaches have not been adequate in analyzing these dynamics; and likewise, as Sterman (2000) explains, "Intuition may enable us to infer the dynamics of isolated loops... But when multiple loops interact, it is not so easy to determine what the dynamics will be" (p. 14). Hierarchy is evident through observation and analysis of systems through which cause and effect interact in only two ways; however, predicting which structures the products of said dynamics within complex systems can present is not possible through a fractured lens.

METAPHOR

The greatest thing by far is to be a master of metaphor; it is the one thing that cannot be learnt from others; and it is also a sign of genius, since a good metaphor implies an intuitive perception of the similarity in the dissimilar.
—Aristotle

Humans must fundamentally reevaluate the metaphors upon which linguistic communication is constructed in order to properly understand, communicate, and demonstrate the true nature of reality. Davidson (1978) defines metaphor as "a dreamwork of language and, like all dreamwork, its interpretation reflects as much on the interpreter as on the originator... all communication by speech assumes the interplay of inventive construction and inventive construal (p. 31). Humans, through cognitive processes, extrapolate reality into elements with which we construct meaning. Metaphor is an essential vehicle through which humans explore our relationship to reality, and convey meaning to each other through linguistic communication. Language is inherently metaphorical, in that it is employed in a collective attempt to analyze and convey the relationship between how one perceives reality, and what actually exists.

Fragmentation presents through accepted linguistic construction, in that,

> the subject-verb-object structure of modern languages implies that all action arises in a separate subject, and acts either on a separate object, or else reflexively on itself. This pervasive structure leads in the whole of life to a function that divides the totality of existence into separate entities, which are considered to be essentially fixed and static in their nature. (Bohm, 1980, pg. xiv)

The general structure exhibited by linguistic communication metaphorically represents the human cognitive processes by which sensory feedback is deconstructed and synthesized, in order to create meaning. Intellectuals such as George Lakoff have conceptualized the cognitive implications of metaphorical usage, developing a model that "conceives of metaphor as a process of 'mapping' from a source domain to some target domain"

(Kirby, 1997, pp. 517–554). This model represents a perspective regarding the rationality of dynamics between human sensory understanding of what is and what is perceived. Given that the cognitive nature of language construction reflects perspective and is simultaneously the primary means by which humans communicate intrinsic and collective perspective, a worldview constructed by alternate definitions of reality will radically alter modes of communication. It also alters human perception of dynamics existing among elements, structures, and systems at all levels of reality.

George Lakoff and Mark Johnson (1980), through their research regarding linguistics, expressed that the system by which humans conceptualize reality is innately metaphorical. We organize various intellectual matters according to these conceptual systems, and as such, they structure perception, navigation, and relationships. Humans are ignorant to many of the ways we exist, in that many of our actions occur more or less instinctively. Through observance of linguistic communication, behavioral motivations can be examined. They both operate via the same conceptual systems.

The concept of the word, "argument," is examined through the expression, "argument is war," which is expressed linguistically and systemically within cultures and societies—for example, the statements, "Your claims are indefensible"; "I demolished his argument"; and "He attacked every weak point in my argument." Lakoff and Johnson (1980) discuss that arguments are not simply talked about in terms of victory and defeat; rather, Western culture operates through dynamics which support this metaphor such that

> many of the things we *do* in arguing are partially structured by the concept of war. Though there is no physical battle, there is a verbal battle and the structure of an argument—attack, defense, counterattack, etc.—reflects this. It is in this sense that the ARGUMENT IS WAR metaphor is one that we live by in this culture; it structures the actions we perform in arguing. (p. 5)

Contrariwise, some cultures view argument as a metaphorical dance which is meant to progress in a manner which values and facilitates balance and harmony. People operating by the rules of this framework will view, experience, and express argument differently than those who accept argument in terms of war and whom would most likely view the dance-like form of discourse as being a completely different activity.

Although normally considered a literary trope, metaphor is a mechanism by which humans rationalize existence. Conceptually speaking, "The essence of metaphor is understanding and experiencing one kind of thing in terms of another... The concept is metaphorically structured, the activity is metaphorically structured, and, consequently, the language is metaphorically structured" (Lakoff & Johnson, 1980, p. 6). Literary and linguistic usage of metaphor are merely communicative presentations of the innate processual human conceptual construction. Metaphorical expression through language interacts systemically with conceptual metaphor, which allows for the examination of linguistic metaphorical construction as a means to understanding metaphorical concepts that influence the nature of human behavior.

Western culture commoditizes the concept of time through the metaphorical statement, "time is money." Culturally speaking, Lakoff and Johnson (1980) surmise that time

> is a limited resource that we use to accomplish our goals. Because of the way that the concept of work has developed in modern Western culture, where work is typically associated with the time it takes and time is precisely quantified, it has become customary to pay people by the hour, week, or year. (p. 8)

Lakoff and Johnson (1980) further explain that this metaphorical image of money is unique to Western culture, and has

> arisen in modern industrialized societies and structure our basic everyday activities in a very profound way. Corresponding to the fact that we act as if time is a valuable commodity—a limited resource, even money—we conceive of time that way. Thus, we understand and experience time as the kind of thing that can be spent, wasted, budgeted, invested wisely or poorly, saved, or squandered. (p. 8)

Those cohabitating to make up modern Western society employ metaphorical equations of time to commodities, resources, and currency, in order to conceptualize and relate its function. These concepts, as Lakoff and Johnson (1980) state, "form a single system based on subcategorization, since in our society money is a limited resource and limited resources are Valuable commodities. These subcategorization relationships characterize entailment relationships between the Metaphors" (p. 9). In this case, the metaphor, "time is money," being the most specific correlation, determines the nature of its systemic employment, within which we spend, invest, budget (money), use, have, run out of (resource), have, give, and lose (commodity) time. Metaphorical evocation can determine that nature of rational systems of understanding and expression.

Lakoff and Johnson (1980) describe orientational metaphor in terms of spatiality, explaining that it

> does not structure one concept in terms of another but instead organizes a whole system of concepts with respect to one another... have to do with spatial orientation: up–down, in–out, front–back, on–off, deep–shallow, central–peripheral... give(s) a concept a spatial orientation; for example, HAPPY IS UP. The fact that the concept HAPPY is oriented up leads to English expressions like "I'm feeling *up* today." (p. 15)

Although spatial orientations are physical in nature, relational significance can vary given cultural context. Furthermore, Western culture dictates that

> to be virtuous is to act in accordance with the standards set by the society/ person to maintain its well-being. VIRTUE IS UP because virtuous actions correlate with social well-being from the society/ person's point of view. Since socially based metaphors are part of the culture, it's the society/person's point of view that counts. (Lakeoff & Johnson, 1980, as cited in Venkartaraman, Dew, & Sarasvathy, 2020, p. 12)

Additionally, rationality is up, whereas emotionality is down. Individual and societal manifestations of orientational metaphor presents physically. For example, Lakoff and Johnson (1980) conceptualized that

> in our culture people view themselves as being in control over animals, plants, and their physical environment, and it is their unique ability to reason that places human beings above other animals and gives them this control. CONTROL IS UP thus providing a basis for MAN IS UP and therefore for RATIONAL IS UP. (p. 18)

It is in this respect that we interact with reality, which presents in many cases as authoritarian hierarchy within closed systems. Societal acceptance of Newtonian science further promotes man as a rational being who is in control of his external environment through cognitive allegiance to designation and structure, and through disregard for context.

THE QUANTUM WORLD

The unavoidable influence on atomic phenomena caused by observing them corresponds to the well-known change of the tinge of the psychological experiences which accompanies any direction of the attention to one of their various elements.
—Bohr, 1934, p. 100)

Quantum physics focuses not on individual details within any one structure, but on dynamics and relationships that exist between elements. Elementary particles are defined through their interactions between energy sources, described throughout moments in time, while operating among networks of interactions. In other words, designations of boundaries, and thus, structures are only defined in accordance with the perceivable instance in which they are being observed. Experimentation follows Wheatley's (1994) description, in that "physicists can plot the probability and results of these interactions, but *no particle can be drawn independent from the others.* What is important in any diagram is the overall process by which elements meet and change (Zukav,

1979, 248–250)" (p. 34). Although seemingly impossible, this concept was explored when Thomas Young performed the double-slit experiment in 1803, which proved the previously refuted wave theory of light.

As summarized by Wheatley (1994, p. 64), during this experiment:

> electrons (or any other elementary particles)...must pass through one of two openings (slits) in a surface. After passing through one of these slits, each electron lands on a second surface, where its landing is recorded. A single electron passes through only one of the openings, but how it displays itself on the landing surface is affected by whether one or both slits are open at the time it passes through either one of them. The electron, like all quantum entities, has two forms of being; it is both a wave and a particle. If both slits are open, the single electron acts as a wave, creating a pattern on the recording screen typical of the diffusion caused by a wave. If only one slit is open, the resulting pattern is that of discrete points, or the behavior of a particle. On its way through one slit, the electron acts in a way that indicates it "knows" whether or not the second hole is open. It knows what the scientist is observing for and adjusts its behavior accordingly. If the observer tries to "fool" the subject by opening and shutting slits as the electron approaches the wall, the electron behaves in the manner appropriate for the state of the holes *at the moment* it passes through one. (For a detailed explanation of this experiment, see Gribbin, 1984, pp. 169–174.) The electron also knows if the observer is watching. If the recording apparatus is not on, the electron behaves differently than if it is being recorded. When the electron is not being observed, it exists only as a probability wave; unless someone is watching, "nature herself does not know which hole the electron is going through." (Gribbin, 1984, p. 171)

The double-slit experiment is one of the foundational experiments in quantum physics, and serves to illustrate that what exists is determined by the method and the instance in which it is perceived.

Edward Larenz, along with Margaret Hamilton and Ellen Fetter proposed chaos theory while observing the performance of computer systems designed to track weather developments. Although weather patterns operate according to basic laws of science, small variations in causal intensity can manifest exponentially as time continues. This is termed deterministic chaos. Simulation of deterministic systems, such as whether programs can track systemic evolution, and reflect each instance as a point of light on a screen. As time progresses,

> the system careens back and forth with raucous unpredictability, never showing up in the same spot twice, [but in tracking its motion], this chaotic behavior weaves into a pattern, and before our eyes order emerges on the screen (Wheatley, 1994). The chaotic movements of the system have formed themselves into a shape. The shape is a "strange attractor," and what has appeared on the screen is the order inherent in chaos. (Weatley, 1994, p. 130)

Chaos theory serves to illustrate the connection between structure and time. Humans, through the use of our five senses, are seemingly only capable of interpreting the dynamics between predictability and chaos (change), with respect to single instances, in the sense that our interpretation of time is synonymous with that of change. The existence of strange attractors, in which paths never intersect but instead weave and convolute to form symmetrical patterns, suggests that predictability is related to temporality.

Humans employ the use of structures and describe predictable processes in order to categorize phenomena into hierarchies. Nature is inherently orderly, the nature of which is observable through the respective context of capacity, diversity, scope, and time. Order is discernible through an evaluation of change. Wheatley (1994) translates Prigogine's concept of dissipative structures as

> a process of energy gradually ebbing away, while structure describes embodied order. [He] discovered that the dissipative activity of loss was necessary to create new order. Dissipation did not lead to the death of a system. It was part of the process by which the system let go of its present form so that it could reorganize in a form better suited to the demands of its changed environment. (p. 20)

Hierarchy is often depicted as an unyielding, vertical, "climbing the ladder" approach while using authoritative and control driven methods. Despite its negative connotation, hierarchy is fundamental to existence. A linear connotation of hierarchy, denotes immediacy in congruency with importance; however, Koestler (1970) explains

> its correct symbol is not a rigid ladder but a living tree—a multileveled, stratified, out-branching pattern of organization, a system branching into sub-systems, which branch into sub-systems of a lower order, and so on; a structure encapsulating substructures and so on; a process activating sub-processes and so on. (p. 132)

Reality is structured in such a way that systemic construction reflects the makeup of the elements of which it is comprised, while these elements are simultaneously formed in accordance with presented system dynamics. In this way, reality is holonic, and hierarchy manifests through structures formed in observance of elemental change over time, which occurs in response to various environmental states.

INTEGRAL THEORY

Mankind must recognize diverse perspectives, in order to foster innovation within ourselves, organizations, and society. Fragmentation can be useful when operating within simple systems and situations wherein time is of the essence; however, this viewpoint has proven detrimental when dealing with complex system dynamics, in which the presence of multiple networks of loops make prediction irrelevant, if not impossible. Ken Wilber's AQAL and integral theory is a practical perceptual kaleidoscope through which to view phenomena as existing separately, while considering the quantum, holonic view of reality. Similarly, Quinn's competing values illustrate possible forms which organizations can take in order to accommodate environmental dynamics.

THE AQAL MODEL

> ... that imagination is the capacity to shift from one perspective to another—
> from the political to the psychological; from examination of a single family
> to comparative assessments of the national budgets of the world.
>
> —C. Wright Mills (1959, p. 71)

Wilber's (2005) "all quadrants, all levels" (AQAL) model suggests five elements: states, stages, levels, lines, types, and quadrants. The term "states" derives from the major states of consciousness: waking, dreaming deep sleep, meditative, altered, and so forth, which are alternatively referred to as peak experiences. These states can be triggered by intense experiences and can result in temporary access to spiritual awakening and wisdom. Wilber (2005) states, "Everybody experiences various sorts of states of consciousness, and these states often provide profound motivation, meaning, and drives, in both yourself and others" (p. 6). States, although impactful under the right conditions, are fleeting, serving as temporary glimpses into stages or levels of consciousness, which represent "the actual milestones of growth and development. Once you are at a stage, it is an enduring acquisition" (p. 7); that is, linguistic development occurs in stages. Once a stage of development is reached, the aspects contained therein are virtually always accessible. Furthermore, each stage denotes a different level of complexity.

Derived from Howard Gardner's concept of multiple intelligences, Wilber (2005) explains that humans perceive reality in terms of "cognitive intelligence, emotional intelligence, musical intelligence, kinesthetic intelligence, and so on. Most people excel in one or two of those, but do poorly in the others" (p. 10). The AQAL model employs these intelligences as a means to track lines of development, and to increase awareness of the many conceptual and tangible presentations existing through cognition and perception. Development among intelligences (cognitive, interpersonal, moral, emotional, and aesthetic) presents via progressive stages.

The term "type" refers to masculinity or femininity. A designated type can present regardless of stage or state, and as Wilber (2005) describes,

> One common typology, for example, is the Myers-Briggs (whose main types are feeling, thinking, sensing, and intuiting). *You can be any of those types at virtually any stage of development.* These kind of "horizontal typologies" can be very useful, especially when combined with levels, lines, and states. To show what is involved, we can use "masculine" and "feminine." (p. 15)

Masculinity tends to be

> based on terms of autonomy, justice, and rights; whereas women's logic or voice tends to be based on terms of relationship, care, and responsibility. Men tend toward agency; women tend toward communion. Men follow rules; women follow connections. Men look; women touch. Men tend toward individualism, women toward relationship. (p. 15)

These types reflect in stages, states, and lines, wherein the highest stages involve an integrated involvement of these two typologies. This dynamic is presented through observation of the caduceus, a staff showcasing images of two serpents intertwined creating the shape of a double helix. The staff is meant to represent the spinal column, and the snakes the solar (masculine) and lunar (feminine) chakras (food, sex, and power, relational heart, communication, psychic, and spiritual) moving from low to high.

The quadrants of the AQAL model derive from linguistics, in that language employs first-person, second-person, and third-person, in order to specify perspective. The quadrants are labeled, "I," "We," "It," and "Its" and as Wilber (2005) states,

> First-person means "the person who is speaking," so that includes pronouns like *I, me, mine* (in the singular), and *we, us, ours* (in the plural). Second person means "the person who is spoken to," which includes pronouns like *you* and *yours*. Third-person means "the person or thing being spoken about," such as *he, him, she, her, they, them, it,* and *its.* (p. 23)

The purpose of these distinctions is to determine in which perspective existing states, stages, lines, and types interact to foster development and growth. The AQAL model is thus divided into subjective and objective (left and right); individual and collective (top, bottom).

The AQAL model is an integral map of human potentials and development, regarding inherent individual motivations, organizational values, and measurable elements—the dynamics of which influence the world's cultures and traditions. An integral approach is useful not as a rulebook to be scrutinized, but as a framework for awareness among known perspectives.

The bottom left, or "We" quadrant is perhaps the most difficult perspectives for man to evaluate, being that we are egotistical and ethnocentric by nature; and that when in groups, we tend to stagnate rather than innovate.

Quinn's Competing Values Model

Robert Quinn's competing values framework (Cameron & Quinn, 2006) is an organizational assessment construct depicted as a Cartesian graph. Its vertical dialectic (adaptation at the top, stability at the bottom) intersects with its horizontal dialectic (internal focus at the left, external focus at the right). The resulting four quadrants in the competing values framework (CVF) are named for their motivations—"Collaborate" (internal/adaptive motivation), "Create" (external/adaptive motivation), "Compete" (external/stability motivation), and "Control" (internal/stability motivation).

Cameron and Quinn (2006) state that, through empirical research of organizational effectiveness,

> it was discovered that some organizations were effective if they demonstrated flexibility and adaptability, but other organizations were effective if they demonstrated stability and control. Similarly, some organizations were effective if they maintained efficient internal processes whereas others were effective if they maintained competitive external positioning relative to customers and clients. (Cameron & Quinn, 2006, p. 2)

These motivational differences constitute the competing values presented by the interaction between two dimensions, for which the model is named; and the respective quadrants represent four different perceptions of organizational management theories and practices.

The quadrant labeled "Collaborate" constitutes perspectives and processes which value and promote collaboration. According to Cameron and Quinn (2006), individuals and organizations existing primarily within this quadrant, "tend to be committed to their community, focusing on shared values and communication. Their culture is oriented towards involvement and building commitment over time... Driving purposes include cohesion and commitment" (p. 3). Leaders within collaborative organizations typically focus on nurturing community through trusting relationships and communicate the importance of unified behavior as a means to establishing a unified organizational image. Within organizations embodying these characteristics, it is not uncommon for the consumer to be treated as a partner or extended community member, but, as Cameron and Quinn (2006) examine; like any perspective, too much time spent in the "collaborate" quadrant "becomes negative and turns into a permissive, lax environment where outcomes and results are underemphasized" (p. 3). Time dictates the need for change, and organizations must be agile enough to adjust for context.

Organizations functioning mainly within the "create" quadrant tend to value creative perspectives and practices by communicating an emphasis on innovation and growth through organizational vision. Change and idea generation are both focal points within this quadrant, which can manifest through the employment of entrepreneurial endeavors. Cameron and Quinn (2006) explore creative organizations, which are energized by instability and "strive to orient their products, services, and ideas to the future. Managers build the organization by developing a compelling vision and emphasizing new ideas and technologies, flexibility, and adaptability" (p. 3). A drawback for organizations within the "create" quadrant is constant chaos that can distract from organizational goals. Idea generation may become unmanageable and unproductive. Creative organizations must accept that predictable outcomes are at times essential in navigation, and that the use of predetermined processes are necessary in situations where time is of the essence.

Environments geared toward aggressive competition and achievement exist within the "compete" quadrant, which is result oriented. Winning and losing are significant themes in organizations such as these, both of which are used to emphasize performance speed in order to increase profits, market share, brand equity, and so forth. Leadership presents within competitive organizations through prioritizing objectives and improving the firm's competitive position through hard work and productivity. These companies seek to deliver results to stakeholders as quickly as possible. Values centered around victory are present not only within competitive organizations, but in the perception of other organizations being the competition which must be destroyed in order for organizational survival to continue. Organizations functioning primarily within the "compete" quadrant fall into perpetual internal and external conflict as self-interest is valued over humanity.

Values, processes, and practices within the "control" quadrant prioritize predictable performance through predetermined processes meant to illicit dependable behavior. Planning compliance becomes processual necessities within this paradigm, as efficiency through high optimization is emphasized. Cameron and Quinn (2006) describe the manner in which managers within control oriented organizations promote said values by "cutting costs, and establishing policies and procedures. Clear role definitions are important. These companies tend to elaborate or extend existing products with minor variations" (p. 3). Organizational stagnation is an inevitable end, leading cultures to focus on control; meanwhile endless bureaucracy will confuse and delay the flow of production. The CVF "is consistent, for example, with the psychology of Jung, the sociology of Parsons, the philosophy of Wilber, and the brain physiology of Lawrence" (Cameron & Quinn, 2006,

p. 3). Necessity dictates that humans consider the effect of collective values and behavior, while demonstrating an understanding of the intrapersonal processes which present through observable behavior.

MORGAN'S ORGANIZATIONAL METAPHOR

In his foundational work, Gareth Morgan presented several metaphors of organizations. He argued that the importance of metaphor could not be understated in understanding organizations.

Organizations Are Machines

Organizations functioning mechanistically view its members as parts which operate within a series of closed systems. Rules and procedure are emphasized, as a means toward autocracy. Leaders utilize machine-like organizations as a device by structuring its members into various hierarchies, and defining processes for tasks to be executed toward their designated ends. Concepts of authority in mechanistic organizations correlate to those within "the military from which it borrowed ranks and uniforms, standardized regulations, task specialization, standardized equipment, systematic training, and command language. Bureaucracies produce routine administration in the same way as machines in factories" (Morgan, n.d., p. 1).

Leadership within mechanistic organizations present control via procedural planning and functional departmentalization. Communication is primarily top–down as barriers exist between departments. Authoritative systems which thrive on efficiency and predictability are best employed among simple systems wherein commencement and execution are temporally proximal. Mechanistic organizations "adapt poorly to change,... [foster] bureaucracy,... [and] can have unanticipated, unwanted consequences, [as they are] dehumanizing" toward their members (Morgan, n.d., p. 2). Autocracies often fail contextually, because as systemic growth occurs, complexity and unpredictability increase.

Organizations Are Brains

Morgan states, learning organizations are intuitive, communicative information processing systems (Morgan, n.d.). According to Carlsen and Gjersvik (1997), flexibility and self-organization are emergent qualities of the brain, which are present in this type of organization. As internal systems inevitably break down, organization resembling the brain are able to repair flawed processes and/or substitute underperforming employees with members more suited to a particular task because, as stated by Carlsen and Gjersvik (1997), "A necessity for this self-organization is the ability to learn in order to adapt and (re)configure the various available parts and subsystems" (p. 2). Brain-like organizations are able to self-organize through holographic structure and communication processes, within which, "the holography, as known from physics, shows the possibility of creating processes where the whole is encoded in all parts" (p. 2). Information within such organizations is holonic, thus the production will not halt due to the removal of one organizational aspect because all members, departments, and so forth, reflect the state of the organization as a whole.

Organizations Are Cultures

Organizations are cultures or, as Carlsen and Gjersvik (1997) determine, "patterns of development reflected in a society's system of knowledge, ideology, values, norms, laws, and rituals. Shared meaning, understanding, and sense-making are all ways of describing culture [37]" (p. 2). Organizational members and leaders construct reality through social interaction, communication, and internal cognitive processes. Social construction within an organizational context results in structure, rules, policies, goals, and job descriptions which "all can be viewed as social artifacts whose primary role are to help shape reality construction" (p. 2). Through this lens, scientific and technological advancement is a product of social construction, as "both social context and technical content are essential for understanding scientific activity. 'Science in action,' as opposed to 'ready-made science,' is not only concerned with an objective scientific truth waiting to become discovered, equally important are social processes striving to interest others, create allies, and keep interested groups inline [27]" (p. 2).

Organizations Are in a Constant State of Flux

Carlsen and Gjersvik (1997) explain that "organizations are in a constant state of flux, including permanence and change" (p. 2). Three principle features of biological systems are: autonomy, circularity, and self-reference, which leads to autopoiesis through a process by which "the idea of interacting with an 'external' environment is replaced by the idea of reflecting on one's own organization. Living systems create images of reality as expressions of their own organization, and interact with these images" (p. 3). This metaphorical formation can be seen as organizational intelligence, which is antithetical to the mechanistic organizational metaphor, because there exists only one acceptable organizational image within a mechanistic culture.

Organizations in a constant state of flux embody principles of system dynamics (Forrester, 1969; Sterman, 2000), through, what Carlsen and Gjersvik (1997) summarize as the concept of "loops not lines—the logic of mutual causality: [which] is based on cybernetics and theories of positive and negative feedback loops" (p. 2). Measurements pertaining to the negativity or positivity of various loops that are constantly changing; being that networks of interdependent systems exist, a change in the value of one loop affects the value of corresponding loops. Carlsen and Gjersvik go on to explain that

> contradiction and crisis [or] the logic of dialectical change is based on Marxist dialectical method in studying contradictions and opposites. The three principles of dialectical change are mutual struggle of opposites, the negation of the negation and revolutionary change. This framework provides evidentiary context for the dynamics between stability and chaos pertaining to organizational production.

Modern society has been constructed through the fragmented collaboration of diverse populations, in order to embody an autocratic hierarchical structure wherein a broad mass of laborers foundationally serve the pinnacle of civilization. Urban skylines present the competitive nature of hierarchies encapsulated within closed systems. This ill-conceived structure of systems is showing signs of stagnation, signaling entropy. The most widespread product of modern societal systems has convoluted communication between humans existing within rigidly structured paradigms. Processes primarily driven by expressions of power and control utilize humanity as fuel within inefficient systems which necessitate that fuel cannot deplete in order for machine to operate productively.

The purpose of this chapter is not to advocate for chaos, but to illuminate the need for awareness regarding its role in innovation and knowledge generation. Learning and survival are synonymous within dynamic environments. Humans are the most adaptable species on the planet, and uncertainty necessitates that we evolve intellectually. The mechanistic worldview signifies man's belief in predictable systems that utilize human work, in order to produce stable outcomes which reduce uncertainty and promote security. Rather than build and rebuild flawed systems based on the construction of static elements, innovative leadership calls for managers who are capable of recognizing existing connections where most cannot conceive. Awareness makes possible the ability to see opportunity within unforeseen circumstances, and to imagine alternate applications of familiar concepts. This process promotes idea generation and creation.

Nevertheless, proper analysis of human psychology, behavior, and physiology is a practical means by which to increase efficiency in specialized processes within controlled environments. With respect to the production of structure, hierarchies of processes are necessary, as the product reflects the manner of work employed in its creation. Additionally, hierarchy based on demonstrated skill is perhaps the most important aspect of job performance. Structure exists naturally; however, boundaries are dictated by the existing immediacy of need in regards to development. Leaders must refrain from dictating structure, instead opting to observe where structure presents, and utilize any presented orientation of elements in order to facilitate production beneficial to the environment.

Concepts based on the quantum nature of existence can aid in the conceptualization of dynamics which determine interaction. This endeavor calls for thinkers to further examine the construction of linguistic communication through multiple perspectives, thus increasing individual understanding of the inherent meaning behind their words. By this process, communicative empathy will result. The African philosophy of Ubuntu translates to mean, "I am because we are," which holds true from a cognitive point of view, and through my recognition of "You" being the means by which "I" determine my relationship to objective reality (It). Totality presents itself through the interplay between I, We, It, and Its.

The openness of information in the modern age, probably originally intended to unite us, has caused increased fragmentation of identity, morality, and reality among populations of people who focus more on what qualities designate them as unique, than the abundance of shared characteristics. Dynamics such as this have been instrumental in the unending cycle of human destruction promoted within mechanistic systems. Modern Titans of industry serve as present day towers of Babel meant to elevate their leaders to godlike status, concentrating the energy produced by the masses into economic wealth and stability for the few. With every iteration of this structure comes more and more confusion, because humanity is being utilized, not cultivated, resulting in fractured views of self and reality. The fundamental misunderstanding between humans has less to do with any specific language as it does our collective ignorance pertaining to the multitude of concepts that words can signify. Prior to the implementation of emergent organizational concepts, innovative leaders must reevaluate their understanding of the dynamics of human cognition in regards to rationality, as well as the various organizational forms people will naturally take under certain conditions.

Perhaps chaos could be defined in terms of various elements simultaneously presenting across multiple respective contexts. Humans are presently only capable of consciously experiencing one instance in time followed by another; a fact which is likely systemically linked to collective understanding of consciousness (scientific, philosophical, spiritual), and the framework within which multiple individuals communicate linguistically.

The double-slit experiment personifies the nature of experience in which the slits and corresponding behavior of electrons represent the process of cognition. In the event that only one slit exists, cognition presents as a distinct pattern, formed by discrete particles; whereas the introduction of an additional slit creates alternate iterations of perspective. These perspectives represent "I," "We," "It," "Its" quadrants through an integral framework, as the number and arrangement of perspectives directly affect the presentation taken by elemental phenomena.

Quantum Model for Organizational Development

This model for observing the dynamic nature of organizational development combines Wilber's AQAL model and a diagram of the famous double-slit experiment. Since, in the double-slit experiment, energy is provided via one objective source, I relate it to the "IT" quadrant. In the experiment, the presence of one, or many slits determines the presented interference pattern or lack thereof, therefore I relate that to the "I" quadrant. The subjectivity of the resulting pattern is dependent upon the number of slits and the measurement process. Where the objective source made up the IT quadrant, this subjective source makes up the "We" quadrant. The dynamic totality of this model is the "ITS" quadrant. See Figure 11.1.

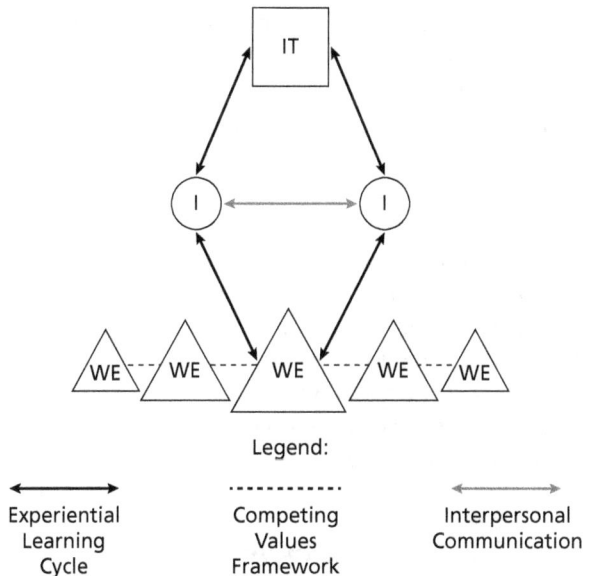

Figure 11.1 Quantum AQAL model. *Note:* This model was created by Daniel Vass-Goosby.

The AQAL model contains four quadrants or perspectives, separated by lines. My goal in presenting this conceptual model is to examine by what processes the perspectives are connected. It is my assertion that the "lines" that represent the distinction between "IT" and "I," and "I" and "WE" are better represented as experiential learning cycles, which according to Kolb and Kolb (2017) are "driven by the integration of action and reflection and experience and concept" (p. 14). In other words, these are processes by which our various perceptions establish metaphorical context.

Communication provides the connection between "I" and "I." Behavioral and linguistic communication provide humans with a basis for understanding. Through this lens, "You" and "I" communicate our respective objective understanding of the organization or "It," which presents as the subjective organizational metaphors "We." Because organizations do not exist solely through the framework of one organizational metaphor, alternate metaphors also present, and decrease distally in intensity. These alternate organizational metaphors are linked via values and can be assessed by utilizing Quinn's CVF. Further, "I" serves as a filter through which "IT" and "We" interact and can be measured via spiral dynamics (Beck & Cowan, 2014). It is my assertion that dynamic change, previously viewed as unmanageable chaos will manifest in structures presented via observation and assessment of the various lines, loops, and levels presented in this model.

In other words, the "IT" quadrant represents the mechanistic, functional organizational processes as exhibited through analysis of production. Quantitative measurement is the primary form of analysis within this quadrant (Philips, 2001) and is understood and conceptualized as it passes through the "I" quadrant. The "We" quadrant is determined through an agreement, or social contract, and the presented metaphor is reflected by the "IT" quadrant, now influenced by the perspectives presented by and the communication between existing "I's." This process is continual and if various models are combined throughout the multiple perspectives, the outputs can be monitored over time. In the context of open communication, limited hierarchies, vigorous recruiting, and extreme individual specialization, this model can allow for insight into what organizational structures materialize in specific situations. Leaders can use this information to remain accountable and understand what practical steps should be taken if the goal is sustainable innovation.

REFERENCES

Ackoff, R. (1994). Systems thinking and thinking systems. *System Dynamics Review*, *10*(2/3), 185–188.

Ali, A. Y. (2016). *Holy Qur'an* (English Translation). Retrieved from https://books.apple.com/us/book/holy-quran-english-translation/id1135959342

Anderson, J. (2010). *Cognitive psychology and its implications.* Pittsburgh, PA: Carnegie Mellon University.

Beck D. E., & Cowan, C. (2014). *Spiral dynamics: Mastering values, leadership and change.* Hoboken, NJ: Wiley-Blackwell.

Bohm, D. (1980). *Wholeness and the implicate order.* London, England: Routledge.

Bohr, N. (1934). *Atomic theory and the description of nature.* Cambridge, England: Cambridge University Press.

Cameron, K., & Quinn, R. (2006). *Diagnosing and changing organizational culture: Based on the competing values framework.* Hoboken, NJ: Wiley.

Carlsen, S., & Gjersvik, R. (1997). Organizational metaphors as lenses for analyzing workflow technology. In S. C. Hayne, W. Prinz, M. Pendergast, & K. Schmidt (Eds.), *GROUP '97: Proceedings of the international ACM SIGGROUP conference on Supporting group work: The integration challenge* (pp. 261–270). New York, NY: Association for Computing Machinery.

Davidson, D. (1978). What metaphors mean. *Critical Inquiry, 5*(1), 31–47.

Forrester, J. (1969). *Urban dynamics.* Cambridge, England: Pegasus.

Gribbin, J. (1984). *In search of Schroedinger's cat: Quantum physics and reality.* New York, NY: Bantam.

Johanessen, J., Olaisen, J., & Olsen, B. (1999). Systemic thinking as the philosophical foundation for knowledge management and organizational learning. *Kybernetes, 28*(1), 24–46.

Kirby, J. (1997). Aristotle on metaphor. *American Journal of Philology, 118*(4), 517–554.

Koestler, A. (1970). Beyond atomism and holism: The concept of the holon. *Perspectives in Biology and Medicine, 13*(2), 131–154.

Kolb, A., & Kolb, D. (2017). Experiential learning theory as a guide for experiential educators in higher education. *ELTHE: A Journal for Engaged Educators, 1*(1), 7–44.

Lakoff, G., & Johnson, M. (1980). *Metaphors we live by.* Chicago, IL: The University of Chicago Press.

Luhman, N. (1992). What is communication? *Communication Theory, 2*(3), 251–259.

Marx, K., & Engels, F. (1848). *The communist manifesto.* New York, NY: International.

Mills, C. (1959). *The sociological imagination.* Oxford, England: Oxford University Press.

Morgan, G. (n.d.). *Machine mataphor* [Student Paper]. Retrieved from https://www.academia.edu/32253656/Machine_Mataphor_by_Gareth_Morgan

Philips, B. (2001). *Beyond sociology's tower of Babel: Reconstructing the scientific method.* New York, NY: Aldine de Gruyter.

Robert E. Quinn's Competing Values Framework. (n.d.). Retrieved from https://www.quinnassociation.com/en/robert_e_quinns_competing_values_framework

Senge, P. (1991). *The fifth discipline: The art and practice of the learning organization.* New York, NY: Doubleday.

Stickland, F. (2002). *The dynamics of change: Insights into organizational transition from the natural world.* London, England: Routledge.

Sterman, J. (2000). *Business dynamics: Systems thinking and for a complex world.* New York, NY: McGraw-Hill.

Thurow, L. (1997). *The future of capitalism: How today's economic forces shape tomorrow's world*. London, England: Penguin.
Venkataraman, S,. Dew, N., & Sarasvathy, S.D. (Eds.). (2020). *Shaping entrepreneurship research: Made, as well as found*. London, England: Routledge.
Wheatley, M. (1994). *Leadership and the new science*. San Francisco, CA: Berrett-Koehler.
Wilber, K. (2005). Introduction to integral theory and practice: IOS basic and the AQAL map. *AQAL Jounral, 1*(1), 1–38.
Zukav, G. (1979). *Dancing wu li masters*. New York, NY: William Morrow.

CHAPTER 12

RELIGIOUS AND WEALTHY

Can One Be Both?

Miles K. Davis
Linfield University

Clifford F. Thies
Shenandoah University

ABSTRACT

If by "religious" is meant taking a vow of poverty; then, by definition, one cannot be both religious and wealthy. On the other hand, if "religious" includes being honest in one's dealings with others, generous with those less fortunate, and using one's wealth for the glory of God; then, yes, one can be both religious and wealthy. Indeed, the question might be asked, can a person be wealthy in a private property-based, free enterprise system without the first two (being honest and generous). This chapter explores the connections between honest dealing and generosity with the amassing of wealth, and also considers the use of wealth for goodness.

Consider the image of businessmen in popular culture. In Frank Capra's (1946) *It's a Wonderful Life*, a decent community banker triumphs over an evil commercial banker. And, in Charles Dickens' (1843) *A Christmas Carol*, an evil businessman learns the spirit of Christmas from a worker whom he had been exploiting. (Both stories are more complex.) "Generally, the role of businessmen and financiers in films is as pantomime villains, ruthlessly pursuing profit at the expense of human life" ("Businessmen Are Always the Villains," 2015, n.p.).

In contrast to the popular image of businessmen, there are real businessmen. Every year, nowadays, *Forbes* compiles a list of the billionaires who died during the prior year. The Americans from a most recent edition are identified in Table 12.1 (Tindera & Berg, 2018).

The first person on the list is Samuel "Si" Newhouse, Jr., who inherited his father's media conglomerate and—refocusing the firm on magazines such as *Vogue, Vanity Fair*, and *The New Yorker*—took the firm to new heights. During his lifetime and in his will, Si Newhouse was a generous giver, most particularly in support of the arts.

Looking over the list, it is clear that every person was involved in philanthropy, some more than others, with recurrent benefactions for the arts, education, medical research, and health care. In addition, many persons

TABLE 12.1 *Forbes* **2018 List of Dead Billionaires, U.S. Citizens (worth in billions)**

Name	Age	Worth ($)	Business	Philanthropy[b]
Samuel Newhouse, Jr.	89	12.1	Media[a]	the arts, education
Bruce Halle	87	6.5	Discount Tire	education, medical research
Leandro Rizzuto	79	4.5	Conair	medical research
Joan Tisch	90	3.8	Loews Corp.[a]	"billionaire matriarch and philanthropist"
David Rockefeller	101	3.3	Chase Manhattan Bank[a]	"a champion of enlightened capitalism"
A. Jerrold Perenchio	86	2.8	Univision	"a generous political donor and philanthropist"
Henry Hillman	98	2.6	Investments	"renowned businessman, investor, and philanthropist"
Sanford Diller	89	1.7	Real Estate	health care, the arts, education
Neal Patterson	67	1.5	Software	health care
Peter Alfond	65	1.4	Dexter Shoes[a]	health care
Dorrance Hill Hamilton	88	1.3	Campbell's Soup[a]	the arts, horticulture, education
Jon Huntsman, Sr.	80	1.0	Chemicals	"one of the world's most generous philanthropists"

[a] largely inherited; [b] various sources

on the list had other forms of civic engagement. The contrast of real businessmen to their depiction in the popular culture couldn't be greater. This chapter examines why businessmen tend to conduct themselves in an ethical manner; and, furthermore, specifically explores the link between businessmen and religion.

Concerning the link between businessmen and religion, possibly the American businessman most famous, recently, for conducting his business in an explicitly religious manner is S. Truett Cathy, founder of the fast-food restaurant chain Chick-fil-A. In an age when fast-food restaurants are open 7 days a week, his restaurants are closed on Sundays, the day of rest for most Christians. When he passed away, in 2014, *Forbes* estimated his worth to be $6 billion.

Other businesses that are explicitly religious include Hobby Lobby, Forever 21, Marriott Hotels, and In and Out Burger (Taylor, 2017). While the religious manners of these companies generally endear them to their clientele, there are recurrent stories reflecting the tension between the slowly moving, more traditional values associated with the religiously observant, with the entire range of values found in a free society. In the case of Forever 21, a retailer of women's apparel, shopping bags are discretely annotated "John 3:16." According to *Forbes*, founders Do Won and Jin Sook Chang are worth $3.4 billion.

Explicitly religious business extends beyond companies that produce goods and services to those involved in finance and insurance. In finance, these businesses include Islamic banks and faith-based mutual funds. Islamic banks organize their business so as to comply with Sharia Law. Significantly, loans must be secured by real assets and otherwise be nonrecourse. For example, a mortgage can be secured by real estate but, in the event of a default, the only option to the lender is to seize the identified property. The lender cannot go after the other property or future earnings of the borrower.

In contrast, with recourse loans, difficulty with repaying loans can lead to burdensome debt. Normally, debtors in default can renegotiate their debts giving their option of filing for bankruptcy. With bankruptcy, a judge will determine what lenders will receive given their priorities of claim, the attachable assets of the borrower, and the borrower's income if higher than the median. But, for various reasons, this arrangement sometimes breaks down. During the financial crash of 2008, the former bank practice of accepting the deed in lieu of foreclosure was tightened. Effectively, this trapped many people into "underwater mortgages," and worsened the recession that followed (Gouldey & Thies, 2012).

Furthermore, certain forms of indebtedness cannot be relieved through bankruptcy, including child and spousal support arrears, tax arrears, and student loan debt. Student loan debt is now the second largest form of household debt, and is subject to high rates of nonpayment. Particularly at risk are college dropouts, students at for-profit schools and Black males (Scott-Clayton, 2018). With recourse loans, the exemption of certain forms of debt from bankruptcy and the breakdown of the creditor–debtor relationship following financial crises make debt problematic for borrowers and even for society as a whole.

A small but growing number of faith-based mutual funds are available to investors. These include funds offered by Aquinas; Ave Maria and Epiphany (Catholic); Guidestone (Southern Baptist); New Covenant (Presbyterian); Praxis (Mennonite); Thrivent (Lutheran); Timothy (nondenominational Christian); and Amana, Azzad, and Iman (Muslim).[1] Similarly to socially responsible investing (SRI) funds, these faith-based funds restrict their assets to those meeting certain criteria. For example, Catholic funds cannot be involved in abortion, contraception, or embryonic stem cell research. Islamic funds must shun firms whose revenues are significantly derived from charging interest, gambling, or pork products, and must purge themselves from any allowed earnings from these activities. Returns on faith-based funds are comparable to returns on both SRI and conventional funds, at least after the size of the fund is considered (Davis, Ghoul, & Thies, 2017).

Among the several cost-sharing nonprofit health ministries grandfathered in by the Affordable Healthcare Act (Obamacare) are four large Christian health ministries (Christian Healthcare Ministries, Liberty Healthshare, Medishare, and Samaritan Ministries). These cost-sharing plans generally feature rules such as abstaining from abuse of alcohol and illegal drugs and regular attendance at an organized house of worship, along with deductibles. Three of these health ministries are explicitly for co-religionists, while one (Liberty Healthshare) is open to adherents of other faith traditions.

By reason of their rules for membership and for reimbursement, these cost-sharing programs actually keep the cost of healthcare low, while many families not qualifying for subsidies find the out-of-pocket costs for premiums and deductibles of Obamacare-compliant plans burdensome.

Men of faith and other civic-minded persons began savings banks 200 years ago as a form of self-help for working-class families. This tradition continues to this day, (e.g., in church-based credit unions). An example is the credit union of Greater Galilee Missionary Baptist Church of Milwaukee, Wisconsin, which serves a poor inner-city community (Ferral, 2018). Although not as numerous as they once were, these credit unions provide credit and other financial services to members whose only alternative for credit might otherwise be payday loan companies. At the global level, there is the Grameen Bank of Bangladesh, founded by Muhammad Yunus, winner of the 2006 Nobel Peace Prize. Grameen Bank makes microloans, almost exclusively to women entrepreneurs. As important as the loans are, the social network developed by the bank may be more important in empowering these women.

THE EYE OF A NEEDLE

While the above survey of explicitly religious businesses argues that religion is not an impediment to pursuing profits, for many, religion connotes suspicion of wealth. This suspicion can be said to stem from Jesus' parable on the eye of a needle; namely, that it is easier for a camel to pass through an eye of a needle than it is for a rich man to enter heaven (Matthew 19:23–24, NIV[2]). It is instructive that immediately after this teaching, Jesus' disciples "were greatly astonished and asked, 'Who then can be saved?'" (Matthew 19:25).

Jesus did not answer them by saying you Jews have it wrong. It's not the rich who go to heaven. It's the poor. Jesus answered, "With man this is impossible, but with God all things are possible" (Matthew 19:26). The rich, just like everyone else, are saved through God's mercy.[3]

That wealth may be a sign of the elect, might be taken from Psalm 112, "Wealth and riches shall be in his house" (i.e., in the house of a righteous man). The Bible is replete with teachings regarding working, saving, honest dealing and prudential management of resources, and associating these with wealth and being generous with those less fortunate. From Proverbs,

> How long wilt thou sleep, O sluggard? When wilt thou arise out of thy sleep. Yet, a little sleep, a little slumber, a little folding of the hands to sleep, so shall thy poverty come on you like a thief, and thy scarcity like an armed man. (6:9–11)
>
> Lazy hands make for poverty, but diligent hands bring wealth. He who gathers crops in summer is a prudent son, but he who sleeps during harvest is a disgraceful son. (10:4–5)
>
> A sluggard's appetite is never filled, but the desires of the diligent are fully satisfied. (13:4)

Religious belief and practice have been shown to be associated with a wide range of outcomes. On the positive side, these outcomes include health and life expectancy, educational attainment, earnings, wealth, marital stability, generosity, and self-reported happiness. On the negative side, these outcomes include *avoiding* unemployment, poverty, drug and alcohol abuse, mental health issues, and suicide. These outcomes are observed both at the individual level in samples of the general population and at the community level (Iannaccone, 1998).

While wealth tends to accrue to those who follow God's laws, there is also recognition that life involves risk; that outcomes are due to more than merely our efforts and intentions.

> As you do not know the path of the wind, or how the body is formed in a mother's womb, so you cannot understand the work of God, the Maker of all

things. Sow your seed in the morning, and in the evening let your hands be not idle, for you do not know which will succeed, whether this or that, or both will do equally well. (Ecclesiastes 11:5–6)

The relationship, then, between goodness and wealth is not one-to-one, and neither is a sure sign of the other.

Indeed, an argument can be made that the great monotheistic religions of the world reconciled human action with risk. Instead of pagan gods playing dice with our lives, the monotheistic religions envision an orderly but complex universe in which the One, True God is sovereign. In such a universe, people can form rational expectations of the probable consequences of decisions (Bernstein, 1996). As this insight was developed, our understanding of the nature of risk, and of business, finance, and entrepreneurship profoundly changed.

Jesus' teaching on the eye of a needle attacked the prejudice that wealth is a sign of the elect. For some, his teaching resulted in an opposite prejudice. Whereas Jesus had to explain to his disciples that the rich, just like everyone else, are totally dependent on God's mercy, it might be necessary, today, to explain that this applies to the poor. This teaching is not so much a new teaching, but a renewed teaching. Psalm 49 says,

> Hear this, all you peoples, listen, all you who live in this world, both low and high, rich and poor alike... no one can redeem the life of another or give to God a ransom for them. (Psalm 49:1–2, 5–6)

THE MANUFACTURE OF NEEDLES

In *The Wealth of Nations*, Adam Smith famously used pin manufacture to illustrate the increase of production enabled by the specialization part of specialization and trade. The pins to which Smith referred were holed at one end, or had an eye, and therefore should be recognized to be needles.

> One man draws out the wire, another straightens it, a third cuts it, a fourth points it, a fifth grinds it at the top for receiving the head; to make the head requires two or three distinct operations; to put it on, is a peculiar business, to whiten the pins is another; it is even a trade by itself to put them into the paper; and the important business of making a pin is, in this manner, divided into about eighteen distinct operations... (Smith, 1937, p. 4)

Smith connected the increase in productivity enabled by specialization to the other part of specialization and trade, trade, with the breakdown of local monopolies allowing places with factories to trade their surplus production for the surplus production of other places. Smith's discussion of specialization and trade was early during the industrial revolution. The great advance in productivity enabled by the industrial revolution was still being mostly absorbed in population. The human race had not yet clearly broken out of the iron law of wages.

Prior to the industrial revolution, the standard of living of ordinary people fluctuated at the subsistence level. Figure 12.1, based on many sources of information concerning the standard of living in past times and on standard sources more recently, demonstrates that low standards of living formerly prevailed throughout the world. Since the industrial revolution, as it spread across the world, more and more places have joined into sustained economic growth and increased standards of living (Deaton, 2013).

Before the industrial revolution, wages above the subsistence level would result in more children surviving to adulthood, increasing the supply of workers relative to the available resources and lowering productivity and wages back down to the subsistence level. And, wages below the subsistence level would result in fewer children surviving to adulthood, decreasing the supply of workers relative to the available resources and raising productivity and wages back up to the subsistence level. Back then, with standards of living constrained by resources, there was a negative correlation between population and standards of living. Gregory Clark (2007), relying on farm records, chronicles the evolution of wages in agriculture in England over

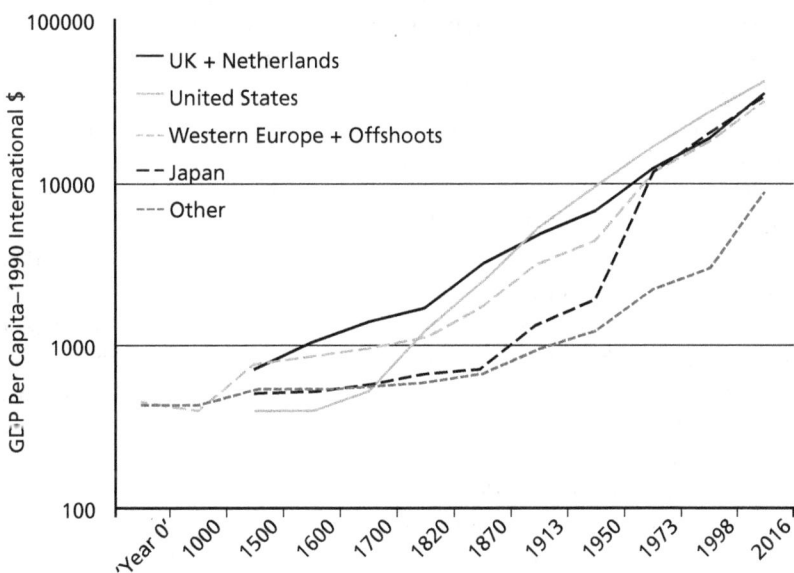

Figure 12.1 GDP per capita, various regions of the world. *Source:* Adapted and updated from Maddison, 2001.

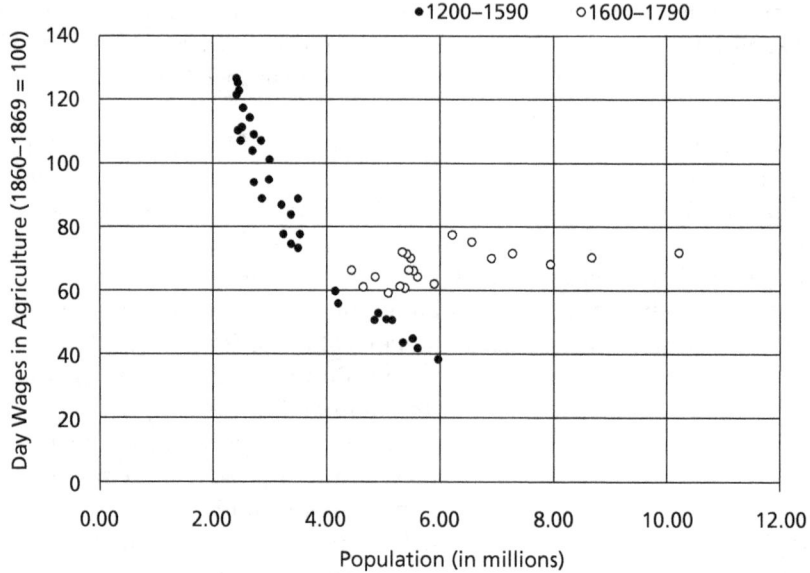

Figure 12.2 Wages, adjusted for prices, versus population in England. *Source:* Adapted from Clark, 2007.

several hundred years. His data are shown in Figure 12.2, juxtapositioned against population. Prior to 1600, the workings of the iron law of wages are clearly exhibited (in the black dots). Following 1600, it is clear (in the gray dots) that something changed. But, through 1800, almost all of the increase in productivity was absorbed by population growth. There was not yet much of an increase in the wages of the masses of workers.

Following 1800, there was an explosion in the wages of the masses of workers. Gregory Clark (2005), this time relying on church records, tracks the wages of laborers and skilled craftsmen in construction in southern England over a period of 800 years. These data are shown in Figure 12.3. Fluctuations in wages prior to 1800 are swamped by the increase in wages after 1800. It is as though the countries that joined into sustained economic growth transitioned to a new world: the "first world," according to terminology that has stayed with us. Countries not making the transition to this first world are described as the "third world," with those in the former communist bloc the "second world." Following the revolution in development economics of the 1990s, the number of low-income countries (using the categories of the World Bank) is down to 31 (Thies, 2018, pp. 209–211), with many formerly low-income countries transitioning to at least middle income. Abject poverty in the world, akin to the subsistence level of prior times, has fallen in half, being practically eliminated outside of Africa south

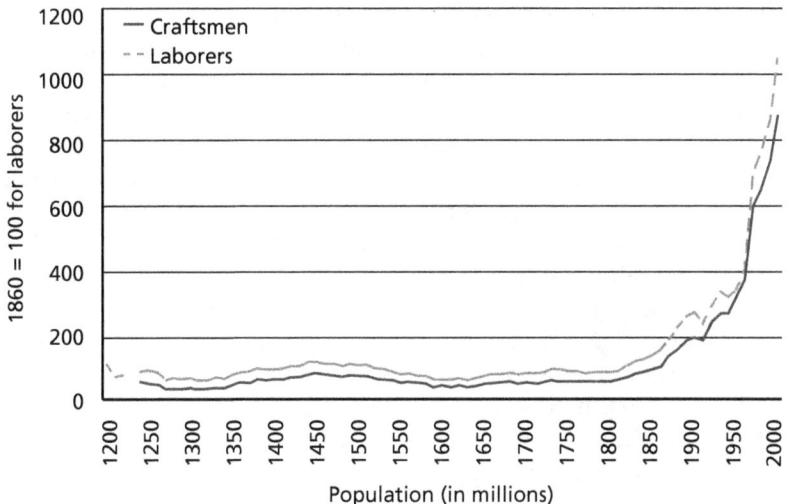

Figure 12.3 Construction wages in Southern England, adjusted for prices. *Source:* Adapted from Clark, 2005.

of the Sahara, and rapidly diminishing there (Pinkowskiy & Sala-i-Martin, 2009, 2010).

The tremendous advance in standards of living now encompassing almost the entire world makes clear that wealth is created even though resources are relatively fixed in their supply. That human beings working together in teams, as these teams are assembled by managers, and outfitted with equipment and knowledge, are capable of producing previously unimaginable wealth. Seeing their part in the great advance of standards of living can sustain the efforts of businessmen who are religious.

HONEST DEALING

In former times, when goods were traded in bazaars, buyers and sellers haggled over price. A buyer didn't buy so many pounds of chicken but rather bought a particular chicken, satisfying herself as to its quality. When value was subject to objective measurement, it was sufficient to have proper weights, and proper measures of dry and liquid volumes. Thus, "Use honest scales and honest weights, an honest ephah and an honest hin. I am the Lord your God, who brought you out of Egypt" (Leviticus 19:36). Today, with differentiated goods and services, honest dealing is harder to describe. Honest dealing means creating an expectation of a good or service, which is referred to as its brand, and then delivering upon that expectation.

The same problem of honest dealing arises when firms hire labor, especially when workers have a mix of levels and types of occupational skills and are hired for indefinitely long terms. Expectations are developed for pay, benefits, and conditions of employment, as well as opportunities for advancement within the firm. Managers of large and complex enterprises produce and sell in a constantly changing and competitive environment, securing consumers, workers, suppliers, creditors, and other stakeholders on the basis partly of price and partly of reputation. Managers do not simply buy and sell commodities in spot markets. They engage a variety of stakeholders in processes that are being continuously changed, dealing with those involved in ways that cannot be completely described by contract. To secure the cooperation of those who are involved in these processes, managers must develop a reputation for treating others fairly.

The stakeholder theory of the firm makes explicit the obligations of firms—especially large and complex firms—to all their stakeholders, and not merely to their shareholders. When the stakeholder theory was promulgated (Freeman, 1984), it appeared to contradict the argument that managers should maximize shareholder value. Stakeholder theory posits that managers must address the needs of all groups having a stake in the firm, not merely its shareholders. "The central task in this process is to manage and integrate the relationships and interests of shareholders, employees, customers, suppliers, communities and other groups in a way that ensures the long-term success of the firm" (Freeman & McVea, 2001, p. 10). While this paradigm evolved over the ensuing several decades, at its core are the "active" management of the business environment and the promotion of shared interest to assure the long-term viability of the firm.

In a series of articles, Michael C. Jensen criticized stakeholder theory for not having an explicit objective function for the firm. He attempted to incorporate the concerns of stakeholder theory into a model featuring the maximization of shareholder value (Jensen, 2001, 2002). Basically, Jensen added a term to the firm's objective function involving benefits provided to nonshareholder stakeholders and the contribution of nonshareholder stakeholders to the value of the firm. Not surprisingly, Jensen found that value-maximizing managers would provide benefits to nonshareholder stakeholders up to the point where $1 in additional benefits equals $1 in additional value creation.

Gouldey, Davis, Thies, and Yevus (2016) derive the implications of the existence of nonshareholder stakeholders from first principles, with the benefits provided to and contributions to value provided by stakeholders incorporated into the structure of the firm. They find that, under fairly general conditions, stakeholder theory is consistent with shareholder value maximization. This is not to say that the job of management is easy. Just the opposite. Managers must continuously intuit the contributions of the many stakeholders of large and complex firms, offering payments and benefits that induce performance, in an environment that is competitive and constantly changing, in order to maximize shareholder value.

Coincident with the rise of stakeholder theory, there has been a change in the dominant view of business ethics. As opposed to the view that "the social responsibility of business is to increase its profits," the new view is that businesses have legal, ethical, and charitable obligations in addition to an obligation, if possible, to be profitable. Much of the distinction can be found in the difference between the title of Milton Friedman's famous article in the *New York Times Magazine*, and his complete statement,

> There is one and only one social responsibility of business—to use its resources and engage in activities designed to increase its profits so long as it stays within the rules of the game, which is to say, engages in open and free competition without deception or fraud. (Friedman, 1970, section SM, p. 17; see also 1962, p. 133)

In the complete statement, profit seeking is constrained by law and honest dealing (two of the three add-ons to profitability found in contemporary business ethics), and also by competition. The part that is missing in the quoted sentence, charity, is alluded to elsewhere in Friedman's (1970) essay, "It may well be in the long run interest of a corporation that is a major employer in a small community to devote resources to providing amenities to that community or to improving its government (1970, section SM, p. 17)." So, all the elements of the social responsibility of business can be found in Friedman's essay, if you read past the title.

In a retrospective on Friedman's essay, John Mackey, founder of Whole Foods Market, made the case for the contemporary view of business ethics.

> I believe that the enlightened corporation should try to create value for *all* of its constituencies. From an investor's perspective, the purpose of the business is to maximize profits. But that's not the purpose for other stakeholders—for customers, employees, suppliers, and the community. Each of those groups will define the purpose of the business in terms of its own needs and desires, and each perspective is valid and legitimate. (Friedman, Mackey, & Rodgers, 2005, para. 7, emphasis in original; cf. Mackey & Sisodia, 2013)

Milton Friedman, commenting on Mackey, said,

> The differences between John Mackey and me regarding the social responsibility of business are for the most part rhetorical. Strip off the camouflage, and it turns out we are in essential agreement. Moreover, his company, Whole Foods Market, behaves in accordance with the principles I spelled out in my 1970 *New York Times Magazine* article. (Friedman et al., 2005, para. 24)

T. J. Rodgers, CEO of Cypress Semiconductor, considered the matter obvious:

> It is also simply good business for a company to cater to its customers, train and retain its employees, build long-term positive relationships with its suppliers, and become a good citizen in its community, including performing some philanthropic activity. (Friedman et al., 2005, para. 42)

We, too, should consider the matter obvious. The modern corporation typically offers products and services that cannot be fully described, about which consumers form expectations largely through marketing. Managers, therefore, are heavily involved in developing the "brands" of their products and services, in addition to organizing production. In a constantly changing environment, managers are also involved in continuous improvement. They do all these things in real time, while buffeted by competition.

In hiring workers, obtaining supplies and securing the cooperation of local governments, managers make offers that involve more than cash payments. These offers include benefits and conditions of employment, and expectations of continuing relations. To deliver upon these expectations, managers must induce relationships. This means managers must commit themselves to treating all their stakeholders fairly, even as they pursue profits, in order to develop reputations worthy of loyalty. Properly understood, management is a calling to service and is honorable. But, the question remains, what to do with profits?

GENEROSITY

Adam Smith (1853), in *The Theory of Moral Sentiments*, developed a certain kind of "fellow-feeling" approach to benevolence. He begins, "How selfish soever man may be supposed there are evidently some principles in his nature, which interest him in the fortune of others (p. 3). This approach to fellow-feeling differs from other approaches, for example, based on kinship or lordship, such as preceded the capitalist era. It involves judgment as people—relating to others on the basis of free association—form expectations of the character of others. At the same time, they sense that they are, themselves, being judged. Indeed, that they are being judged by what Smith calls the "impartial spectator" (p. 27). It is this sense of being judged that induces "self-command" in individuals, tempering selfishness, ambition, and so forth, and exciting what Smith calls the "amiable" virtues such as kindness, tenderness, and humanity (p. 26). As members of a free society, individuals find themselves in a web of exchanges and relations in which it is difficult to say where one ends and the other begins.

Businessmen, in particular, are subject to the discipline of continuous dealings in the marketplace (Tullock, 1985). Gary Becker incorporates a variable representing "social opprobrium and perhaps ostracism" in a model of consumer behavior (Becker, 1974, p 1085). This variable reflects the transactions and relationships offered and withheld by others according to their views of one's benevolence. Becker finds that something like tithing comes out of his model.

The charitable giving and other forms of civic engagement by members of market-oriented economies are famous. In *Democracy in America*, Alexis de Tocqueville (2000, pp. 489–492) discusses the propensity of Americans to form associations. During the 19th century, both in Great Britain (Himmelfarb, 1984, 1991) and the United States (Schwartz, 2000), private giving supported an increasing array of charitable, fraternal, and civic institutions. When Gunnar Myrdal came to study race relations in this country during the 1930s, he described African Americans as "exaggerated Americans" because of their embrace of work, family, church, and social institutions (Myrdal, 1944, p. 712). Most of the richest men of the Gilded Era are associated with philanthropy, John D. Rockefeller and Andrew Carnegie in particular. Rotary International boasts more than 1 million members worldwide.

In 2006, the Charities Aid Foundation published an international study of giving (Clegg & Pharoah, 2006). The findings were roughly in accord with other similar, one-time studies. As Table 12.2 shows, the people of the United States were found to be dramatically more generous than the people of other advanced democracies, with the people of the United Kingdom and other English-tradition countries following, in or near second place.

A few years later, the Charities Aid Foundation developed a World Giving Index from three of the questions asked in the Gallup World Poll (Charities Aid Foundation, 2017). The three questions involve charitable acts done by people during the prior month: (a) donating money, (b) volunteering time, and (c) helping a stranger. The questions each elicit a binary, "Yes" or "No" answer (e.g., did or did not donate money during the past month). The responses do not speak, for example, to the amount of money donated.

TABLE 12.2 National Giving as a Percentage of GDP

United States	1.67	Netherlands	0.45
United Kingdom	0.73	Singapore	0.29
Canada	0.72	New Zealand	0.29
Australia	0.69	Turkey	0.23
South Africa	0.64	Germany	0.22
Ireland	0.47	France	0.14

Source: Charities aid foundation, "International Comparisons of Chartiable Giving," (Clegg & Pharoah, 2006, p. 6)

While the United States was in the top five in the first World Giving Index, Australia and New Zealand finished first and second. Also finishing in the top ten was Sri Lanka, a predominantly Buddhist country. In the 4 years from 2013 to 2016, the #1 and #2 countries were Myanmar, another predominantly Buddhist country, and the United States. In 2017, Myanmar and Indonesia, a predominantly Muslim country, were #1 and #2, and the United States #5.

Figure 12.4 shows that, over the time period 2009 to 2016, countries with higher ratings on the Index of Economic Freedom tended to score higher on the World Giving Index. The relationship appears essentially flat for countries that are not rated and countries with ratings less than 70. The people of countries with ratings in the 70s and especially countries in the 80s give more frequently.

A problem with profit maximization is that money is merely a means, it is not an end. Money, in this sense, is sterile. Without a purpose, the pursuit of profit may be likened to a dog that chases after a fire truck. What does the dog do if he catches the fire truck? It is understandable that a younger person is more involved in the pursuit of profit and not yet focused on the use of wealth. But, with the advance of years, or with the succession of one generation by another in a financial dynasty, a more balanced perspective is appropriate. Friedrich Hayek (2011) says individuals of great wealth can play important roles in cultural amenities, in the fine arts, in education and research, in the preservation of natural beauty and historic treasures, and

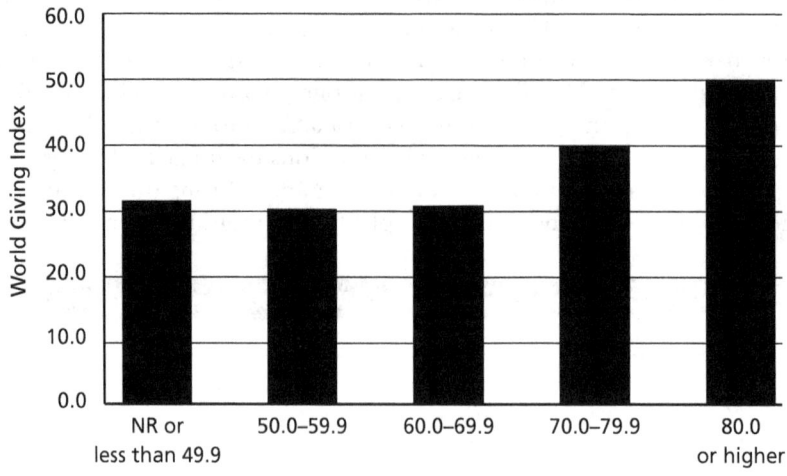

Figure 12.4 World Giving Index, 1,126 country: Years 2009–2016. *Source:* Charities Aid Foundation, 2017.

in the propagation of new ideas in politics, morals, and religion. With the rule of law and a commitment to honest dealing, the pursuit of profit is honorable. Success in this pursuit provides an opportunity for using wealth well. But wealth should have a purpose beyond keeping score in the competitive game that is business.

Self-Interest Versus Self-Denial

In *The Fable of the Bees: Or, Private Vices, Publick Benefits*, Bernard Mandeville (1988) describes how those who are totally selfish and vain advance the public good. For example, without vanity there would be no fashion industry. There would be a fall in the employment of seamstresses and reduced demand for textiles. There would be massive unemployment, collapse of an entire industry, and the banks that lent to this industry would be put at risk. Therefore, says Mandeville, vanity is a good thing. Even thieves give employment to locksmiths, police officers, jailers, and lawyers, and so advance the public good. Thank Lucifer for thieves!

At one level, *The Fable* can be criticized for indulging in the economic heresy of underconsumptionism (Bleaney, 1976). At another level, it can and was criticized as sacrilegious and declared a public nuisance, although not officially censored. For critics of market economics, *The Fable* describes how free markets serve the vulgar interests of the masses and in so doing reinforce those vulgar interests and man's selfishness. As Mandeville himself argued, members of society merely feign to be honest, fair, and generous out of self-interest, like so many poker players at a table each trying to fake the others.

In some religious traditions, the endemic problem of self-interest is addressed by vows of poverty and possibly other acts of self-denial. In Buddhism, asceticism is seen as part of the path to enlightenment. While Buddhist monks commit themselves to this path, they serve a greater community engaged in the "middle path" between extreme self-denial and extreme self-indulgence. Similarly, in the Christian tradition, Saint Francis pursued the life of an ascetic. But, Christians in general are to be "in, but not of" this world (John 17:14–19). Asceticism is not generally found among Baptists, Jews, or Muslims (aside from Sufi Muslims). Within the faith traditions that embrace asceticism, the ascetics live in a symbiotic relation with the egoists of their communities, being supported by the egoists and providing peace to them. Their relationship can be seen as a form of specialization and trade. Within the faith traditions that do not embrace asceticism, the equality of all believers is emphasized, and other means are employed to modulate selfishness. Among the ways that religions induce commitment and, at the same time, minimize free riding is through seemingly arbitrary restrictions on manners, dress, and so forth (Iannaccone, 1994). In her study of intentional communities, Rosabeth Kantor (1972) found that those that were successful tended to employ such restrictions to induce commitment. A statistical analysis of the American experience with intentional communities indicates that a combination of restrictions and concessions to egoistic concerns has been the most successful (Thies, 2000).

With regard to vulgar interests, these are seen as mostly due to one's circumstances in life, a product of one's upbringing and education, and not inherent. In the 19th century, during the heyday of private charity, it was thought that the poor needed to be uplifted, and "visiting" as well as material assistance was provided. In isolation, not engaged with others, man would be antisocial (Dixon & Wilson, 2010); but, when engaged with others including employers and landlords, in hierarchical, fraternal, and social relations, even the "most corrupted and dissolute of the poor people" could be morally elevated (Tuckerman, 1838, p. 88–89). During the 20th century, poverty came to be redefined as a lack of money. The dignity of a job and relating to others on the basis of free association were dismissed as being intangible.

Globalization and automation threaten the jobs of many in the working class, and now there is the prospect of robots. Labor force participation even adjusted for the aging of the population, lags. Many young men seem happy remaining jobless and unmarried, living in their parents' basement playing video games (Thies, 2017). In addition to resulting in "discouraged" workers, prolonged unemployment can cause "learned helplessness" (Beck, 1990, pp. 253–267). Some individuals externalize their continued failure, indulging themselves in self-righteous, while others internalize their continued failure, indulging themselves in self-blame (McClure, 1985). To treat poverty merely as a lack of income ignores the importance of being a productive member of society and of being part of a family and other forms of community. Man, after all, does not live by bread alone.

NOTES

1. Miles Davis discloses that he is an outside director of the Amana Fund.
2. All scripture quoted unless otherwise indicated is from the New International Version.
3. In a slightly different heresy, middle class is taken to be a sign of blessing. "Give me neither poverty nor riches..." Proverbs 30:8.

REFERENCES

Beck, R. (1990). *Motivation: Theories and principles* (3rd ed.). Englewood Cliffs, NJ: Prentice Hall.

Becker, G. (1974). A theory of social interactions. *Journal of Political Economy, 82*(1974), 1063–1093.
Bernstein, P. (1996). *Against the gods: The remarkable story of risk.* New York, NY: Wiley & Sons.
Bleaney, M. (1976). *Underconsumption theories: A history and critical analysis.* New York, NY: International.
Businessmen are always the villains. (2015, October 16). *The Economist.* Retrieved from https://www.economist.com/prospero/2015/10/16/businessmen-are-always-the-villains
Clark, G. (2005). The condition of the working class in England, 1209–2004. *Journal of Political Economy, 113*(6), 1307–1340.
Clark, G. (2007). The long march of history: Farm wages, population, and economic growth, England 1209–1869. *Economic History Review, 60*(1), 97–135.
Clegg, S., & Pharoah, C. (2006). *International comparisons of charitable giving.* Kent, England: Charities Aid Foundation. https://www.cafonline.org/about-us/publications/archive/international-comparisons-of-charitable-giving
Charities Aid Foundation. (2017). *CAF world giving index 2017: A global view of giving trends* (and prior editions). Kent, England: Author.
Davis, M. K., Ghoul, W. A., & Thies, C. F. (2017). The performance of religious and secular SRI funds: A matched-pair approach. *Journal of Applied Business and Economics 19*(7), 75–83.
de Tocqueville, A. (2000). *Democracy in America* (H.C. Mansfield & D. Winthrop, Ed. & Transl.). Chicago, IL: University of Chicago Press. (original work published in 1835 and 1840)
Deaton, A. (2013). *The great escape: Health, wealth, and the origins of inequality.* Princeton, NJ: Princeton University Press.
Dixon, W., & Wilson, D. (2010). Thomas Chalmers: The market, moral conduct, and social order. *History of Political Economy, 42*(2010), 223–246.
Ferral, K. (2018, October 30). Church-run credit unions keep the faith despite challenges. *Religion News Service.* Retrieved from https://religionnews.com/2018/10/30/church-run-credit-unions-keep-the-faith-despite-challenges/
Freeman, R. (1984). *Strategic management: A stakeholder approach.* Boston, MA: Pitman.
Freeman, R., & McVea, J. (2001). *A stakeholder approach to strategic management* (Darden Business School Working Paper No. 01-02). Retrieved from https://papers.ssrn.com/sol3/papers.cfm?abstract_id=263511
Friedman, M. (1962). *Capitalism and freedom.* Chicago, IL: University of Chicago Press.
Friedman, M. (1970, September 13). The social responsibility of business is to increase its profits. *The New York Times.* Retrieved from https://www.nytimes.com/1970/09/13/archives/a-friedman-doctrine-the-social-responsibility-of-business-is-to.html
Friedman, M., Mackey, J., & Rodgers, T. J. (2005, October). Rethinking the social responsibility of business. *Reason.* Retrieved from https://reason.com/2005/10/01/rethinking-the-social-responsi-2/
Gouldey, B., Davis, M., Thies, C., & Yevus, M. (2016). Stakeholder theory and the market value rule. *Financial Decisions, 28,* 1–20.
Gouldey, B., & Thies, C. (2012). Asset bubbles and supply side failures: Where are the qualified sellers? *Cato Journal, 32*(2), 513–538.

Hayek, F. (2011). *The constitution of liberty*. Chicago, IL: University of Chicago Press. (Origianl work published 1960)
Himmelfarb, G. (1984). *The idea of poverty: England in the early industrial age*. New York, NY: Knopf.
Himmelfarb, G. (1991). *Poverty and compassion: The moral imagination of the late Victorians*. New York, NY: Knopf.
Iannaccone, L. (1994). Why strict churches are strong. *American Journal of Sociology, 99*(5), 1180–1211.
Iannaccone, L. (1998). Introduction to the economics of religion. *Journal of Economic Literature, 36*(3), 1465–1496.
Jensen, M. (2001). Value maximization, stakeholder theory, and the corporate objective function. *Journal of Applied Corporate Finance, 14*(3), 8–21.
Jensen, M. C. (2002). Value maximization, stakeholder theory, and the corporate objective function. *Business Ethics Quarterly 12*(2), 235–256.
Kantor, R. (1972). *Commitment and community: Communes and utopias in sociological perspective*. Cambridge, MA: Harvard University Press.
Mackey, J., & Sisodia, R. (2013). *Conscious capitalism*. Cambridge, MA: Harvard Business.
Maddison, A. (2001). *The world economy: A millennial perspective*. Paris, France: Organisation for Economic Cooperation and Development.
Mandeville, B. (1988) *The fable of the bees: Or, private vices, publick benefits*. Indianapolis, IN: Liberty Fund. [Original work published 1723]
McClure, J. (1985). The social parameter of 'learned' helpless: Its recognition and implications. *Journal of Personality and Social Psychology, 48*(6), 1537.
Myrdal, G. (1944). *An American dilemma: The Negro problem and modern democracy*. New York, NY: Harper & Bros.
Pinkowskiy, M., & Sala-i-Martin, X. (2009). *Parametric estimates of the world distribution of income* (NBER Working Paper No. 15433). Retrieved from https://www.nber.org/papers/w15433
Pinkowskiy, M., & Sala-i-Martin, X. (2010). *African poverty is falling... Much faster than you think!* (NBER Working Paper No. 15775). Retrieved from https://www.nber.org/papers/w15775
Schwartz, J. (2000). *Fighting poverty with virtue: Moral reform and America's urban poor, 1825–2000*. Indianapolis: Indiana University Press.
Scott-Clayton, J. (2018, January 10). The looming student loan default crisis is worse than we thought. *Brookings Institution*. Retrieved from https://www.brookings.edu/research/the-looming-student-loan-default-crisis-is-worse-than-we-thought/
Smith A. (1853). *The theory of moral sentiments*. London, England: Henry G. Bohn. (original work published in 1759)
Smith, A., (1937). *An inquiry into the nature and causes of the wealth of nations*. (E. Cannan, Ed.), New York, NY: Modern Library. (original work published in 1776)
Taylor, K. (2017, October 7). 9 American companies with extremely religious roots. *Business Insider*. Retrieved from https://www.businessinsider.in/9-American-companies-with-extremely-religious-roots/articleshow/60986584.cms
Thies, C. (2000). The success of American communes. *Southern Economic Journal, 67*(1), 186–199.

Thies, C. (2017). Slip and drift in labor force statistics since 2007. *Econ Journal Watch, 14*(1), 121–132.
Thies, C. (2018). *The global economy: A holistic approach.* Lanham, MD: Lexington Books.
Tindera, M., & Berg, M. (2018, March 31). From the world's richest woman to a strangled mogul: The billionaires who died last year. *Forbes.* https://www.forbes.com/sites/maddieberg/2018/03/06/from-the-worlds-richest-woman-to-a-strangled-mogul-the-billionaires-who-died-in-the-last-year/#20eee97f6b2f
Tuckerman, J. (1838). *Principles and results of the ministry at large in Boston* (pp. 88–89). Boston, MA: James Munroe.
Tullock, G. (1985). Adam Smith and the prisoners' dilemma. *Quarterly Journal of Economics, 100,* 1073–1081.

CHAPTER 13

HOW CAN AN UNDERSTANDING OF AND ACKNOWLEDGMENT OF THE EFFECTS OF SIN AND EVIL INFORM SOLUTIONS TO ORGANIZATIONAL AND SOCIETAL PROBLEMS?

Larry G. Daniel
University of Texas Permian Basin

ABSTRACT

Building on Karl Menninger's (1973) seminal work, *Whatever Became of Sin?* and other subsequent theological and social science writings, I argue for more inclusion of the topics of evil, sin, and redemption in discussions about solutions to organizational and societal problems. In doing so, I explore perspectives of sin from Christian, Jewish, Muslim, Buddhist, and secularist traditions and discuss various factors that must be taken into consideration when discussing sin and evil. Leaders developing solutions to organizational problems would be wise to apply knowledge of the nature of sin, evil, and redemption as a springboard for positive organizational action.

Society, institutions, and organizations are plagued with myriad social and moral problems. These problems regularly capture the attention of the media, government, religious leaders, educators, law enforcement officials, and the general public. Indeed, a cursory review of daily news headlines yields reports on problems as broad as violent crime, theft, corporate malfeasance, and human rights violations. Explanations for these problems are many and varied. Violent offenders are said to have anger management issues, lack impulse control, or suffer from mental illness; misdemeanors and white-collar crimes are explained as crimes of opportunity; and violations of human rights are said to result from poor social conditioning. Although there is relative truth in all these explanations, questions remain about the more generalized explanation for crime, interpersonal problems, and the general ills of society. Indeed, it has become rare to hear explanations of these problems focused on the impact of sin, evil, or lack of personal responsibility.

In this chapter, I argue for the importance of understanding sin and acknowledging the effects of sin on human behavior, relationships, and larger problems in organizations and society. I present evidence that an understanding of sin requires acknowledgement of (a) the existence of evil, (b) the religious and moral roots of sin, and (c) the importance of personal responsibility. Next, I explore a variety of ineffectual methods commonly used for addressing personal and societal problems of a moral nature, none of which typically considers sin and evil as underlying causes of aberrant behaviors. I then propose better alternatives for addressing problems that acknowledge and apply an understanding of sin and evil. In doing so, I explore perspectives of sin from Christian, Jewish, Muslim, Buddhist, and secularist traditions. I then provide several examples of how leaders developing solutions to organizational problems might apply knowledge of the nature of sin, evil, and redemption as a springboard for positive organizational action.

THINKING ABOUT SIN AND EVIL

In 1973, Karl Menninger's provocative book—*Whatever Became of Sin?*—made its appearance on the American social scene. Menninger, a psychiatrist, lamented that the rise of psychoanalysis and other "talking cures" had objectified behavior to the point that actions long considered sinful or immoral were now regarded as normal. In effect, the descriptive social sciences had progressively become prescriptive sciences. Specifically, Menninger (1973) noted,

> The very word, "sin," which seems to have disappeared, was a proud word. It was once a strong word, an ominous and serious word. It described a central point in every civilized human being's life plan and lifestyle. But the word went away. It has almost disappeared—the word, along with the notion. Why? Doesn't anyone sin anymore? Doesn't anyone believe in sin? (p. 14)

Menninger's astute observations about sin are relevant today, and, in fact, society's aversion to acknowledging sin has continuously grown more intense over the several decades since Menninger penned his treatise. For example, Ragen (1994) lamented that "the idea of being a sinner has been so trivialized in American culture that no one need mind being called one or admitting that he or she is one" (p. 9). More recently, Portmann (2007) contended that "sin did not fare well in the heady 1980s and 1990s as fewer and fewer Westerners seemed to think about it" (p. xvi). For example, sin has been omitted from the dialogue surrounding many important moral issues, including bioethics (Collange, 2005). Portmann (2007) acknowledged further that Americans suffer from a sense of "sin fatigue" in which behaviors previously regarded as sins are socially or legally removed of that label. Indeed, perceptions of sin change over time (Capps & Haupt, 2011), and many people just are not that interested in talking or hearing about sin; in fact, they suffer from related "atonement fatigue" that limits their interest in doing what it takes to seek forgiveness and get beyond the effects of sin (Portmann, 2007). General lack of interest in acknowledging sin is prevalent for at least three reasons: (a) acknowledging sin means acknowledging the existence of evil, (b) acknowledging sin means acknowledging religion, and (c) acknowledging sin means acknowledging personal responsibility.

Acknowledging the Existence of Evil

Acknowledging sin forces one to acknowledge the existence of evil. Evil is an ever-present force. Indeed, the notion that evil exists in a metaphysical sense is difficult for some to swallow whereas an evil act is more tangible and easier to acknowledge. Likewise, people are often more comfortable talking about *sins* rather than *sin*. Sins, as individual evil deeds or poorly motivated acts, are wrongdoings, and no one would doubt that people commit multiple wrongs on a regular basis. Sin, as a state, infers the existence of evil in a metaphysical sense within the human experience in general and within the hearts and minds of individual persons more specifically. Despite this important distinction, it is difficult to acknowledge a given sin without linking that individual sin to metaphysical sin. For example, Peters

(1994) observed, "When we commit a sin, we do not present evil for the first time to a previously innocent world. Sin was here before we arrived. We are drawn into it by forces that surround us" (p. 24). Likewise, Portmann (2007) acknowledged the cyclical nature of sin and sins: "Personal sins lead to sinful social structures, and sinful social structures encourage personal sins" (p. xvi).

In talking about evil, synonyms such as wickedness, immorality, depravity, and the like come to the fore. Further, conversations about evil evoke thoughts about the converse of evil: goodness, ethics, and morality. Jordan (2018) argued that moralists reflect regularly on the nature of evil, concluding that "the occurrence of evil is [often] necessary for bringing about a greater good or preventing an equally bad or worse evil from occurring" (p. 11). Collectively, the concepts of good and evil, sin, morality, and ethics have, over many centuries, been the focus of dialogue, debate, and a good deal of controversy. Fisher (2011) distinguished three forms of ethics, namely, applied ethics, which focuses on moral questions about specific issues involving decisions of right and wrong; normative ethics, which focuses on underlying principles defining behavior or conduct; and metaethics, which focuses on second-order understanding of the process of ethics. Although understanding ethics at these three levels can be useful when thinking about sin and evil, the topic of ethical systems is beyond my scope and will only be given this cursory mention. I encourage interested readers to study Fisher's (2011) fine book in detail.

Menninger (1973) identified a number of terms that have been commonly used to describe the motivation underlying aberrant behavior:

> Egocentricity is one name for it. Selfishness, narcissism, pride, and other terms have also been used...The popular leaning is away from notions of guilt and morality. Some politicians, groping for a word, have chanced on the silly misnomer, permissiveness...Disease and treatment have been the watchwords of the day and little is said about selfishness or guilt or the "morality gap." And certainly no one talks about sin! (pp. 227–228)

Portmann (2007) noted further that even "Christians continue to slip and slide between permissiveness and repressiveness" (p. xiii). Peters (1994), reflecting on wrongful thinking among many religious leaders, similarly lamented, "The theological establishment has consigned the human predicament to structure of political and economic oppression or to such systemic evils as race and gender discrimination. In the process, theologians lost interest in the internal workings of the human soul" (p. 2). Likewise, Holifield (1983) observed that the thrust of pastoral counseling has unfortunately shifted its focus from "the cure of souls" to the lifting of self-esteem.

So where does evil come from? It is possible to reduce aberrant behavior to cognitive decision-making, with the focus on the making of "bad choices" or "poor decisions." Scientific evolutionists have posited "selfish gene" and other sociobiological theories to explain that violence is rooted in the evolutionary history of the human race (Peters, 2018). However, the motivation behind aberrant actions is explained, few would deny the importance of understanding people's motivations for action as well as attempts to shape those motivations. Menninger (1973), in getting to the heart of aberrant behavior and its consequences, acknowledged:

> I believe there is "sin" which is expressed in ways which cannot be subsumed under verbal artifacts such as "crime," "disease," "delinquency," "deviancy." There *is* immorality; there *is* unethical behavior; there *is* wrongdoing... There is usefulness in retaining the concept, and indeed the word, SIN, which now shows some signs of returning to public acceptance. (p. 46, emphasis in original)

Likewise, Keltner (2005) focused on ways in which sinful behavior has impacted society, including its deleterious effects on mental health. Specifically, he noted that some individuals with mental health problems "have willfully acted in ways that have compromised them emotionally. Those individuals may well suffer from a soul disorder" (p. 142).

Acknowledging Religion

Because the concept of sin has its roots in religion, it is necessary that one think about religion when thinking about sin. Although a moral "antirealist" would argue that there are no moral facts, Miller (2018) posited that moral facts do indeed exist even though they may not be empirically verifiable. Further, Kellenberger (2018) noted that anthropologists have largely denied the plausibility of cultural moral relativism. There are universal moral truths or facts, and understanding these moral facts means investigating their roots, which often means examining cultural and religious propositions underlying them (even though moral evil can also be examined outside of a religious context [Kellenberger, 2018]). Understanding moral facts means examining the religious roots of sin. This does not mean that it is essential to accept the tenets of any given religion, but rather, that to appropriately understand sin, religious thinking about sin must be considered.

In a 1989 *Atlantic Monthly* article, Tinder queried, "Can we be good without God?" Tinder (1989) explored links between spirituality and politics, concluding, after reflecting on historical roots of intellectual thinking that "only in modern times has it come to be taken for granted that politics is entirely secular. The inevitable result is the demoralization of politics" (p. 1). Sacred social and political values, maintained Tinder (1989), become hard to maintain apart from a belief in God. Likewise, Portmann (2007) noted, "Sin doesn't really make much sense divorced from the concept of God" (p. 4).

Acknowledging Personal Responsibility

Acknowledging sin forces one to face the realities of personal responsibility (or human agency) underlying individuals' actions. The human character includes both positive and negative features (Miller, 2018), and human beings, as free moral agents, may select behaviors consistent with either of these character extremes or with mixed motivation. This sense of "agent causation" is the result of individuals doing something rather than having something done to them (McCann, 2018). Menninger (1973) argued that just as the concept of sin has largely disappeared from conversations about morality so has the concept of personal responsibility:

> Notions of guilt and sin which formerly served as some restraint on aggression have become eroded by the presumption that the individual has less to do with his actions than we had [previously] assumed, and hence any sense of personal responsibility (or guilt) is inappropriate. (p. 177)

Rather than asking an individual to take responsibility for aggressive behavior, society has come up with a multitude of explanations and treatments for it. For instance, an explanation of psychological disorder means that therapy, drugs, or other treatments are the primary intervention with minimal attention on how an individual's aggressive behavior has hurt others or caused damage. Likewise, an explanation of social factors means that the offender is punished lightly or not at all with focus instead on improving the situation in which the offense has occurred.

Keltner (2005), a psychiatric nurse, noted that the general quality of psychiatric care has suffered as a result of "the erosion of personal responsibility.... Multiple individuals have interpreted psychodynamic theories as *raison d'etre* for shifting personal responsibility to childhood events or to others" (p. 143). Although, personal responsibility alone cannot account for all aberrant behavior, the tendency to downplay the significance of personal responsibility in favor of viewing individuals as controlled by others is equally problematic. Consequently, Menninger (1973) argued for

> the revival or reassertion of personal responsibility in all human acts, good or bad. Not total responsibility, but not zero either.... To revive the half-submerged idea of personal responsibility and to seek appropriate measures of reparation might turn the tide of our aggressions.... We will see our world dilemmas more and more as expressing *internal* personal moral problems

instead of seeing them only as *external*, social legal, or environmental complexities. (p. 178)

Failure to take personal responsibility may also result in "collective irresponsibility" which can bring about the sins of groupthink—war, slavery, denial of the Holocaust, environmental sins, and sins of corporations to name a few (Menninger, 1973; Portmann, 2007). Peters (1994) contended that the unwillingness of many to accept responsibility for the broader evils of society has created an "us–them" mentality in which it becomes convenient to blame some other group of people (e.g., those who have a different worldview or who lack "our" level of enlightenment) for the evils of society. Conversely, giving attention to sin within social discourse "enables us to better understand the human predicament and so enables us to better respond to it" (Weaver, 2001, p. 475).

COMMON INEFFECTUAL METHODS FOR ADDRESSING PROBLEMS

Menninger (1973) contended that mental illness, crime, nonfunctioning, aggression, alienation, death, and sin are all subsumed under the larger umbrella of "separation." If the greater problem is indeed separation, in all possible senses of the word, it would make sense that some sense of "joining" or "reconnecting" should be a common way of dealing with these matters. Indeed, Philpott (2013) noted that this concept is consistently visible in religious thinking, regardless of the particular religion. Judaism, Christianity, and Islam share some version of the concept of restoration of right relationship with God and other people as part of a complete religious experience (Philpott, 2013). However, in society's conventional approaches, the methods used to address problems often drive a further wedge between the people involved. Following are several examples of how society deals with problems of separation by means that result in further separation.

Incarceration and Recidivism

Convicted criminals are frequently sentenced to jail or prison for a specified period of time following commission of a crime. Although there is certainly a place for incarceration in the broader criminal justice system, the effectiveness of long-term incarceration, as typically practiced, has been called to question. For example, Baca (2012) has noted:

> Correctional institutions have operated as warehouses for too long, simply locking up offenders without any real effort to rehabilitate or educate. The results have been unacceptably high rates of recidivism throughout the nation, with a national average of more than 68%. This means that for every 10 people released from custody, 7 individuals will be rearrested, reconvicted, and resentenced for a new crime within 3 years. (p. xv)

All of this results in further separation of individuals from society and their families and ignores the fact that "the relational impacts of incarceration create the very risk factors that impede and make rehabilitation difficult" (Sexton, 2016, p. 63). The result is a relatively unsuccessful means for changing offenders' aberrant behavior.

Media Bias and Sensationalism

The media and various groups within society have become famous for uncovering, and in some cases, engineering scandals regarding high profile persons. Although investigative journalism can be a valuable means for pointing out crime, such efforts often smack of political motivation and as a means for garnering viewership and ratings (Vettehen, Nuijten, & Peeters, 2008). Further, the constant replaying of disturbing video footage related to controversial events only serves to build the sensationalism of such events. The media regularly takes on the roles of prosecutor, judge, jury, and executioner, giving no regard to the accused person's Fifth and Sixth Amendment rights and the responsibility of the courts to handle matters involving criminal behavior. Although more research is needed, there is at least some evidence (and clear popular opinion) that pretrial publicity may result in jury bias (Studebaker & Penrod, 1997). Further, when court verdicts are rendered, if they are contrary to the media's own sense of what a verdict should be, there is little respect given to the courts and their responsibility for handling matters according to rule of law rather than popular opinion. The end result of these processes is complete demonization of the accused individual whether in the end the individual is actually convicted of any particular wrong. Even if there is a conviction, and legal punishment of the individual is warranted, the focus is more on full damnation of the convicted person than on fit of the punishment to the crimes committed. In other words, the focus is on isolation: The public is conditioned to distance itself from the offending individual and anything with which the individual is associated. However, simply separating the offending person from society will not, in and of itself, serve to rectify the larger problem.

Psychodynamics and Passing of Blame

Psychodynamic therapies have been used as a major family of approaches among mental health professionals since the early days of psychiatry. Psychodynamic therapy focuses on the patient's relationship with other people and the external world. Psychodynamic therapists may encourage patients to examine issues or concerns based on recollections or events in their early childhood and/or relationships within their family of origin. In its most positive intention, psychodynamic theory allows for new understandings of current issues or problems by reflecting on their origins and provides valuable information useful for designing treatment protocols. However, psychodynamic therapy may have unintended negative consequences. With the focus on shifting blame, it "gives rise to thousands of people who view themselves as controlled by others. In other words, it is a socially inflicted external locus of control" (Keltner, 2005, p. 143).

True victimization aside (and victimization is a genuine issue for certain members of society), routinely blaming one's father, mother, birth order, or a childhood mishap for one's present troubles may become an excuse for not taking affirmative steps to regulate one's own life and behavior. This passing of blame may actually result in further separation of the individual from others. If one deems mistreatment by one's mother as the cause for one's problems, why maintain a relationship with such a domineering and abusive mother? If all one knows is failed relationships, why would that person engage in any future relationships with others?

Organizational Malfeasance and Compensatory Practices

Mandalaki and O'Sullivan (2016) provided an interesting treatise on the unethical actions of large corporations, noting that there is a tendency for these organizations to increase good deeds in one domain of their operation following publicized bad deeds in a different domain. The authors likened this practice to the Catholic concept of the granting of indulgences. Indulgences in the ancient Catholic tradition were a means for reducing the punishment one would receive for sins committed. Indulgences generally involved recitation of a certain prayer a given number of times, performance of a compensatory good action, and public confession of sin. In effect, the process involved true repentance of the wrongdoing followed by redirection of actions in a positive direction. Although indulgences were generally a form of individual penance, Church history provides examples of organizations being granted indulgences by the Church.

By the 16th century, the practice of indulgences had fallen into abuse, with religious officials engaging in the selling of indulgences. Mandalaki and O'Sullivan (2016) noted that the present-day Mafia in Sicily still operates in the spirit of the practice:

> The Sicilian Mafia still engage in this practice of generous donation to the church which they appear to see as some kind of insurance against eternal damnation.... The contemporary belief is based more on superstition rather than a tenable religious position, since the Church while gladly accepting the donations does not of course today officially grant such indulgences. (p. 210)

Current day corporate "indulgences," though designed to restore public confidence and erase the effects of past sins, typically serve to drive wedges between the customers and publics the corporations intend to serve. (Note that corporate indulgences are distinct from "redemptive acts" [Elster, 2006] that individuals or organizations may do as a true about-face to a previously adversarial posture.) As Mandalaki and O'Sullivan (2016) have noted, "When contemporary companies and organizations engage in philanthropy, they rarely have the slightest intention of correcting the initial wrongdoing which triggers the philanthropic attempt to gain indulgence" (p. 211). This obvious corporate hypocrisy is easy to see through, and many customers react by taking their business elsewhere.

As examples of this practice, Mandalaki and O'Sullivan (2016) offered up the philanthropic activities of tobacco firms which can never compensate for the ill-health effects caused by deceptive practices and the dangers of their products; the involvement of Shell Oil in community development projects in Nigeria, at the same time it was being sued in international courts for multiple environmentally debilitating oil spills in the region; the investments by McDonald's in the Ronald McDonald House Foundation at the same time the company continues to offer menu choices that have contributed to the obesity epidemic; and the "green company" marketing campaign and activities conducted by BP Oil at the same time their poorly maintained oil wells were on the verge of malfunctioning. Using BP as the example, the authors illustrated how these hypocritical practices further separate corporations from their publics, noting that the actions have "damaged the company's ethical reputation with ethical investors" (p. 220).

CHRISTIAN, JEWISH, ISLAMIST, AND BUDDHIST PERSPECTIVES ON SIN, EVIL, AND REDEMPTION

As previously noted, understanding sin requires delving into conventional religious thinking about sin. The prevalence of Christian thought within American society has led many to perceive sin as a uniquely Christian concept. However, as Peters (1994) has noted, "Sin and evil are topics well known beyond the fences of Christian doctrine" (p. 5). Understanding the

Christian perspective is important, but it is equally important to view sin from the perspectives of other religions. To this end, I will, in turn, provide brief conceptualizations of sin from Christian, Jewish, Muslim, and Buddhist perspectives.

A Christian Perspective

Though exact views of sin vary across Christian denominations, common elements are that all human beings are sinful and in need of a savior, namely Christ; that sin separates a person from God; and that sin has consequences in this life and in the world to come. Several Greek words are translated as "sin" in the New Testament, including "*hamartia*, meaning 'to miss the mark' as if an archer's arrow were to miss hitting the target; *adikia*, meaning 'injustice' or 'unrighteousness'; and *anomia* meaning 'to be without the law' or 'lawlessness'" (Peters, 1994, p. 7). McFarland (2018) noted differences in definitions of sin across Christian traditions, concluding that "sin is better described as the contradiction of the good rather than its privation" (p. 329). Christians often speak of the distinction between sin and suffering; whereas the former is displeasing to God, the latter may simply be a reality of the human condition. Burroughs (1654/1992) argued from a Christian point of view that suffering and sin are comingled throughout one's life; to make a choice to sin in an attempt to avoid suffering is the "evil of evils" (p. 1).

Differences exist within various Christian traditions regarding "original sin" (Portmann, 2007). Original sin as a doctrine states that, as a result of the sin of Adam and Eve, all human beings are born with a predisposition toward sin. The sin of the original humans upset the primordial perfection of creation, resulting in an imperfect, sinful state. Original sin serves as a reminder to Christians that they are regularly subject to the effects of sin and that fully relying on God, through Christ, is the only way to live above sin's effects. Those Christians who place less emphasis on original sin still acknowledge that believers must come to terms with their own sinfulness, regularly guard against committing sin, and regularly seek God's forgiveness for any sins committed. Further, the Christian perspective always parallels the realities of sin and evil with the themes of repentance, grace, and redemption (i.e., salvation). Redemption is perhaps the most powerful theme within Christianity, for it allows belief that the most iniquitous and reprobated of individuals, following genuine repentance of sin and an encounter with a divine Savior, can experience a "new birth" and become an exemplar of the love of God to others.

The central focus of sin and its effects within Christian teaching is perhaps the most uncomfortable of all Christian teachings to the non-Christian;

nevertheless, the existence of sin provides a powerful explanation for certain human experiences. As Tinder (1989) has observed:

> Nothing in Christian doctrine so offends people today as the stress on sin. It is morbid and self-destructive, supposedly, to depreciate ourselves in this way. Yet the Christian view is not implausible. The twentieth century, not to speak of earlier ages (often assumed to be more barbaric), has displayed human evil in extravagant forms. Wars, massacres, systematic torture and internment in concentration camps have become everyday occurrences in the decades since 1914...Thus our own experience indicates that we should not casually dismiss the Christian concept of sin. (p. 8)

A Jewish Perspective

The Genesis account of creation affirms that when God created man, man was made as a *nephesh hayah* or "living soul." The immortality of the soul and, consequentially, the importance of personal accountability for one's actions are central to Judaism. Jews believe, as Christians, in the primordial goodness of all things. Repentance, or atonement, for one's sins and wrongdoings is essential. Although Jews typically reject the doctrines of original sin and redemption, they acknowledge that people are sinners and that the potential for rebellion against God resides in the hearts of all.

In ancient Judaism, there was the strong belief that sin resulted in death. The Israelites, as descendants of Abraham, were a covenant people, and violation of God's covenant and laws earned the penalty of death. Rather than the individual him/herself dying, a blood sacrifice of an animal was offered at designated times to atone for individual and corporate sins. As Portmann (2007) observed, "People came to believe that sacrificing [alone] could atone for all sins" (p. 37). The writings of the Hebrew prophets are replete with admonitions that repentance must be truly from the heart and an act of the will, not simply a ritual sacrifice. Portmann (2007) noted that when the Jewish Temple in Jerusalem was destroyed in AD 70, the Jewish system of sacrifices ended. In modern-day Jewish practice, repentance is most formally acknowledged on Yom Kippur, the most holy day of the Jewish year, in which believers joyfully celebrate God's willingness to forgive their moral failures.

An Islamist Perspective

In examining the root beliefs of Islam, it is important to draw both parallels to and contrasts with the beliefs of Judaism and Christianity. Katsch (1963) observed that Islam might never have developed were it not for the

Jews and Christians living on the Arabian Peninsula who influenced Muhammad, founder of the Islamist faith. The five important doctrines (Articles of Faith) in Islam are belief in God (Allah), angels, books, prophets, and the Last Day. These doctrines and other important teachings of Muhammad are contained in the Qur'an, the central religious text of Islam, which Muslims regard as divinely inspired. Muslims see humans as pure and able to reach salvation by faith and good practice, seeking the mercy of God, and relying on the intercession of prophets, imams, and other revered Muslims (Meftah & Rabbini, 2015; Miner, Ghobary, Dowson, & Proctor, 2014). Though acknowledging humans are subject to sin, Muslims reject the concept of original sin. They view sin as disobedience to God rather than transgression against a divine standard (Nigosian, 2003). Further, Philpott (2013) noted, "Islam also teaches that forgiveness restores right relationship, both between God and humans and between humans" (p. 404).

In Muslim belief, people of the faith have a special attachment to God (Allah) based on their relationships with key human intermediaries. Miner et al. (2014) noted, "Believers develop relational knowledge of God as merciful and compassionate through relational knowledge of mediators such as prophets and spiritual leaders" (p. 89). Believers approach God directly and through these key representatives. Muslims regard all things created are from God, including human actions; however, humans possess the ability to perform actions, and that is where wrongdoing, or sin, may occur (Burrell, 1997). Forgiveness may sometimes involve lengthy lamentation. Further, Nigosian (2003) indicated that Muslims acknowledge the primacy of the sin of apostasy: "Apostasy—abandonment of Islam for another religion—was equivalent to the denial of God and of his unity. To deny God in this way was to forfeit one's status as a member of the Islamic community" (p. 94).

A Buddhist Perspective

Buddhism holds that time is both beginningless and endless. There is no creator God and therefore no final judge of the world. Good and evil coexist and are constantly at war with one another. The Buddhist moral law of *kamma* (or karma) is an outgrowth of this sense of the duality of good and evil. Kamma is essentially an external action driven by intentionality which leads to future consequences—good or bad. In the Buddhist sense, sin is defined as an act or deed rather than a state, and outward sinfulness is the result of corrupt motives or wrong thinking. The consequences of kamma may reveal themselves in the present life or in future lives.

There is considerable focus in Buddhist dogma on suffering:

> Suffering is a reality that sentient beings are unable to escape...Each instance of suffering has a cause that brought it about...The Buddha also tells us that suffering can cease, and that there are means to achieve the cessation of suffering. (Cattoi, 2017, p. 34)

Personal enlightenment is the way to escape sin and its consequential suffering. Enlightenment is a means for transcending the good–evil duality—moving beyond the realm of good and evil to an "empty" place where good and evil do not exist. Kamma may result in both personal and social consequences. Moe (2015) noted a distinction between Buddhist and Christian perspectives as regards the origin of catastrophic events:

> Since evils result from tyranny, Buddhists emphasize more on the question of how the ridding of evils can be solved by human efforts than the question of how God would react to them. Buddhists argue that evil calamities are human-made, whereas Christians claim that evil calamities are both divine-made and human-made. (p. 34)

A SECULARIZED VIEW OF SIN AND EVIL

Obviously, not all who approach problem-solving come from a religious perspective, and the very notion that traditional views about sin come from religious thinking turns off some secularists. Indeed, some secularists maintain that religion itself defies intelligence; hence, they may reject any notion of the existence of sin and evil. However, it is equally well argued that "the intellectual justifiability of religious faith in today's world is a hotter topic than it has been for decades" (Joas, 2014, para. 2), and secularists would do well to consider religious views about the nature of humanity even if they choose to reject religious thinking in the larger sense. Likewise, Weaver (2001) noted, "The discourse of sin offers a moral language of accountability that refers to experiences and struggles human beings can recognize and resolve without reference to religious convictions" (p. 482). Further, Peters (1994) suggested there may be more common ground between the religious and secularists than realized relative to perceptions about sin and evil, noting "people of every cultural tradition and religious persuasion are able to recognize the blindness of unbridled greed and the destructive power of pride" (p. 5).

Lugg (1996) drew parallels between the political philosophy of "social traditionalism," one of the prominent political movements in the United States, and Christianity. Although she acknowledged that "not all devout Christians are social traditionalists, nor are all social traditionalists

Christians," she observed that social traditionalists are more likely to view social problems as the result of moral failings of individuals than as a consequence of the flaws of the political, social, and economic order (p. 6). Hence, social traditionalists act on the notion that personal flaws, or sins, must be addressed in order for society to advance and effectively address its major issues. Social traditionalists often employ religious sentiments in their thinking; for example, they may promote the notion "that individuals would rather feel guilty, when disaster strikes, than helpless" (p. 8). Hence, traditionalists view acknowledgement of past failure and personal responsibility as the most effective means for advancing society.

APPLYING KNOWLEDGE OF SIN AND EVIL TO THE BEHAVIOR REPERTOIRE OF LEADERS

Regardless of one's personal philosophical or religious slant, it would behoove all leaders to incorporate a knowledge of sin and evil into their understanding of issues involving people and their actions considering that wrongdoing within organizational contexts is, unfortunately, both prevalent and normative (Palmer, 2013). Specifically, an understanding of sin and evil would serve leaders well when having discussions about ethics and ethical behavior. By no means does this infer that leaders should go about judging and labeling individuals or individuals' actions as sinful; rather, they should acknowledge that concepts involving the nature of sin, evil, goodness, and redemption can be a springboard for positive organizational action. Corporate wrongdoing results in human suffering (Palmer, 2013), and approaches to eliminating causes of suffering imply identifying the perpetrators of wrong actions. As Weaver (2001) has noted:

> Religious ethics should not appropriate sin-talk in its more general or doctrinal expressions as a device to "fix" persons or the world, nor as a device for lowering expectations... Religious ethics should appropriate sin-talk and pay nuanced attention to particular sins because doing so reveals the limits of, as well as the necessity for and the promise of, ethics. Through a constant, creative and (self-)critical envisioning of the good, and through equally vigilant, imaginative, and open reflection on the acts and relations that order us to the good, ethics can be chastened by the recognition of sin and empowered by the grace to respond to it. (p. 499)

Although an understanding of sin might be helpful to leaders in dealing with a variety of issues, I will discuss three here, namely handling disputes, offering public apologies, and dispensing restorative and intergenerational justice.

Handling Disputes

When human beings interact, conflict is inevitable. Leaders in any group or organization find themselves addressing conflicts with some regularity as part of "the business of managing change" (Brubaker, Noble, Fincher, Park, & Press, 2014, p. 382). Conflict resolution may involve two people, groups of individuals within organizational or social settings, or two or more nations. Leaders understand that unresolved conflict is costly in a variety of ways (Brubaker et al., 2014). There are seldom pat answers in the resolution of conflict considering that each scenario presents its own uniqueness in terms of the needs and interests of the parties, the nature and severity of the issue(s) causing conflict, and the length of time the conflict has gone on unresolved.

Often, there is the illusion of resolution to conflict when no resolution is really accomplished. For example, one party may become fatigued and give in to the other, or both parties may get distracted from the conflict because of other important issues. On the other hand, conflict may fail to be resolved due to the way that one party treats the other. Linder (2008) discussed the matter of "humiliation" as a major stumbling block to the process of conflict resolution. In effect, if one party treats the other contemptibly such that there is "an offensive violation of humanity" (p. 165), the injured party may withdraw. This may give the other party the guise of resolution. Although Linder (2008) does not discuss this topic in terms of behaviors being sinful, the links to sin could easily be made. Consider the following examples:

> A husband who habitually beats his wife and children, believing that domestic chastisement of disobedient family members is his duty, will define "successful reconciliation" as the "quiet submission" of his family members under his routine domination. If we extrapolate this example to larger political contexts at macro levels, the path to reconciliation may entail everything from violence and war to a shrewd mix of arm-twisting and deceptive Machiavellian "negotiation" of "conflicts of interest" (be it disputes over access to water, land, or other resources). Reconciliation is seen as accomplished when defeated opponents "understand" that it is in their "interest" to acquiesce to the victor's domination, and submissively enter the ranks of underlings. (p. 164)

Acknowledging the impact of individual sinfulness (especially one's own) can go a long way in making conflict resolution productive. Although the literature on conflict resolution generally avoids the topic of sin, it is common to see language such as "misconduct," "aberrant behavior," or "transgressions," all of which can be considered synonyms of sin. In fact, Palmer (2013) advanced the notion that wrongdoing, rather than being considered an abnormal phenomenon, is quite normal in organizational life. Otherwise upstanding individuals may at times commit wrongdoings. Unfortunately, wrongdoings may cause people to suffer in various ways (Palmer, 2013). Therefore, beginning resolution of conflict with ground rules stressing mutual dignity is a valuable first step. Conflict resolution should ideally focus on productive and mutually beneficial dialogue. Too often, when conversations get tense, one party will resort to domination, threats, or intimidation, or, alternately, may try to "buy off" the other party materially or with favors. These strategies, unfortunately, usually result in deepening the conflict. When wrongdoings by one party against another occur, it is important to recognize the value of apologies and forgiveness. However, forcing an individual to offer an apology when that person is unwilling to do so is counterproductive. Likewise, forgiveness can also be a tricky enterprise.

Adams, Zou, Inesi, and Pillutla (2014) noted, when "there is high potential for disagreement about the transgressor's ostensible blameworthiness for wrongdoing," the person expressing the forgiveness may actually be avoided in the future by the transgressor (p. 131). In any case, clearly recognizing the specific transgression (i.e., sin) that has occurred is an important first step. All members of an organization, including leaders, must be regularly cognizant of their own potential for wrongdoing: "It is important for managers to develop a better understanding of the forces that operate on all organizational participants, including themselves, that can cause them to cross the line separating right from wrong" (Palmer, 2013, pp. 21–22).

Offering Public Apologies

The American public has become increasingly familiar with televised and social-media-shared apologies from celebrities, corporate executives, governmental officials, and other high-profile individuals. These apologies often follow a personal moral failure, an embarrassing remark or episode, a cover-up exposed, or some other major mistake. Quality of the apologies and their emotional impact vary appreciably. Some spokespersons gloss over wrongdoings, fail to provide enough information about what has occurred, or, worse yet, pass blame on to others. Other spokespersons more appropriately describe incidents in detail, fully accept blame, apologize sincerely, and promise corrective action. Although there are many elements of an effective apology, the acknowledgement of "sin" is a crucial part of the process. As noted previously in the section on handling disputes, it is uncommon in the literature to see the word "sin" used when discussing public apologies; however, the concept is there, and it is clear that good apologies address sin whereas poor apologies either ignore it or fail to recognize its impact.

When public apologies involve a moral failure, bad actions of a member or members of a corporate group, systematic organizational wrongdoing, or leadership failure, the apology should ideally be sincere, timely, and detailed. According to Cels (2017), apologies should include at least three ethical components: (a) acknowledgment of the moral consequences of the wrongdoing (i.e., the harm done), (b) level of responsibility of the apologizer for the wrongdoing (i.e., degree of personal involvement), and (c) prior relationship between the apologizer/organization and the victims. Obviously, apologies are also typically accompanied by a promise of future actions to rectify the wrongdoing (Kim, Park, Cha, & Jeong, 2015). In essence, using the language of sin, these steps include an admission of sin and its consequences, request for forgiveness, and hope of reconciliation.

Often, it becomes important to apologize for offensive events that occurred in a society's past. Celermajer (2013) presented an excellent treatise on this subject, focusing on the difference between individual guilt for a wrong personally committed and collective shame for an act committed by society in the past that has caused one or more groups of people to suffer long-term negative consequences. Here again, the apology should focus specifically on the wrong done (historically), the consequences of the wrong, and a desire to take a new course of action. The apology, if provided sincerely and with enough specificity to provide full acknowledgement of wrongs done, would ideally be followed by a promise by all persons and groups involved to move beyond the painful events of the past with the goal of building a positive future. Public apologies of this type can be controversial as some would regard asking a present person or group to make the apology is forcing that person or group to assume the guilt of the event even though no one of them particularly was involved. Celermajer (2013) countered this position:

> If guilt (especially criminal guilt) adheres uniquely to actions, then shame adheres to our identity, or to the ways in which we partake in the world in which the specific wrongs are rendered possible if not likely... Shame, and the expression of shame in the form of the apology, are then the means through which we take responsibility for recasting our political culture. (pp. 51–52)

Dispensing Restorative and Intergenerational Justice

The term "restorative justice" is often used within the confines of criminal justice to refer to ways that an offender or society can make whole the victim of a crime; in this sense it is similar to the legal concept of restitution, but it also includes attention to restoring of relationships. However, the term has also been used more broadly to focus on the steps a society can take to deal with the harm caused to groups within society by the evils of past policies, laws, or actions. Braithwaite (2000) noted that "healing relationships, as opposed to balancing hurt with hurt, is one core value of restorative justice" (p. 185). Further, restorative justice focuses on the larger problem or concern rather than the offender or the victim even though it ideally will benefit all parties involved.

Restorative justice at the societal level is a tedious subject. As previously noted, many individuals have a hard time understanding why institutions, governments, and other organizations feel they must take action today in response to actions that took place years before when no one involved in the original actions is even alive anymore. Nevertheless, sins of previous generations (i.e., what Peters [1994] refers to as "socially inherited sins") frequently demand action by a current generation. Portmann (2007), reflecting on issues as broad as the environment, national debt, and college admission policies, observed,

> Young people in America pay for the sins of their fathers in a variety of ways, and older Americans ought to think long and hard about the consequences of their actions as well as how to foot the bill equitably. (p. 167)

Indeed, young adults in the twenty-first century are shouldering the burden of past errors of discrimination, pollution, corruption, greed, and the like.

Intergenerational justice is closely related to restorative justice; however, its focus is more on "reducing harms to future generations" (Hendlin, 2014, p. 25) than on correcting the effects of past misdeeds. Intergenerational justice is built on a foundation of human dignity (Riley, 2016). Intergenerational justice is designed to

> respect future generations such that we commit no injustice against them either in terms of distributive justice (equitable distribution of goods between generations) or in terms of more basic wrongs (namely, destroying the conditions of their existence or their potential for levels of well-being equivalent to our own). (Riley, 2016, p. 275)

In determining how to dispense restorative or intergenerational justice, leaders, by necessity, must identify the exact sins and evils that have taken place. This is usually fairly easy to do. Determining the long-term effects of those past sins is more difficult, and determining what, if any, corrective actions are needed is yet more difficult. Institutionalized racism is a particularly thorny problem for those concerned with intergenerational justice. Portmann (2007) observed that "original sin serves as an excellent model through which to understand this problem of intergenerational justice" (p. 163). Just as the doctrine of original sin acknowledges, due to the sins of forebears, the moral imperfections with which humans are born, some may view (rightly or wrongly) innocent White infants being born with a stain of racism based on the past actions of persons of their race. Simply by being White, a child may be assumed to be an oppressor. Unfortunately, many young White people may "blame themselves for the nagging problem of racism, even though young white people may feel it wildly unfair—immoral even—to blame themselves" (Portmann, 2007, p. 163).

Good leaders understand these issues surrounding racism. They work with others to understand and clarify the sins of the past and the consequences of those sins. They understand that individuals within the current generation must sometimes stand as proxies for those who may have sinned in the past. They work collaboratively, in the mode of restorative justice, to focus on the problem and to heal relationships among those who have been disadvantaged by racism and those whose forbears created racist structures and practiced racist behaviors. Effective restorative justice measures help to ensure social justice (Braithwaite, 2000).

CONCLUSIONS AND REMAINING UNANSWERED QUESTIONS

Sin is a moral reality that affects the lives of people every day. Every person has the capacity to sin; no one is immune. Whether one acknowledges original sin, individually committed sins, and/or the existence of sinful states, it is hard to ignore this powerful moral force. Sin affects everyone and has consequences that impact people as individuals and in groups. Current generations frequently must deal with the fallout caused by sins of previous generations. In a nutshell, "Sin belongs to the human condition" (Peters, 1994, p. 276).

I have attempted, in this chapter, to provide examples of how acknowledgement of sin and its effects can be a useful tool in addressing a host of problems and issues encountered in homes, the workplace, government, and society in general. Menninger (1973) noted that sin must be dealt with in many places but ultimately within "the private courts of the individual heart" (p. 180). This is true whether a person is religious or areligious; Christian, Jewish, Muslim, Buddhist, or a follower of another religion; spiritualist or secularist.

Grappling with contemporary problems demands attention to sin and its effects. Questions of personal morality are not explained away adequately by addressing an individual's poor decision making. Likewise, corporate and governmental wrongdoings are not simply the actions of nameless, faceless bureaucracies. Individual persons set policies, take actions, and respond to the people served. People, even "good" people, make errors and mistakes, commit wrongdoings, and hurt others. The consequences of sin are great. Injuries and broken relationships separate people from one another. Although people may be quick to intervene, the methods used to address sin often drive a further wedge of separation between the people involved, leaving a general feeling of alienation and hopelessness.

In the midst of this doom and gloom, I have hoped to provide some important information that might assist leaders in more effectively addressing organizational and societal problems. As an educator and leader, I maintain my optimism and my passion to be a force for positive change in the world around me. Knowledge is power, and knowledge about sin and evil can be a powerful tool in helping leaders develop creative solutions to problems. Menninger (1973) lamented that the biggest problem with sin is failing to admit that it exists. Conversely, openly talking about sin and its implications will serve to understand it better. I have provided three specific arenas in which leaders can benefit by an understanding of sin and evil—handling disputes, offering public apologies, and dispensing restorative and intergenerational justice. The possibilities for applying knowledge about sin to other areas of importance to organizations and leaders are endless. Portmann (2007) summarized his treatise on sin as follows:

> People will remain the signal constant for sin. They will spur us to sin sometimes and deter us from it at others. More than natural disasters or terrorist attacks, individuals (and groups of them) will disrupt our rest and drive us to ponder unspeakable acts. At the same time, individuals (and groups of them) will deliver consolation more powerful than we are likely to find in Prozac or technological gadgets. *People are more important than sin* [emphasis added]. (pp. 200–201)

Tough times call for courageous leaders. Though the problems leaders encounter in the 21st century are, at times, ominous, it is encouraging that leaders, due to the explosion of knowledge and advances in technology, have more tools at their disposal than ever before. Leaders should employ every tool in their warehouse, but they should also wisely employ incontrovertible information about topics as old as the history of humankind. Sin and evil are such topics.

REFERENCES

Adams, G. S., Zou, X., Inesi, M. E., & Pillutla, M. M. (2014). Forgiveness is not always divine: When expressing forgiveness makes others avoid you. *Organizational Behavior and Human Decision Processes, 126*, 130–141.

Baca, L. D. (2012). Foreword. In A. H. Normore & B. D. Fitch (Eds.), *Education-based incarceration and recidivism: The ultimate social justice crime-fighting tool* (pp. xv–xvi). Charlotte, NC: Information Age.

Braithwaite, J. (2000). Restorative justice and social justice. *Saskatchewan Law Review, 63*(1), 185–194.
Brubaker, D., Noble, C., Fincher, R., Park, S. K.-Y., & Press, S. (2014). Conflict resolution in the workplace: What will the future bring? *Conflict Resolution Quarterly, 31*(4), 357–386.
Burrell, D. B. (1997). The pillars of Islamic faith: What we should know & why. *Commonweal, 124,* 17–19.
Burroughs, J. (1992). *Evil of evils, or the exceeding sinfulness of sin.* Morgan, PA: Solio Deo Gloria. (Original work published 1654)
Celermajer, D. (2013). Apology and the possibility of the ethical nation. In D. Cuypers, D. Janssen, J. Haers, & B. Segaert (Eds.), *Public apology between ritual and regret: Symbolic excuses on false pretenses or true reconciliation out of true regret?* (pp. 45–64). Amsterdam, The Netherlands: Rodopi.
Cels, S. (2017). Saying sorry: Ethical leadership and the act of public apology. *The Leadership Quarterly, 28*(6), 759–779.
Capps, D., & Haupt, M. (2011). The deadly sins: How they are viewed and experienced today. *Pastoral Psychology, 60*(6), 791–807.
Cattoi, T. (2017). Flawed subjectivities: Cyril of Alexandria and Mahāyāna Buddhism on individual volition, sin, and karma. *Buddhist-Christian Studies, 37*(1), 29–39.
Collange, J.-F. (2005). Bioethics and sin. *Christian Bioethics, 11*(2), 175–182.
Elster, J. (2006). Redemption for wrongdoing: The fate of collaborators after 1945. *Journal of Conflict Resolution, 50*(3), 324–338.
Fisher, A. (2011). *Metaethics: An introduction.* London, England: Routledge.
Hendlin, Y. H. (2014). The threshold problem in intergenerational justice. *Ethics and the Environment, 19*(2), 1–38.
Holifield, E. B. (1983). *A history of pastoral care in America: From salvation to self-realization.* Eugene, OR: Wipf and Stock.
Joas, H. (2014, November 18). Is being religious "intellectually dishonest"? How the dialogue between believers and nonbelievers is changing—for the better [Web log post]. *Stamford University Press.* Retrieved from http://stanfordpress.typepad.com/blog/2014/11/is-being-religious-intellectually-dishonest.html
Jordan, J. (2018). The evidential argument from evil. In J. Gellman, C. Meister, & C. Taliaferro (Eds.), *The history of evil from the mid-twentieth century to today: 1950–2018 C. E.* (pp. 11–27). London, England: Routledge.
Katsch, A. I. (1963). Judaism and Islam. *Journal of Educational Sociology, 36*(8), 400–406.
Kellenberger, J. (2018). Moral relativism. In J. Gellman, C. Meister, & C. Taliaferro (Eds.), *The history of evil from the mid-twentieth century to today: 1950–2018 C. E.* (pp. 344–361). London, England: Routledge.
Keltner, N. L. (2005). Whatever became of sin? Revisiting Menninger's question. *Perspectives in Psychiatric Care, 41*(3), 142–145.
Kim, H., Park, J., Cha, M., & Jeong, J. (2015). The effect of bad news and CEO apology of corporations on user responses in social media. *PLos One, 10*(5), 1–21. https://doi.org/10.1371/journal.pone.0126358
Linder, E. G. (2008). Why there can be no conflict resolution as long as people are being humiliated. *International Review of Education, 55*(2/3), 157–181.

Lugg, C. A. (1996). Calling for community in a conservative age. *Planning and Changing, 27*(1/2), 2–14.
Mandalaki, E., & O'Sullivan, P. (2016). Organisational indulgences or abuse of indulgences: Can good actions wipe out corporate sins? *M@n@gement, 19*(3), 203–227.
McCann, H. J. (2018). Free will theodicy. In J. Gellman, C. Meister, & C. Taliaferro (Eds.), *The history of evil from the mid-twentieth century to today: 1950–2018 C. E.* (pp. 104–119). London, England: Routledge.
McFarland, I. A. (2018). The problem with evil. *Theology Today, 74*(4), 321–339.
Meftah, A. R., & Rabbini, M. (2015). A comparison between the concepts of redemption in Christianity and intercession in Shia Islam. *Comparative Theology, 5*(12), 143–160.
Menninger, K. (1973). *Whatever became of sin?* New York, NY: Hawthorn.
Miller, C. (2018). Moral realism and anti-realism. In J. Gellman, C. Meister, & C. Taliaferro (Eds.), *The history of evil from the mid-twentieth century to today: 1950–2018 C. E.* (pp. 323–342). London, England: Routledge.
Miner, M., Ghobary, B., Dowson, M., & Proctor, M.-T. (2014). Spiritual attachment in Islam and Christianity: Similarities and differences. *Mental Health, Religion, & Culture, 17*(1), 79–93.
Moe, D. T. (2015). Sin and evil in Christian and Buddhist perspectives: A quest for theodicy. *Asia Journal of Theology, 29*(1), 22–46.
Nigosian, S. A. (2003). *Islam: Its history, teaching, and practices*. Bloomington: Indiana University Press.
Palmer, D. A. (2013). The new perspective on organizational wrongdoing. *California Management Review, 56*(1), 5–23.
Peters, T. (1994). *Sin: Radical evil in soul and society*. Grand Rapids, MI: William B. Eerdmans.
Peters, T. (2018). The science of evil and the evil of science. In J. Gellman, C. Meister, & C. Taliaferro (Eds.), *The history of evil from the mid-twentieth century to today: 1950–2018 C. E.* (pp. 221–241). London, England: Routledge.
Philpott, D. (2013). The justice of forgiveness. *Journal of Religious Ethics, 41*(3), 400–416.
Portmann, J. (2007). *A history of sin: Its evolution to today and beyond*. Lanham, MA: Rowman & Littlefield.
Ragen, B. A. (1994, January 29). A wretch like who? *America, CLXXX*(3), 8–11.
Riley, S. (2016). Architecture of intergenerational justice: Human dignity, international law, and duties to future generations. *Journal of Human Rights, 15*(2), 272–290.
Sexton, T. L. (2016). Incarceration as a family affair: Thinking beyond the individual. *Couple and Family Psychology: Research and Practice, 5*(2), 61–64.
Studebaker, C. A., & Penrod, S. D. (1997). Pretrial publicity: The media, the law, and common sense. *Psychology, Public Policy, and Law, 3*(2/3), 428–460.
Tinder, G. (1989, December). Can we be good without God? *The Atlantic*. Retrieved from https://www.theatlantic.com/magazine/archive/1989/12/can-we-be-good-without-god/306721/

Vettehen, P. H., Nuijten, K., & Peeters, A. (2008). Explaining effects of sensationalism on liking of television news stories: The role of emotional arousal. *Communication Research, 35*(3), 319–338.

Weaver, D. F. (2001). How sin works: A review essay. *Journal of Religious Ethics, 29*(3), 473–501.

CHAPTER 14

HOW CAN THE NEWEST GLOBAL RELIGION—THE BAHA'I FAITH—IMPACT THE FUTURE OF BUSINESS?

Payam Zamani
Founder, Chairman & CEO at One Planet Group

This chapter, in a departure from the academic and scholarly style of the other essays in *Blessed*, presents my own personal reflection on my spiritual experience as it relates to my entrepreneurial career. I do not profess to be a scholar, either academically or of the Baha'i Faith, so have chosen to write instead from my own personal belief perspective about how my religion and its spiritual and moral teachings have impacted the business decisions I have made and the career choices I have pursued.

In this chapter, I will endeavor to cover:

- my values and the values of my faith,
- the general principles found in the Baha'i teachings,
- how those principles impact business in general, and

- finally, I will share the six spiritual conclusions I have reached as a successful Silicon Valley entrepreneur, using the Baha'i principles and my own business experience:
  - Share your profits.
  - Be a business—but with social impact.
  - Strive for goodness, not bigness.
  - Do not let competition make you compromise.
  - Build a new vision for business.
  - See humanity as one.

SPIRITUAL VALUES

Every business—small, midsized, or gigantic—operates from a set of spiritual values, whether stated or not. Those values typically contribute heavily to the culture of the organization and its workplaces. Of course, most workplaces are made up of a diverse set of individuals who collaborate, work together, set goals, make decisions—and socialize, too. From that mix of an organization's culture and the individual personalities who work within that culture, growth and development occur—for the employer and the employees, for the work itself, and for the relationships formed within that culture.

For a Baha'i like me, the workplace culture, the relationships it engenders and the products or services the organization delivers all ideally combine to form a collective contribution to the common good.

The Baha'i Faith teaches a unique set of spiritual and social principles. Those principles provide guidance for organizational relationships that sustain themselves and generate healthy profit margins—while maintaining an ongoing sense of mission, meaning, and individual fulfillment for their owners, employees, and the community.

THE BAHA'I PRINCIPLES THAT GUIDE MY WORK

Some of the Baha'i principles that have always guided my work ethic, and my philosophy of business, include:

- the oneness of the entire human race;
- the need for the valuing of justice as a primary operating principle;
- the eradication of prejudices of all kinds;
- eliminating the societal custom of backbiting and gossip;
- enhancing the interrelationship of unity and diversity;
- realizing the power of true consultation for decision-making;
- the equality of men and women;

- work, done in the spirit of service, is a form of worship;
- the need for universal education and philanthropy;
- honesty and trustworthiness in all dealings; and
- spiritual solutions to economic problems.

Baha'is worldwide, including myself, are learning to translate these principles into action in business. The democratically elected global governing body of the Baha'i, the Universal House of Justice, recently gave the worldwide Baha'i community advice on the issue of economics and business when it wrote:

> The welfare of any segment of humanity is inextricably bound up with the welfare of the whole. Humanity's collective life suffers when any one group thinks of its own well-being in isolation from that of its neighbours or pursues economic gain without regard for how the natural environment, which provides sustenance for all, is affected. A stubborn obstruction, then, stands in the way of meaningful social progress: time and again, avarice and self-interest prevail at the expense of the common good. Unconscionable quantities of wealth are being amassed, and the instability this creates is made worse by how income and opportunity are spread so unevenly both between nations and within nations. But it need not be so. However much such conditions are the outcome of history, they do not have to define the future, and even if current approaches to economic life satisfied humanity's stage of adolescence, they are certainly inadequate for its dawning age of maturity. There is no justification for continuing to perpetuate structures, rules, and systems that manifestly fail to serve the interests of all peoples. The teachings of the Faith leave no room for doubt: there is an inherent moral dimension to the generation, distribution, and utilization of wealth and resources. (The Universal House of Justice, 2017, para. 4)

I view these spiritual and moral principles as uncompromising anchors through which new realities—including in the business world—can emerge and develop. Throughout my 20+ years as an entrepreneur in Silicon Valley, I have gained firsthand experience how such principles shape or disrupt our views around sharing profits, social impact, philanthropy, and competition.

SIX SPIRITUAL BUSINESS GUIDELINES

In this section, I want to share some of my views on business success combined with spirituality and explain the thinking behind them. I hope my experience will help business creators, executives, and owners in their quest for success, and in fostering the positive long-term impact they have on the world and the human family. In this section, you will find my six specific suggestions:

- Share your profits.
- Be a business—but with social impact.
- Strive for goodness, not bigness.
- Do not let competition make you compromise.
- Build a new vision for business.
- See humanity as one.

Share Your Profits

A century ago, megacorporations, conglomerates, and monopolies were called "trusts." They dominated whole industries and even entire nations through their rapacious business practices. The trusts became unassailable monopolies, restraining trade and raising their prices to unfair levels—after they had decimated and destroyed or swallowed up their business rivals. Alarmed, many governments created antitrust laws to regulate and control the trusts—but corporate mergers and takeovers found ways to get around those laws. Does that still sound familiar today?

In the early part of the 20th century, Abdu'l-Baha—the son of Baha'u'llah, the prophet and founder of the Baha'i Faith, and its leader after Baha'u'llah's passing—visited North America and spoke in cities across the United States and Canada for 8 months. On June 3rd and 4th, 1912, he was invited to visit the Milford, New York estate of Gifford Pinchot, the former United States cabinet secretary and head of the U.S. Forest Service, and later the Governor of Pennsylvania. Pinchot, one of the founders of the Progressive Party along with U.S. President Theodore Roosevelt, assembled a group of national leaders who engaged Abdu'l-Baha in a lengthy, detailed question-and-answer session. One of those leaders asked Abdu'l-Baha about economic conditions, including the issues of labor unions and the trusts. He answered:

> The owners of properties, mines, and factories should share their incomes with their employees and give a fairly certain percentage of their products to their workingmen in order that the employees may receive, beside their wages, some of the general income of the factory so that the employee may strive with his soul in the work. (Abdu'l-Baha, p. 84)

These spiritual principles of fairness and justice, reflected throughout the Baha'i teachings, honor the work of all people, ask corporations to share their wealth, and by doing so inherently limit the out-of-control growth of megacorporations and monopolies that make huge profits, hoard their resources and don't reward their workers commensurately.

Typically, emerging companies and even established ones, especially in Silicon Valley, incentivize their workforces by offering a profit-sharing model based on ownership of stock. Simply granting stock options to those involved in the building or growth of a business has a significant downside; however, it often incentivizes greed by focusing on the short term. This dynamic works by utilizing the "build and flip" business model so many startups subscribe to—quickly ramping up the stock valuation via rapid growth, and then selling the company to benefit the heavy stock option holders. In some ways, this model mimics the old, illegal "pump and dump" schemes that artificially inflated the stock price of a given enterprise and then took large profits out by selling that stock all at once.

This, of course, is not a healthy recipe for longevity or real business success.

At my company, One Planet Ops, Inc., we have tried to build long-term value, not by granting stock options, but by actually meaningfully sharing the quarterly profits of the company with our employees. That way, stock ownership does not become a short-term and sometimes ephemeral mirage dependent only on the market's valuation at the moment. Instead, we try to follow our best understanding of the Baha'i model of actual profit sharing, which calls upon the owners of any given company to share a significant percentage of that company's profits with the workers:

> Laws and regulations should be enacted which would grant the workers both a daily wage and a share in a fourth or fifth of the profits... or which would have the workers equitably share in some other way in the profits with the owners. For the capital and the management come from the latter and the toil and labour from the former. (Abdu'l-Baha, 2014, p. 317)

At One Planet we have learned that this model—which emphasizes building an operation that offers real service and creating actual versus paper valuation—has many advantages. It generates long-term rather than fleeting, short-term valuation; it incentivizes all employees instead of just a select few; it creates commitment to the actual mission of the organization and not just to its fluctuating share price; and it leads to stability and permanence rather than shaky impermanence. We have found that this profit-sharing model also creates better customer service and a much higher level of job satisfaction, as well

Be a Business—But With Social Impact

Companies, we all know, need to focus on business fundamentals—generating profits and doing their best to provide a healthy return for investors. That is a given, and nothing to apologize for or shy away from.

But is profitability a company's only goal? Does financial performance serve as the sole benchmark for the success of an organization? Increasingly, experts including CEOs understand that companies, no matter their size or scope, need something more than just the profit motive to sustain them.

In fact, I believe that doing the right thing, and considering the impact of our work on humanity, represents a natural, healthy ingredient currently missing from many of our profitable endeavors. By including these ingredients, we will build better companies, better products, and better societies, and the outcome will in fact be more valuable and more profitable businesses.

This is not just a theory—I have seen it happen, time and time again.

Accordingly, we should stop segregating businesses into social impact enterprises and traditional for-profits. Often social impact businesses get lumped into a secondary category: the ones with inferior business models and smaller opportunities for growth. Our best businesses should proactively consider their social impact and build sacrificial philanthropy into their core.

Businesses today need to recognize their role in shaping the wider social fabric, and then drive their enterprise with a constant eye on dramatically improving it. As a Silicon Valley entrepreneur, I believe our biggest problem is that success here—and all across the business world—is often only measured in financial terms. We need to change that. We need to measure success by how likely we are to spend our resources to help and serve others, by how many lives we touch in a positive way, and by how successful we are with the positive impact we can have on the betterment of our communities and the world around us.

I am not talking about a $40 billion company giving 1% of their profits away, just so they can check the "socially responsible" box. Our companies need to go way beyond simply creating a façade of being good, and actually examine their core beliefs and change their hearts—so they, with all their might, will want to actually demonstrate their deep concern for humanity and help shape a better future.

The Baha'i teachings say that the impact we each can have on the betterment of the world will ultimately determine what truly matters. Abdu'l-Baha (1957) wrote:

> We must now highly resolve to arise and lay hold of all those instrumentalities that promote the peace and well-being and happiness, the knowledge, culture and industry, the dignity, value and station, of the entire human race. Thus, through the restoring waters of pure intention and unselfish effort, the earth of human potentialities will blossom with its own latent excellence and flower into praiseworthy qualities. (p. 4)

After all, let us not forget that the majority of entrepreneurs are highly focused on building massive amounts of wealth. But the Baha'i teachings say that wealth earned through our efforts is really only admirable and praiseworthy if we choose to spend it for the well-being of humankind. I mean, what is wealth for? If we accept the fact that we are spiritual beings, if we agree that we all belong to one human family, shouldn't we concern ourselves with the welfare of all people? Abdu'l-Baha continued:

> Wealth is praiseworthy in the highest degree, if it is acquired by an individual's own efforts and the grace of God, in commerce, agriculture, art and industry, and if it be expended for philanthropic purposes... if it is dedicated to the welfare of society—its possessor will stand out before God and man as the most excellent of all who live on earth and will be accounted as one of the people of paradise. (pp. 24–25)

Do we see the overall welfare of our society as a priority—or are we too busy maximizing personal wealth? This quote from Baha'u'llah ought to answer that question: "Blessed and happy is he that ariseth to promote the best interests of the peoples and the kindreds of the earth" (Baha'u'llah, 1978, p. 167).

So what leads to this kind of social impact, to that happiness which comes from promoting "the best interests of the peoples and kindreds of the earth?" In my experience, the answer to that question lies in the difference between ends and means. In the end, most of us want to have a positive impact on humanity and its problems. We want to contribute. But many of us get stuck in this kind of thinking: "I'll do all that good once I am big and mighty." That idea presumes that only huge megacorporations can really have an impact on the world, and nothing could be further from the truth. In fact, that reasoning is almost like a driver saying, "Let me drive fast, break laws along the way, show road rage if necessary, but once I get to my destination, I will do good." In other words, it is the process that really counts—the means, not the ends. One ancient philosopher, Epictetus, said, "There are no ends—only means."

Having a social impact should be part of every company's fabric from Day One. When we structure an organization with social impact as part of its original mission, that will in fact help us build better companies that attract the right people and give us the necessary North Star for all of our decision-making efforts.

Strive for Goodness, Not Bigness

Does your enterprise have to become huge before you can have a measurable impact on society? I have to be honest—over the years, as an entrepreneur I have dreamt about building a company that could become a major global force. Many entrepreneurs have those dreams. We want to build something of consequence, a company that can have a real impact on the world, an influential, trendsetting institution that pioneers true change.

But here is the question I have asked myself recently: Does a corporation have to grow extremely large and powerful to function as a global force? Do we all have to bow down to the god of perpetual growth? In other words, does bigness equate to goodness?

That seems like a stretch, right? If you look at some of the world's largest corporations—Google, Apple, Amazon, Microsoft, Exxon, Walmart—and closely examine their overall impact on the world, it's predictably a mix of good, not-so-good, and downright bad, with downright bad leading the way sometimes. But why is this important?

The World Bank reported in 2016 that of the world's 100 largest economies, 31 were countries and 69 were corporations. The tenth largest economy in the world was Walmart. This means we need to start thinking of multinational megacorporations as entities responsible for more than just their own bottom line.

Yes, the big corporations employ many people, providing them and those who depend on them with their livelihoods. They help support national and international economies. In some cases, they, or their founders and executives, might contribute to worthy charities.

But if you are aware of the basic motivations of those megacorporations, you will also soon come to understand that often greed and world domination drive a significant part of their agendas. Many big public corporations, because they are primarily motivated by the bottom line and by the ever-present profit demands of their shareholders, do not seem to have much of a focus on their impact on humanity whether in their local area or the broader world. Instead, they seem to be driven by the Darwinian concept of self-interest and relentless, no-holds-barred competition, the old survival-of-the-fittest doctrine that can obviate human altruism and conscience when it comes to business.

How can we overcome that lack of ethical thinking? The Baha'i teachings say we need "a shared ethic, a sure framework for addressing the crises that gather like storm clouds":

> [T]he world is in desperate need of a shared ethic, a sure framework for addressing the crises that gather like storm clouds. The vision of Baha'u'llah challenges many of the assumptions that are allowed to shape contemporary discourse—for instance, that self-interest, far from needing to be restrained, drives prosperity, and that progress depends upon its expression through relentless competition. To view the worth of an individual chiefly in terms of how much one can accumulate and how many goods one can consume relative to others is wholly alien to Baha'i thought. But neither are the teachings

in sympathy with sweeping dismissals of wealth as inherently distasteful or immoral, and asceticism is prohibited. Wealth must serve humanity. Its use must accord with spiritual principles; systems must be created in their light. (The Universal House of Justice, 2017, para. 5)

The big multinational corporations, when they do not have much concern for the future of humanity and focus solely on their bottom lines, have tremendous unintended impacts on the rest of the world. What can solve that dilemma?

To answer those questions, we need to look at the process of corporate growth and what drives the mentality that prompts it. Think about it this way: Imagine if corporations shared their profits from the start rather than planning to enrich only a select few, if they were less aggressive in terms of killing their competition, if they cared more about their impact on unemployment caused by the companies they take over or run out of business, if they adopted a serious social impact agenda from the very beginning, if they gave sacrificially to charitable causes—then perhaps those moral and spiritual standards, enforced in the company's culture since its inception, would permeate its leadership and mitigate its negative impact on the world.

Also, if those more altruistic goals became an integral part of the company's original mission, then perhaps the accumulation of its own material advantage would become less obsessive and primary, or at least the maximization would take place within the parameters set by these first principles.

Should we cease polluting the Earth or make more money? Should we change our employment and human rights practices, or should we ignore those issues and make more money? Should we capitalize on products or services that are not ultimately good for humankind? When corporations ask themselves these tough questions, too often the answers come down on the side of money. Ask those questions to any random megacorporation CEO, and you will probably hear some version of this canned answer: "We exist to maximize profit for our shareholders, not to solve the world's problems—that's someone else's responsibility."

So you have to wonder: Would the world's megacorporations even be able to grow so large if they actually checked their true intentions and had a "shared ethic and a sure framework?" If they really intended to make the world a better place and do so through their service at scale, all while making a great profit, but did not have greed and world domination as the number one agenda item, would they still strive to become so big? Or would growing, profitable corporations with a conscience be willing to slow their growth rate a bit so they could treat their employees well, do good things for everyone and give back to society?

It is not the sheer size of the megacorporations that is objectionable—it is how they get there. If corporations did profit share, participate in programs that help humanity and give to charity sacrificially—if they operated without the goal of growing so large that they put others, especially small business owners, out of business—but instead cared about their global and local impact and actually did something about it, could they even become megacorporations?

These days I have begun to believe that the Baha'i teachings, through love rather than force, foster an environment that automatically limits how large businesses can and should get, and how much control a single corporation could possibly exert over humanity as a whole:

> Love is heaven's kindly light, the Holy Spirit's eternal breath that vivifieth the human soul. Love is the cause of God's revelation unto man, the vital bond inherent, in accordance with the divine creation, in the realities of things. Love is the one means that ensureth true felicity both in this world and the next. Love is the light that guideth in darkness, the living link that uniteth God with man, that assureth the progress of every illumined soul. Love is the greatest law that ruleth this mighty and heavenly cycle, the unique power that bindeth together the divers elements of this material world, the supreme magnetic force that directeth the movements of the spheres in the celestial realms. Love revealeth with unfailing and limitless power the mysteries latent in the universe. Love is the spirit of life unto the adorned body of mankind, the establisher of true civilization in this mortal world, and the shedder of imperishable glory upon every high-aiming race and nation. (Abdu'l-Baha, 1982a, p. 27)

Don't Let Competition Make You Compromise

The approach discussed in the previous section will probably inherently limit corporate growth, not through force and laws, but through building a new value system based on an infusion of love and altruism. The outcome? An environment where corporations will not be so powerful that they can impact the entire world beyond what should be a reasonable level of influence from a business—which will also leave the market open to small business owners, including many who are currently headed toward extinction.

These spiritual limits to corporate growth will allow for diversity in our choices, the family touch in many enterprises, and opportunity for everyone. In business, we can probably agree that healthy competition is a good thing but compromising your moral and spiritual values to completely ruin your competition stains the entire playing field.

If one or two companies grow so large and become such massive platform plays, they can completely block all others and not only reduce choices for consumers but drive higher prices, stunt ingenuity and create unreasonable and potentially catastrophic corporate power and liability, just like the trusts did a century ago. When monopolies take over, no one is safe. We got a bitter taste of that excess with the recent global financial crisis, when some megacorporations in the financial sector famously became "too big to fail."

This problem of sheer corporate bigness now afflicts not just the business world itself, but the world at large. Megacorporations like Apple have market caps of a trillion dollars, large enough to include them in G7 meetings. Monopolies in many economic sectors produce enormous wealth for a few, but actually result in the net loss of livelihood for many. With money comes power, and with power comes—well, everyone already knows about the problems power usually produces.

Much of this global affliction, however, comes from the spiritual disease of materialism. The Universal House of Justice (2017) characterized that disease this way:

> The forces of materialism promote a quite contrary line of thinking: that happiness comes from constant acquisition, that the more one has the better, that worry for the environment is for another day. These seductive messages fuel an increasingly entrenched sense of personal entitlement, which uses the language of justice and rights to disguise self-interest. Indifference to the hardship experienced by others becomes commonplace while entertainment and distracting amusements are voraciously consumed. The enervating influence of materialism seeps into every culture, and all Baha'is recognize that, unless they strive to remain conscious of its effects, they may to one degree or another unwittingly adopt its ways of seeing the world.... With the approach of adulthood comes a responsibility, shared by one's generation, not to allow worldly pursuits to blind one's eyes to injustice and privation. (para. 11)

The Baha'i teachings say the world is approaching adulthood—a new period of human maturation, in which we will learn to cooperate and communicate effectively, building the potential to bring about global peace and harmony among all peoples. That spiritual and moral maturation calls on us all to begin to consider others, not only as equals, but as part of our human family. After all, biological science reliably informs us that we are all related—57th cousins, at most. If we begin to think of one another in that new way, the Baha'i teachings say, it will ultimately change things:

> Consider the harmful effect of discord and dissension in a family; then reflect upon the favors and blessings which descend upon that family when unity exists among its various members. What incalculable benefits and blessings would descend upon the great human family if unity and brotherhood were established! (Abdu'l-Baha, 1982b, p. 229)

Can you imagine this new, unified state of society the Baha'i teachings envision? If you can, you already recognize the interdependence of the world, and you may understand what that growing interdependence really means for insightful business leaders and entrepreneurs.

This movement toward unification, which the Baha'i teachings have predicted and encouraged since the 19th century, is happening all around us. In a more unified world, we will transcend borders, ethnicity, nationality, and skin color. In a more unified world, markets will expand. In a more unified world, the arena for new and innovative businesses will grow. I predict that in a more unified world, entrepreneurs will play a much more vital role in society. In a more unified world, interdependence will become more and more important. Here is a quote from Abdu'l-Baha from over one hundred years ago:

> In cycles gone by, though harmony was established, yet, owing to the absence of means, the unity of all mankind could not have been achieved. Continents remained widely divided, nay even among the peoples of one and the same continent association and interchange of thought were well-nigh impossible. Consequently intercourse, understanding and unity amongst all the peoples and kindreds of the earth were unattainable. In this day, however, means of communication have multiplied...In like manner all the members of the human family, whether peoples or governments, cities or villages, have become increasingly interdependent. For none is self-sufficiency any longer possible, inasmuch as political ties unite all peoples and nations, and the bonds of trade and industry, of agriculture and education, are being strengthened every day. Hence the unity of all mankind can in this day be achieved. (1982a, pp. 31–32)

My business success, in other words, should not depend on the death of someone else's business. We are interdependent. In healthy ecosystems, which support a wide variety and diversity of life, plants, and animals have to cooperate, intermingle, and coexist. In a healthy business ecosystem, the same dynamic applies. Instead of some of the vicious business practices we have seen recently—hostile takeovers, predatory pricing strategies, employee poaching, negative advertising, and the like, we should hope for the success of our competitors, and simply do our best to provide better service to our customers. That kind of friendly, wholesome competition only makes things better, not worse. So let's welcome healthy competition rather than trying to stamp it out—we will all be better for it.

Build a New Vision for Business

Many people think of religion as antibusiness, but with the Baha'i Faith, that is simply not true. Let us be clear—the Baha'i teachings have absolutely nothing against business, success, and wealth, as long as that success is achieved through hard work, honesty, and diligence; and the resulting wealth is spent on the welfare of all humanity:

> Man's merit lieth in service and virtue and not in the pageantry of wealth and riches... Be generous in your days of plenty, and be patient in the hour of loss. (Baha'u'llah, 1978, p. 138)

> Economic life is an arena for the expression of honesty, integrity, trustworthiness, generosity, and other qualities of the spirit. The individual is not merely a self-interested economic unit, striving to claim an ever-greater share of the world's material resources... By consecrating oneself to the service of others, one finds meaning and purpose in life and contributes to the upliftment of society itself. (The Universal House of Justice, 2017, para. 8)

More and more, people and companies are integrating this progressive Baha'i viewpoint—that wealth can be creatively utilized to uplift society itself—into their consciousness. After all, one of the most creative arenas available to us as human beings is our ability to generate ideas and build organizations that produce security, sustenance, and wealth for all of us. When we catch the entrepreneurial spirit, and that spirit includes the moral and spiritual motivation to do good for all, the results can be spectacular.

We can become the source of wealth and well-being for many, many other people. We can support families, villages, towns, and cities with an infusion of jobs, productive work, and economic well-being. We can bring about flourishing communities, alleviate poverty, educate children, and encourage the cultural aspects of human existence. We can build business ecosystems that spin off other ventures, ideas, and enterprises. In short, we can inject new vigor and vitality into our lives and the lives of everyone around us. What could be more creative, more satisfying, and more altruistic?

Once corporations and their leaders consider their intentions, de-emphasize greed as a main motivator, and cease being driven by the push for global domination, a better business environment will inevitably result, where small businesses will flourish alongside many more midsize companies with maybe a few billion in revenue—but not hundreds of billions and valuations approaching or exceeding trillions.

As a CEO, I see many wealthy entrepreneurs and executives who have built huge organizations, enjoyed financial success beyond their wildest dreams, and accomplished a great deal, but remain terribly unhappy. It is as if they expected their financial and business success to somehow make them whole, to fill in a missing part in their inner lives. They seek meaning and happiness in all kinds of places, from yoga retreats to sweat camps to adventure vacations, but nothing external seems to fill that void inside.

Here is my prescription for filling it: serve others. That is the eternal advice of every great faith and the Baha'i teachings, too:

> Economic life is an arena for the expression of honesty, integrity, trustworthiness, generosity, and other qualities of the spirit. The individual is not merely a self-interested economic unit, striving to claim an ever-greater share

of the world's material resources. "Man's merit lieth in service and virtue," Bahá'u'lláh avers, "and not in the pageantry of wealth and riches." And further: "Dissipate not the wealth of your precious lives in the pursuit of evil and corrupt affection, nor let your endeavors be spent in promoting your personal interest." By consecrating oneself to the service of others, one finds meaning and purpose in life and contributes to the upliftment of society itself. (The Universal House of Justice, 2017, para. 8)

If you make service to humanity a fundamental part of your organization's mission statement, your everyday work will inevitably benefit others and you will reap the joyous rewards of those interactions.

I am confident, with a bit more focus on what will uplift others versus what benefits us personally and materially, that implementing a deep service ethic in our souls and our companies will bring more happiness and fulfillment to all of us.

See Humanity as One

As I mentioned earlier in this chapter, the recognition of humanity as one family drives much of the economic and business guidance in the Baha'i teachings.

That vision of human oneness affects the Baha'i view of capitalism, of prejudice, sexism, and racism in the workplace, of labor vs. management struggles, and of economic justice. It deeply impacts the Baha'i view of alleviating poverty through world unity and humanistic policies of globalization. As the Baha'i writings say:

> The harvest comes forth for everyone. The rain showers upon everybody and the heat of the sun is destined to warm everyone. The verdure of the earth is for everyone. Therefore, there should be for all humanity the utmost happiness, the utmost comfort, the utmost well-being.
>
> But if conditions are such that some are happy and comfortable and some in misery, some are accumulating exorbitant wealth and others are in dire want—under such a system it is impossible for man to be happy and impossible for him to win the good pleasure of God. God is kind to all. The good pleasure of God consists in the welfare of all the individual members of mankind. (Abdu'l-Baha, 1982b, p. 312)

What is your vision for your business? Do you want to be a mogul, a captain of industry, a rainmaker? Or do you want to truly impact and alleviate the suffering of your fellow human beings? Search your conscience with those questions and see how it responds.

The Baha'i teachings say that humility, spirituality, and a real desire to serve others count as each human soul's real success, that the mere accumulation of riches is only temporary, while service to the world of humanity lasts forever.

The world runs on business. To create a new kind of business—human-centered organizations with a conscience and a commitment to helping others—means we may not become giants of the business world and hopefully the business world will not be made up of globe-dominating giants. The goal should be that we achieve maximum success for ourselves and our businesses, while remaining true to our commitments that ensure betterment of the world is not just a slogan—but part of the fabric of our business life and our guiding North Star.

I will leave you with a few bullet points that will hopefully help summarize this chapter:

- We are one. Our race—the human race—has an inescapable mutuality and interdependence.
- Because we are one, the human race operates like any other linked, interdependent ecosystem: It depends on diversity and variety to function optimally.
- Because we are one, we also have an inherent desire to altruistically help others.
- Business organizations that fail to recognize that vital human component—altruism—might make a good product or deliver good value, but they ultimately lack a critical component.
- Every business organization, if it hopes to become sustainable and truly succeed, must adopt a serious social impact agenda.

I hope your endeavors in this fertile field will bear fruit.

REFERENCES

Abdu'l-Baha. (1957). *The secret of divine civilization.* Wilmette, IL: Baha'i Publishing Trust.

Abdu'l Baha. (1982a). *Selections from the writings of Abdu'l-Baha.* Haifa, Israel. Baha'i World Center.

Abdu'l-Baha. (1982b). *The promulgation of universal peace.* Wilmette, IL: Baha'i Publishing Trust.

Abdu'l-Baha. (2014). *Some answered questions* (2nd ed.). Haifa, Israel: Baha'i World Centre.

Baha'u'llah. (1978). *Tablets of Baha'u'llah.* Haifa, Israel: Baha'i World Center.

The Universal House of Justice. (2017, March 1). To the Baha'is of the world. *Baha'i Reference Library*. Retrieved from https://www.bahai.org/library/authoritative-texts/the-universal-house-of-justice/messages/20170301_001/1#712004157

CHAPTER 15

"NUNS" TO NONES?

Revisiting Management, Spirituality, and Religion in the Workplace for the New Generation

Latha Poonamallee
*Milano School of Policy, Management, and Environment
The New School*

ABSTRACT

The religious "nones" or ones who have no religious affiliation is a fast-growing demographic category in the United States. But management and organizational research has not considered the implications of this trend towards irreligiousness for organizations and workplaces. In this chapter, I introduce the nones, their profile characteristics, and position them as a persecuted minority given their deep differences from the mainstream U.S. culture, which is high on religiosity, especially among the developed nations. I also explore two lines of thought about their presence in the workplace: (a) how the inclinations of the nones could be at odds with organizations that seek to create affective commitment in its employees and (b) how they are well positioned to facilitate the next transformation of our work and society.

> *For we know that our patchwork heritage is a strength, not a weakness. We are a nation of Christians and Muslims, Jews and Hindus and non-believers. We are shaped by every language and culture, drawn from every end of this Earth; and because we have tasted the bitter swill of civil war and segregation, and emerged from that dark chapter stronger and more united, we cannot help but believe that the old hatreds shall someday pass; that the lines of tribe shall soon dissolve; that as the world grows smaller, our common humanity shall reveal itself; and that America must play its role in ushering in a new era of peace.*
>
> —Obama, 2009

For what may have been the first time in modern U.S. history, an American president rescued a large demographic category from obscurity, thrust them on a national stage and included them to expand and reiterate the definition of who we are as a collective and what our highest good was. It was a significant moment that echoed, acknowledged, and honored the changing tide of religiosity in America. The group that President Obama termed the nonbelievers is more commonly referred to as the "nones" (Vernon, 1968) and is made up of a hotchpotch of atheists, agnostics, spiritual but not religious, and nothing in particular (The Pew Forum, 2016). At 22.8%, this group called the religious nones make up almost a quarter of the U.S. adult population (Lipka & Gecewicz, 2017). At 54 million people, this group is more numerous than Catholics and Mainline Protestants and second only to Evangelical Protestants who make up 25.4% of the U.S. population. According to the same survey, this segment is growing especially rapidly among the millennials. About 35% of the millennials call themselves the nones and this number goes up to 39% in people in the 30–49 age group. This trend is seen in all demographic groups including those with college degrees or high school diplomas, men and women, and all ethnic groups among the younger population and globally, including even predominantly religious countries such as India (Quack, 2012). This group has invited an increasing interest by researchers in social sciences (Baker & Smith, 2015; McClure, 2017; Silver, Coleman, Hood, & Holcome, 2014) but has eluded the attention of organization and management scholars. In this chapter, I contribute to addressing this gap by examining the implications of this growing group for workplace organizing, especially in the area of meaning making and affective commitment.

Modern organizations encourage a vocational attitude among its employees to increase their engagement and organizational citizenship behaviors and discourage attrition and dysfunctional behaviors within organizations. Faith-based organizations exemplify this approach in engaging its employees and volunteers, especially in areas of social welfare such as education and healthcare. Many secular organizations try to mimic building this type of deep connections with and among its employees to promote affective commitment, job satisfaction, and organizational citizenship through various positive organizational psychology approaches such as organizational compassion and religious practices such as mindfulness. Whether it is multinational businesses honoring and marking new offices with poojas in India, celebrating Christmas and Hanukkah elsewhere, embedding spiritually grounded mindfulness practices to serve secular ends such as stress reduction, organizations contend with the role of spirituality and religion in its stakeholder groups. Scholarship has followed suit by systematically examining the role of spirituality and religion in the workplace. If the general consensus is that spirituality and religion shape organizational life, we don't yet know how the nones, the second largest demographic group in the United States shape or expect to shape organizational life and how organizations should prepare to deal with this group.

In this chapter, I introduce this growing demographic category, describe the nuances of subcategories within the group, and then, I examine the unexamined: How do the nones shape the organizational life today? How are they expected to shape the future of organizations? How should organizations support them? I conclude by laying out implications for research and practice.

DEMYSTIFYING THE NONES

At 54 million people, the nones as a group are more numerous than Catholics and Mainline Protestants and second only to Evangelical Protestants in the United States. A fast-growing group, its membership jumped from 7.5% in 1973 to 25% of American adults in 2017 (Lipka & Gecewicz, 2017) and worldwide, there are anywhere between 500 and 700 million individuals with no religious affiliation (Zuckerman, 2007). About 20% of the population do not attend services of any kind (Norris & Ingleheart, 2011; Roozen, 2011). Further, among the millennials, this segment is growing especially rapidly. About 35% in the 18–29 and 37% in the 30–49 age groups are unaffiliated to any religions. Although the term, nones is used to represent all those who check the box of no religion, there is a valid criticism that nones are wrongly treated as a homogenous group (Frost & Edgell, 2017) but include atheists, agnostics, nothing in particular (NIP), spiritual but not religious (Lee, 2014), and different ways of being irreligious (Frost & Edgell, 2017). This is further complicated by gender, race, and other intersectional identities that play a part in this mix. However, in general, all the nones share a preoccupation with disaffiliation from any engagement with religion and religious culture in general (Lee, 2014, p. 474) and their mindsets characterized by tolerance for diversity in terms of group membership and participation (Kettell, 2013).

Of these strains, atheists are the most organized, vocal, and visible (Blankholm, 2014; Cimino & Smith, 2014) and the spiritual but not religious (SBNR), most loosely defined and organized. Among the atheists, LaDrew (2012, 2013) distinguishes between the contemporary or new atheists who are more aligned to scientific or enlightenment rationalism/atheism than the humanist atheists more aligned to the rise of Marxist social scientists. Secular humanists seek accommodation similar to those with a declared religious affiliation, but contemporary or new atheists are more eliminationists. In the same vein, Langston, Hammer, and Cragun (2015) identify three important subsets: secular affiliates, secular nonaffiliates, and the sizable portion of nonbelievers who are not involved in any group because to them, their nonbelief does not matter. Their approaches to formal, organized religion spans from the range from eliminationism, substitutionalism, and accommodationism. These nones (SBNR) believe in a God or some form of higher power (Kosmin & Keysar, 2008). About half of the nones describe themselves as spiritual, 41% pray more than once a month, and 68% believe in a God or universal spirit (Lipka, 2015). Even if they do not participate in organized religion, the SBNR population maintains a personal sense of spirituality (Davie, 1994; Heelas, 2006). Ammerman (2013) describes four primary cultural packages in which people construct meaning of spirituality. Theistic, that is, relationships with personal deities; extra-theistic, that is, naturalistic forms of transcendence; ethical, that is, focused on everyday compassion; and belief and belonging spirituality, that is, cultural notions of religiosity such as cultural Jews or cultural Hindus. Nonreligious are more likely to use extra-theistic terms. However, in this category, the empirical boundary between spirituality and religion is far more porous than the moral and political one. (O'Brian Baker & Smith, 2009). When it comes to political identification and attitudes related to religiously infused topics, SBNR people are more aligned with the atheists than with the religious. Although there is a surge of new groups and movements across the nones (Baker & Smith, 2015; Beaman & Tomlins, 2015), scholars examining this category need to be sensitive to their different stances to religion and gods, but also to race, gender, and class, thus making intersectionality an essential part of understanding this category (Cornwall, 2009).

Within the nones, atheists are more at social risk than others who declaim religious identification (Edgell, Frost, & Stewart, 2017; Edgell, Hartmann, Frost, Stewart, & Gerteis, 2016). This explains why more self-identified atheists are from privileged identity groups—White, male, with a college degree (Furseth, 2009); perhaps because they have the resources to avoid or deal with the stigma associated with nonreligion (Link & Phelan, 2001). This may also explain why men tend to identify more as atheists (Furseth, 2009) than women, especially given that women who are vocal about lack of religiosity are viewed as less womanly (Hutchinson, 2011; Schutz & Roth, 2015).

Even if they do not believe in the supernatural or a universal spirit, older and nonwhite women tend to soften the social blow by identifying as spiritual but not religious (Aune, 2015; Brown, Taylor, & Chatters, 2015; Wilcox, 2009). Similarly, almost 81% of African Americans characterize themselves as spiritual *and* religious. Brown et al. (2015) find that non-Hispanic White, Hispanic, and Asian Americans are more likely than African Americans and African Caribbean Americans to identify as less religiously involved. A quarter of Asian Americans identify with non-theistic religions and engage in private practices like shrines at home, meditation and private worship services at home, and this doesn't usually get captured in the church attendance data. This group also tends to use religious practices as cultural practices in raising their younger generations. However, this group is also an overrepresented minority among the affluent and highly educated (Macartney, Bishaw, & Fontenot, 2013) and rank highest among all racial/ethnic groups on almost all measures of economic well-being (Callis & Kresin, 2014; Macartney et al., 2013), thus confounding the matter even further.

Age is another salient factor in understanding the profile of the nones. Younger cohorts tend to be more religiously uninvolved (Putnam & Campbell, 2012) thus adding to the swelling numbers. Even among African Americans, a highly religious group in the United States, age plays a role. Younger African Americans are more likely to say rarely attend services compared to older African Americans. Merino (2013) finds that recent cohorts with secular upbringing tend to stay unaffiliated as adults and are likely to have an unaffiliated spouse; they also tend to be more secular, liberal, and wary of organized religion as adults. Similarly, Nelson (1990) confirmed that religious intermarriage led to children being more likely to claim no religious affiliation. One of the strongest predictors to having no religion is marrying a similarly unaffiliated partner (Baker & Smith, 2009) thus increasing the pool of the nones should prevent defection to religion and keep the growth of the unaffiliated stable and rising, thus making this group an important phenomenon and worthy of inquiry.

Why is there such a surge of nonbelievers in the United States? Scholars offer several theories. One is that the recent increased politicization of religion, that is, especially the rise of the fundamentalist right and their conservative positions on cultural issues claiming more public space (Davie, 2013) put them at odds with young adults (Hout & Fischer, 2002; Putnam & Campbell, 2012). A second theory is that secularization is an offshoot of increased economic security (Norris & Ingleheart, 2011). Although this theory wouldn't explain why the millennials, the most financially precarious generation yet, would not quell their anxiety through religious affiliation, it explains why women and poorer communities of color with fewer opportunities and less power are more risk averse and have higher religiosity (Levin, Taylor, & Chatters, 1994; Miller & Hoffmann, 1995; Norris & Ingleheart, 2011; Taylor,

1988). Further, faith communities have played an historical role of providing succor and resources for individual and community well-being among the less privileged. Lacking social obligations used to be considered another source of atheism (Stark & Bainbridge, 1987). However, with the increasing population of nonreligious couples raising children who are nones as well, this theory does not hold its ground anymore. Finally, modernization theorists argue that higher levels of education and acceptance of empiricism reduces religious involvement (Wilson, 1976) and an increasing acceptance of the view that religion is not universal. This development "counters the notion that all people—as people—are somehow intrinsically religious or that religion is some sort of necessary, universal, or inextricable component of the human condition" (Zuckerman, 2015, p. 172).

GODLESS AS THE "OTHER"

Zuckerman (2009) asks, "Can people reject god and still have strong beliefs and values?" Negative view of atheists is pervasive in the United States (D'Andrea & Sprenger, 2007; Downey, 2004; Ehrlich & Van Tubergen, 1971; Harper, 2007; Heiner, 1992; Hwang, 2008; Koproske, 2006; Newport, 2006; Pew Research, 2019). In a society which views religiosity as a proxy for moral worth that underpins cultural membership in our increasingly multicultural society (Edgell et al., 2017, p. 508), atheists are perceived as immoral (Gervais et al., 2017; Lamont & Molnar, 2002) and remain persistent cultural outsiders (Edgell et al., 2017, p. 609). Discrimination against atheists has been documented by several scholars (Dawkins & Flynn, 2007; Downey, 2004; Goodstein, 2000; Hammer, Cragun, Hwang, & Smith, 2012; Heiner 1992; Hunsberger, 2006; Koproske, 2006; Pollitt, 2011; Reisberg, 1998; Zorn, 2008). A survey by Edgell et al. (2006) found that the nonreligious are often characterized as immoral, elitist, and antisocial. Researchers found the following: 44% of Americans would disapprove if their child married an atheist, 42% believe that the nonbelievers do not share their vision of American society, 36% of Americans say that atheists lack a moral center, 22% think that they are more likely to engage in criminal activity behavior (Edgell, Gerteis, & Hartmann, 2006; Gervais, Shariff, & Norenzayan, 2011). These assumptions and perceptions are far from the truth and are not supported by any evidence.

Atheists and seculars are less nationalistic, less prejudiced, less anti-Semitic, less racist, less dogmatic, less ethnocentric, less close-minded, and less authoritarian (Altemeyer, 2003, 2009; Altemeyer & Hunsberger, 1992, 1997; Argyle, 2000; Batson, Schonerade, & Ventis, 1993; Beit-Hallahmi, 2007; Beit-Hallahmi & Argyle, 1997; Jackson & Hunsberger, 1999; Sider, 2005; Wulff, 1991; as cited in Zuckerman, 2009). They are more supportive of gender equity

(Hayes, 1995) and more accepting of homosexuality and support for gay rights (Burdette, Ellison, & Hall, 2005; Hayes, 1995; Lewis, 2003; Linneman & Clendenen, 2009; Loftus, 2001; Roof & McKinney, 1987; Sherkat, Powell, & Williams, 2011; Sherkat, 2008). They are also anti-war. Only 32% of secular Americans found the Iraq war justified compared to 89% of Mormons, 87% of Evangelicals, 73% of Mainline Protestants, and 84% of Catholics (Guth, Green, Kellstedt, & Smidt, 2005). Secular/nones are least supportive of torture and less likely to favor harsh sentencing compared to religious people (Grasmick, Davenport, Chamlin, & Bursik, 1992). Although atheists tend to break the law in minor crimes such as underage alcohol consumption and illegal use of drugs (Benson, 1992; Gorusch, 1995; Stark & Bainbridge, 1996), only 0.2% of prisoners in the United States are atheists (Zuckerman, 2009). While race and class do play a part in who gets incarcerated in the United States, all evidence indicates that atheists and secular people seem to possess very clear values and beliefs and a well-defined sense of right and wrong, (i.e., morality) and demonstrate greater self-regulation.

Secular individuals donate less than religious individuals, but secular countries donate the most money per capita to poorer nations (Center for Global Development, 2017). Even though at an individual level, religious people are said to be happier than the secular people (Altemeyer, 2009), at a societal level, the secular nations report the highest level of happiness among their citizens (Beit-Hallahami, 2009; Harris, 2018; Zuckerman, 2008). Secular nations are also more environmentally progressive, more peaceful, and far more prosperous. For a more detailed review, refer to Zuckerman (2008, 2009).

Despite these statistics, according to Edgell, Gereis, and Hartmann (2006), Americans report more antipathy towards atheists than they do towards other religious groups, or other racial and ethnic groups such as recent immigrants, Asian Americans, African Americans, Hispanics, or homosexuals. For example, Furnham et al. (1998) found that participants would assign lower priority to atheist or agnostic patients on a kidney transfer waitlist. Americans would not vote for nonreligious presidential candidates (Joyner, 2007; Hunter, 1990). Divorced parents get custody denied because of their atheism (Volokh, 2006). Non-Christian immigrants feel pressure to be more religious to be considered "true" Americans (Jacobs & Theiss-Morse, 2013). Discrimination contexts and types vary but discrimination occurs in several contexts including college campuses (Goodman & Mueller, 2009). Younger atheists tend to experience discrimination in family contexts while older or adult atheists tend to experience discrimination in work contexts. In work contexts, discrimination gets couched in other explanations such as showing up late (Huang & Kleiner, 2001).

Interestingly, other nones, such as SBNR, tend to be interpreted differently than atheists and agnostics. SBNR are seen as being more dissatisfied with organized religion, but atheists or agnostics evoke strong reactions and are perceived to lack morality and pose a danger to the society (Edgell, Gerteis, & Hartmann, 2006; Jenks, 1986). Like discrimination perceived by minorities such as Jews (Rosenfield, 1982; Shapiro, 1997), Mormons (Messer, 2009), Sikhs (The Pluralism Project, 2013), Muslims (Bloul, 2008; El Hamel, 2002; Montgomery, 2008), and Catholics (Hirschman, 2004), the nones and atheists in particular report strong discrimination (Cragun, Kosmin, Keysar, Hammer, & Nielsen, 2012; Downey, 2004; Franks & Scherr, 2014; Swan & Heesacker, 2012; Wallace, Wright, & Hall, 2014; Wright, Wallace, Bailey, & Hyde, 2013). However, unlike racial identity and in some cases, religious identities (e.g., Sikhs), this group has no external identifiers. A better comparison group may be homosexuals and bisexuals (Herek & Glunt, 1993; Meyer, 2003) because like them, atheists need to be out to experience discrimination and like the homosexuals, atheists also attempt to pass (Garfinkel, 1985). Nonreligious may identify as religious "to complement other social and emotional experiences of 'belonging'" (Day, 2011, pp. 191–192). Day (2011) also writes that coercion of the nonreligious is a human rights issue and that freedom of religion and freedom from religion must coexist in a just world. However, unlike homosexuality, being an atheist is thought of as more of a choice, that is, controllable and variable (Ghumman, Ryan, & Park, 2016) and hence the ungodly deserve mistreatment and mistrust.

In sum, completely undeservedly, American perception of those who do not believe in God and/or irreligious, is one of mistrust and suspicion. Given the growing numbers of nones in the workplace, this perception needs to be challenged and changed to build a more inclusive workplace. This is not an easy task because belief and belonging go together. And most Americans prefer people with belief in "a/any" religion to people with no belief in god or religion.

THE NONES, ENGAGEMENT, AND AFFECTIVE COMMITMENT

Nones are said to be less likely to be engaged in civic and community activities and demonstrate reduced institutional participation (Kosmin et al., 2009; Putnam & Campbell, 2012). This attribute has implications for organizational citizenship and commitment behaviors and relationship to work in general. Those who are emotionally connected to God also emotionally commit to fellow employees and workplace organizations (Kent, Bradshaw, & Doughtery, 2016). Dik and Duffy (2009) characterize work as transcendent summons and Volf (2001) defines work as cooperation with God. This approach is not new. Catholic church caught up with the

Protestant work ethic (Weber, 1905/2001) when Paul IV (1964) upheld the pursuit of holiness through work (and not just priestly careers) and the relationship between theology and organizational commitment has been well demonstrated (Neubert & Halbesleben, 2015). It is also well known that religious involvement fosters volunteering and civic engagement (Son & Wilson, 2012) because religion is seen as a feeder system into volunteering activities (Johnston, 2013).

A potential line of inquiry then is to see if there is a connection between the younger workers eschewing organized religion and their attitude towards employment and careers and the challenges faced in retaining them (Deloitte, 2015). To understand this, we may want to consider the construct of affective commitment in organizational management literature. Affective commitment is the measure of emotional bond between a person and an organization (Allen & Meyer, 1990). Employees with high affective commitment feel attached to their organization and assign personal meaning to their work context (Neubert & Halbesleben, 2015). Kent (2017) found that a strong attachment to God is correlated with higher levels of affective commitment than those with average and low levels. The underlying logic here is that attachment to God/religious domain is likely to spill over and may affect psychosocial adjustment and attachment in the secular domain (Granqvist & Kirkpatrik, 2013; Hazan & Shaver, 1990). High attachment in the Catholic Church despite the troubled times is owed to the strong identity created through the bureaucratic structure (Kent, 2017). Evangelicals connect work with spiritual meaning as well (Park, 2014), but their attachment to God is not associated with high affective commitment to their work organizations (Kent, 2017). This may be because of the more distributed nature of the evangelical church in which people church shop and do not belong to the same "big church" and the strong identity surrounding such membership and belonging (Perrin, Kennedy, & Miller, 1997). It is also possible that evangelicals may privilege religious commitments over work commitments.

So, the question here is: Do the godless then evince lower affective commitment? Is God an untapped resource for retaining the unaffiliated? Low attachment to God and religion means God plays an insignificant role in their lives. Does that then translate to low organizational commitment? What are the options here? Why do we need to care?

Religion is central to one's self-concept (Alidadi, 2012; Fernando & Jackson, 2006; Gebert et al., 2014) and work (Benefiel, Fry, & Giegle, 2014). Religious identity is a powerful self-concept creation and maintenance tool and can supersede other common identities such as organizational identity (Weeks & Vincent, 2007). Religion provides a psychological scaffolding for sensemaking (Blogowska & Saroglou, 2011). In fact, most of the modern-day conflicts may be attributed to strong and inflexible religious identities of individuals and groups and differences in making and assigning personal and collective meanings. While the U.S. workplace is supposed to be secular and separate from personal faith, this wall gets breached in two ways. One, organizations that focus on work–life integration and spirituality at work tend to abolish the distinction between the private and public spaces (Tourish & Tourish, 2010) because values and beliefs of the owners and managers shape the organizational values and are used to lead the followers. Second, in the United States, there is a continuously increasing desire for religious expression (Beane, Ponnapalli, & Viswesvaran, 2017; King & Holmes, 2012) combined with several others who do not appreciate the same from people who represent the organizations leading to a managerial bewilderment (Turnbull, 2007). Religious discrimination claims have doubled in the last 10 years (Dean et al., 2014; Ghumman, Ryan, Barclay, & Markel, 2013). More than even active discrimination, it is the workplace unpreparedness to deal with employees' need for religious expression (Atkinson, 2004) that leads to these claims. Exploring this dynamic using empirical data is a fertile line for inquiry for organizational and management scholars, especially the ones dealing with research about generations and cohorts.

I present the following three approaches to adopt while considering the role of nones in contemporary and future workplaces.

Let the Godless Come In/Out

Human connections at work matter (Dutton, Roberts, & Bednar, 2010) for the nones just like for the religious people (Kent et al., 2016). Frost and Edgell (2017) explore the variations in how nonreligious identification, belief, and behaviors affect civic engagement. Among the various subgroups, the NIP is less likely to be civically engaged than atheists, agnostics, and the SBNR. Moreover, the image of the nonreligious as not engaged in civic participation is inaccurate in recent times. There are 1,390 organizations in the United States devoted to nonreligious belief (Garcia & Blankholm, 2016). Thirty-three percent of 1,000 secular group members see social or political participation as a significant source of meaning in their lives (Pasquale, 2010). In fact, social and communal spaces of even nonreligious sometimes mimic religious group institutional models (Cimino & Smith, 2014; Smith, 2017) and provide similar incentives and resources (Lewis, MacGregor, & Putnam, 2010). Therefore, taking this approach means organizations can adopt an inclusion framework like it is being attempted with minorities and women to foster a collective identity and engender the affective commitment of the godless.

Are the Godless Cohort the Next Messiah?

In a more radical approach, I propose that these cohorts of the godless have the potential, inclination, and mindsets to transform the world of work as we know it. They are free of authoritarian ideas, willing to challenge and overthrow received wisdom such as capitalism and unfettered growth, and nonmaterialistic enough to engage in personal sacrifice for the greater good and their principles. As a group, compared to the faithful, the nones are uniformly more open-minded, progressive, believe in science, and more environmentally responsible (Alidadi, 2012; Cash & Gray 2000; Wuthnow, 2004). Millennials, in particular, are in search for a career that provides purpose or helps them create a more meaningful life (Deloitte, 2015) and a life that integrates work and life (Tien & Wang, 2015). They tend to be more collectivistic in orientation (the Bernie Sanders movement, for example) and invest in social and political activities. Secular activism has focused on battling discrimination, speaking race, gender, and injustice to power more successfully in recent decades and has become the bulwark of resistance against the increasing conservatism of the religious groups encroaching into public and private spaces. In this context, it is no wonder that the younger nones define their careers and impact differently than the previous generations. Perhaps they will create alternate models of workplace that are progressive, equitable, and postcapitalistic in that they aim to bridge inequalities, protect the environment, and advance a more just world.

The Middle Route

Perhaps the answer lies in the middle. Either way, a defining characteristic of affective commitments in organizations or social movements, is the collective identity construction. It is clear that a well-defined identity, both at individual and collective levels leads to more engagement (Frost & Edgell, 2017). Unlike the NIP, all other subgroups of the nones—atheists, agnostics, and SBNR—value civic engagement and volunteer at similar or higher rates than religious individuals because they are also interested in the search for a personal meaning (Giacalone & Jurkewics, 2010; Pawar, 2009). However, a robust but flexible identity system can promote the ability to hold cognitively complex mental models (Poonamallee & Goltz, 2014) essential for building bridges across divides. Self-referencing theory (SRT; Buri & Mueller, 1993; Cantone, 2012) explains how identities are created through mental models or self-schemata. These mental models or self-schemata (Markus & Nurius, 1986) or internal working models (Bowlby, 1969, 1973, 1980; Johnson-Laird, 2010) are powerful in shaping how we view the world, engage with it, and how individuals develop relational identities at work (Sluss & Ashforth, 2007). People tend to resist internalizing information that counters their own self-schema (Burnkrant & Unnava, 1989; Cantone, 2012). Further, people hold multiple identities at the same time or move from one identity to another (Cotter, 2015). This is especially true of the nones who move between labels freely and fluidly. This could be a very productive model of engagement for the workplace to cope with the enormous pace of change in the market, economy, and technology.

Meaning making is the starting point for identity construction and shifts. "Finding (or losing) oneself in the ocean of a common human spirit" (Ammerman, 2013, p. 269) or experiencing the fullness when the ordinary life is touched by meaning (Taylor, 2007) is a shared common experience whether one is religious or irreligious. Guenther, Mulligan, and Papp's (2013) work on boundary permeability for understanding collective identity in atheist movement organization is perhaps equally applicable to work organizations that are trying to cultivate collective identities that bind instead of divide. These organizations show how the nones and, in particular, atheists seek solidarity and belonging very much like a churchgoer seeks brotherhood and community. Stressing differences and developing a distinct identity in opposition like the fundamentalist religious or the New Atheists may help in the mobilization of a core identity, but it also could come in the way of collective identity at an organizational or societal level perpetuating the "us" vs "them" template that an early emphasis on religion tends to produce (Altemeyer & Hunsberger, 1997).

REFERENCES

Alidadi, K. (2012, May 1). *Religious diversity and secular models in Europe: Innovative approaches to law and policy: A comparative legal study addressing religion or belief discrimination in employment and reasonable accommodations for employees' religious or philosophical beliefs or practices.* http://dx.doi.org/10.2139/ssrn.2843026

Allen, N. J., & Meyer, J. P. (1990.) The measurement and antecedents of affective, continuance, and normative commitment to the organization. *Journal of Occupational Psychology, 63*(1), 1–18.

Altemeyer, B. (2003). Why do religious fundamentalists tend to be prejudiced? *International Journal for the Psychology of Religion, 13*(1), 17–28.

Altemeyer, B. (2009). Non-belief and secularity in North America. In P. Zuckerman (Ed.), *Atheism and Secularity, Volume 2* (pp. 1–22). Westport, CT: Praeger.

Altemeyer, B., & Hunsberger, B. (1992). Authoritarianism, religious fundamentalism, quest, and prejudice. *International Journal for the Psychology of Religion, 2*(2), 113–133.

Altemeyer, B., & Hunsberger, B. (1997). *Amazing conversions: Why some turn to faith and others abandon religion.* Amherst, NY: Prometheus.

Ammerman, N. T. (2013). Spiritual but not religious? Beyond binary choices in the study of religion. *Journal for the Scientific Study of Religion. 52*(2), 258–278.
Argyle, M. (2000). *Psychology and religion: An introduction.* London, England: Routledge.
Atkinson, W. (2004). Religion in the workplace: Faith versus liability. *Risk Management, 15*(1), 18–23.
Aune, K. (2015). Feminist spirituality as lived religion: How UK feminists forge religio-spiritual lives. *Gender & Society, 29*(1), 122–145.
Baker, J. O., & Smith, B. G. (2009). The nones: Social characteristics of the religiously Unaffiliated. *Social Forces, 87*(3), 1–14.
Baker, J., & Smith, B. (2015). *American secularism: Cultural contours of nonreligious belief systems.* New York, NY: New York University Press.
Batson, C. D., Schonerade, P., & Ventis, W. L. (1993). *Religion and the individual: A social-psychological perspective.* New York, NY: Oxford University Press.
Beaman, L., & Tomlins, S. (Eds.). (2015). *Atheist identities: Spaces and social contexts.* Cham, Switzerland: Springer International.
Beane, D., Ponnapalli, A., & Viswesvaran, C. (2017). Workplace religious displays and perceptions of organization attractiveness. *Employer Responsibility Rights Journal, 29*(2), 73–88.
Beit-Hallahami, B. (2007). Atheists: A psychological profile. In M. Martin (Ed.), *The Cambridge companion to atheism* (pp. 300–318). New York, NY: Cambridge University Press.
Beit-Hallahami, B. (2009). Morality and immorality among the irreligious. In P. Zuckerman (Ed.), *Atheism and secularity* (pp. 113–148). Westport, CT: Praeger.
Beit-Hallahami, B., & Argyle, M. (1997). *The psychology of religious behavior, belief, and experience.* London, England: Routledge.
Benefiel, M., Fry, L. W., & Giegle, D. (2014). Spirituality and religion in the workplace: History, theory, and research. *Psychology of Religion and Spirituality, 6*(3), 175–187.
Benson, P. L. (1992). Religion as substance abuse. In J. F. Schumaker (Ed.), *Religion and mental health,* New York, NY: Oxford University Press.
Blankholm, J. (2014). The political advantages of a polysemous secular. *Journal for the Scientific Study of Religion, 53*(4), 775–790. Retrieved from https://escholarship.org/uc/item/4390d3wm
Blogowska, J., & Saroglou, V. (2011). Religious fundamentalism and limited prosociality as a function of target. *Journal for the Scientific Study of Religion, 50*(1), 44–60.
Bloul, R. D. (2008). Anti-discrimination laws, Islamaphobia, and ethnicization of Muslim identities in Europe and Australia. *Journal of Muslim Minority Affairs, 28*(1), 7–25.
Bowlby, J. (1969). *Attachment and loss (Vol. 1): Attachment.* New York, NY: Basic Books.
Bowlby, J. (1973). *Attachment and loss (Vol. 2): Separation: Anxiety and anger.* New York, NY: Basic Books.
Bowlby, J. (1980). *Attachment and loss (Vol. 3): Loss.* New York, NY: Basic Books.
Brown, R., Taylor, R. K., & Chatters, L. (2015). Race/ethnic and social-demographic correlates of religious non-involvement in America: Findings from three national surveys. *Journal of Black Studies, 46*(4), 335–362.

Burdette, A., Ellison, C., & Hall, T. (2005). Conservative protestantism and tolerance toward homosexuals: An examination of potential mechanisms. *Sociological Inquiry, 75*(2), 177–196.

Buri, J. R., & Mueller, R. A. (1993). Psychoanalytic theory and loving God concepts: Parent referencing versus self-referencing. *The Journal of Psychology, 127*(1), 17–27.

Burnkrant, R. E., & Unnava, H. R. (1989). Self-referencing: A strategy for increasing processing of messaging content. *Personality and Social Psychology Bulletin, 15*(4), 628–638.

Callis, R. R., & Kresin, M. (2014). *Residential vacancies and home ownership in the first quarter 2014. U.S. Department of Commerce, Social, Economic, and Housing Statistics Division.* Washington, DC: U.S. Census Bureau.

Cantone, J. A. (2012). *Religion at work: Evaluating hostile work environment religious discrimination claims* (Unpublished docrotral dissertation). University of Nebraska, Omaha. Retrieved from https://digitalcommons.unl.edu/dissertations/AAI3469383

Cash, C., & Gray, G. (2000). A framework for accommodating religion and spirituality in the workplace. *Academy of Management Executive, 14*(3), 124–133.

Center for Global Development. (2017). *Commitment to development index 2017.* Retrieved from https://www.cgdev.org/commitment-development-index-2017

Cimino, R., & Smith, C. (2014). *Atheist awakening: Secular activism and community in America.* New York, NY: Oxford University Press.

Cooperman, A. & Gray, G.A. (2016). The factors driving the growth of religions 'nones' in the US. *Pew Research Center.* https://www.pewresearch.org/fact-tank/2016/09/14/the-factors-driving-the-growth-of-religious-nones-in-the-u-s/

Cornwall, M. (2009). Reifying sex differences isn't the answer: Gendering processes, risk, and religiosity. *Journal for the Scientific Study of Religion, 48*(2), 252–255.

Cotter, C. (2015). Without god yet not without nuance: A qualitative study of atheism and nonreligion among Scottish university students. In L. Beaman & S. Tomlins (Eds.), *Atheist identities—Spaces and social contexts* (pp. 171–196). Cham, Switzerland: Springer International.

Cragun, R. T., Kosmin, B., Keysar, A., Hammer, J. H., & Nielsen, M. (2012). On the receiving end: Discrimination towards the non-religious in the United States. *Journal of Contemporary Religion, 27*(1), 1–44.

D'Andrea, L., & Sprenger, J. (2007). Atheism and nonspirituality as Diversity Issues in Counseling. *Counseling and Values, 51*(2), 149–158.

Davie, G. (1994). *Religion in Britain since 1945: Believing without belonging.* Oxford, England: Blackwell.

Davie, G. (2013). *The sociology of religion: A critical edition.* London, England: SAGE.

Dawkins, R. (2007). Foreword. In T. Flynn (Ed.), *The new encyclopedia of unbelief* (pp. 10–12). Buffalo, NY: Prometheus Books.

Day, A. (2011). *Believing in belonging: Belief and social identity in the modern world.* Oxford, England: Oxford University Press.

Dean, K. L., Safranski, S. R., & Lee, E. S. (2014). Religious accommodation in the workplace: Understanding religious identity threat and workplace behaviors in legal disputes. *Employee Responsibilities and Rights Journal, 26*(2), 75–94.

Deloitte. (2015). *The millennial survey*. Retrieved from https://www2.deloitte.com/content/dam/Deloitte/global/Documents/About-Deloitte/gx-wef-2015-millennial-survey-executivesummary.pdf

Dik, B. J., & Duffy, R. D. (2009). Calling and vocation at work. *The Counseling Psychologist, 37*(3), 424–450.

Downey, M. (2004). Discrimination against atheists: The facts. *Free Inquiry, 24*(4), 41–43.

Dutton, J. E., Roberts, L. M., & Bednar, J. (2010). Pathways for positive identity construction at work: Four types of positive identity and the building of social resources. *Academy of Management Review, 35*(2), 265–293.

Edgell, P., Frost, J., & Stewart, E. (2017). From existential to social understandings of risk: Examining gender differences in nonreligion. *Social Currents, 4*(6), 556–574.

Edgell, P., Gerteis, J., & Hartmann, D. (2006). Atheists as 'Other': Moral boundaries and cultural membership in American society. *American Sociological Review. 71*(2), 211–234.

Edgell, P., Hartmann, D., Frost, J., Stewart, E., & Gerteis, J. (2016). Atheist and other cultural outsiders: Moral boundaries and the non-religious in the United States. *Social Forces, 95*(2), 607–638.

Ehrlich, H. J., & Van Tubergen, G. N. (1971). Exploring the structure and salience of stereotypes. *Journal of Social Psychology, 83*(1), 113–127.

El Hamel, C. (2002). Muslim diaspora in Western Europe: The Islamic headscarf (Hijab), the media, and Muslims' integration in France. *Citizenship Studies, 6*(3), 293–308.

Fernando, M., & Jackson, B. (2006). The influence of religion-based workplace spirituality on business leaders' decision-making: An inter-faith study. *Journal of Management & Organization, 12*(1), 23–39.

Franks, A. S., & Scherr, K. C. (2014). Anti-atheist prejudice at the polls. *Journal of Applied Social Psychololgy, 44,* 681–691. https://doi.org/10.1111/jasp.12259

Frost, J., & Edgell, P. (2017). Rescuing nones from the reference category: Civic engagement among the nonreligious in America. *Nonprofit and Voluntary Sector Quarterly, 47*(2), 417–438. https://www.doi.org/10.1177/0899764017746251

Furnham, A., Meader, N., & McClelland, A. (1998). Factors affecting nonmedical participants' allocation of scarce medical resources. *Journal of Social Behavior and Personality, 13*(4), 735–746.

Furseth, I. (2009). Atheism, secularity, and gender. In P. Zuckerman (Ed.), *Atheism and secularity* (pp. 209–228). Westport, CT: Praeger.

Garcia, A., & Blackholm, J. (2016). The social context of organized nonbelief county-level predictors of nonbeliever organizations in the United States. *Journal of the Scientific Study of Religion, 55*(1), 70–90.

Garfinkel, H. (1985). *Studies in ethnomethodology.* Cambridge, England: Polity Press.

Gebert, D., Boemer, S., Kearney, E., King, J. E., Jr., Zhang, K., & Song, L. J. (2014). Expressing religious identities in the workplace: Analyzing a neglected diversity dimension. *Human Relations, 67*(5), 543–563.

Gervais, W. M., Shariff, A. F., & Norenzayan, A. (2011). Do you believe in atheists? Distrust is central to anti-atheist prejudice. *Journal of Personality and Social Psychology, 101*(6), 1189–1206. https://doi.org/10.1037/a0025882

Gervais, W., Xygalatas, D., McKay, R., van Elk, M., Buchtel, E. E., Aveyard, M. . . . Bulbulia, J. (2017). Global evidence of extreme intuitive moral prejudice against atheists. *Nat Hum Behavior, 1,* 0151. https://doi.org/10.1038/s41562-017-0151

Ghumman, S., Ryan, A. M., Barclay, L. A., & Markel, K. S. (2013). Religious discrimination in the workplace: A review and examination of current and future trends. *Journal of Business and Psychology, 28*(4), 439–454.

Ghumman, S., Ryan, A. M., & Park, J. S. (2016). Religious harassment in the workplace: An examination of observer intervention. *Journal of Organizational Behavior, 37*(2), 279–306. https://doi.org/10.1002/job.2044

Giacalaone, R. A., & Jurkiewiscz, C. A. (Eds.). (2010). *Handbook of workplace spirituality and organizational performance.* Armonk, ME: Sharpe.

Goodman, K. M., & Mueller, J. A. (2009). Invisible, marginalized, and stigmatized: Understanding and addressing the needs of atheist students. *New Directions for Student Services, 125,* 55–63.

Goodstein, L. (2000, September 16). PUBLIC LIVES; It's a harsh political climate for a believer in nonbelief. *The New York Times.* Retrieved from https://www.nytimes.com/2000/09/16/us/public-lives-it-s-a-harsh-political-climate-for-a-believer-in-nonbelief.html

Gorusch, R. L. (1995). Religious aspects of substance abuse and recovery. *Journal of Social Issues, 51*(2), 65–83.

Granqvist, P., & Kirkpatrick, L. A. (2013). Religion, spirituality and attachment. In K. I. Pargmanet, J. J. Exline, & J. W. Jones (Eds.), *APA handbook of psychology, religion, and spirituality (Vol. 1): Content, theory, and research* (pp. 139–155). Washington, DC: American Psychological Association.

Grasmick, H., Davenport, E., Chamlin, M., & Bursik, R. (1992). Protestant fundamentalism and the retributive doctrine of punishment. *Criminology, 30,* 21–45.

Guenther, K. M., Mulligan, K., & Papp, C. (2013). From the outside in: Crossing boundaries to build collective identity in the new atheist movement. *Social Problems, 60*(4), 457–475.

Guth, J., Green, J., Kellstedt, L., & Smidt, C. (2005). Faith and foreign policy: A view from the pews. *Review of Faith and International Affairs, 3*(2), 3–9.

Hammer, J. H., Cragun, R. T., Hwang, K., & Smith, J. M. (2012). Forms, frequency, and correlates of perceived anti-atheist discrimination. *Secularism and Nonreligion, 1,* 43–67. http://doi.org/10.5334/snr.ad

Harper, M. (2007). The stereotyping of nonreligious people by religious students: Contents and subtypes. *Journal for the Scientific Study of Religion, 46*(4), 539–552.

Harris, B. (2018, March 16). These are the happiest countries in the world. *World Economic Forum.* Retrieved from https://www.weforum.org/agenda/2018/03/these-are-the-happiest-countries-in-the-world/

Hayes, B. (1995). Religious identification and moral attitudes: The British case. *British Journal of Sociology, 46*(3), 457–474.

Hazan, C., & Shaver, P. (1990). Love and work: An attachment-theoretical perspective. *Journal of Personality and Social Psychology, 59*(2), 270–80.

Heelas, P. (2006). The infirmity debate: On the viability of new age spiritualities in life. *Journal of Contemporary Religion, 21*(2), 223–240.

Heiner, R. (1992). Evangelical heathens: The deviant status of freethinkers in Southland. *Deviant Behavior: An Interdisciplinary Journal, 13,* 1–20.

Herek, G. M., & Glunt, E. K. (1993). Interpersonal contact and heterosexuals' attitudes towards gay men: Results from a national survey. *The Journal of Sex Research, 30*(3), 239–244.

Hirschman, C. (2004). The role of religion in the origins and adaptation of immigrant groups in the United States. *International Migration Review, 38*(3), 1206–1233.

Hout, M., & Fischer, C. S. (2002). Why more Americans have no religious preference: Politics and generations. *American Sociological Review, 67*(2), 165–190.

Huang, C. C., & Kleiner, B. H. (2001). New developments concerning religions discrimination in the workplace. *International Journal of Sociology and Social Policy, 21*, 128–136.

Hunsberger, B. (2006). *Atheists: A groundbreaking study of America's nonbelievers*. Amherst, NY: Prometheus Books.

Hunter, J. D. (1990). The Williamsburg Charter Survey: Methodology and findings. *Journal of Law and Religion, 8*(4), 257–272.

Hutchinson, S. (2011). *Moral combat: Black atheists, gender politics, and the values wars*. Los Angeles, CA: Infidel Books.

Hwang, K. (2008). Experiences of atheists with spinal cord injury: Results of an internet-based exploratory survey. *SCI Psychosocial Process, 20*(2), 4–28.

Jackson, L., & Hunsberger, B. (1999). An intergroup perspective on religion and prejudice. *Journal for the Scientific Study of Religions, 38*(4), 509–523.

Jacobs, C., & Theiss-Morse, E. (2013). Belonging in a "Christian nation": The explicit and implicit associations between religion and national group membership. *Politics and Religion, 6*(2), 373–401.

Jenks, R. J. (1986). Perceptions of two deviant and two nondeviant groups. *The Journal of Social Psychology, 126*(6), 783–790.

Johnson-Laird, P. N. (2010). Mental models and human reasoning. *Proceedings of the National Academy of Sciences, 107*(43) 18243–18250. https://www.doi.org/10.1073/pnas.1012933107

Johnston, H. (2013). Religion and volunteering over the adult life. *Journal for Scientific Study of Religion, 52*(4), 733–752.

Joyner, J. (2007, February 20). Black resident more likely than Mormon or Atheist. *Outside the Beltway*. Retrieved from https://www.outsidethebeltway.com/black_president_more_likely_than_mormon_or_atheist_/

Kent, B. V. (2017). Attachment to God, religious tradition, and firm attributes in workplace commitment. *The Journal of Social Psychology, 157*(4), 485–501.

Kent, B. V., Bradshaw, M., & Dougherty, K. D. (2016). Attachment to god, vocational calling, and worker contentment. *Review of Religious Research, 58*(3), 343–364.

Kettell, S. (2013). Faithless: The politics of new atheism. *Secularism and Nonreligion, 2*, 61–72.

King, J. E., Jr., & Holmes, I. O. (2012). Spirituality, recruiting, and total wellness: Overcoming challenges to organizational attraction. *Journal of Management, Spirituality, and Religion, 9*(3), 237–253.

Koproske, C. 2006. Living without Religion: The Secular Stigma. *Free Inquiry, 27*(1), 49–50.

Kosmin, B. A., Keysar, A., Cragun, R., & Navarro-Rivera, J. (2009). *American nones: The profile of the no religion population*. Hartford, CT: Trinity College.

LaDrew, S. (2012). The evolution of atheism: Scientific and humanistic approaches. *History of the Human Sciences, 24*(3), 70–87.
LaDrew, S. (2013). Discovering atheism: Heterogeneity in trajectories to atheist identity and activism. *Sociology of Religion, 74*(4), 431–453.
Lamont, M., & Molnár, V. (2002). The study of boundaries in the social sciences. *Annual Review of Sociology, 28*, 167–195.
Langston, J., Hammer, J., & Cragun, R. T. (2015). Atheism looking in: On the goals and strategies of organized nonbelief. *Science, Religion, and Culture, 2*(3), 70–85.
Lee, L. (2014). Secular or nonreligious? Investigating and interpreting generic "not religions categories and populations. *Religion, 44*(3), 466–382.
Levin, J. S., Taylor, R. J., & Chatters, L. M. (1994). Race and gender differences in religiosity among older adults. *Sociology of Religion, 66*(1), 23–43.
Lewis, G. (2003). Black–White differences in attitudes toward homosexuality and gay rights. *Public Opinion Quarterly, 67*, 59–78.
Lewis, V., MacGregor, C. A, & Putnam, R. (2010). Secular and liminal: Discovering heterogeneity among religious nones. *Journal for the Scientific Study of Religion, 49*(4), 596–618.
Link, B., & Phelan, J. (2001). Conceptualizing stigma. *Annual Review of Sociology, 27*(1), 363–385.
Linneman, T., & Clendenen, M. (2009). Sexuality and the secular. In P. Zuckeman (Ed.), *Atheism and secularity* (pp. 89–112). Westport, CT: Praeger.
Lipka, M. (2015. November 4). American's faith in God may be eroding. *Pew Research Center.* Retrieved from https://www.pewresearch.org/fact-tank/2015/11/04/americans-faith-in-god-may-be-eroding/
Lipka, M., & Gecewicz, C. (2017, September 6). More Americans now say they're spiritual but not religious. *Pew Research Center.* Retrieved from https://www.pewresearch.org/fact-tank/2017/09/06/more-americans-now-say-theyre-spiritual-but-not-religious/
Loftus, J. (2001). America's liberalization in attitudes towards homosexuality, 1973–1998. *American Sociological Review 66*(5), 762–782.
Macartney, S., Bishaw, A., & Fontenot, K. (2013). *Poverty rates for selected detailed race and Hispanic groups by state and place. 2007–2011.* Washington, DC: U.S. Department of Commerce, United States Census Bureau.
Markus, H., & Nurius, P. (1986). Possible selves. *American Psychologist, 41*(9), 954–969. https://doi.org/10.1037/0003-066X.41.9.954
McClure, P. (2017). Something besides monotheism: Sociotheological boundary work among the spiritual, but not religions. *Poetics, 62*, 53–65.
Merino, S. M. (2013). Irreligious socialization? The adult religious preferences of individuals raised with no religion. *Secularism & Nonreligion, 1*, 1–16.
Messer, T. M. (2009). *The price of prop 8.* Washington, DC: The Heritage Foundation.
Meyer, I. H. (2003). Prejudice, social stress, and mental health in lesbian, gay, and bisexual populations: Conceptual issues and research evidence. *Psychological Bulletin, 129*(5), 674–697. https://doi.org/10.1037/0033-2909.129.5.674
Miller, A. S., & Hoffman, J. P. (1995). Risk and religion: An explanation of gender differences in religiosity. *Journal of the Scientific Study of Religion, 34*(1), 63–75.

Montgomery, E. (2008). Long-term effects of organized violence on young Middle Eastern refugees' mental health. *Social Science & Medicine, 67*(10), 1596–1603.

Nelson, M. H. (1990). The religious identification of children of interfaith marriages. *Review of Religious Research, 32*(2), 122–134.

Neubert, M. J., & Halbesleben, K. (2015). Called to commitment: An examination of relationships between spiritual calling, job satisfaction, and organizational commitment. *Journal of Business Ethics, 132*(4), 859–872.

Newport, F. (2006). Democrats view religious groups less positively than Republicans. *Gallup Report.* Retrieved from https://news.gallup.com/poll/24385/democrats-view-religious-groups-less-positively-than-republicans.aspx

Norris, P., & Ingleheart, R. (2011). *Sacred and the secular: Religion and politics worldwide.* New York, NY: Cambridge University Press.

Obama. B. (2009, January 21). President Barack Obama's inaugural address. *The White House.* Retrieved from https://obamawhitehouse.archives.gov/blog/2009/01/21/president-barack-obamas-inaugural-address

O'Brian Baker, J., & Smith, B. (2009). None too simple: Examining issues of religious nonbelief and nonbelonging in the United States. *Journal for the Scientific Study of Religion, 48*(4), 719–733.

Park, J. Z. (2014, November). *The Bible in the workplace.* Paper presented at the Society for the Scientific Study of Religion, Indianapolis, IN.

Pasquale, F. (2010). A portrait of secular group affiliates. In P. Zuckerman (Ed.), *Atheism and secularity, Volume I* (pp. 43–87). Santa Barbara, CA: Praeger ABC-CLIO.

Paul IV. (1964). *Dogmatic constitution of the church.* Rome, Italy: The Vatican.

Pawar, B. (2009). Workplace spirituality facilitation: A comprehensive model. *Journal of Business Ethics, 90*(3), 375–386.

Perrin, R. D., Kennedy, P., & Miller, D. E. (1997). Examining the sources of conservative church growth: Where are the new evangelical movements getting their numbers? *Journal for the Scientific Study of Religion, 36,* 71–80.

Pew Forum. (2019, July 23). *Feeling towards religious groups.* Retrieved from https://www.pewforum.org/2019/07/23/feelings-toward-religious-groups/

Pollitt, K. (2005). *Brooklyn prof in godless shocker.* Retrieved from https://www.thenation.com/article/brooklyn-prof-godless-shocker/

Poonamallee, L. C., & Goltz, S. M. (2014). Beyond social exchange theory: An integrative look at transcendent mental models for engagement. *Integral Theory, 10*(1), 63–90.

Putnam, R. D., & Campbell, D. E. (2012). *American grace: How religion divides and unites us.* New York, NY: Simon & Schuster.

Quack, J. (2012). Organized atheism in India: An overview. *Journal of Contemporary Religion, 27*(1), 67–85.

Reisberg, L. (1998). New groups unite in belief that one needn't believe in god. *Chronicle of Higher Education, 44*(32), 43–44.

Roof, W. C., & McKinney, W. (1987). *Mainline American religion: Its changing shape and future.* New Brunswick, NJ: Rutgers University Press.

Roozen, D. A. (2011). *A decade of change in American congregations 2000–2010.* Hartford, CT: Hartford Institute for Religion Research.

Rosenfield, G. (1982). The polls: Attitudes toward American Jews. *Public Opinion Quarterly, 46*(3), 1245–1251.

Schutz, A., & Roth, L. M. (2015, August). *Reconceptualizing religious risk: Gender differences in the Atheist experience.* Working paper presented at the American Sociology Association Annual Meeting, San Francisco, CA.

Shapiro, S. (1997). The uncanny Jew: A brief history of an image. *Judaism, 46*(1), 63–78.

Sherkat, D. E. (2008). Beyond belief: Atheism, agnosticism, and theistic certainty in the United States. *Sociological Spectrum, 28*(5), 438–459.

Sherkat, D., Powell-Williams, M., & Maddox, G. (2011). Religion, politics, and support for same-sex marriage in the United States, 1988–2008. *Social Science Research, 40*(1), 167–180. https://doi.org/10.1016/j.ssresearch.2010.08.009

Shook, J. (2006). In M. Martin (Ed.), *The Cambridge companion to atheism* (pp. 230–233). New York, NY: Cambridge University Press.

Sider, D. (2005). *The scandal of the evangelical conscience: Why are Christians just like the rest of the world?* Grand Rapids, MI: Baker Books.

Silver, C., Coleman, T., Hood, R., & Holcome, J. (2014). The six types of nonbelief: A qualitative and quantitative study of type and narrative. *Mental Health, Religion, & Culture, 17*(10), 990–1001.

Sluss, D. M., & Ashforth, B. E. (2007). Relational identity and identification: Defining ourselves through work relationships. *Academy of Management Review, 32*(1), 9–32.

Smith, J. (2017). Can the secular be the object of belief and belonging? The Sunday Assembly. *Qualitative Sociology, 40*(1), 83–109.

Son, J., & Wilson, J. (2012). Using normative theory to explain the effect of religion and education on volunteering. *Sociological Perspectives, 55*, 473–499.

Stark, R., & Bainbridge, W. S. (1987). *A theory of religion.* New York, NY: Peter Lang.

Stark, R., & Bainbridge, W. S. (1996). *Religion, deviance, and social control.* New York, NY: Routledge.

Swan, L. K., & Heesacker, M. (2012). Anti-atheist bias in the United States: Testing two critical assumptions. *Secularism and Nonreligion, 1*, 32–42. https://doi.org/10.5334/snr.ac

Taylor, C. (2007). *A secular age.* Cambridge, MA: Belknap Press.

Taylor, R. J. (1988). Correlates of religious non-involvement among Black Americans. *Review of Religious Research, 30*(2), 126–139.

The Pluralism Project. (2013). *Research report: Post 9/11 hate crime trends: Muslims, Sikhs, Hindus, and Jews in the US.* Cambridge, MA: Harvard University Press.

Tien, H. S., & Wang, Y. C. (2015). Work and family: Conflict, balance, and life satisfaction in Asia. In L. Luo & C. Cooper (Eds.), *Handbook of research on work–life balance in Asia* (pp. 35–60). Cheltenham, England: Edward Elgar.

Tourish, D., & Tourish, N. (2010). Spirituality at work, and its implications for leadership and followership: A Post-structuralist perspective. *Leadership, 6*(2), 207–224. https://doi.org/10.1177/1742715010363210

Turnbull, L. (2007, February 15). Religious tension in the workplace on the rise. *The Seattle Times* https://www.seattletimes.com/seattle-news/religious-tension-in-workplace-on-the-rise/

Vernon, G. M. (1968). The religious "nones": A neglected category. *Journal for the Scientific Study of Religion, 7*(2), 219–229.

Volf, M. (2001). *Work in the spirit: Toward a theology of work.* Eugene, OR: Wipf & Stock.

Volokh, E. (2006). Parent–child speech and child custody speed restrictions. *The British Journal of Sociology, 49,* 640–660.

Wallace, M., Wright, B. R. E., & Hyde, A. (2014). Religious affiliation and hiring discrimination in the American South: A field experiment. *Social Currents, 1*(2), 189–207. https://doi.org/10.1177/2329496514524541

Weber, M. (2001). *The protestant ethic and the spirit of capitalism.* Chicago, IL: Fitzroy Dearborn. (Originally published in 1905)

Weeks, M., & Vincent, M. A. (2007). Using religious affiliation to spontaneously categorize others. *The International Journal for the Psychology of Religion, 17*(4), 317–331.

Wilcox, M. (2009). *Queer women and religious individualism.* Bloomington: Indiana University Press.

Wilson, B. R. (1976). Aspects of secularization in the West. *Japanese Journal of Religious Studies, 3*(3/4), 259–276.

Wright, B., Wallace, M., Bailey, J., & Hyde, A. (2013). Religious affiliation and hiring discrimination in New England: A field experiment. *Research in Social Stratification and Mobility, 34,* 111–126.

Wulff, D. M. (1991). *Psychology of religion: Classical and contemporary views.* New York, NY: Wiley.

Wuthnow, R. (2004). Presidential address: The challenge of diversity. *Journal for the Scientific Study of Religion, 43*(2), 159–170.

Zorn, E. (2008, April 3). Change of subject: Rep Monique Davis to atheist Rob Sherman: It's dangerous for our children to even know that your philosophy exists. *Chicago Tribune.* Retrieved from http://blogs.chicagotribune.com/news_columnists_ezorn/2008/04/rep-monique-dav.html

Zuckerman, P. (2007). Atheism: Contemporary numbers and patterns. In M. Martin (Ed.), *Cambridge companions to philosophy: The Cambridge companion to atheism* (pp. 47–65). Cambridge, England: Cambridge University Press. https://doi.org/10.1017/CCOL0521842700.004

Zuckerman, P. (2008). *Society without God: What the least religious nations can tell us about contentment.* New York, NY: New York University Press.

Zuckerman, P. (2009). Atheism, secularity, and well-being: How the finds of social science counter negative stereotypes and assumptions. *Sociology Compass, 3*(6), 949–971.

Zuckerman, P. (2015). *Faith no more: Why people reject religion.* Oxford, England: Oxford University Press.

ABOUT THE CONTRIBUTORS

Joi Carr, professor of English and Film Studies, serves as the director of the Film Studies and as an academic director of the Institute for Entertainment, Media, Sports, and Culture, Pepperdine University. As the creative and program director of the Multicultural Theatre Project, Dr. Carr leads students in a theatrical exploration of diversity through her transdisciplinary, arts-based, critical pedagogical work, which is the subject of her first monograph, *Encountering Texts: The Multicultural Theatre Project and "Minority" Literature* (Peter Lang, 2015). Her second release, *Boyz N the Hood: Shifting Hollywood Terrain* (Peter Lang, 2018), examines John Singleton's aesthetic voice and his iconic film, *Boyz N the Hood*. Dr. Carr's latest monographs focus on Black female voice, *Voice: African American Women and Vocation* and *She's Not Reel: Constructing Black Female Cinematic Voice*. She is a singer-songwriter, actress, and playwright and earned her PhD in English and Film from Claremont Graduate University.

Raymond Carr describes his research interests as theologically ecumenical, historically sensitive, and radically inclusive. He earned his PhD at Graduate Theological Union in Systematic and Philosophical Theology. As an assistant professor of theology at Pepperdine University, Carr taught courses on the theology of Martin Luther and Theologies Born of Struggle. He is currently developing a trilogy in theological aesthetics. The first book, *Theology in the Mode of Monk. An Aesthetics of Barth and Cone on Revelation and Freedom*, integrates his research interests and deploys the music of Thelonious Monk as a form of parabolic suggestiveness (Cascade, forthcoming). Previous publications include "Merton and Barth in Dialogue on Faith and Understanding: A Hermeneutics of Freedom and Ambiguity," *The Merton Annual: Studies in Culture, Spirituality, and Social Concerns* and "Fired in the Crucible of Oppression: Toward a Theology of Spiritual Freedom" in *With This Root About My Person: Charles H. Long and New Directions in the Study of Religion.*

Tom Clark serves as the executive director of the Krause Center for Leadership and Ethics at The Citadel, the Military College of South Carolina in Charleston. He graduated from The Citadel in 1985, earning a BS in mathematics and computer science, and served 30 years as a Marine Corps pilot flying the F/A-18 Hornet. He is currently enrolled in the organizational leadership PhD program at Regent University.

Larry G. Daniel serves as professor and dean in the College of Education at The University of Texas Permian Basin (UTPB). A career educator, he has worked with students at the middle, secondary, undergraduate, and graduate levels. He is a leader in UTPB's implementation of US PREP, a national model for reform of teacher education, serves of a variety of community boards and councils, and chairs the Government Relations and Advocacy Committee of the American Association of Colleges for Teacher Education. He serves as an organizational consultant, program evaluator, and accreditation site reviewer. His teaching and research interests include educational leadership, teacher education, middle grades, and research and statistics. Larry and his wife, Caren, reside in Odessa, Texas. They have four adult children and six grandchildren.

Miles Davis is the president of Linfield University. Previously, he was the dean of the Harry F. Byrd, Jr. School of Business and the George Edward Durell Chair of Management. He also was the founding director of the Institute of Entrepreneurship at Shenandoah University. Dr. Davis is an active scholar and has published scholarly articles on the intersection of entrepreneurship and faith-based practices. He has been presented with the "Silver Good Citizenship Medal" from the Sons of the American Revolution and recognized as being a "Drum Major for Justice" by the United Covenant Churches of Christ. Dr. Davis was the first person outside of the UK appointed to the "Society of Leadership Fellows," Saint George's House, Windsor Castle and is a dean emeritus at Shenandoah University. Dr. Davis sits on the board of the Amana Mutual Fund Trust.

Matthew Waritay Guah is full professor and chair of the Business Administration & Information Systems Department at South Carolina State University. He also serves as the interim director for the MBA Program. Dr. Guah returned to the chair position in August 2019, after contributing as acting associate provost for Academic Affairs for three years. Dr. Guah continues to serve as faculty athletic representative for MEAC/NCAA—a position he's held since 2016. Prior to joining SC State in 2014, Dr. Guah was director for MBA program at Claflin University, where he spear-headed major changes at Claflin Business School—wining two excellence awards for research (in 2012) and services (in 2013). With a PhD in Information Systems and Management Controls from Warwick University (United Kingdom), Dr. Guah has previously worked at Erasmus School of Economics (Rotterdam), University of Hawaii (Honolulu), Warwick University and Brunel University (London). Dr. Guah's primary research focuses on business systems in healthcare organizations—reforming healthcare delivery process and performance evaluation. Dr. Guah currently teaches Management Information Systems and Integrated Business Decision within the School of Business. He is also researching claims that Big Data is the next frontier for innovation, competition, and productivity. From his previous life, Dr. Guah brings into the classroom industry experience that include United Nations, British Airways, British Standards Institute and Merrill Lynch Bank. Dr. Guah has published 4 books and over 75 journal articles, book chapters and international conference papers, mostly in healthcare management, project management and business accountability. Dr. Guah currently serves on editorial boards for several academic journals as well as track chair, session chair, and panelist for many international conferences. Dr. Matthew Guah is Eucharistic Minister at Holy Trinity Catholic Church in Orangeburg, where he also serves as a member of the Parish Council. He is married with two children currently in college.

Quintus R. Jett, PhD is a consultant, educator, and organizer of public causes. He has a doctorate in Organizations from Stanford University, and he has a faculty career which spans business, engineering, liberal studies, public and nonprofit management, and theological seminaries. Dr. Jett is an innovator in higher education, bridging the divide between academic research and the other priorities of the modern university, including student access and diversity, community engagement, and providing foundations for life-long learning in today's rapidly changing world. Since 2016, Dr. Jett has served on the Resilient America Roundtable, a convening of the National Academies of Sciences, Engineering, and Medicine to address whole-community preparation and response to extreme events.

Dorothy M. Kirkman is a tenured associate professor of management and an associate dean in the College of Business at the University of Houston–Clear Lake. She received her PhD in Organized Management from Rutgers University; an MBA from Carnegie Mellon University and a BA from North Carolina State University. Her current research interests include technology innovation, social entrepreneurship, and program evaluation. Her work has been published in the *International Journal of Technology Transfer*, the

Administrative Issues Journal, the *American Evaluation Journal,* and the *Organizational Management Journal.*

Mike Mlynarczyk is a Department of Defense (DoD) program manager. In addition, he teaches and develops graduate-level management and public administration courses in the Colorado Christian University (CCU) College of Adult and Graduate Studies (CAGS). He is a 15-year veteran of the United States Air Force where he served as a Space and Missile Operations Officer. Dr. Mlynarczyk has focused his research on leadership efficacy, servant leadership, and organizational development and change leadership and management during merger and acquisition (M&A) activities. He has been a peer reviewer and editor for the *Academy of Management* (AOM) in support of the annual conference. In 2016, he was a Presidential Management Fellow Program, Semi-Finalist.

Valerie L. Myers is an Organizational Psychologist, scholar, and consultant with 20 years of academic and corporate achievements. Rigorous, creative, and results-oriented, Myers currently delivers high-impact learning in MBA and Executive Education programs at the University of Michigan's Ross School of Business and through her consulting firm. Myers has taught graduate courses in Inclusive Leadership, Healthcare Management, Strategy, and Organizational Behavior. She's also conducted research and published scholarly insights in academic journals (e.g., *Organizational Dynamics,* the *Journal of Healthcare Management*), book chapters, and her sole-authored book, *Conversations About Calling: Advancing Management Perspectives* (Routledge, 2014), which contributes to the fields of Positive Organizational Scholarship and Management, Spirituality and Religion. Through her teaching, consulting, and public speaking, Valerie seeks to cultivate leaders worth following and organizations that serve humanity. Dr. Myers earned a dual doctoral degree in Organizational Psychology & Social Work Policy from the University of Michigan (Ann Arbor).

Richard Peters is an associate professor of management at Xavier University of Louisiana and the current faculty director of the core curriculum. His research interests are in Corporate Social Responsibility and Sustainability (CSRS) with a recent emphasis on social innovation and the role of institutions in CSRS evolution and implementation. He has published articles in business-related journal and has presented at numerous international, national, and regional conferences. He is also a reviewer for academic journals and an associate editor of *Business and Society Review* as well as sitting on the advisory board of the *Global Jesuit Case Series.* He is passionate about bringing impactful change to communities and environments. He has worked with organizations and students on issue related to strategic planning, social responsibility and sustainability planning/implementation, business ethics, international management, supply chain management, and innovation.

Latha Poonamallee is associate professor and chair of management and innovation and faculty fellow at the New School in New York City. She also serves as the editor-in-chief of the Society for Advancement of Management's scholarly journal. Latha's scholarship and practice builds organizational capacities towards a more just, sustainable, and prosperous world with two primary areas: *Socio-Tech Innovation: Harnessing Technology for Social Good* (Palgrave, 2020); how mindfulness and contemplative practice can be utilized to advance prosocial mental models and move leadership development beyond the competency approach. As a Fulbright Fellow, she worked with the Botswana Civil Society, Botswana Government, U.S. Embassy in Botswana, USAID and private sector in Botswana to develop a social entrepreneurship ecosystem and leadership capacity building for the civil society. She also a technology entrepreneur. Dr. Poonamallee received her PhD in organizational behavior from Case Western Reserve University.

Erin D. Renslow currently serves as a program assistant for the Department of Leadership Studies at The Citadel, The Military College of South Carolina in Charleston. She received her BS from Ohio University and her MEd from Wright State University. On an unrelated research trip to Blessed in the U.K. in 2018, Renslow learned about many different religions and more about non-believers. This trip caused a spiritual transformation to occur and changed her worldview. After hearing about the book, she became invested in the project and its vision, it's authors, and it's content being shared with the world.

Joe M. Ricks, Jr., is the chair of the Division of Business and is the J.P. Morgan Chase Professor of Sales & Marketing at Xavier University of Louisiana. Dr. Ricks earned a PhD in marketing from Louisiana State University, and researches Corporate Philanthropy and Social Responsibility, Sales and Sales Leadership, and Christianity in Business Strategy and Operations. He has been a visiting professor at Young & Rubicam Advertising and in multiple divisions at 3M Company. Dr. Ricks serves as chair of the Ethics Review Board for the City of New Orleans and sits on the board of the Louisiana Quality Foundation and the Friends of the Fisher House for Southeast Louisiana. He is a member of the Franklin Avenue Baptist Church.

Shalei V. K. Simms is an associate professor of management at SUNY College at Old Westbury. Her work has been featured in such publications as *Group Decisions and Negotiations* journal and *International Perspectives of Social Entrepreneurship Research*. She has presented her research both nationally and internationally. She holds a PhD from Rutgers University and a BA from Wesleyan University. She and her husband live with their twin daughters in Brooklyn, NY.

J. Goosby Smith ("Dr. J") serves in several capacities at The Citadel, The Military College of South Carolina in Charleston. She serves as assistant provost for diversity, equity, and inclusion; director of the campus Truth, Racial Healing, and Transformation Center; associate professor of management in the Baker School of Business; and associate professor of leadership in the Department of Leadership Studies. She holds MBA and PhD degrees in Organizational Behavior from the Weatherhead School of Management at Case Western Reserve University and a BS in Computer Science from Spelman College. She is completing her MDiv at The Interdenominational Theological Center.

Clifford F. Thies is the Eldon R. Lindsey Chair of Free Enterprise and Professor of Economics and Finance at Shenandoah University. He is the author or coauthor of 92 articles in scholarly journals; and, author or other contributor to eight books. His most recent is *Global Economics: A Holistic Approach*, published by Lexington Books. Dr. Thies regularly writes and speaks on the moral foundations of free enterprise, the intersection of religion and economics, the social responsibility of business, intentional communities, and cooperation.

Shoaib Ul-Haq is an associate professor at Karachi School of Business & Leadership, Pakistan. Shoaib's research focuses on understanding the complexities of the human condition and its Eastern as well as Western theoretical explanations. His work has been published in top journals including *Organization, Long Range Planning, Human Resource Development International*, and *Third World Quarterly*. He is also an editorial board member of the prestigious *Journal of Business Ethics*. He is currently writing a chapter on the Eastern philosopher-poet, Allama Iqbal, and how his ideas of self-hood (khudi) provides an important metaphysical perspective. Shoaib received his doctoral training in business management and postcolonialism from Lahore University of Management Sciences, Pakistan and then held an assistant professor position at Sejong University, South Korea.

Daniel Vass-Goosby is a personal trainer in Los Angeles, California, who holds a BA in Organizational Communication Studies from Sacramento State University. He has worked extensively in the entertainment industry, as well as financial services. He employs his understanding of messages, investment principles, and personal development to cognitive and organizational contexts. As a former college athlete, Daniel became interested in the various leadership processes, and assessment methods that exist within organizations. He hopes to further his research in areas such as, cognitive development, organizational learning and leadership, and linguistics.

Payam Zamani is the founder, chairman, and CEO of One Planet Group, a hybrid tech firm that owns and operates a suite of online technology and media businesses, the co-founder and editor-in-chief of BahaiTeachings.org, and is an early stage investor. He is a visionary entrepreneur who has built and managed global companies. His first company, Autoweb, was the first online car buying service. Its market cap post IPO reached $1.2 billion. Payam came to the United States as a 16-year-old Baha'i refugee. He's built One Planet on a model not focused solely on financial success, but with an ethos of sacrificial giving and universal philanthropy, believing that businesses should consider the betterment of the world and be a source of good.

CPSIA information can be obtained
at www.ICGtesting.com
Printed in the USA
JSHW051901280521
15339JS00001B/2